British Dramatists

British Drama

Gordon Craig: Design for a Theatre open to the Air, the Sun, and the Moon

ALLARDYCE NICOLL , 1894-

British Drama.

Fifth edition revised
and reset.

BARNES & NOBLE, Inc. · New York
Booksellers · Publishers · Founded 1873

First published in the United States 1963, © 1962
© Allardyce Nicoll 1962

Made in Great Britain

Preface

The title of this book sufficiently indicates its purpose—to provide a general survey of the drama in Great Britain from earliest times to the present. In this edition the original text has been revised throughout, and extended so as to include reference to the latest dramatic movements of our own time.

It should be observed that, in this revision, quotations from medieval and Elizabethan plays are now given in modernized form and that, with one or two necessary exceptions, the spelling of play-titles has similarly been modernized. The select bibliography printed as an appendix has been designed to serve both as a guide to essential reference works and to suggest further reading for those anxious to delve more deeply into the history of the drama during particular periods.

A. N.

Acknowledgments

For this fifth revised edition, I wish to thank the following for permission to quote from plays: Messrs Curtis Brown, Ltd, and Messrs Chatto and Windus, Ltd, for a stage direction from *Success*, by A. A. Milne; Messrs Evans Brothers, Ltd, Evans Plays, and Messrs Faber and Faber, Ltd, for an extract from *Epitaph for George Dillon*, by John Osborne (written in collaboration with Anthony Creighton); Messrs Gerald Duckworth and Co., Ltd, for stage directions from *The Fugitive, The Mob*, and *A Family Man*, by John Galsworthy; Messrs Faber and Faber, Ltd, for an extract from *Murder in the Cathedral*, by T. S. Eliot; Messrs Macmillan and Co., Ltd, for an extract from *Mrs Dane's Defence*, by Henry Arthur Jones; Mr W. Somerset Maugham, Messrs William Heinemann, Ltd, and Messrs Doubleday and Company, Inc. (New York), for an extract from W. Somerset Maugham's *Our Betters* (copyright 1921 by W. Somerset Maugham); Oxford University Press for an extract from *Curtmantle*, by Christopher Fry; The Public Trustee, The Society of Authors, and Messrs Constable and Co., Ltd, for an extract from *Too True to Be Good*, by George Bernard Shaw; the Author's Representatives and Messrs Sidgwick and Jackson, Ltd, for an extract from *Hindle Wakes*, by Stanley Houghton; and The Society of Authors and Dr John Masefield, O.M., for an extract from *The Tragedy of Nan*, by John Masefield.

A. N.

Contents

I

THE BEGINNINGS TO SHAKESPEARE

II

ELIZABETHAN DRAMA

III

THE JACOBEAN AND CAROLINE DRAMA

IV
RESTORATION DRAMA

V
DRAMA IN THE EIGHTEENTH CENTURY

VI
DRAMA IN THE NINETEENTH CENTURY

VII
DRAMA IN THE TWENTIETH CENTURY

Illustrations

Design for a Theatre open to the Air, the Sun, and
the Moon   *frontispiece*

> From Gordon Craig's *The Theatre Advancing* (1921), by permis-
> sion of the author and Messrs Constable & Co., Ltd.

Medieval Pageants   *page* 30

> Although these may represent puppet-plays, it seems probable
> that they are intended to depict pageant plays with a curtained
> lower room and an elevated acting platform.

The Bankside, Southwark   31

> Four theatres, presumably the Swan, Hope, Rose, and Globe, are
> shown in the foreground with their flags flying.

The Swan Theatre   96

> This, the de Witt drawing, is the only definite contemporary
> pictorial evidence relating to the interior of any particular
> Elizabethan playhouse.

Two Elizabethan Stages   97

> The right-hand design is an enlarged portion of the frontispiece
> to William Alabaster's *Roxana* (1632); the left-hand design
> similarly reproduces part of the frontispiece to N. Richard's
> *Messalina* (1640). Both, no doubt, are intended to illustrate the
> stages of 'private' theatres.

Proscenium Arch and Scene I for *The Queen of Arragon*   128

> Prepared by Inigo Jones for a production in 1639 of William
> Habington's *The Queen of Arragon*. This indicates how the
> typical 'masque' scenery came to be applied to the presentation
> of plays. Reproduced by kind permission of the Duke of Devon-
> shire. Photograph by the Victoria and Albert Museum.

An illustration in Charles Hoole's translation of the *Orbis sensualium pictus* (1658) of Johan Amos Comenius. The description is as follows:

In a Playhouse 1 (which is trimmed with Hangings 2 and covered with Curtains 3) Comedies, and Tragedies are acted, wherein memorable things are represented; as here the History of the Prodigal Son 4 and his Father 5 by whom he is entertained, being returned home. The Players act being in disguise; the Fool 6 maketh jests. The chief of the Spectators sit in the Gallery 7, the common sort stand on the ground 8 and clap their hands if any thing pleases them.

An engraving in Francis Kirkman's *The Wits* (1673), a collection of 'drolls.' It probably is a rough representation of the kind of stage used by the players in the Commonwealth period.

This shows the interior of Dorset Garden Theatre in 1673. Note should be taken of the ornate proscenium arch, the projecting apron stage, and the costumes of the actors.

Frontispiece to the 1713 duodecimo edition. The blending of contemporary and Roman dress is of particular interest.

This print well illustrates the atmosphere in the 'minor' theatres in the early nineteenth century.

A 'realistic' setting typical of the Edwardian stage. From *The Stage Year Book*, 1909.

This was executed for the production in 1923 at the Birmingham Repertory Theatre. It well shows the 'new movement' in scenic design which reacted against earlier realism.

I

The Beginnings to Shakespeare

1. INTRODUCTORY: THE CLASSICAL HERITAGE

THE mimetic instinct is confined to no single nation; it is universal in its appeal and reveals itself as one of the most primitive of human emotions. The desire of men and women to garb themselves in the semblance of attendants upon a god, even to take upon themselves the god-form in its august majesty; the desire to re-enact the sacred stories, whether they be of Grecian deities or of Jehovah and Christ; the later desire of the peasant to place himself, if but for a fleeting moment, in the position of a courtier, or of the courtier to forget for a time the intrigues and the cares of his state in a fondly imagined Arcady —all of these are manifestations of the one primeval passion which reveals itself in church liturgy, in folk-mummings, and in masquerades, no less than in the tragedies of Æschylus and of Shakespeare. This universal nature of acting and of drama renders a study of the stage at once more fascinating and more difficult than the study of almost any other type of literature. It demands, in the first place, a careful investigation of religious ritual and of folk-customs, and, in the second, an equally careful investigation of the literatures of diverse races. No account of English drama can possibly be complete unless reference be made to the services of the early Church, to the relics of pagan ceremonials preserved in half-fossilized forms among the peasantry, and to the development of dramatic activities in other lands.

At the very start of our inquiry into the origin and growth of the English stage, the necessity of looking beyond the immediate to the general becomes apparent. Drama in England does not begin until the tenth century, and the impulse which brought it into being was completely independent, uninfluenced by any force from without. At the same time, we cannot dismiss from our minds the thought that, centuries before, the ancient Athenians had seen the stage evolving in their own culture and had brought that stage to a high level of achievement. From Greece, this stage was passed on to Rome and, although there it lost its initial power, it pursued its activities up to the time when the Empire eventually fell, in the fourth century, under the attacks of the barbarian hordes. Three aspects of the earlier dramatic movement demand that at least some brief attention should be given to it before we pass to consideration of the native English theatre. First, there is the interest which arises from observing that, in essence, the ultimate source of the drama which arose in the tenth century is similar to that which brought the Athenian drama into existence. Secondly, there is corresponding interest in finding that, without any direct impress of the one upon the other, many of the same features are to be discerned in both. And thirdly, there is the fact that, while the earliest efforts of the English drama were wholly native and innocent of classical influence, we cannot escape references to the Greek and the Roman after the period when, in the sixteenth century, knowledge of their theatrical activities was brought to the attention of English playwrights.

In Greece, both comedy and tragedy took their rise from religious ceremonial. We may think of the latter as starting from a chorus of worshippers standing or moving in a circle round the altar of a god, chanting in unison and indulging in unrehearsed dance. The first movement towards the dramatic came when one member of the chorus separated himself from the rest, uttering lines to which the chorus collectively replied. Once this single 'actor' had established his position, the rest was simple. Two actors, and then three, made their appearance, and with them formal dialogue took shape. On them the attention of spectators focused, and the chorus lost its original function as the protagonist.

Thus tragedy emerged out of a religious observance, and to

the end it remained integrally related to the service of the gods. Audiences were attracted to the performances because of the entertainment to be derived from them, but with the sense of delight was associated a feeling of awe and wonder. As a consequence, only a formal august tone could be permitted in the elaboration of plot and dialogue. The stories told in these tragic dramas were for the most part restricted to a set series of legendary themes; the chorus, even when removed from its central position, helped to preserve a ritual element; the scenes took shape according to a set plan.

The formalism inherent in the Greek drama was further encouraged by the theatres in which the tragedies were produced. Since these tragedies were fundamentally religious exercises, they were presented on special days of festival when all the inhabitants of the city state, rich and poor, aristocratic and humble, flocked to witness them. At the start, the theatre consisted of no more than a sloping hillside, which provided accommodation for the spectators, and a level tract, marked out in a circle, on which the players moved and spoke. Soon, however, these primitive conditions were improved: a semicircle of stone seats became an auditorium; the space for the chorus became an 'orchestra,' with the altar in its centre; and, facing the spectators, arose a building the front of which came to serve as a background for the performers. In the forepart of this building a long, narrow raised stage offered a platform for the actors, while the chorus stood below them. These theatres were vast, and accordingly they encouraged statuesque methods of production. The actors wore high boots (the *cothurnus*) to give them added height; over their faces they had huge masks. Thus they could indulge in no violent movement, and for practical reasons their speech had to be stately and majestic.

Betweeen the conditions operative in this Greek theatre and the conditions which prevailed in the bustling, secular playhouses of Shakespeare's time there is a vast measure of difference, and in comparing the two our first thoughts must be of the distinctions which separate the one from the other. Yet the extraordinary thing is that, despite these distinctions, the Athenian and Elizabethan stages came to produce similar kinds of tragic expression. It may be assumed that for Shakespeare the Greek masters, Æschylus, Sophocles, and Euripides, were no more than names, but his great tragedies may be critically discussed on the same terms as theirs. It is almost as though the spirit of the theatre itself, independent of time and place, had worked to realize identical ends.

In Athens, at other festivals, comedy also flourished—a comedy lyrical and fantastic which found its master in Aristophanes. These satirical, exuberant, and often burlesque plays formed the fitting complement of the tragic drama, but, unlike them, they find but few counterparts in later ages. Nevertheless, although in themselves they stand almost unique, other comic forms arose out of their inspiration which do have reflections in Elizabethan and other periods. Aristophanes' comedies are generally described as the 'Old Comedy'; when the city state of Athens moved into its decline and different social conditions were operative, a 'New Comedy' took shape. In this type of play, associated with the name of Menander, the fantastic, lyric element vanished; the extravagant characters—the Birds and the Frogs and the rest of Aristophanes' imaginary figures—were abandoned; the wildly impossible plots were laid aside. Instead, 'realistic' plots based on contemporary social life were chosen, and the audience's attention was held by clever twists and turns in the action; the characters were no longer grotesques, but stage images of types such as might have been found in any Hellenic city. Menander's play-world points forward towards more than one kind of later comic endeavour; it may be associated with the comedy of social manners which flourished in the seventeenth century, and it may also be seen to have connexions with the Elizabethan comedy of romance. His *Dyskolos*, after lying in obscurity for more than two thousand years, has come to light only recently, but many of its scenes summon forth thoughts of Shakespeare's sixteenth-century works.

This drama of Greece proved to be the chief model for the Roman theatre, and in the first instance it was through Rome that the classical achievements of Greece were handed down to later generations. Ancient tragedy meant, not the plays of Sophocles, but the closet dramas of Seneca; Menander remained unknown during periods when Terence was read and admired. When, however, we turn to consider the forces which inspired the upsurge of a fresh dramatic development in the medieval period, we must put even these Latin playwrights out of our minds. With the fall of Rome in the fourth century the theatre virtually vanished; perhaps wandering entertainers carried on some of its traditions in a crude form amid their juggling and their jesting; but the production of drama, which in any case had been almost completely given over during the last years of the Empire, disappeared. While it is true that manuscripts of the Roman comedies and tragedies were still preserved in monastic libraries and were read there for the sake of their polished style, hardly anyone thought of them as plays. Indeed, the common idea was that these pieces were merely recited by the poet or by one of his friends, while entertainers mimed some of their actions on the ground below the platform on which he stood. There is no question of imitation here. Later on, Seneca and Terence and Sophocles came to influence the English drama, but that time lay several centuries ahead. In the tenth century, when the medieval plays first came into being, a completely fresh start had to be made.

2. THE GROWTH OF NATIVE DRAMA: TROPES AND LITURGICAL PLAYS

The prime interest of this fresh start is that it almost exactly paralleled the start of the Athenian drama. The drama of the Greeks had begun with the extension of religious observance, and in similar manner the medieval theatre developed, without conscious effort, out of the religious services of its time. Distinctively it was a creation of the Church.

For men and women of the Middle Ages, apart from the round of their daily affairs, the Church was virtually everything. There may have been grumblings concerning corruption among the clergy, and even anger at all the rabble of lecherous and greedy hypocrites who sought, under its cloak, to fleece the poor; but here, after all, was rest for the weary, solace for the afflicted, bread for the hungry, succour for the oppressed; here was not only the church, but the school, the meeting-place, the centre of art and, still more important, of amusement. The religion of the Middle Ages was a broad religion. It was serious and mystical, but it allowed of laughter. Beside the real bishop stood the boy bishop with his riotous crowd of hilarious attendants. The Church was ready and eager to provide for the people all the delight as well as the spiritual uplifting it could by means of art and letters. Moreover, it was ready to show to an uneducated folk the Scriptural story in visible wise, thus counteracting the lack of vernacular versions of the Holy Writ.

The very Mass itself is an effort in this direction. The whole of this service with its accompanying ritual is a symbolic represen-tation of the most arresting episodes in the life of Christ, and it is but natural that the clergy should have attempted to make it even more outwardly symbolic as the knowledge of Latin among the ordinary people passed farther and farther into the back-ground. More especially they must have seen the necessity, on the great feast-days of Christmas and of Easter, of bringing be-fore the congregation the salient facts of the New Testament story.

From a very early period various liturgical developments may be traced, all potentially conducive to the establishment of a dramatic form. Of these most significant were the so-called 'tropes' which, particularly in the ninth century, permitted an extension, in music and even in language, of the service appro-priate to the Easter ceremonials. It was out of such tropes that there arose, in the tenth century, the very first modern play, the *Quem Quæritis*. To call this a play may seem strange, since it consisted of only four lines; yet when we examine it carefully we must come to realize that it includes all the essential ingredi-ents of drama—the setting of a place of action, the presentation of fictional persons interpreted by performers, and the use of dia-logue. One priest, standing near the altar, personates the Angel guarding the tomb of Christ, and towards him walk three other priests, personating the three Maries. Chants the Angel:

Quem quæritis in sepulchro, O Christicolæ?
[Whom do ye seek in the sepulchre, O Christian women?]

The others reply:

> Iesum Nazarenum crucifixum, O cælicola.
> [Jesus of Nazareth who was crucified. O heavenly one.]

And the Angel tells them:

> Non est hic, surrexit sicut prædixerat.
> Ite, nuntiate quia surrexit de sepulchro.
> [He is not here; He has risen even as He foretold.
> Go; proclaim that He has risen from the sepulchre.]

Simple as this piece is, it gives us the embryo of drama. Once born, it possessed all the elements necessary for further growth; and that growth was fed in four chief ways. First, there was what we may style histrionic elaboration by which the time taken in the chanting of the three brief speeches was lengthened. Already, by the close of the tenth century, a *Concordia Regularis*, prepared by Ethelwold, Bishop of Winchester, for the use of the Benedictines, clearly indicates how this was accomplished even at a period when the primitive drama remained part of the Church's service. While the third lesson was being intoned, we are told, four of the monks proceeded to dress themselves. One, clad in an alb, quietly moved to the altar and seated himself there, palm in hand. The other three, wearing copes and carrying thuribles of incense, then slowly approached the altar, "stepping lightly in the similitude of persons seeking something." After this came the question from the Angel, the reply of the Maries, and the Angel's announcement; and at its conclusion the trio of priests turned to the choir, crying, "*Alleluia: resurrexit Dominus* [Halleluia, the Lord has arisen!]" while the Angel called them back, intoning the anthem "*Venite et videte locum* [Come, see the place]," at the same time lifting a veil and showing them "the place bare of the Cross, but only the cloths lying there in which the Cross had been enfolded." Whereupon the Maries lifted up the cloth as though they would reveal to all that the Lord had arisen, and sang the anthem *Surrexit dominus de sepulchro*. Finally, the ceremony ended with the singing of the *Te Deum* and a joyful pealing of the bells.

A second force leading towards further development was the expansion of the tiny playlet from within, in two directions. One

of these was the splitting of the choral three Maries into individuals and the giving them each their own speeches, sometimes running into many stanzas. The other was to attach to the
central theme various subsidiary episodes. Thus, for example, the
Maries were supposed to bear spices with which to anoint Jesus'
body, and we soon hear of the introduction of an additional
character, an Unguent-seller, some of whose wares they pretend
to purchase before stepping up to the altar.

It will easily be imagined how in these ways the original little
Easter ceremony came to be lengthened and diversified, but here
we must take into account something still more important.
Obviously what was being done for the Easter story could also
be done for other cardinal episodes in the New Testament. Thus,
for instance, the question "Whom seek ye in the sepulchre?"
could without effort be changed into "Whom seek ye in the
manger, O shepherds?" and applied to the Christmas services.
And the Christmas playlet offered as many opportunities for
elaboration as the other: the shepherds could be shown chatting
together, the star could be made to appear to them, they could
be addressed by an Angel, they could seek for the rustic gifts
they were to carry to the child Christ.

And, lastly, a fourth force was that which we may style the
'theatrical,' or the 'scenic.' At the very start, no attempt was
made to suggest, even by the most primitive means, the supposed locality of the action: the words alone indicated that this
was presumed to be near or at the tomb of Christ. As the liturgical plays developed, however, and particularly as various episodes came to be included in them, a step was taken which ultimately was to lead to the association of 'scenery' with the
priests' performances. An architectural structure was erected
close to the altar in the similitude of the tomb; a throne was provided for the Angel; and for the Unguent-seller a seat or stall was
set up in another part of the church. By devices such as this, as
we shall see, the principle of later medieval staging was established.

Although there existed all these several forces leading towards
dramatic elaboration, however, quite obviously the play as play
could not hope to reach far so long as it remained part of a larger

religious service, nor could it develop freely while its dialogue was in Latin, not spoken but chanted. The very last force, therefore, and the most important of all, was that exerted by the separation of these playlets from the liturgy and their consequent secularization.

3. MYSTERIES AND MIRACLES

This secularization of the drama arose largely because of the circumstances of the production. Medieval folk were lacking in means of entertainment, and naturally they flocked in to watch these liturgical performances: thus very soon the churches were found inadequate for the accommodation of all the men and women anxious to see the shows. The obvious solution was to carry the performances outside into the spaces surrounding the church itself. This meant, however, that, even though the clergy still provided the actors, the plays were inevitably divorced from the services of which originally they formed part. At the same time, some of the monks and priests, eager to make these dramatic pieces more appealing to an unlettered public, began to introduce the vernacular into the dialogue—sometimes by reciting lines in Latin immediately followed by a translation, sometimes by uttering certain speeches in Latin with other speeches in tongues familiar to the spectators.

When this stage had been reached the ecclesiastical authorities recognized a danger lying ahead of them, and in diverse ways they sought to suppress that which the Church itself had brought into being. Strict orders were promulgated, so that, as Robert Mannyng puts it in his *Handlyng Synne*, the cleric was forbidden by decree

> Miracles for to make and see:
> For miracles if thou begin,
> It is a gathering, a sight of sin.
> He may in the church through this reason
> Play the Resurrection . . .
> If thou do it in ways or greens,
> A sight of sin truly it seems.

The result of this prohibition, however, was distinctly not that which was desired: when the clergy was instructed not to take part in these performances the laity eagerly seized upon the drama, naturally abandoned the use of Latin dialogue, substituted vernacular speech throughout, and proceeded to expand the plays both in form and content. In many European countries this happened, and the interest which the Biblical performances had aroused in the medieval mind is amply demonstrated by the foundation in France and Italy of societies specifically created for the purpose of acting and producing such pieces and by the willingness of the English trade guilds to become responsible for their presentation to the public.

The actors, then, were no longer restricted groups of priests and monks; large bodies of eager amateurs had taken their place; and it is by no means surprising that, in their hands, the scope of the drama was mightily extended. The medieval theatre had started with a brief four-line playlet introducing as characters only an Angel and the three Maries; very soon the whole story of the Bible, from the creation of Adam on to the Resurrection of Christ or the Last Judgment, was being given dramatic shape. For the performance of the plays impetus was offered through the establishment of a Corpus Christi festival due to be held each year on the Thursday after Trinity Sunday; first set by a papal decree of 1264, and later, in 1311, placed more formally in the calendar by an order of the Council of Vienne, that day was selected for the presentation of the amateur shows, and numerous records both in England and abroad indicate that the months between performance and performance were busily spent in preparing for these eagerly awaited holiday events. In those days, when recreations and amusements were relatively rare, the Corpus Christi productions were evidently red-letter occasions for actors and audience alike.

In this way, during the thirteenth, fourteenth, and fifteenth centuries the mystery cycles, generally called 'miracle plays' in England, came into being. The term 'mystery' is somewhat difficult to explain and define, but in all probability it embraced the concept both of a religious ceremonial (as in the 'mysteries' of the Passion) and of a special art, skill, or function (as in the trade 'mysteries' of the guilds). Abroad, scores of such compilations are extant; in England only four cycles have been preserved, but these, taken in association with other relevant records, are sufficient to demonstrate that the English dramatic activities were fundamentally the same as those which can be more fully traced in France and Italy. While it is true that we have nothing equivalent to the elaborate prompt-book which outlines the theatrical marvels aimed at in the presentation of the Mons cycle, the general picture is the same—and before turning to consider the cycles themselves it is this production method which we have to examine.

Rarely were the mystery plays exhibited anywhere except out of doors, and no attempt was made to construct for them any 'theatre,' in the modern sense of the term. The fundamental principle utilized by the actors was the application in an elaborated form of the staging device used for the liturgical and related plays in the churches. As we have seen, this involved the setting-up of special locations—often called *sedes*, or seats, *loci*, or places, *domus*, or houses—assigned to the chief characters or events. Within the church all such stations or locations were in view of the audience throughout the entire time of the performance, and thus was established that method of stage representation to which has been given the name of 'simultaneous setting,' or 'multiple setting.' What happened, of course, was that when the Maries stopped to buy unguents at a stall, only this stall attracted the attention of the congregation-audience; and when they proceeded towards the station of the tomb the existence of the stall was completely ignored. Two further things have to be observed. The first is that the simultaneous setting constantly foreshortened distance; in a Christmas play, for example, the shepherds might first be shown tending their flocks and then later coming to the manger; in actuality the meadow where their sheep grazed would have been in the country, the manger would have been in an inn at Nazareth, but the spectators of the liturgical play saw these two places standing side by side. The second thing to note is that the area on which the individual stations were set up itself became part of the 'setting'; it could imaginatively be taken as representing the territory between location and location, so that the shepherds, in walking the few yards from their meadow to Christ's manger, might be supposed to have journeyed many miles, and on other occasions the actors could be made to establish a specific location on any part of this open area by simply using words alone. The liturgical plays, therefore, did not merely employ a series of stations visually presented to the spectators by means of seats or small platforms, but they also had available the *platea*, or place, on which these stations were set.

When the liturgical plays ceded their position to the mystery cycles what happened was that the seats or small platforms were elaborated into 'mansions'—sometimes made into little rooms by provision of curtains at the sides and back, sometimes decorated with pieces of carved and painted 'scenery'; and at the same time the *platea* continued to serve its original function. In the placing of the mansions, two chief methods were employed. The first, generally styled the 'stationary' set, presented the mansions in a curving row facing the audience or else arranged them within a circle or a rectangular space. The second involved the placing of the mansions on wheels, so that they became 'pageants' which could be drawn from spot to spot; these, according to one contemporary, were fashioned "like a house with two rooms, being open at the top"; in the lower room the actors "apparelled and dressed themselves, and in the higher room they played."

No doubt, in England at least, many of the effects aimed at were of a simple kind, yet we have ample evidence that as the years passed by numerous scenic tricks were introduced. The records, however, seem to demonstrate that greatest attention was paid to costuming. At Canterbury we hear of "a pair of new gloves for St Thomas"; at Chelmsford a certain John Wright was paid for "making a coat of leather for Christ." In 1564 an inventory includes "two Vices' coats and two scalps, five Prophets' caps, three flaps for Devils, four sheephooks, and four whips." From Coventry we learn that in 1544 "a new coat and a pair of hose for Gabriel" cost three shillings and fourpence, while at Hull in 1494 "three skins for Noah's coat, making it, and a rope to hang the ship in the kirk" amounted to seven shillings; "a pair of new mittens to Noah" cost fourpence. In 1504, at Leices-

ter, "linen cloth for the Angels' heads, and Jesus' hose" involved
an expense of ninepence, and the painting of the Angels' wings
cost eightpence. At Norwich, in 1565, an inventory of property
belonging to the Grocers' Company listed, among many other
items:

> 2 coats and a pair of hose for Eve.
> A coat and hose for Adam.
> A coat with hose and tail for the Serpent.
> An Angel's coat and over-hose.
> A face and hair [i.e., a mask and wig] for the Father.
> 2 hairs [i.e., wigs] for Adam and Eve.

No doubt increasing efforts were made by the great guilds to vie
with one another in the presentation of the separate plays, and
these inventories give us some idea as to how they went about
their work.

The actors in these pieces, as has been said, were all amateurs
—members of the various companies who for a time put aside
their labour to perform in the sacred mysteries. They were generally paid for their services, but never looked upon their work as
a regular profession. At Coventry in 1573 a certain Fawson
received from one of the companies fourpence "for hanging
Judas" and fourpence "for cock-crowing." An anonymous actor
received as much as three shillings and fourpence "for playing
God," and five shillings went to "three white [i.e., saved] souls"
and five shillings to "three black [i.e., damned] souls." "Two
worms of conscience" earned sixteenpence between them. In
1483 at Hull Noah received one shilling; in 1494 in the same
town Thomas Sawyr for personating God was given tenpence,
while Noah's wife received eightpence. The plays and their
performances were, therefore, distinctly the creation of the
common people, with all the defects and the virtues consequent upon that fact. The naïveté visible in the few extracts from
the records given above may prepare us for a similar naïveté in
the treatment of the subject-matter of the plays—both, of course,
ultimately dependent upon the people who wrote and who witnessed these dramas. The audience was profoundly devout and
sincere, but at the same time it unconsciously sought for ways of
escape from its piety in all manner of licence. One way is to be

seen in the incredibly coarse *fabliaux* of the time, and even in certain ceremonies of misrule actually sanctioned by the Church, such as the notorious Feast of Fools and the Feast of the Boy Bishop. Here piety was thrown to the winds, and licence reigned. The gargoyles in the medieval cathedrals which grin down cynically on the worshippers are but another expression of this mood of abandon—a mood, however, which rarely becomes permanent. The gargoyles are but little outbursts of freakishness and gaiety in the midst of the mysterious grandeur of the vaulted nave and the solemn choir. For these people of the Middle Ages there was no such thing as form, as form is known in classic and in neoclassic art. With them drunkenness is found with the most mystic adoration, debauchery with the most lofty moral idealism, cynical ridicule with passionate worship, laughter with the solemnity of sacred thoughts.

It is natural that this grotesquerie should be reproduced in what is in some ways the most typical of medieval creations, the mystery or miracle play. The seriousness is there in the figures of God and of His angels, in the terrible passion of Christ and in His resurrection from the dead, but there is also the laughter and the abandon, the escape from too high majesty. At one of the solemnest moments, as, for example, when the shepherds watch the star that is to herald the coming of a King over kings, this laughter breaks out, and we are treated to a fascinating little episode of the thievish Mak and his companions. The general satire of women could not be stilled even in face of the worship of the Virgin Mary, and Noah's wife becomes a shrew, jeering at her husband and flouting him uproariously. Even the flaming terror of Satan was not exempt; rapidly he developed into an almost comic figure, roaring and lashing his tail, attended by groups of minor devils which, in their grotesquely monstrous attire, were designed to arouse both thrills of terror and shouts of laughter. Herod, too, suffered in dignity. This slayer of infants, this murderer of murderers, developed into a comic type. His roaring and ranting became a recognized part of the performances of the time, and Shakespeare remembered him in later days. Formless were the plays in which these characters appeared, lacking literary style often, and always wanting in 'correct' artistic proportions—the work, as eighteenth-century critics would have said, of the "Gothick imagination."

In these dramas, however, lay the seeds that were later to blossom out into the plays of Shakespeare and his contemporaries. There is freshness of fancy here, a free treatment of the material, a rich fund of humour, and at times a true sense of the profound and the tragic. If with the mysteries we are but on the borders of drama proper we can see clearly the various traditions which later were brought to culmination in the time of Queen Elizabeth I.

These mystery plays were not confined to any one district of England. No doubt the record of many of them has perished, but acting can be traced during the thirteenth, fourteenth, and fifteenth centuries in over one hundred and twenty-five towns and villages of Britain, extending from the south of England to the north, from the Welsh mountains to Edinburgh and Aberdeen, even across the sea to Dublin and Kilkenny. Some of these towns, no doubt, had no regular series of mystery plays of their own, but numbers must have treasured for centuries their specially prepared individual cycles. Those which have come down to us are unquestionably merely an infinitesimal portion of a literary activity once vast and far-reaching in its extent. Four such cycles have been preserved—those of Chester (twenty-five plays, with an extra drama probably abandoned at the time of the Reformation), York (forty-eight plays and a small fragment of another), "Towneley" or Wakefield (thirty-two plays), and Coventry (forty-two plays in the *Ludus Coventriæ* and two separate dramas from the Coventry Corpus Christi cycle). Besides these there are extant a Grocers' play of *The Fall* from Norwich; two dramas of *Abraham and Isaac*, one belonging probably to Northampton; a Shipwrights' play from Newcastle-upon-Tyne; the so-called *Croxton Sacrament*, dating from the second half of the fifteenth century; the "Digby" plays of unknown origin; a stray drama of the *Burial and Resurrection*; the Shrewsbury fragments; and a set of five plays in the Cornish tongue, presenting interesting parallels with extant English examples.

It is impossible here to deal with all or even many of these plays in detail. First, to get an impression of their scope, we may turn to the best-preserved of the series, the York cycle, and, allowing for individual variations, treat it as a type for all. This cycle, as has been indicated, contains forty-eight separate dramas, as well as a solitary fragment which was probably added towards the close of the fifteenth century. In it the various component parts are clearly apportioned to the various guilds:

(1) Barkers. *The Creation, Fall of Lucifer.*
(2) Plasterers. *The Creation to the Fifth Day.*
(3) Cardmakers. *The Creation of Adam and Eve.*
(4) Fullers. *Adam and Eve in the Garden of Eden.*
(5) Coopers. *The Disobedience and Fall.*
(6) Armourers. *The Expulsion from Eden.*
(7) Glovers. *Cain and Abel.*
(8) Shipwrights. *The Building of the Ark.*
(9) Fishers and Mariners. *Noah and the Flood.*
(10) Parchminers and Bookbinders. *Abraham's Sacrifice.*
(11) Hosiers. *Israelites in Egypt, Ten Plagues and the Passage of the Red Sea.*
(12) Spicers. *The Annunciation.*
(13) Pewterers and Founders. *Joseph and Mary.*
(14) Tile-thatchers. *The Journey to Bethlehem.*
(15) Chandlers. *The Shepherds.*
(16) Masons. *The Coming of the Three Kings to Herod.*
(17) Goldsmiths. *The Adoration.*
(18) Marchals [*i.e.*, men who shod horses]. *The Flight into Egypt.*
(19) Girdlers and Nailers. *Massacre of the Innocents.*
(20) Spurriers and Lorimers [*i.e.*, makers of bits for horses]. *The Disputation in the Temple.*
(21) Barbers. *The Baptism of Christ.*
(22) Smiths. *The Temptation of Christ.*
(23) Curriers. *The Transfiguration.*
(24) Capmakers. *The Woman taken in Adultery and the Raising of Lazarus.*
(25) Skinners. *Entry into Jerusalem.*
(26) Cutlers. *The Conspiracy.*
(27) Bakers. *The Last Supper.*
(28) Cordwainers. *The Agony and Betrayal.*
(29) Makers of bows and arrows. *Peter's Denial and Christ before Caiaphas.*
(30) Tapestry-makers and Couchers. *The Dream of Pilate's Wife and Christ before Pilate.*

(31) Lytsterers [*i.e.*, dyers]. *The Trial before Herod.*
(32) Cooks and Waterleaders. *The Second Accusation before Pilate with the Remorse of Judas.*
(33) Tilemakers. *The Judgment on Christ.*
(34) Shearmen. *Calvary.*
(35) Pinners [*i.e.*, makers of pins] and Painters. *The Crucifixion.*
(36) Butchers. *The Mortification of Christ.*
(37) Sadlers. *The Harrowing of Hell.*
(38) Carpenters. *The Resurrection.*
(39) Winedrawers. *Christ appears to Mary Magdalen.*
(40) Sledmen. *Travellers to Emmaus.*
(41) Hatmakers, Masons, and Labourers. *The Purification of Mary.*
(42) Scriveners. *The Incredulity of Thomas.*
(43) Tailors. *The Ascension.*
(44) Potters. *The Descent of the Holy Spirit.*
(45) Drapers. *The Death of Mary.*
(46) Weavers. *The Appearance of Our Lady to Thomas.*
(47) Ostlers. *The Assumption and Coronation of the Virgin.*
(48) Mercers. *The Judgment Day.*
(49) [fragment]. Innholders. *The Coronation of Our Lady.*

The first point of interest in this list is the close connexion of the plays with the guilds. It will be noted how in many instances plays were given to men specially qualified to deal with them; thus the mariners took the Flood, and the goldsmiths the Adoration. Secondly, from this list it will be appreciated that these plays cannot be judged critically on any standards such as are applicable to other dramas. Each play stands alone, yet all are but parts in a vast cycle. We cannot indulge in a critical study of either plays or cycles such as would be appropriate for the dramas of Marlowe or of Shakespeare. The mystery plays have no author, or countless authors, put it in which way we will. The cycles were constantly changing. Unquestionably portions were periodically added to or taken away from particular plays. The whole cycles are typically medieval in their almost complete anonymity and general formlessness. All we may do, therefore, is to indicate some of the chief points in one or two of the dramas or separate cycles, stressing chiefly those elements which might be held to offer hints to the dramatists of later years.

From the literary point of view the York cycle is possibly the least entertaining. Its high-water mark of excellence is to be found in the last few plays dealing with the Passion of Christ, but even here there is little that strikes us as possessing the potentialities of greatness. The value of this cycle is largely historic and linguistic. The Chester cycle presents, on the other hand, certain features of interest. This series may have been influenced slightly by the plays of York, and certainly something seems taken from the great French *Mystère du Vieil Testament*, but there is about these dramas a genuine devoutness of tone which gives it a distinction of its own. Not that the grotesque elements are wanting. They are displayed here clearly in the Water-leaders' pageant of *The Deluge*, where Noah's wife appears in her traditional guise of a scolding shrew:

> *Noah.* Wife, come in! Why standest thou here?
> Thou art ever forward, that dare I swear.
> Come in, on God's half! Time it were,
> For fear lest that we drown.
>   *Noah's Wife.* Yea, sir, set up your sail
> And row forth with evil hale!
> For, without any fail,
> I will not out of this town.
> Unless I have my gossips every one
> One foot further I will not gone.
> They shall not drown, by St John,
> If I may save their life.
> They loved me full well, by Christ.
> Unless thou wilt let them in thy chest.
> Else row forth, Noah, whither thou list,
> And get thee a new wife.
>   *Noah.* Sem, son, lo! thy mother is wrath;
> Forsooth such another I do not know.
>   *Sem.* Father, I shall fetch her in, I trow,
> Without any fail.
> Mother, my father after thee sends,
> And bids thee into yonder ship wend.
> Look up and see the wind,
> For we be ready to sail.
>   *Noah's Wife.* Son, go again to him and say
> I will not come therein to-day.

Medieval Pageants

30

The Bankside, Southwark

The four theatres, indicated by flags, are presumably the Swan, Hope, Rose, and Glob

Noah. Come in, wife, in twenty devils' way,
Or else stand there without. . . .
　　Noah's Wife. That will I not for all your call,
Unless I have my gossips all.
　　Sem. In faith, mother, yet you shall,
Whether you will or not.　　[*She is forced into the Ark.*
　　Noah. Welcome, wife, into this boat.
　　Noah's Wife. And have thou that for thy meed!
　　　　　　　　　　　　　　　[*She gives him a slap.*
　　Noah. Ah! Ha! Marry, this is hot.

Whatever jollification may appear in scenes such as this, it is,
however, the emotion appearing in these Chester plays that
calls for most attention. It is nowhere better expressed than in
the play of *Abraham's Sacrifice*, performed by the Barbers and
the Wax-chandlers. The portraits of Abraham and Isaac are well
drawn, and there is charm in the childlike presentation of this
heart-touching story:

　　Abraham. Make thee ready, my darling,
For we must do a little thing.
This wood upon thy back thou bring.
We must not long abide. . . .
　　Isaac. Father, I am all ready
To do your bidding meekly.
To bear this wood full ready am I,
As you command me.
　　Abraham. O Isaac, Isaac, my darling dear,
My blessing now I give thee here.
Take up this faggot with good cheer
And on thy back it bring;
And fire with me I will take.
　　Isaac. Your bidding I will not forsake,
Father, I will never slack to fulfil your bidding.
　　　　　　[*Here Isaac takes up the wood on his back,
　　　　　　　　and they both go off to the hill.*
　　Abraham. Now, Isaac son, go we our way
To yonder mountain, if that we may.
　　Isaac. My dear father, I will assay
To follow you full fain.
　　Abraham. Oh, my heart will break in three!

To hear thy words I have pity.
As Thou wilt, Lord, so must it be:
To Thee I will be bound.
Lay down thy faggot, my own dear son.
　　Isaac. All ready, father, lo! it is here.
But why make you so heavy cheer?
Father, if it be your will,
Where is the beast that we shall kill?
　　Abraham. There is none, son, upon this hill
That I see here in this place. . . .
　　Isaac. Father, tell me of this case,
Why you your sword drawn has
And bear it naked in this place?
Thereof I have great wonder.
　　Abraham. Isaac, son, peace! I pray thee.
Thou breakest my heart even in three.
　　Isaac. I pray you, father, keep nothing from me.
But tell me what you think.
　　Abraham. O Isaac, Isaac, I must thee kill.
　　Isaac. Alas! father, is that your will—
Your own child here for to kill
Upon this hill's brink? . . .
　　Abraham. O my son, I am sorry
To do to thee this great annoy.
God's commandment do must I;
His works are aye full mild.
　　Isaac. Would God my mother were here with me!
She would kneel upon her knee,
Praying you, father, if it might be,
For to save my life.
　　Abraham. O comely creature! unless I thee kill
I grieve my God, and that full ill.
I may not work against His will,
But ever obedient be.
O Isaac, son, to thee I say,
God has commanded me this day
Sacrifice—this is no nay—
To make of thy body.
　　Isaac. Is it God's will I should be slain?
　　Abraham. Yea, son, there is no denying:
To his bidding I will be bound,

Ever to His pleasing. . . .
   Isaac. Marry, father, God forbid
But you do your offering.
Father, at home your sons you shall find
That you must love by course of kind.
Be I once out of your mind,
Your sorrow may soon cease.
But you must do God's bidding.
Father, tell my mother for nothing.

It is easy to see here the emotional power, even if expressed in crude phraseology, which was to be exploited by later dramatists.

Clear marks of composite authorship are afforded in the so-called "Towneley" cycle, which probably belongs to the town of Wakefield. Some of the plays are evidently taken over from the York series or belong to some common source; others are independent, but of small literary value; and a few (plays iii, xii, xiii, xiv, and xxi) are characterized by a humour freer and bolder than anything visible in the other mystery cycles. Indeed, in those five plays we have the first sure signs of the hand of a writer possessing independent thought and individual expression. The five plays deal with Noah, the Shepherds, the Adoration, and the last days of Christ. Of these unquestionably that which possesses most interest is the so-called *Second Shepherds' Play* (Nos. xii and xiii are both shepherds' plays), in which occurs the delightful pastoral farce of Mak and his companions. The shepherds are shown chatting "in rustic row"; Mak enters to them, and, when they lie down to sleep, he succeeds in stealing a lamb. His companions awake, and find their loss. Together they troop down to Mak's cottage and knock at the door. Mak lets them in, and they see a cradle (in which the sheep is wrapped up). The third shepherd wishes to see the supposed child:

Give me leave him to kiss and lift up the clout.
What the devil is this? He has a long snout!
   1st *Shepherd.* He is marked amiss. We wait ill about.
   2nd *Shepherd.* Ill-spun woof, iwys, aye comes foul out.
Aye, so.
He is like to our sheep!

3rd Shepherd. How, Gyb? May I peep?
1st Shepherd. I trow kind will creep
Where it may not go. . . .
   Mak. Peace! bid I. What? Let be your fare.
I am he that him got and yond woman him bare.
   1st Shepherd. What the devil shall he be called? Mak? Lo, God.
Mak's heir!
   2nd Shepherd. Let be all that. Now God give him care, I say.
   Wife. A pretty child is he
As sits on a woman's knee.
A-dillydown, perde,
To make a man laugh.
   3rd Shepherd. I know him by the ear mark. That is a good token.
   Mak. I tell you, sirs, his nose was broken.
Once told me a clerk that he was forspoken [*i.e.,* bewitched] . . .
   Wife. He was taken with an elf;
I saw it myself.
When the clock struck twelve
Was he forshapen.
   2nd Shepherd. Ye two are both in the plot.
   3rd Shepherd. Since they maintain their theft, let's do them to
      death.
   Mak. If I trespass again, take off my head. . . .
   1st Shepherd. Sirs, do as I say.
For this trespass
We will neither curse nor quarrel,
Fight nor chide,
But get it over quickly
And toss him in a blanket.

This scene, because of its vivacity and realism, has become
well known, but, although it cannot be matched elsewhere, it is
typical of many other scenes in which a crude kind of native
comedy may be seen struggling to birth. Thus in the most terrible
scene of the *Crucifixion* humour is introduced in the persons of
four torturers. They work away at the cross, and start hauling
it to its place:

> *3rd Torturer.* So, that is well, it will not burst.
> But let us see who does the best
>   With any sleight of hand.
> *4th Torturer.* Go we now unto the other end.

Fellows, fasten on fast your hands
    And pull well at this band.
    1st Torturer. I say, fellows, by this weather,
That we draw all once together
    And look how it will fare.
    2nd Torturer. Let's now see, and leave your din!
And draw we each sinew from sinew.
    For nothing let us spare.
    3rd Torturer. Nay, fellows, this is no game!
We will no longer draw all together—
    So much have I espied.
    4th Torturer. No, for as I may have bliss
Some can tweak, whosoever it is,
    And seek ease on one side or other.
    1st Torturer. It is better, as I hope,
Each by himself to draw this rope
    And then may we see
    Who it is that ere while
    All his fellows can beguile
    Of this company.
    2nd Torturer. Since thou wilt so have, here for me!
Now draw I, as might thou thrive!
    3rd Torturer. Thou drewest right well.
Have here for me half a foot!
    4th Torturer. Alas, man! I trow thou dotest!
Thou moved it never a bit!
But have here for me that I may!
    1st Torturer. Well drawn, son, by this day!
    Thou goest well to thy work!
    2nd Torturer. Once more, whilst thy hand is in!
Pull thereat with some good will!
    3rd Torturer. Yea, and bring it to the mark!
    4th Torturer. Pull! Pull!
    1st Torturer.   Have at it now!
    2nd Torturer.   Let us see!
    3rd Torturer.   Ah ha!
    4th Torturer. Yet one more draw!
    1st Torturer.   Thereto with all thy might!
    2nd Torturer. Ah ha! Hold still there!
    3rd Torturer. So, fellows!

The other stray examples of mysteries need not detain us much further, although the *Ludus Coventriæ*, if only for its peculiar character as an unattached cycle and for its fanciful theology, deserves close attention. This series of forty-two plays has nothing to do with the regular Coventry Corpus Christi cycle, of which all but a fragment has perished, and was most probably performed at more than one town. Apart from these major series the most interesting relics we possess are the actors' parts for three little playlets of an exceedingly primitive type. These actors' parts were discovered at Shrewsbury in 1890 and show clearly how the Latin anthems at Christmas and Easter were gradually adorned with fragments of dialogue in the vernacular. The *Officium Pastorum* gives us the basis of the later shepherds' plays, the *Officium Resurrectionis* the elaboration of the *Quem Quæritis* trope, and the *Officium Peregrinorum* the first stage of development in the ever-popular story of Christ's appearance before his disciples. The majority of the other extant mysteries and miracles have less intrinsic value. The Newcastle Shipwrights' play is in the ordinary tradition; the *Abraham and Isaac* probably belonging to Northampton is interesting for its association with the French *Mystère du Vieil Testament*; and the "Digby" plays of *The Conversion of St Paul*, *St Mary Magdalene*, and *The Massacre of the Innocents* show evidence of capable authorship. None, however, deserves detailed mention here.

What, it may be asked in conclusion, is to be our final judgment on this mystery tradition so far as it concerns the development of dramatic art? Obviously there are many defects in the plays. They are chaotic in construction, the cycles forbidding the more ordered presentation of dramatic material. Conservatism, moreover, rules these dramas. The stories and the types were already there before the authors when they sat down to write. Hardly any scope was offered to the dramatist who might have superabundant dramatic inventiveness. The stiltedness of the language affects us also; clearly the writers are fettered by the various rimes and measures in which the dialogue is cast. On the other hand, we see many possibilities for future advance. The mysteries gave to the people of England a taste for theatrical shows; they prepared the ground for the Elizabethan drama of later date; they provided the basis for further development. Despite the restrictions, too, some of the authors displayed a real liveliness: Cain becomes an English peasant, grasping and rapacious; the shepherds are not the shepherds of Palestine, but the shepherds of an English countryside; Noah's wife is a "cursed shrew" of some provincial town. The serious scenes, too, have frequently realistic flavour. The murderers who surround Christ in the Wakefield play of *The Crucifixion* are native types and owe nothing to their historical surroundings. It is the freshness, then, of the mystery plays which deserves our attention, for it was this freshness added to a sense of form borrowed from a study of classical art which gave to us the glories of the Shakespearian drama.

4. THE DEVELOPMENT OF PROFESSIONAL DRAMA: MORALITIES AND INTERLUDES

In some of the mystery plays occasionally one or two personifications, such as Dolor or Misery, intrude, and the appearance of such characters leads us towards the next development in drama —that of the morality play. Already in the fourteenth century there are records of Paternoster dramas, designed to reveal the triumph of the Virtues over the Vices, and the first years of the fifteenth century bring to us the interesting *Castle of Perseverance*, which shows us the principle of the mystery plays being applied to a new kind of subject-matter. For this production a series of mansions (or, as they are here called, 'scaffolds') were placed roughly in a circle, with one mansion at the centre. Midmost stood the Castle itself, and round about were the scaffolds of Caro, Mundus, Belial, Covetousness, and Deus. The method of staging is the same as that which had been used for the Biblical plays throughout many long years; but clearly the characters here are not taken from the Bible. Instead, the spectators had before them a drama the protagonist of which was Humanum Genus, mankind at large. To one side of him were grouped the persons of an evil angel, Malus Angelus, Mundus (the World), Belial, and Caro (the Flesh), whose minions were the Seven Deadly Sins; to the other side came a good angel, Bonus Angelus, associated with Confessio, Shrift, Penitencia, and six Divine Graces. At the drama's conclusion a heavenly debate involved Misericordia (Mercy), Iustitia (Justice), Pax (Peace), and Veritas (Truth) before the person of God (Deus), seated on his imperial throne. Clearly in this play we have moved to another dramatic world, one in which the plot, instead of being taken from a Biblical source, has been invented by the playwright and in which the characters are all allegorically conceived.

Within the course of the fifteenth century two other dramas of a similar kind show how the morality was developing. About 1450 came *Mankind*, in which the generic hero listens for a time to the beguilements of a rascally crew consisting of Mischief, New Guise, Nought, and Now-a-days and is eventually brought to repentance, receiving the blessing of Mercy; while towards the close of the period Henry Medwall produced a two-part play called *Nature* wherein the hero, at first brought up by Nature, Reason, and Innocency, turns to Worldly Affection, Pride, and Sensuality, rioting with them until finally Meekness, Charity, Patience, Occupation, and Liberality become his guides.

When we think of the term 'morality,' and when we consider that all the characters are abstractions, we may be inclined to suppose that in this kind of dramatic development was to be seen retrogression rather than progress. The persons of the mystery plays, we might say, were nearly all given individual names and, even although the primitive style of the authors was insufficient to make of them real characters in their own right, the basis was there for a drama rooted in reality; no such basis, we might continue, was to be found in the world of ideas and moral concepts presented in such plays as *Mankind* and *Nature*. To dismiss these works thus summarily would, however, be false; the surprising thing is that in moving into this realm of abstractions the playwrights paradoxically came closer to the world around them, and in their technique they introduced certain elements which were to exercise considerable force on the later Elizabethan drama. The personifications were given contemporary features, and the audience was drawn into association with them. Even in these two early pieces the scenes offer proof of the latent vitality possessed by this dramatic form. In *Mankind* Now-a-days, on his first entry, justles his way on to the acting area through the very midst of the spectators:

> Make room, sirs, for we have been long!
> We will come give you a Christmas song.

Not satisfied with that, his companion Nought actually draws these spectators into their merriment:

> Now I pray all the yeomandry that is here
> To sing with us a merry cheer.

Later, we hear the roar of Titivillus, the devil, and his cry,

> I come with my legs under me!

whereupon the rascally crew determine that this will serve as an excellent opportunity for proferring the collection-bag: "We shall gather money unto," says New-Guise, "Else there shall no man him see"—

> Now ghostly to our purpose, worshipful sovereigns,
> We intend to gather money, if it please your negligence,
> For a man with a head that is of great omnipotence.
> > Now-a-days. Keep your tail, in goodness, I pray you, good
> > brother!
> He is a worshipful man, sirs, saving your reverence.
> He loveth no groats, nor pence, or twopence;
> Give us red royals if ye will see his abominable presence!
> > New Guise. Not so! Ye that may not pay the one, pay the
> > t'other!

The episode is racy, and the audience is caught up within the play. So, in Nature, Pride is not simply an abstract figure ideally conceived; he is an extravagant Osric of his day:

> I love it well to have side hair
> Half a wote beneath mine ear,
> For evermore I stand in fear
> > That mine neck should take cold.
> I knit it up all the night,
> And the daytime comb it down right;
> And then it crispeth and shineth as bright
> > As any purlèd gold.

My doublet is unlaced before—
A stomacher of satin and no more;
Rain it, snow it, never so sore,
    Methinketh I am too hot.
Then have I such a short gown,
With wide sleeves that hang a-down—
They would make some lad in this town
    A doublet and a coat.

And as we listen to these persons chatting among themselves, we realize that their words are the current speech of life. Sensuality is told by Man that he will rejoin the rioting crew. "Oh then," he says,

> shall ye them comfort
> And yourself also.
> Wot ye who will be very glad?
>   *Man.* Who?
>   *Sensuality.* Margery!
>   *Man.* Why, was she sad?
>   *Sensuality.* Yea, by the mass! She was stark mad
> Even for very woe
> When she heard talk of this chance;
> And because she would live in penance
> Her sorrow for to quench,
> She hath entered into a religious place
> At the Green Friars hereby.
>   *Man.* Yea, has she?
> Alack, good little wench!
> Is it an house of strict religion?
>   *Sensuality.* Yea, as any that ever was bygone
> Sith the world stood.
>   *Man.* Be they close nuns as others be?
>   *Sensuality.* Close, quod a? nay, nay, perde!
> That guise were not good—
> Ye must beware of that gear!
> Nay, all is open that they do there,
> As open as a goose eye!
>   *Man.* And cometh any man into their cells?
>   *Sensuality.* Yea, yea, God forbid else!
> It is free for everybody . . .

Man. Be they not wedded, as other folk be?
Sensuality. Wedded, quod a! No, so may I thrive!
They will not tarry therefor;
They can wed themselves alone.
'Come, kiss me, John'—'Gramercy, Joan,'
Thus wed they evermore.

These two or three early moralities, then, introduce us to something new—to plays which stand as independent entities and are not simply parts of larger cycles; which call for the invention of plots and not only for the retreatment of Biblical narrative; which move from a world of ancient history into a contemporary environment; which, especially in their scenes of riot, reflect the conditions of life known to those audiences drawn by the actors into their play-universe. Moreover, and still more importantly, they bring us from the milieu of the trade guilds into a completely different theatrical environment.

The Castle of Perseverance, it is true, was performed with a setting similar to that used for the mystery plays, and its large collection of dramatic characters must have been interpreted by a group of amateurs. Amateurs, too, no doubt presented *Mankind* and *Nature*. But here there is a difference. Neither of these plays makes use of scenery; both must have been produced, without any attempt at the providing of a background, on the floor of a hall; in the latter the characters come in and out of doors, while the former was certainly a Christmas piece, and when the collection-bag is passed round New Guise remarks that

At the good man of the house first we will assay.

We have not yet reached the world of true professionalism, but we are very close to it; probably the performers consisted of a group of local amateurs, not just members of some trade guild engaged in an annual festivity, but rather an association formed for the specific purpose of acting—in other words, a fifteenth-century amateur dramatic society.

Theatrical records of this period, although sparse, offer confirmation. During the latter years of the century, associations of 'players' called by the names of their towns or districts are recorded as receiving rewards for their services, and soon these tended to lose their amateur status. What probably happened was that the privileged group of minstrels attached to the houses of the gentry, seeing what the amateurs could do and looking enviously on the awards made to them, gradually proceeded to engage in theatrical activities, so that in many districts small companies, most of them including no more than some four players, sprang into being; some of their members no doubt were already professionals, drawn from the minstrel class, others were carpenters and weavers caught by the glamour of the stage. In order to protect themselves, most of these put themselves under the patronage of prominent lords; at these lords' mansions they presented their Christmas shows and for many months of the year they wandered round from place to place as strolling actors. An act of 1464 definitely associates 'players' of this kind with minstrels, and by the eighties of the century we hear not only of the King's players but also of others such as those under the patronage of the Earl of Essex and of Richard, Duke of Gloucester (later King Richard III).

The act of 1464 refers to "players in their interludes," and in 1494 King Henry VII's actors were described as "pleyars of the Kyngs enterluds"; and here we first encounter a dramatic term of very considerable importance. The word 'interlude,' strangely, seems to be exclusively English. Whether in origin it meant only a play (or *ludus*) carried on between (or *inter*) several characters need not concern us; what is important is the fact that from the close of the fifteenth century on until about 1575 it came to have a quite definite significance as the type of play, relatively short, suitable for performance by a small acting company at a lord's house. It was therefore the term used to describe the typical pieces which made up the repertory of the professionals coming into being during these years.

It must not, of course, be assumed that with the appearance of the small professional troupes all other theatrical activities declined or vanished. Well into the sixteenth century mystery plays continued to be performed just as they had been for generations, and the conditions which were fruitful for the arising of the strolling actors were also fruitful for the cultivation of performances of other kinds. In fact, the early years of the sixteenth century show us a vast and variegated growth of all sorts of theatrical ventures. From the eighties of the preceding century the University of Oxford was displaying an interest in academic shows, and Cambridge soon followed suit; the members of the Inns of Court early discovered the delights of dramatic activities; several of the larger schools brought play-acting into their curricula; the children of the royal chapels similarly were encouraged to present their stage offerings; the household of Sir Thomas More may not have been singular in the attention it paid to these early theatricals; and, at a slightly later date, at least a few worthy religious teachers, such as John Bale, recognized that the drama could provide an excellent means of promulgating moral or theological opinions. Certainly the central element amid all this diverse activity was that of the small professional companies, yet it must be remembered that between 1475 and 1575 the drama was being fed from all these several sources.

In seeking to trace the growth of dramatic writing during this period it is not possible either to follow a strictly chronological progress or to keep distinct the various types of play cultivated by the different kinds of performers. All we can do is to treat the early Tudor plays, roughly from the beginning of the sixteenth century up to near the accession of Elizabeth in 1559, as one general group, and then to consider the contributions of the sixties and early seventies, when the professional companies were enlarging their scope, as the transition between the old world and the world of Shakespeare and his companions.

A start may be made with the first three plays extant in printed form—*Everyman*, *Fulgens and Lucrece*, and *Hick Scorner*. The first of these, a play still esteemed and acted, stands with one foot in the fifteenth century and one in the sixteenth. Related in some way with the Dutch *Elckerlijk*, it associates itself with the moralities; yet in its form, more consciously 'dramatic' than that of *The Castle of Perseverance*, *Mankind*, or *Nature*, it points towards something new. With a kind of subdued and simple passion it shows us Death, commanded by God, approaching Everyman; anxiously Everyman seeks solace and help from his companions, but Fellowship, Kindred, Goods, and all worldly things forsake him; in the end only Good Deeds, frail and faint-ing, accompanies him over the passage of the grave. We cannot be quite sure what actors were in the anonymous writer's mind when he penned this work, but almost certainly the second play, *Fulgens and Lucrece*, was intended for presentation by a group of amateurs in a private house. In it a humanistic theme is ex-ploited, a maiden Lucrece being confronted by two lovers—Publius Cornelius, an aristocratic gallant, and the more lowly born but virtuous Flaminius. To a certain extent the piece might be regarded as a kind of dramatic debate, the lovers arguing their cases and the maiden finally deciding the question by offering her hand to Flaminius. This brief description of the plot does not suggest that it has much vital interest, yet as soon as we turn to the text and listen to two boys, called simply A and B, chattering to each other, we recognize that we have before us the work of a skilful dramatist. The pair have just come from a banquet pro-vided by a cardinal, and they are full of excitement about a play which is to be performed for the delectation of his guests. They are not supposed to be actors, but B knows the plot of the piece and tells it to his friend A (and incidentally, of course, conveni-ently provides the audience with the 'argument'). Then, when the main performers come to speak their lines, A takes service with one of the wooers and B with the other, introducing an ele-ment of light comedy both by their comments on the debate and by their own wooing of Lucrece's maid. To a certain extent the device is no more than a development of the technique used in *Mankind* for the purpose of drawing the spectators into the play-world, but obviously it is much more adroitly employed, and indicates well how dramatic craftsmanship was being polished even in these early days.

The third play, *Hick Scorner*, differs from the other two, and almost certainly was intended for performance by professionals. In it, Pity, Contemplation, and Perseverance meet to bewail the evils of the time, when suddenly Freewill pushes his way in:

> Away, fellows, and stand a-room!
> How say you? Am not I a goodly person?
> I trow you know not such a guest.
> What, sirs? I tell you my name is Freewill.

Soon he is joined by Imagination, and later by Hick Scorner him-self—a merry character who regales the spectators with an account of his adventures:

> Sirs, I have been in many a country—
> As in France, Ireland and in Spain,
> Portugal, Seville, also in Almaine,
> Friesland, Flanders and in Burgoyne,
> Calabria, Pugle and Arragon.

This trio band together and put Pity in the stocks, where he sadly laments his fate in almost lyrical terms:

> Lo, lords, they may curse the time they were born,
> For the weeds that overgroweth the corn.
> They troubled me guiltless and wot not why.
> For God's love yet will I suffer patiently.
> We all may say 'Well-away' for sin that is now-aday.
> Lo! virtue is vanished for ever and aye—
>   Worse was it never.

After all this grieving and this irreverent merriment, suddenly the plot turns to a happy conclusion. Perseverance and Contem-plation return to rescue Pity from the stocks, while Freewill is converted from his evil ways.

If we take these three plays as pointers it is possible to see in general outline the varied courses which the drama was taking during the first half of the sixteenth century. The tradition of what may be styled the 'amateur morality,' established in *The Castle of Perseverance, Mankind,* and *Nature,* and showing one form of development in *Everyman,* continued in several direc-tions. In the hands of some writers it tended to shift its orienta-tion towards political rather than religious themes, although, of course, in noting this, we must also remember that in the Tudor age matters of Church and State were inextricably intertwined. Here comes John Skelton's *Magnificence* (probably about 1515), which introduces as central character a prince, Magnificence, led astray by Counterfeit Countenance, Cloaked Collusion, Courtly Abusion, and Folly, brought to Poverty and Despair, and eventu-ally embracing Good Hope and Redress. Skelton was a poet, and his scenes are vitally conceived, but his work must cede place to the

still more vital *Satire of the Three Estates* (1540–50), written by
Sir David Lyndsay, and produced several times in Scotland. The
core of this lengthy and ambitious drama is a disputation, with
Rex Humanitas in the centre, between Diligence and Wanton-
ness, a disputation richly embroidered by episodes which, attacking corruptions ecclesiastical and political, have as their central
figure "Pauper, the Poor Man." Vigorous and forthright, Lyndsay's lines display an imaginative power going considerably beyond anything of a similar kind to be found in the contemporary
English moralities, but unfortunately it stands alone in the Scotland of its time. Somewhat akin to it is an anonymous *Respub-
lica*, acted as a "Christmas device" by a company of boys in
1553. In this play, too, the common folk find their representative
in the People, an abstract character who, speaking in dialect, does
not hesitate to complain of the evils of the age. "Then let poor
volk ha some part," he says,

> Vor we ignoram people, whom ich do perzent,
> Wer ne'er zo i-polld, so wrong, and so i-torment,
> Lord Jhese Christ, when he was i-pounst and i-pilate,
> Was ner zo i-trounst as we have been of years late.

These political moralities at first may seem to exist in a sphere
far removed from that of the Shakespearian drama, yet their significance in connexion with what was to come is great. Out of
them eventually developed the chronicle history play, and how
that happened finds excellent illustration in a drama, *Kynge
Johan*, written by the worthy proselytizing vicar, John Bale,
shortly before the middle of the century. In essence it does not
differ overmuch from the other political moralities even although
its main emphasis is upon the evils of Catholicism rather than
upon pride and magnificence, but the method that Bale employed in its construction makes it the clear link between the old
and the new, the abstract and the concrete. When we look at
some of the scenes, and encounter dramatic persons such as
'Ynglond' (England), Sedicion, Civil Order, Commonalty, Private Wealth, and Dissimulation, we might think that it is
exactly the same as the other morality plays. The essential thing
to note, however, is that Bale, in order to make his arguments

more potent, has deliberately avoided making his central figure a Prince Magnificence or a Rex Humanitas; instead, he has turned to English history and set King John on his stage throne, associating him not only with a collection of abstract virtues and vices, but also with individually named characters such as Stephen Langton, Cardinal Pandulphus, and Symon of Swynsett. All that was required for the creation of the chronicle history was for a later dramatist to banish the personifications and stick more closely to the actual historical events.

Alongside the plays of this kind, others of the morality type sought to promulgate humanistic concepts and to plead for the pursuit of learning. To a certain extent that had been the object of Medwall's *Nature*, and the tradition was carried on in later works exemplified by John Redford's *Wit and Science* (c. 1540) and John Rastell's *Nature of the Four Elements* (c. 1517). In the former, Wit, the central character, enters with Study, Diligence, and Instruction. Very soon Tediousness destroys his power, and he is trapped by the ensnaring wiles of Idleness until, at the close, Shame comes to him, and he returns to the arms of Science and Reason. In Rastell's play, science also becomes the prime virtue, conceived mainly in terms of the discoveries currently being made by the voyagers across the vast Atlantic Ocean.

John Rastell introduces us to an interesting company. He himself married Elizabeth, the daughter of Sir Thomas More, and his daughter Joan became the wife of John Heywood, the author of several plays which connect themselves with the tradition to which *Fulgens and Lucrece* belonged. We are in the midst here of the More circle, and the More circle was interested humanistically in the theatre. Besides penning his own play, Rastell, a printer-publisher by trade, issued an anonymous adaptation of a Spanish work, *Celestina* (1499), under the title of *Calisto and Melebea*, thus bringing to the attention of English readers a narrative-drama which played a not unimportant part in the growth of the European theatre as a whole. The story of this piece tells how Calisto has become enamoured of Melebea, and how he confides in his servant Sempronio, who arranges to see the bawd Celestina. The heroine is almost persuaded to agree to an assignation with the hero when her father, Danio, tells her of an ominous dream he has had. In horror Melebea confesses her sinful thought, and the action ends with exhortations to virtue. The English version thus has a thoroughly moral conclusion, but quite obviously the author's attention is directed mainly towards the intrigue, and the liveliest portions are those in which Celestina, a kind of prototype of Juliet's nurse, indulges in her lusty speeches. She can tell a tale lengthily and with evident gusto:

Now the blessing that Our Lady gave her son
That same blessing I give now to you all. . . .
Sempronio for me about doth enquire,
And it was told me I should have found him here.
I am sure he will come hither anon,
But the whilst I shall tell you a pretty game.
I have a wench of Sempronio's, a pretty one,
But the last day we were both nigh a stark shame . . .
She loveth one Crito better or as well.
This Crito and Elecea sat drinking
In my house, and I also making merry,
And, as the devil would, far from our thinking,
Sempronio almost came on us suddenly.
But then wrought I my craft of bawdery.
I had Crito go up and make himself room
To hide him in my chamber among the broom;
Then made I Elecea sit down a-sewing,
And I with my rock began for to spin
As who sayeth of Sempronio we had no knowing.
He knocked at the door and I let him in,
And for a countenance I did begin
To catch him in mine arms, and said 'See, see,
Who kisseth me, Elecea, and will not kiss thee.'
Elecea for a countenance made her grieved,
And would not speak, but still did sew.
'Why speak ye not,' quod Sempronio. 'Be ye moved?'
'Have I not a cause,' quod she. 'No,' quod he. 'I trow.'
'Ah, traitor,' quod she, 'full well dost thou know.
Where hast thou been these days from me—
That the imposthume and evil death take thee!'
'Peace, mine Elecea,' quod he. 'Why say ye thus?
Alas, why put you yourself in this woe?
The hot fire of love so burneth between us

That my heart is with yours wherever I go.
And for three days' absence to say to me so,
In faith me thinketh ye be to blame.'
But now hark well, for here beginneth the game.
Crito in my chamber above that was hidden
I think lay not easily and began to rumble.
Sempronio heard that and asked who was within
Above in the chamber that so did jumble.
'Who?' quod she. 'A lover of mine.' 'Mayhap ye stumble,'
Quod he, 'on the truth as many one doth.'
'Go up,' quod she, 'and look whether it be sooth.'
'Well,' quod he, 'I go.' Nay, thought I, not so;
I said, 'Come, Sempronio, let this fool alone,
For of thy long absence she is in such woe,
And half beside herself, and her wit nigh gone.'
'Well,' quod he, 'above yet there is one.'
'Wilt thou know?' quod I. 'Yea,' quod he, 'I thee require.'
'It is a wench,' quod I, 'sent me by a friar....'
Then he laughed. 'Yea,' quod I, 'no more words of this,
For this time too long we spend here amiss.'

The language is racy, and we can well appreciate how knowledge of such a piece might well stimulate the playwrights of the time towards fashioning and enriching their comic styles.

Heywood's dramatic essays breathe the same air. Their plots are simple, but their dialogue has liveliness, jauntiness, and skill. *Witty and Witless* (c. 1533) takes shape as a simple debate between an intellectual and his opposite; *The Play of Love* (printed 1533) shows the debate in a slightly more elaborate form, involving four characters—the Lover-not-Loved, the Woman-Beloved-not-Loving, the Lover-Loved, and Neither-Lover-nor-Loved. Although the persons are not given individual proper names, the world they live in is the same as that of *Calisto and Melebea*; indeed, as we listen to the tongue of Neither-Lover-nor-Loved wagging while he goes to the door—

'Knock soft,' quoth one who the same unlocked,
An ancient wise woman who was never
From this said, 'Sweeting, but about her ever.'
'Mother,' quoth I, 'how doth my dear darling?'
'Dead, wretch,' cried she, 'even by thine absenting'—

we might well have the impression that Celestina is still rattling
on. Yet a further advance is made in *The Play of the Weather*
(printed 1533), where the debate is extended and associated with
groups of characters. Jupiter, we learn, is more than a little worried to hear that many humans are grumbling about the weather
he supplies to them, and he summons Merry Report to inquire
into the matter. A Gentleman asks for days "Dry and misty, the
wind calm and still," a Merchant prays for the weather to be
"Stormy nor misty, the wind measurable," a Ranger wants "good
rage of blustering and blowing," a Water Miller seeks rain but
is confronted by a Wind Miller who desires only breezes to move
his sails; these are followed by a Gentlewoman, who demands
"weather close and temperate," a Launderer, who craves for
sunshine, and finally by a little Boy whose sole interest is in
"plenty of snow to make my snow-balls." In the face of all these
suits what can poor Jupiter do save provide variety of weather at
his own good will? Obviously here we are moving away from
the world of abstractions and of didacticism; genuine farce and
comedy are in the making.

This farce and comedy emerge even more clearly in three other
short plays which, although their authorship is not absolutely
certain, may also have come from Heywood's witty pen. In *The
Pardoner and the Friar* (c. 1519) a Friar steps on stage and to his
disgust encounters a Pardoner; they quarrel about their respective virtues and functions, and each starts to deliver a sermon,
the one seeking to outbellow the other—

> *Friar. Date et dabitur vobis.*
>   Good devout people, this place of Scripture——
>   *Pardoner.* Worshipful masters, ye shall understand——
>   *Friar.* Is to you that have no literature——
>   *Pardoner.* That Pope Leo the Tenth hath granted with his
>   hand——
>   *Friar.* Is to say in our English tongue——
>   *Pardoner.* And by his Bulls confirmed under lead . . .

A Curate and Neighbour Pratt vainly attempt to still their
clamour. There is no real plot here, nor is there in *The Four PP*
(c. 1520), but the dialogue is vigorous and the fictional situation

offers ample opportunity for the introduction of just such tale-telling as gives raciness to *Calisto and Melebea* and *The Play of Love*. A Palmer, a Pardoner, a 'Poticary, and a Pedler meet and, in the course of argument, agree to have a competition in the narrating of lies. Towards the end, the Pardoner explains that a certain lady-friend of his had died, and declares that he went down to Hell to seek her. There he encountered a genial Satan:

> 'Ho, ho!' quoth the devil, 'we are well pleased.
> What is his name thou wouldst have eased?'
> 'Nay,' quoth I, 'be it good or evil,
> My coming is for a she-devil.'
> 'What calls her,' quoth he, 'thou whoreson?'
> 'Forsooth,' quoth I, 'Margery Carson,'
> 'Now by our honour,' said Lucifer,
> 'No devil in Hell shall withold her—
> And if thou wouldest have twenty more,
> Wert not for justice, they should go.'

Women, explains this devil, are such shrews that life in Hell is becoming most uncomfortable. As the Pardoner reaches this part of his story it seems as though he must surely win the prize; but very quietly the Palmer interrupts to remark that he considers the narrative most peculiar since in the whole of his varied experience he has never yet found any woman out of patience. For this lie the laurels are immediately awarded to him.

Finally, in *Johan Johan* (c. 1520) the debate is integrated into a simple plot. The piece opens excellently. On to the stage wanders the henpecked husband whose name gives the title to the play, and at once he takes the audience into his confidence:

> God speed you, masters, every one.
> Wot ye not whither my wife is gone?

He tells them that she is continually gadding about, and, working himself up into a passion, he promises that when she comes home he will beat her soundly,

> And at every stroke lay her on the ground
> And train her by the hair about the house round.
> I am even mad that I beat her not now.

> But I shall reward her, hardily, well enow.
> There is never a wife between heaven and hell
> Which was ever beaten half so well.

Then a doubt strikes him:

> Beaten, quotha? Yea, but what if she thereof die?
> Then I may chance to be hanged shortly.
> And when I have beaten her till she smoke
> And given her many a hundred stroke,
> Think ye that she will amend yet?
> Nay, by Our Lady, the devil a bit!
> Therefore I will not beat her at all.

This reflection, however, brings him back to his anger at her ways: he determines that he must punish her. Then the thought occurs to him of what his fellows will say: he imagines one of his neighbours asking:

> 'Whom chidest thou, Johan Johan?'
> 'Marry,' will I say, 'I chide my curst wife,
> The veriest drab that ever bare life,
> Which doth nothing but go and come,
> And I cannot make her keep her at home.'
> Then I think he will say by and by,
> 'Walk her cote, Johan Johan, and beat her hardily.'
> But then unto him mine answer shall be,
> 'The more I beat her the worse is she,
> And worse and worse make her I shall.'
> He will say then, 'Beat her not at all.'
> 'And why?' shall I say, 'This would be wist,
> Is she not mine to chastise as I list?'
>   But this is another point worst of all,
> The folks will mock me when they hear me brawl.
> But for all that, shall I cease therefore
> To chastise my wife ever the more
> And to make her at home for to tarry?
> Is not that well done? Yes, by Saint Mary,
> That is the point of an honest man.
> For to beat his wife well now and then.

Thus he works himself up into his passion once again, and at this opportune moment Tyb, his wife, enters on the stage behind him:

Tyb. Why, whom wilt thou beat, I say, thou knave?
Johan. Who, I, Tyb? None, so God me save.
Tyb. Yes, I heard thee say thou wouldst one beat.
Johan. Marry, wife, it was stockfish in Thames Street,
Which will be good meat against Lent.
Why, Tyb, what haddest thou thought that I had meant?
    Tyb. Marry, I thought I heard thee bawling.
Wilt thou never leave this wawling?
How the devil dost thou thyself behave?
Shall we ever have this work, thou knave?
    Johan. What, wife, how sayest thou? Was it well guessed
      of me
That thou wouldest be come home in safety
As soon as I had kindled a fire?
Come, warm thee, sweet Tyb, I thee require.

The sense of what will be effective on the stage is clearly evident
in this introduction to the play, and its subsequent action well
keeps up the promise of the opening episode. The wretched husband is sent off, much against his will, to invite the local priest
to share in the eating of a pie which Tyb has baked. Just as they
are all about to sit down to the repast, he is commanded to draw
some water from the well; when he returns he discovers that the
pail has a hole in it and consequently he is forced to sit down by
the fire, painfully softening wax for the purpose of mending it,
while the amorous priest and the wife gobble up the last morsels
of the pie. The action ends when, unable to bear his indignities
any longer, he suddenly goes berserk and drives the pair from
his house.

At the same time as playlets of this kind were being written
for amateurs, the professional actors were constantly adding to
their own repertories, for the most part specializing in interludes akin to *Hick Scorner*. Most of their plays have vanished,
and consequently there is no sure basis for the formulating of
absolutely certain judgments concerning the material they presented to their audiences either in lordly hall or on village green;
but at least enough remains to suggest what they had to offer.
Such interludes as have come down to us indicate that an effort
was made to combine good healthy instruction with much comic
business, and in them two technical elements in particular call

for our attention, the use of disguise and the establishment of the dramatic character called the Vice. To a certain extent the disguise device seems to have arisen chiefly out of the morality-play pattern. The hero, or at least the central figure in a play, is approached by some evil characters who wish to get him into their clutches; if they come to him in their own shapes he may be induced to dismiss them summarily, and so they pretend to be other than they are. This device is constantly being employed, and we may well believe that the familiarizing of sixteenth-century spectators with the convention helps to explain the popularity of the disguise element in the later Elizabethan drama. Often this disguise device is associated with the person of the Vice, a dramatic type ubiquitous in early Tudor plays but one somewhat difficult to analyse. Most modern dramatic historians have inclined to interpret this Vice as having his origin in the Seven Deadly Sins of the morality tradition, and, largely because of Shakespeare's allusion to the Vice with his dagger of wrath belabouring the Devil, there has been a tendency to see him as having diabolic associations. For neither of these assumptions is there any real evidence. It is true that frequently the Vice is connected with the morality-play Vices, but he remains distinct from them; and the only two plays wherein the Vice and the Devil are brought together are late in date. It is also to be observed that the term 'Vice' often appears applied to characters, such as Neither-Lover-nor-Loved and Merry Report, who are in no wise connected with the Vices at all. In fact, the names Neither-Lover-nor Loved and Merry Report offer us an excellent clue to his dramatic function. While at times he may come upon the stage as Politic Persuasion or even as Sin, fundamentally he is a completely amoral figure existing primarily, and sometimes only, for the purpose of arousing laughter. He is the character who keeps the spectators bound up in the play, crying "Make room, make room!" as he enters, and continually turning to them with comment and question. His share in the dialogue, generally more extensive than that of any of his companions, is regularly enriched by an effervescent bubbling-over of words; he loves to rattle off lists of place-names, just as he also loves to have long catalogues of words come tumbling from his lips—

The offals, the refuse, the rags, the parings;
The baggage, the trash, the fragments, the sharings;
The odd ends, the crumbs, the driblets, the chippings;
The patches, the pieces, the broklets, the drippings;
The flittance, the scrapings, the wild waifs and strays;
The skimmings, the gubbings of booties and preys;
The gleanings, the casualities, the blind escheats;
The forging of forfeits, the scape of extreats;
Th'excess, the waste, the spoils, the superfluities;
The windfalls, the shreddings, the fleecings, the petty fees;
With a thousand things more which she might well lack
Would fill all these same purses that hang on my back.

Clad like the Fool in folk-dances and entertainments, he delights to sing and prance, and perhaps his name, as has been suggested, does not connect itself at all with the Vices but derives from his wearing of a visor, or vise. Many a scene in these early plays he richly enlivens, and long after he disappeared in his own person from the stage his spirit continued to haunt the later drama.

5. COMEDY, TRAGEDY, AND TRAGICOMEDY

Our brief glance at early Tudor drama has carried us just a little past the mid-point of the century. During this period men were slowly coming to be aware of plays in other tongues both ancient and contemporary. A school-piece such as the farce of *Jack Juggler* (c. 1550) bases its farcical plot on Plautus' *Amphitruo* and at the same time introduces Jack as a native Vice constantly taking the audience into his confidence:

Our Lord of Heaven and sweet Saint John
Rest you merry, my masters every one . . .
And you too, sir, and you, and you also . . .
How say you, masters, I pray you tell,
Have I not requited my merchant well?

It was precisely this combination of native elements with elements classical and classically inspired that led to the development of the stage which gave birth to Shakespeare; and as we pass the century's mid-point, arriving at the years immediately preceding the accession of Queen Elizabeth in 1559, we find our-

selves accelerating our steps. Even more rapid becomes the pace
when we reach the decade following her enthronement. Suddenly
the forms of drama which had been so slowly evolving began to
assume a new shape, partly due to further efforts of the amateurs, partly due to a fresh scope of activity won by the professionals.

About the year 1553 two plays were performed, both
comedies, which mark a sharp break with the past. One is
Gammer Gurton's Needle, written by a "Mr S." and presented
at Christ's College, Cambridge; the other, intended for school
production (probably at Westminster), is Nicholas Udall's *Ralph
Roister Doister*.

In *Ralph Roister Doister* the impress of the two forces—that
of the interlude and that of classical comedy—may readily be
traced. So far as the play's form is concerned, Terence is the
master, and we realize how much the playwrights of the time
were to learn from him in two particular directions. Terence
taught them how to shape, not merely a farcical episode, but a
fully developed comic plot; *Ralph Roister Doister* is neither farce
nor debate; it is a comedy full of incident and intrigue, well ordered and well planned. In addition, Terence showed the English
playwrights how to vary and depict stage characters; the witty
lovers, the testy old fathers, the intriguing servants, the blustering soldiers of late sixteenth-century drama were largely to take
their inspiration from his example. Mere imitation of Terence,
however, might well have led towards nothing save dullness and
insipidity, and, as *Ralph Roister Doister* demonstrates, the English authors of this time happily had their own fully established
native dramatic tradition to keep their scenes lively. Roister
Doister himself may be simply a version of the bombastic, boasting soldier of the Roman plays, but his companion, Matthew
Merygreeke, manifestly owes his being to the popular Vice.

The vitality in this new dramatic development may be seen
even more clearly in *Gammer Gurton's Needle*. Again the influence of Terence is patent, but, instead of finding ourselves in an
urban environment, we are carried off to a rustic setting, peopled
by English village characters who owe little or nothing to ancient
example. The plot is simple—just the story of the loss of a pre-

cious needle and the resultant suspicions and jealousies, aggravated by the merry-making proclivities of the Vice-like Diccon—and the author's skill is demonstrated in the adroit manner by which he has succeeded in keeping the audience's attention alert by the turns of his action and by the vigour of his dialogue.

This reference to dialogue reminds us that, while effective dramatic expression requires careful and skilful planning of scenes, architectural form alone cannot create good plays either comic or tragic: the author must have at his command an adequate and forceful medium for his dialogue. In the days of the mystery plays many of the speeches were cast in lines of varied, and often complicated, stanzaic structure, and the tradition of these stanza forms was passed on to the sixteenth century. During the early Tudor period, however, two things happened: more and more the playwrights tended to seek for simpler rhythmic measures and gradually they started to grasp the fact that effective dramatic values could accrue from the apportionment of certain measures to particular situations or characters. Thus, in addition to a toning down of the 'poetic' style, a vague principle was established whereby external rhythmic forms were used to express outwardly the playwrights' purposes. Heywood's *The Play of the Weather* illustrates this well. For Jupiter, as an omnipotent god, the dignified rime royal is reserved:

> Right far too long, as now, were to recite
>   The ancient estate wherein ourself hath reigned,
> What honour, what laud, given us of very right,
>   What glory we have had, duly unfeigned
>   Of each creature which duty hath constrained;
> For above all gods since our father's fall
> We, Jupiter, were ever principal.

No other person is permitted to use this form. The more cultured among the human characters, such as the Gentleman, are given two media of expression. When they address Jupiter they frame their lines in quatrains:

> Most mighty prince and god of every nation,
>   Pleaseth your highness to vouchsafe the hearing
> Of me, which, according to your proclamation,

> Doth make appearance in way of beseeching,.
> Not sole for myself, but generally
> For all come of noble and ancient stock,
> Which sort above all doth most thankfully
> Daily take pain for wealth of the common stock.

But when they are conversing with their fellows they descend for the most part to simple couplets. Thus, immediately after uttering the lines quoted above, the Gentleman has some speech with Merry Report, concluding:

> Then give me thy hand. That promise I take.
> And if for my sake any suit thou do make,
> I promise thy pain to be requited.
> More largely than now shall be recited.

In contrast with these, the merry Vice Merry Report inclines to allow his speeches to fall into irregularly stressed couplets:

> Yea, farewell, good son, with all my heart.
> Now such another sort as here hath been,
> In all the days of my life I have not seen.
> No suitors now but women, knaves, and boys,
> And all their suits are in fancies and toys.
> If that there come no wiser after this cry,
> I will to the god and make an end quickly.
> O yes! if that any knave here
> Be willing to appear,
> For weather foul or clear,
> Come in before this flock;
> And be he whole or sickly,
> Come, show his mind quickly.

The principle, an excellent one, was to prove of immense service to Shakespeare and his companions at the close of the century; but it had one fundamental weakness. It was, as it were, set too high; on its top notes the dialogue rose to the artificial and undramatic rime royal, and its lowest notes did not reach beyond Merry Report's erratic couplets. Quite clearly, further advance was not possible without a recasting of the range in dialogue forms. Such recasting was, fortunately, adumbrated during the period of the fifties and sixties, and the methods employed are plainly indicated by two plays—a comedy called *The Supposes*, performed in 1566 by the members of Gray's Inn, written by George Gascoigne, and a tragedy, *Gorboduc* or *Ferrex and Porrex*, presented by the Inner Temple in 1562, penned by two authors, Thomas Norton and Thomas Sackville. In the latter, the unprecedented step was taken of using blank verse throughout; in the former the comic dialogue was expressed entirely in prose, a medium which previously had almost never been employed for stage purposes. If we take these together, we realize that the dramatists, instead of being dependent upon a scale running from rime royal to irregular couplets, now had available another scale extending from blank verse to prose and that they could still make use, for occasional special effects, of such forms as couplets, quatrains, and the like. In fact this was the scale on which the Shakespearian drama was to rely.

In the tragic realm, *Gorboduc* occupies a position akin to that occupied by *Ralph Roister Doister* and *Gammer Gurton's Needle* in the comic. Just as these plays were fashioned according to Terentian principles, so it owed its shape to the study of Seneca, an author who suddenly assumed prominence in the early sixties. The translation of his works began with the efforts of Jasper Heywood; no less a person than Queen Elizabeth tried her hand, in 1561, at versifying some passages from *Hercules Œtæus*; and within a few years all the tragedies were to appear in English costume. Sackville and Norton, therefore, were being thoroughly up to date in seeking to adapt his methods to the needs of the English stage. These needs, however, were not for mere imitation; and the pair of authors showed their awareness of what the public wanted by their deliberate departures from what Seneca had to offer. They refrained from dealing with a theme taken from classic myth, substituting instead a plot based on ancient British history; instead of resting content with the exhibition of high passions and monstrous 'tragic' events, they made their play into a message for their own times. Their tale of a monarch who made ill arrangements for the succession to his throne was one which obviously had direct pertinence at a time when all men, remembering the terrible days of the Wars of the Roses, were concerned and worried about the future of the kingdom.

To a certain extent, therefore, *Gorboduc*, although it has abandoned the use of personifications, may be regarded as a 'morality
play,' and this draws attention to the continuing force of the
morality tradition, not only during this early period, but also
later when Shakespeare was turning from his comic realm to the
realm of the tragedies.

All these plays were 'academic,' and they were accompanied
by numerous others designed for performance at universities,
Inns of Court, or schools. Gascoigne's *The Supposes*, adapted from
I suppositi by the Italian dramatist and poet Lodovico Ariosto,
was companioned by an anonymous *Bugbears*, similarly adapted
from another Italian comedy, A. F. Grazzini's *La spiritata*. A few
years after *Gorboduc*, in 1566, the Inner Temple put on a second
Senecan drama, the horrific *Gismond of Salerne*, which also
deviated from the strict classic pattern by selecting a plot from
one of Boccaccio's romantic tales. The significance of such
comedies and tragedies was great; yet at the same time we must
observe that the professionals, too, were playing their part in the
enlargement of dramatic form and style, and that, in particular,
they were extending their resources in such a way as to permit
them to make use of what the academics had to offer. During the
first part of the century, as we have seen, the professional companies were very small, usually consisting of only four men or
of four men and a boy; and it was obviously with such groups in
view that publishers inserted on many title-pages of plays the
statement that "four men may easily play this interlude." Sometimes careful examination of the texts indicates that statements
of this kind were over-optimistic, but clearly the publishers themselves felt that the little blurb had sales value. As we move into
the early decades of Elizabeth's reign, interesting signs of change
become evident; the references to the number of actors who, by
doubling their parts, could perform the published dramas are
extended to include six, seven, and even eight players, while at
the same time the length of the popular plays tends to become
greater. Even although this is a period when comparatively little
has come down to us for the forming of sure judgments, sufficient remains to convince us that by 1575 the actors were finding a public considerably larger than anything they had enjoyed

in the past, that as a result they were approaching the status of the great companies of Shakespeare's time and that they were able to put on shows far in advance of the short interludes with which the earlier spectators had been regaled. Alongside of the growth of the adult companies, we must also take into account the activities of the children of Paul's and the Chapel. These continued to orient their productions towards the Court, but, as the years pass by, we realize that more and more they, too, were becoming 'professional.' Some time was to elapse before their performances were to offer serious rivalry to the adults, but already steps had been taken in that direction.

The public which attended shows given both by the men actors and by the children clearly were attracted by lyricism, wit, action, and variety rather than by any stiffly 'classical' style; and as we look upon such plays of the period as have come down to us we see before us diverse essays in the 'tragicomic' form rather than unrelieved tragedies from which lighter things have been banished or comedies barren of serious thought. The dramatic works of this kind fall into more than one group. First come a series of moral interludes like *Nice Wanton* (c. 1550), *Wealth and Health* (c. 1555), *The Longer Thou Livest the More Fool Thou* (c. 1560), William Wager's *Enough is as Good as a Feast* (c. 1565), *New Custom* (c. 1565), *The Contention between Liberality and Prodigality* (c. 1568), *The Trial of Treasure* (printed 1567), and George Wapull's *The Tide tarrieth No Man* (printed 1576). Not all of these are definitely associated with professional players, but all are of the type which we know from numerous sources formed a large part of the offerings of the popular stage. All exhibit common features: a moral theme is presented by means of abstractly named characters; farcical-comic business is plentiful; at the centre of the merriment is a gay fleering person usually named specifically as the Vice. Moreover, most of them make considerable use of song, and this musical element is developed in such a way as to demonstrate that at least some of the playwrights had glimpsed the dramatic possibilities inherent in the use of lyrical material; in some plays the songs are introduced solely for the purpose of providing variety, but in others they are made to serve a definite function either in forwarding the course of the plot or in evoking atmosphere. Still further, several of the pieces in this group introduce stage directions of a sort rarely to be met with in earlier years—directions which suggest an increased awareness of theatrical effect. When, for example, in *The Longer Thou Livest* Moros is bidden to enter "counterfeiting a vain gesture and a foolish countenance," or when Worldly Man, in *Enough is as Good as a Feast*, is told to appear "stout and frolic" and later to sport "a strange attire," we realize that the authors, no doubt due to greater familiarity with the professional productions, are writing in terms different from those pertaining in many of the earlier interludes.

In scope these plays are being brought to a level near to that of the later Elizabethan drama, and an excellent example of this is provided by *Liberality and Prodigality*. Almost certainly that piece was originally acted, probably by boys, in 1567 or 1568, but when it was printed in 1602 we are informed on the title page that it was revived at Court before Elizabeth in 1601—the year when Shakespeare was engaged in the writing of his *Hamlet*. We are therefore concerned here, not with something so primitive as to possess only historical value, but with a dramatic form which could still appeal to audiences thirty years later, and which, in fact, exercised a potent force in the formation of the stage in 'Shakespearian' times.

A second group of plays shows the mixture of the serious and the comic in another way. Here we meet *Horestes* (printed 1567) by John Pikeryng, Thomas Preston's "lamentable tragedy mixed full of pleasant mirth," *Cambises* (printed c. 1570), Thomas Garter's *Susanna* (c. 1569), Richard Edwardes' *Damon and Pythias* (c. 1565), R. B.'s *Apius and Virginia* (c. 1565), and George Whetstone's *Promos and Cassandra* (printed 1578). In each of these the style is 'romantic,' and in most the influence of the morality tradition is apparent. Haphazard in *Apius and Virginia* is the old rattling Vice; in *Cambises* the amoral Ambidexter carries on the ancient tradition of keeping in direct touch with the spectators, at one moment pretending he sees a pickpocket plying his trade—

> Is not my cousin Cutpurse with you in the meantime?
> To it! To it! cousin, and do your office fine . . .

> How like ye now, my masters? Doth not this gear cotton? . . .
> But how now, cousin Cutpurse, with whom play you?
> Take heed, for his hand is groping even now!——

at another moment turning to address an individual girl in the audience—

> I care not if I be married before to-morrow at noon,
> If marriage be a thing that so may be had.
> How say you, maid? To marry me will ye be glad?

At the same time, the plots are for the most part taken from classical sources, directly or indirectly: *Horestes* is simply Orestes with a cockney accent, and all the authors show that they are familiar with Terentian and Senecan styles.

Apius and Virginia is the most 'tragical' and also the most primitive in form. Here we are presented with a little *Measure for Measure* picture. Virginia, daughter of Virginius, fires the heart of the judge Apius. With the aid of Mansipulus and Haphazard he contrives to pass a decree that Virginia shall be given to him, but she prefers death at her father's hands to shame. The serious plot, written throughout in a jogging rhythm, has little virtue save in its moral; but when he turns to comedy the author's lines suddenly acquire a spirited liveliness. "Very well, sir," says Haphazard, on his entry upon the stage,

> Very well, sir, it shall be done
> As fast as ever I can prepare.
> Who dips with the devil he had need of a long spoon,
> Or else full small will be his fare.
> Yet a proper gentleman I am of truth—
> Yea, that may ye see by my long side gown.
> Yea, but what am I? A scholar, or a schoolmaster, or else
>   some youth?
> A lawyer, a student, or else a country clown?
> A broom-man, a basket-maker, or a baker of pies,
> A flesh- or a fish-monger, or a sower of lies?
> A louse or a louser, a leek or a lark,
> A dreamer, a drommel, a fire, or a spark?
> A caitiff, a cut-throat, a creeper in corners,
> A herbrain, a hangman, or a grafter of horners? . . .

The words go gushing forth in a long, amusing stream, and, ridiculous though they may be, they serve to give individuality to a rogue who might be regarded as the ancestor of Autolycus. Even to his death he goes gaily:

> Must I needs hang? By the gods, it doth spite me
> To think how crabbedly this silk lass will bite me.
> Then come, cousin Cutpurse, come run, haste and follow me;
> Haphazard must hang—come follow the livery.

A similar quality is apparent in *Horestes*. The mythical tale of Clytemnestra's murder moves heavily with its long, crudely constructed, trailing couplets, but as soon as the Vice comes on stage pretending to be deep in thought and then addresses the spectators—

> Ah, sirrah! Nay soft. What? Let me see.
> Good morrow to you, sir. How do you fare?—

we find ourselves in a different realm, a realm of impertinent laughter and practical joking.

The juxtaposition of murder, assassination and cruel vengeance and of rollicking impudence reaches its most blatant expression in *Cambises*, a play in which the author exhibits his passion for theatrical effects both in the dialogue and in the extraordinarily lengthy stage directions. The main plot concerns the ambitious wars of Persia's monarch and the ugly intrigues of his court. Cambises himself, the judge Sisamnes, prince Smirdis, and other 'historical' characters here justle with numbers of personifications—Cruelty, Murder, Shame, Counsel, Diligence, Preparation, Commons Cry and Commons Complaint, 'Small Hability' and Execution—and with two classical deities, Venus and Cupid. Alongside of these serious persons others carry on business of a vastly different kind—Huf, Ruf, and Snuf, three comic Soldiers with a Meretrix, the rustic Hob and Lob, accompanied by Hob's wife, Marian-May-Be-Good. And mingling with both the farcical and the heroic figures the Vice Ambidexter laughs his way through the action. Never for a moment is the stage still: the Meretrix has a comic fight with Huf, Ruf, and Snuf; one of the characters is smitten "in the neck with a sword to signify his death"; "a little bag of vinegar is pricked" to simulate bleeding; there is bombastic boasting, and wild fits of anger, and pleading, and lamentation. Obviously this was the kind of thing which excited and appealed to the spectators of the time.

Promos and Cassandra and *Damon and Pythias* introduce us to still another sort of tragicomic drama. The former, based on a play by Giraldi Cinthio and on Claude Rouillet's *Philanira*, deals with the *Measure for Measure* theme. The choice of sources here is significant, since both the Italian playwright and the French were men who had critically deplored the over-dependence of their contemporaries upon classical material and had pleaded for the cultivation of a romantic drama more appropriate to the spirit of the world they lived in. Quite clearly Whetstone was similarly intent on familiarizing English audiences with the atmosphere of romance. Edwardes, in *Damon and Pythias*, pursued the same course and indeed went so far as to style his work a "tragical comedy." The story here is one of friendship. Damon and Pythias arrive at Syracuse, and the former, having unwittingly allowed himself to give cause for suspicion to Carisophus, a parasite and informer, is condemned to death. On his begging leave of the monarch Dionysius to return for a short time to Greece before his execution, he is permitted to go provided that Pythias remains in custody as his pledge of return. On the day appointed for the execution Damon has not appeared: Pythias is about to perish when his friend rushes in, embraces him, and demands to take his place. The king is so affected by this exhibition of loyalty that he pardons Damon and takes the pair into his court. The story is expanded and lightened by several comic elements—by the pleasant humours of the kindhearted but self-seeking philosopher Aristippus (a kind of transformed Vice), by the pranks of the merry serving-boys Jack and Will, and by the rustic adventures of Grim the Collier.

This development of romantic themes must be associated with the exploitation of another form of romance, the chivalric, which seems to have been widely popular in the early seventies. The titles of numerous now lost plays from this period are known to us, and among them we find many, such as *Cloridon and Radiamanta, Paris and Vienna, Mamillia, Predor and Lucia, Her-*

petulus the Blue Knight, Panecia, Phedrastus, Phignon and Lucia, Philemon and Felicia, Pretestus, and The Red Knight, which certainly or probably dealt with material of this sort. One extant piece gives us a good idea of what these were like—The History of the Two Valiant Knights, Sir Clyomon Knight of the Golden Shield, Son to the King of Denmark, and Clamydes the White Knight, Son to the King of Suavia (c. 1577). As produced by the Queen's company, this must have been an exciting show, with its varied scenes of love and rivalry, of farcical humour, of high adventure, and with its rich array of characters extending from comic servants, noble heroes, distressed maidens, cruel giants, to the imperial Alexander the Great. The gallimaufry of episodes and persons might at first make us deem the drama unworthy of serious consideration, but when we read the text with the stage of the seventies in mind we are bound to acknowledge that it has been well constructed in a form apt to appeal to the growing theatrical audience of the age.

The growing theatrical audience was responsible for many things and for none more important than the building of London's first permanent playhouse in 1576. With its establishment, an old world gave place to a new. Of this a prime sign was the disappearance of the term which previously had been used to describe professional plays; up to 1576 more than half the printed plays had been described on their title pages as 'interludes'; after 1576 not a single one was so styled. The 'interludes' belonged to the time when the professionals were strolling actors, usually including only three men and a boy in each company, able to perform short morals and farces but incapable of presenting anything more elaborate. Now, in the new age, professional associations, established in permanent homes, could offer to the public works of extended scope—works for which the word 'interlude' no longer was appropriate. We are rapidly approaching the time of Shakespeare.

II

The Elizabethan Drama

1. THE THEATRES

IN 1576 Elizabeth had been on the throne for seventeen years, but in so far as the stage is concerned we may consider the erection of The Theatre in Shoreditch as marking the start of that great dramatic development which is styled by her name. What happened during the first part of her reign was of prime significance; nevertheless, it formed a basis rather than a firm structure; it was a foundation, not the building itself.

Shoreditch was selected as the location for this first permanent playhouse because, although it was convenient of access to those living in the city, it lay outside the jurisdiction of the civic authorities. During the time when the professional actors were establishing their position, the Queen herself and numbers of her lords had displayed a real, if somewhat erratic, interest in theatrical affairs, and as a result the actors were enabled to carry on their activities with a certain amount of freedom, and even of support. So long as the monarch and members of the nobility protected the players, allowing them to form companies which went under such titles as the Queen's Men, Lord Sussex's Men, Lord Essex's Men, and the like, the actors were not only at liberty to move from place to place without running the risk of arrest as vagabonds, they were also provided with warrants likely to induce local officials to give them assistance in the pursuit of their histrionic activities. This, however, by no means meant that these local officials, many of them puritanically inclined looked upon the stage with favour; and in particular London's civic authorities had always shown themselves opposed to the stage. Their objections to it were numerous—religious, medical, and economic. They tended to regard play-acting as ungodly, and the more severe among them were prepared to describe the theatre as the home of the Devil. With dismay they observed that greater crowds could be assembled for a performance than for a worthy sermon. Not unjustifiably they pointed out that such crowds added materially to the spread of infection during times of plague. And, above all, they claimed that attendance at plays had the effect of encouraging apprentices to slip away from their appointed tasks and of giving to others an excuse for idleness. Consequently the fathers of the city constantly sought to put such obstacles as they could in the path of those players who attempted to act within London's boundaries.

Established in Shoreditch, however, The Theatre was in a position to carry on its work unmolested, and as other playhouses came to be erected the localities chosen were all outside the walls. Some of them were built to the east, like the original Theatre itself; others were placed on the far side of the Thames, to the south, where they might be reached either by crossing the old bridge or by ferrying over the river. In the one district or the other rival houses—the Rose, the Swan, the Globe, and the Fortune—soon were called for by the steadily increasing audiences of the time.

During the period immediately before the erection of The Theatre, we have evidence that the players frequently made use of inn-yards for their performances, no doubt setting up some kind of trestle-stage at one end and accommodating spectators both in the yard itself and in the galleries which commonly ran round the walls. This may well have formed a partial model in 1576 for the first building specifically set up to house an acting company, although it is possible that some of its features may have been influenced by what was known concerning theatrical experimentation in Italy and elsewhere on the Continent. Basically, the open-air structure provided a benchless standing area for the less affluent members of the audience, while galleries offered more comfortable accommodation for those who could afford the additional cost; the limited few willing to pay still more were catered for in a 'lords' room,' no doubt part of the lower gallery boxed off near the stage. These spectators saw before them a wide open platform, jutting out into the middle of the yard and some forty feet square, with a half-roof supported on pillars giving some protection to the actors during inclement weather. Above this was placed a tiny turret on which a flag was flown, and from which a trumpeter announced to all the commencement of a performance.

The main stage was bare, backed by a façade broken by two or more doors, through which the actors made their entrances and exits. In general, no attempt was made to localize the place of action by means of scenery, although the use of movable properties might imaginatively suggest indoor or outdoor settings as well as scenes supposed to take place in darkness. Thus a small tree could, if necessary, stand for a forest, a table and benches give the impression of a tavern, a bed wheeled in indicate that the setting was a chamber, while the carrying-on of a flaring torch might suggest in the warmth of a June sun the darkness of night. This conventional method of production had several results. Usually it meant that the players did not seek to localize their scenes with the exactitude common in modern dramas; the audience were content if they knew that a particular episode was presumed to take place out of doors or indoors, during the day or during the night. Secondly, it imposed upon the playwrights the necessity of doing in words what now is done by the scene-designer; Elizabethan tragedies and comedies include a considerable amount of descriptive material which would be entirely inappropriate in modern dramatic writing. At the same time, it offered to the authors very great freedom; not having to consider the problem of stage settings, they could, in effect, introduce into a play as many separate scenes as they cared—and, if need be, they could make an individual scene as short as a dozen lines. Finally, for those concerned with the productions there could be no worrying thoughts regarding scenic expense.

The shape of the theatre also meant that the close association of actors and audience which was a familiar feature of early

Tudor performances remained unaltered. The spectators almost surrounded the players and, as it were, they came *within* the play that was being presented. Certain dramatic conventions, therefore, which would be inappropriate for the modern picture-frame theatre, were in perfect harmony with the style of Elizabethan productions. The soliloquy, for instance, has been banished from the stage in our times, partly because it is out of keeping with to-day's realism, partly because a soliloquy mouthed by an actor who stands at a distance from his audience must inevitably lose its effect. The Elizabethan actor stood on a conventional platform almost in the midst of the spectators, and the uttering of his thoughts, addressed to those in close physical proximity to him, was completely in concord with his surroundings. So, too, with the aside. In the modern theatre the actor usually is separated from the spectators, and consequently the uttering of an aside seems artificial and absurd; in the Elizabethan playhouse the aside was merely an extension of generally prevailing audience-actor communion.

Besides the main stage, the actors had two other playing areas which they could use on occasion—some kind of rear stage and some kind of upper stage. How precisely the rear-stage was formed is by no means certain, but the precise mechanics involved in its construction are of no present consequence. All that matters here is that, by drawing a curtain, by opening a large door, or by setting forth a tent-like structure, the players could provide the suggestion of an interior—a bedroom, a cave, or a prison. The other area available to the actors consisted of a portion of the lower gallery immediately above the stage façade, an area which might be localized at will as Juliet's balcony, or as the walls of Calais, or as a castle's battlements. While, however, the stage direction "enter above" occurs frequently in play-texts of this period, it is worthy of note that hardly ever do we find scenes proceeding on the gallery floor alone; almost invariably when characters are bidden to enter above they are kept in contact with other characters standing on the main stage below. Perhaps even a third acting area was also at their service; evidence is now accumulating to show that quite frequently performers made entries directly into the yard and thence ascended to the stage—a practice which clearly was inherited from their predecessors, the interlude players.

The essential thing to bear in mind while we are reading Elizabethan plays is that they were written for an audience trained to accept a conventional treatment of reality and to permit free scope for their own imaginative powers. One or two examples may serve to make this clear. A situation that not infrequently occurs in both tragedies and comedies is that wherein some character is supposed to be in a room, pursued by his enemies. He dashes in and locks a door while his foes clamour without. On the Elizabethan stage quite obviously this had to be done conventionally. All the doors in the façade could not be locked, and in effect the spectators put out of their minds the existence of all save the one immediately in use; fundamentally the situation was the same as that in medieval productions, when mansions not actually in dramatic service were dismissed from the spectators' attention. So, too, the old medieval convention of foreshortening space remained in familiar use. A dramatist, for instance, wishes to show two characters in Rome and then to carry them to Venice; he bids them go out by one door and in by another, and the voyage is done.

If those responsible for the productions did not have to spend much money on scenic effects they certainly laid out considerable sums on clothes. From the last years of the century we have some inventory lists of properties owned by the Lord Admiral's company, and these amply testify to the riches of the theatre's wardrobe. Here are doublets of orange-tawny satin and carnation satin and white satin and peach-colour satin, all "laid thick with gold lace"; here are senators' gowns, hoods and caps; here are green jackets for Robin Hood's men, costumes for classical deities, suits for particular characters such as Herod, Henry V, and Tamburlaine; there is even a "ghost's suit and bodice." The lists are lengthy and demonstrate the sartorial wealth possessed by the greater companies. And properties, too, are here in profusion— globes, sceptres, clubs, wooden heads and masks, Cupid's bow and quiver, snakes, pictures, armour, dragons, lions, popes' mitres, imperial crowns, and crowns for ghosts—a miscellaneous collection revealing the resources now readily available for players who no longer had to trudge wearily with their bundles from stance to stance.

In endeavouring to make a mental picture of productions in Elizabethan times we must not permit ourselves to be misled by the absence of scenery. The main stage may have been bare and the façade unchanging; but we may well imagine that the audiences saw before them a rich colourful display of actors jetting round the platform in their silks and satins, equipped with all the properties they required for the appropriate presentation of their scenes.

2. SHAKESPEARE'S IMMEDIATE FORERUNNERS

When we pass beyond the year 1576 we have an impression of accelerated time. Through five long decades, from 1500 to 1550, the drama had moved forward with slow and unchanging pace, and between 1550 and 1575, even although many new theatrical experiments were being indulged in, the speed is not materially advanced. After the establishment of The Theatre, on the other hand, we are rushed forward precipitately towards the triumphs of the century's final years. The progress is steady and rapid, requiring to be looked at as a whole; at the same time it may be convenient here to divide these last twenty-five years of the century into three, considering first the period from about 1576 to 1588, going on from that to the sudden burst of energy which came during the years 1588–92, and then finally examining the sure accomplishments of the last decade of Queen Elizabeth's reign.

It was during the first of these periods that John Lyly introduced a fresh kind of comedy to the English stage. *Alexander, Campaspe, and Diogenes* and *Sapho and Phao* appeared in 1584, *Galathea* about 1586, *Endimion* in 1588, and these were followed by others of similar qualities—*Midas* (1589), *Mother Bombie* (c. 1590), *Love's Metamorphosis* (c. 1590), and *The Woman in the Moon* (c. 1592). In approaching these works, we must remember that Lyly's career, from first to last, was associated with the child actors of Elizabeth's Court. It is important to bear this fact in mind for several reasons. Their methods of staging were not the same as the methods employed by the adult players; in effect, they utilized a kind of simplified 'simultaneous setting' reminiscent of medieval practice, identifying various parts of the stage with such fictional localities as were required. Thus, for example, in *Alexander, Campaspe, and Diogenes* there are three locations —Alexander's house, Diogenes' tub, and the shop of Apelles the painter—all exhibited to the audience at one time. It will readily be understood that if we try to read Lyly's plays in terms of Shakespeare's stagecraft we shall form an entirely erroneous idea of their structure; an awareness of Lyly's dramatic skill can come only when we consider his scenes in the light of the 'simultaneous setting' for which they were designed. Apart from this, we must realize that the audience for whom he wrote was different from that which was to be found flocking to The Theatre and its successors. His plays were oriented more towards courtly spectators, men and women less apt to make demand for bold effects, more likely to appreciate delicate turns and subtle nuances.

It was Lyly who was largely responsible for the first refined elaboration of romantic sentiment. As a university man, he was well acquainted with the classical playwrights, and his comedies show that his imagination was continually stirred by memories of ancient Greek myth. Yet he was no more inclined than the authors of the popular tragicomedies to pursue a wholly imitative path. Where he differed from them was in his basic approach. They had mingled comic scenes with serious, paying little attention to congruity; their Hufs and Rufs and Snufs were crudely justled in alongside a Cambises and a Praxaspes. He clearly sought for some atmosphere or for some method of treatment which might make a harmony of apparently antagonistic spheres of interest. There is, accordingly, in his comedies a mellowed spirit under which seriousness and laughter meet, a poetic fancy wherein the deities of classical mythology live and move by the side of human figures, wherein the clownish is made kin to the courtly. We might almost say that all his characters are viewed through an idealistic coloured glass, bringing them together under the one single illumination. Above all, he largely limits his dramatic themes to the exploitation of romantic love, and this romantic love he develops, not in its chivalric form, but in a form which led directly on to Shakespeare's. Here are delicate colourings, a certain mellowed sadness, a spirit which the author himself described as "delight."

In pursuing this method, Lyly was enabled to make important advances in character-drawing. No doubt many of his stage persons are reminiscent of types to be found in the plays of Terence and elsewhere, but rarely do we find dully conceived replicas, and many are given subtle individualistic touches. Maestius and Serena in *Mother Bombie*, Eumenides and Semele in *Endimion*, Alexander and Campaspe and Apelles obviously anticipate romantic characters in the years to come.

Unfortunately, the feature in his comedies which perhaps gave them their greatest attractive power for contemporaries is precisely that which makes them rather difficult to read to-day. In his novel called *Euphues*, published in 1578, Lyly had exploited a new and highly artifical prose style—a style which rapidly became so popular in courtly speech and in the writings of other authors that it has won notoriety under the title "euphuistic." Basically, this prose form depends upon the constant use of antithetical clauses, often underlined by rather blatant alliteration, and upon the unending flow of similes, most of them derived from what has been called the "unnatural natural history" beloved of the age. For us to-day, the euphuistic style seems dull, monotonous, and uninteresting, but we must not forget that in its own time it appeared fascinating and exciting. In it men found a prose utterance clearly based on artistry, possessing an element of grace, cultivating refinement of thought and of phrase instead of blundering blindly forward. All men and women of culture started to converse in euphuistic style, and the commoners tried at least to ape the aristocrats.

This style Lyly has used for the dialogue of his plays. True, he has modified considerably the artificialities of his original *Euphues*, and in many scenes the speeches he gives to his characters are reasonably effective; but sufficient remains to make the greater part of his dramatic work seem to modern ears somewhat boring. In reading his comedies, therefore, we distinctly require to exercise our historical imagination. We must take these plays as they were taken by their first audiences. We read, for example, such a passage as this:

> Dromio. Now, if I could meet with Risio, it were a world of waggery.
>
> Risio. O that it were my chance, *obviam dare Dromio*, to stumble upon Dromio, on whom I do nothing but dream.
>
> Dromio. His knavery and my wit should make our masters that are wise, fools; their children that are fools, beggars; and us two that are bond, free.
>
> Risio. He to cozen and I to conjure would make such alterations that our masters should serve themselves—the idiots, their children serve us—and we to wake our wits between them all.

Its artificially balanced cadences, repeating themselves from scene to scene, may have a soporific effect upon us, yet we have to create in our imagination the delight they occasioned to those for whom they were novel and fresh. Some years later Shakespeare might indulge in good-humoured satire of the euphuistic style; nevertheless, his own precise prose owed as much to Lyly as did his maidens in men's habits, his romantic lovers, his grotesques, such as Don Armado with his page.

What precisely the adult players were offering to the public during these years we do not know, since this is a period from which few texts have been preserved for us; but several plays which are extant give us at least a glimpse of their repertory. *Common Conditions*, published during the very year when The Theatre was built, shows us the old methods being employed for the treatment of romantic adventure. We are here introduced to three tinkers, Thrift, Drift, and Shift, planning to hold up and rob some traveller. Sedmond comes in, accompanied by Clarisia and his servant Common Conditions; they indulge in conversation cast in the dreary kind of serious verse which had been usual in plays of the *Clyomon and Clamydes* school:

> The silly traveller that is attach'd through wearied toil
> And forc'd through mere necessity to trace from native soil,
> Though wearied at his journey's end with painful travail past,
> Is glad in heart he hath attain'd his journey's end at last.

Then the fun begins. The tinkers surround the small party of travellers and decide that Common Conditions must be hanged. He, however, begs leave to do this office for himself and succeeds in persuading his captors to allow him to climb a tree with a halter in his hand. Once he has reached a bough far above their heads he promptly starts to raise such vociferous halloos for help that the robbers hastily decamp in terror. This adventure leads to others in which romantic love and strange dangers and hilarious mirth are freely exploited. As in the much later *Cymbeline*, a Duchess finds herself consumed with jealousy because the fair, innocent, gentle heroine is beloved by the people more than her own children are; as in *The Two Gentlemen of Verona*, one of the characters (Common Conditions) is seized by bandits who, immediately recognizing his cleverness, ask him to be their captain; as in *Pericles*, the heroine is lost at sea, taken by mariners, and sold into servitude. Despite the dullness of much of the serious talk and the crudity of the comic, no one can avoid seeing here some of the foundations of Shakespeare's world of romance.

With *Common Conditions* may be associated two interesting pieces, *The Three Ladies of London* and *The Three Lords and Ladies of London*, important because they were both written by one man, Robert Wilson, because that man was a popular actor, and because they can be dated with assurance, the first appearing about 1581 and the second in 1588. Even when all allowance is made for the maturing power of the author, therefore, there is the possibility of catching a glimpse here of the way in which dramatic progress was being effected during the passage from the beginning to the end of the eighties. Both plays derive their being from the moral-interlude tradition, but there is a marked distinction between them. *The Three Ladies*, making use of the ancient abstractions, such as Fame, Love, Conscience, Dissimulation, Fraud, and Simplicity, attacks the prevalent vices of the age, and in the course of its action it introduces several episodes which attract our attention. Of these, the most significant is the story of a merchant, Mercadore, who goes off to Turkey in the service of Lucre; there he meets and cheats a Jew called Gerontus; brought to court, he discovers that in law a Turk cannot be forced to pay his debts to a foreigner; at once he declares his

willingness to abandon the Christian faith and become a Moham-
medan; whereupon Gerontus, shocked by his proposed apostacy,
offers to absolve him from the debt so that Mercadore may not
be tempted to commit such a crime. Incidents like these display
Wilson's quality of mind, but it must be confessed that for the
most part the writing of his dialogue is awkward, cramped, and
old-fashioned. While we cannot acclaim *The Three Lords* as a
play of outstanding worth, it does exhibit an ease and assurance
lacking in the earlier work. The abstractions are handled with
greater skill, the scenes are more elaborate, the story is made
more complex, and the style of dialogue definitely moves forward
from the patterns set in the older interludes to those which were
being established at the time when Shakespeare first applied himself to the stage. Perhaps these two plays may be taken as symbolic of what was happening generally to the drama during this
decade.

Still further variations on the theme of romance appear in *The
Rare Triumphs of Love and Fortune* (1582), a tragicomical drama
which anticipates several later Elizabethan plays in presenting
its main action within a fully developed 'framework,' so that, as
in *The Taming of the Shrew*, for example, the play itself takes
shape in the form of a theatrical representation given before or
by another group of characters. In *The Rare Triumphs* we are
first introduced to a meeting of mythological deities during the
course of which Venus and Fortune quarrel about their respective powers over humanity. The main play thus becomes, as it
were, a test of these powers—the first episode revealing Fortune's
strength, the second that of Venus, with a concluding finale
wherein the influences of both are displayed. Romantic love and
magic are predominant in the scenes. The hero, Hermione, apparently of low birth, is devoted to Fidelia, daughter of Duke
Phizantius. The girl's brother, Armenio, in a jealous rage, chal-
lenges him to fight, and as a result of their combat the lover is
exiled. Wandering abroad in despair, he comes to a cave wherein
his high-born father Bomelio, also banished, lives in seclusion
poring over his magical books, and by Bomelio's aid a happy
conclusion eventually is reached. We are looking forward here
to *The Tempest*, and, although the anonymous author was no

great poet, the varied style of the dialogue gives a clear sign leading towards the poetic subtleties on which Shakespeare's achievements were to be based.

Finally, we come to *Fedele and Fortunio, or The Two Italian Gentlemen* (1584). If, as seems probable, this was the work of Anthony Munday, then it introduces us to a man whom at least one contemporary acclaimed as "the best for comedy" in his time and "our best plotter." Most of his dramatic writings have perished, but one other at least, *John a Kent and John a Cumber*, was penned some time before 1590 and accordingly may also be dealt with here. *The Two Italian Gentlemen* is only a modified version of an Italian *Il Fedele* (1576) by Luigi Pasquaglio, and hence does not call for special attention; but the other play has unquestioned importance. Once again the main plot revels in romantic love and rare adventure, and these Munday has enveloped in a richly variegated atmosphere. Continually complicating the plot come two magicians—the Welsh John a Kent and his morose Scots rival, John a Cumber. Says one of them:

> Here's love and love, good Lord, was never the like.
> But must these joys so quickly be concluded?
> Must the first scene make absolute the play?
> No cross? No change? What? No variety?

and these words might almost be taken as a motto, giving expression to what appealed most to the audiences of the time and to what Munday was seeking to give them. In addition to these two active wizards, other characters add to the diversity of the play. Among these, particularly significant are the group of quaint 'Antiques,' fairies or spirits, in the service of one of the magicians, and the group of clownish humans, Turnop and his rustic crew, busily engaged in rehearsing a rude entertainment for the delectation of their lord. If *The Rare Triumphs* calls *The Tempest* to mind, here *A Midsummer Night's Dream* is manifestly being anticipated.

3. THE ARRIVAL OF SHAKESPEARE

Precisely when Shakespeare started to work for the London stage cannot be accurately determined; all we know for certain is that by 1592 he had won such success as to arouse his rival, Robert Greene, to utter a jealous attack upon him. Some believe that Shakespeare had presented his first plays as early as 1585; others would place his advent some five years later. Perhaps the exact date does not particularly matter: what is important is the fact that he stands out as a central figure in the swift dramatic movement which between about 1587 and 1592 laid a sure and firm basis for the great dramatic development which enriched the last years of Elizabeth's reign.

In 1592 the dying Robert Greene had called Shakespeare a 'Johannes Factotum,' a Jack-of-all-Trades, and the epithet was not without justification. During the immediately preceding theatrical seasons Shakespeare had gained popularity in diverse spheres—tragedy (*Titus Andronicus*), chronicle history (the three parts of *Henry VI*), and comedy (*The Comedy of Errors, The Two Gentlemen of Verona*, perhaps a first version of *Love's Labour's Lost* and other pieces). In fact, these early plays of his reflected accurately the three kinds of drama which characterized the period as a whole. No other playwright of the time exhibited such a range, even although his own dramatic power was aided by the efforts of others, contemporaries or immediate predecessors.

In the realm of tragedy two such companions set the pace, Christopher Marlowe and Thomas Kyd. When the former, about 1587, sent his prologue-speaker to introduce *Tamburlaine* to the public, providing him with an aggressive and self-confident challenge:

> From jigging veins of riming mother-wits
> And such conceits as clownage keeps in pay,
> We'll lead you to the stately tent of war
> Where you shall hear the Scythian Tamburlaine
> Threatening the world with high-astounding terms,

at one stroke he established a new theatrical realm. Up to that

time no author had invigorated the stage with poetic fervour.
The prevaling styles in dialogue were rhythmical and metrical,
and some writers succeeded in making these mildly effective; but
before the appearance of *Tamburlaine* audiences had never had
the chance of listening to the majestic and lyrical speech which
Marlowe offered to his actors. Fundamentally, his greatest contribution to the playhouse of his age was stylistic. From 1587
onward, blank verse became the established norm for serious
dramatic dialogue; other playwrights, and most notably Shakespeare, were to modify and make more varied its basic rhythms;
but it was Marlowe who stood forward as the precursor and
prophet.

Tamburlaine was quickly followed by *Dr Faustus* (*c.* 1588)
and *The Jew of Malta* (*c.* 1589), and these three works have
qualities in common. In the first two particularly we recognize
at once Marlowe's power of self-identification with his heroes.
Tamburlaine seizes upon our imaginations because, in presenting
him, the poet has dreamed a vision of military grandeur; and the
fusing of the author's own personality and that of the fictional
character becomes patent in the lines. Thus at one and the same
time Marlowe can identify himself with his hero and also cause
his hero to identify his being with that of the poet. Suddenly,
amid scenes of conquest and carnage, Tamburlaine starts his
speech beginning

> If all the pens that ever poets held
> Had fed the feeling of their masters' thoughts,

and concluding with the concept of a poetic vision beyond the
power of words to express; obviously this is not the victorious
monarch speaking but Marlowe himself. Similarly, Tamburlaine's passionate seizing of Meander's line:

> And ride in triumph through Persepolis

in his

> 'And ride in triumph through Persepolis?'
> Is it not brave to be a king, Techelles,
> Usumcasane and Theridamas?
> Is it not passing brave to be a king,
> And ride in triumph through Persepolis?

reflects the poet's and not the prince's delight in rich, sonorous phrases. This fusion of the author and the hero becomes even threefold in *Dr Faustus*. Faust is a scholar, not an ambitious conqueror; but he and Tamburlaine and Marlowe all meet at times in one:

> Nature, that fram'd us of four elements
> Warring within our breasts for regiment,
> Doth teach us all to have aspiring minds.
> Our souls, whose faculties can comprehend
> The wondrous architecture of the world
> And measure every wandering planet's course,
> Still climbing after knowledge infinite
> And always moving as the restless spheres,
> Will us to wear ourselves and never rest
> Until we reach the ripest fruit of all,
> That perfect bliss and sole felicity,
> The sweet fruition of an earthly crown.

The Marlovian approach, therefore, brings intensity, admiration, and wonder into tragedy. It must, at the same time, be realized that these qualities exist for their own sake. The impression we have after reading *Tamburlaine* is that Marlowe is intoxicated by the fascination exerted upon his mind by contemplation of the aspiring man who, starting as a simple Scythian shepherd, ends as a king over kings. Nevertheless, the admiration thus aroused could not banish the thought that Tamburlaine himself was a monster of cruelty. Wonder at Faustus' aspiring courage in making his pact with Mephistopheles could not deny the fact that this action damned his soul. The admiration and the wonder, accordingly, were stimulated, not by appreciation of moral virtues, but solely by the exhibition of individualistic striving, in spite of humanity's weakness, towards superhuman power. This means that the intensity, admiration, and wonder could come as easily from watching extreme villainy as it could from looking at virtuous aspiration. Thus, after presenting Tamburlaine and Faustus, Marlowe appropriately completed the trio of dramas by devoting attention to his thoroughly evil Barabas in *The Jew of Malta*.

This concentration upon intensity and this self-identification of the poet with his central characters offered much to Shakespeare and his fellow tragedians, but in concentrating upon those qualities Marlowe's own dramatic achievement was seriously restricted. Not only was he so involved in the creatures of his imagination that they tended to become lyrical rather than theatrically poetic characters, he was also inhibited from creating a larger and comprehensive dramatic universe. *Tamburlaine*, it might be said, exists solely for Tamburlaine, *Dr Faustus* exclusively for Faust. All the other characters are mere dummies, inanimate figures, whose only excuse is to offer opportunities for the hero's eloquence; the play's structure has no significance apart from that hero's being. Marlowe was incapable of giving life to an Horatio, a Cassio, a Banquo, or a Kent; he could not have imagined the architectural complexities of a *Hamlet*.

That, however, is precisely what his companion Kyd was fitted to do. In the same year when *Tamburlaine* appeared on the stage, *The Spanish Tragedy* captured the excited attention of the public, and its dramatic, as opposed to poetic, power is amply demonstrated both by its immediate success and by its long-continuing popularity. There are no heroics here: the element of wonder and admiration is absent; although Kyd's blank verse has a variety and at times an appealing quality of a kind not to be found in Marlowe's dialogue, it lacks entirely the fierce passion and lyrical fervour which his possessed; instead of concentrating upon one single hero, the author presents to us something in the nature of a psychological thriller. The play opens with the soliloquy of a ghost and proceeds to tell a story of love, murder, and vengeance. Bellimperia, daughter of the Duke of Castile, exchanges vows with Horatio, son of Hieronimo, but her brother Lorenzo, having planned his sister for his friend Balthazar, breaks in upon their amorous conversation and hangs the lover in an arbour. Awakened by the noise, old Hieronimo finds his son dead and the shock deranges his brains. He seeks revenge, but at first he cannot be sure of the identity of those responsible; when he determines the truth the attainment of his objective is delayed both by the fits of madness which come upon him and by the fact that his enemies are lords of high estate. Only after numerous hesitating steps does he succeed in enticing them to take part in the performance of a play and in killing them during the course of its action. To a certain extent this is a Senecan drama; the ghost, the revenge element, many stylistic features testify to its ultimate origin. But Kyd knew the tastes of his audience, and he adapted what he took from the Latin dramatist to popular demands. The play has a strong, well-developed, and at times intricate, plot; the stage effects are excellently managed; throughout, the scenes are varied and built so as to hold the spectators' attention; and the whole tragedy rises at the end to a thrilling climax of interest in the play-within-the-play scene.

Quite clearly, the plot and development of *The Spanish Tragedy* are the same as those of *Hamlet*; in the one a father seeks to avenge his son's murder and is afflicted with madness; in the other a son endeavours to avenge a father's murder and exhibits both feigned and real disturbance of mind. The indebtedness of Shakespeare to Kyd is patent. However, even although a Hamlet play was in existence by 1590, the *Hamlet* we know did not come into being until the beginning of the seventeenth century, and it is only with Shakespeare's youthful works that we are at present concerned. During this period he penned his gruesome *Titus Andronicus*, a tragedy in which, as it were, he combined the essential qualities of Marlowe and of Kyd. Its story, replete with death, horror, vengeance, links it with *The Spanish Tragedy* in the planning of well-constructed scenes and in the exploitation of intrigue; in addition, attention is not concentrated upon one person alone but is spread over a group of characters skilfully contrasted. At the same time, Shakespeare has infused into the play something of Marlowe's intensity; the figure of Aaron the Moor grips the imagination by its display of vigorous and self-centred wickedness. While no one would be prepared to say that *Titus* is one of Shakespeare's masterpieces, it manifestly shows the hand of a playwright greater than either of the other two. The distinctive contributions of these men have been seized upon and used as a foundation; but the structure raised upon that foundation demonstrates the craft and the dramatic potency of its author. The style has a directness, a subtlety, and a diversity of its own, matching Marlowe's high-astounding terms and yet allowing itself to express the qualities

of characters far removed from those on whom alone that lyric
author had lavished his attention.

The public was fascinated by these tragedies, but it was also
much attracted by historical dramas of all kinds, some of them
certainly concerned with 'tragic' material but others giving more
weight to romantic adventure. Once more, the loss of so many
plays does not permit us to say with confidence when and by
whom the chronicle history was inaugurated; perhaps several
authors concurrently contributed to its establishment, but if so
Shakespeare was assuredly one of the first. His three parts of
Henry VI, in spite of their patent immaturity in style and in
grasp of character, bring before us an ordered dramatic presentation of historical events such as cannot be discerned in any similar extant plays which might possibly have been produced before
their time. If we find ourselves inclined to dismiss this trilogy as
unworthy of theatrical attention we need only compare it with
the contemporary *Edward I* of George Peele in order to appreciate
its virtues. *Edward I* makes every attempt to win popularity; it is
spectacular and patriotic, and the strands of its plot are woven
into a complicated pattern. But the pattern itself has no design;
historical matter has here been mixed up with folk-lore elements
and with romantically conceived inventions; there exists no sense
of purpose beyond an effort to make an immediately popular
appeal. More of an historical sense of purpose appears in *Jack
Straw*, but the handling of its simple story of Wat Tyler's rebellion and of Richard II's endeavour to avoid bloodshed shows the
history play hardly advanced to a structure richer than that of
the interludes. *Henry VI*, despite the lack of assurance apparent
in many of its scenes, displays a masterly grasp of complex
chronicle material and at the same time an innate sense of
dramatic requirements. Even if we assume that other writers
before Shakespeare had taken the step of dealing with English
history without the introduction of Bale's abstractions there can
be little doubt that *Henry VI* was the force which inspired the
subsequent popular development of the chronicle play.

Henry VI, of course, was completed by Shakespeare's own
Richard III, a drama planned more in Marlowe's tragic form.
Eminently 'theatrical' in conception, it focuses all its attention

upon the central figure, presented as a monster of villainy. The difference between the true dramatist and the lyrical poet, however, becomes apparent just as soon as we compare this character with Tamburlaine, Faust, or Barabas. Their portraits are all humourless, drawn in hard unshaded lines, beings to be wondered at, no doubt, but lacking human features. On the surface, Richard seems to be delineated in a similar way, but, when we look at his speeches carefully, we realize that what gives him his peculiar theatrical vigour derives from something other than mere intensity. A grim sense of humour animates his words and actions from his first maliciously mocking soliloquy. The wooing of Anne certainly has been undertaken in order to further his own political ends, but it is enlivened by the evident delight he takes in his own consummate skill. While it would be impossible to discuss Richard's personality as we discuss the personality of Hamlet, unquestionably Richard possesses an individuality of character such as is absent in Marlowe's heroes; and basically that derives from the fact that he has not been conceived by a poet anxious lyrically to identify himself with the figment he has created, but by a dramatist able to hold himself apart from his fictional persons.

Marlowe tried his hand at one work of this kind, dealing in *Edward II* with a young king whose impolitic and unhealthy devotion to a favourite brings him to ruin. This play has no heroics, and it might seem that in it Marlowe was showing himself possessed of a genuine dramatic power distinct from the lyrical intensity of his other three plays. With the disappearance of the aspiring hero, however, this poet-playwright's virtue fades. No one who has seen *Edward II* in performance can deny that, compared even with Shakespeare's apprentice efforts, it is dull and uninspired. Although it offers some affecting scenes, and although one or two episodes permit the poet to indulge in arias, as a whole its dialogue lacks distinction; while the fact that the author has ignored larger issues in order to deal with a private story of a homosexual infatuation leaves it without the broader quality which gives distinction to Shakespeare's chronicle histories. No doubt it is true that *Richard II* was strongly influenced by *Edward II*, but recognition of this fact merely serves to emphasize the essential dramatic difference between the two plays.

Tragedy and chronicle history excited spectators during these years, but it would appear that the staple repertory of the playhouse consisted mainly of essays in the treatment of romance. In this sphere Marlowe's companion, Robert Greene, stands out as the leader. Lyly, as we have seen, had contributed much to romantic comedy during the early eighties; his writings, however, were cast in a form suitable for interpretation by child actors rather than by adults; and it was left to Greene to fashion the romance material into a more popular mould. His method, in *Friar Bacon and Friar Bungay* (*c.* 1588) and *James IV* (*c.* 1590), was to select a vaguely historical setting and within its framework to weave a variegated design of love, adventure, and magic. In adopting this course he was clearly following on from earlier experiments in the romantic style, yet his plays remain distinct from anything which had gone before because of their effective dialogue, their strongly drawn characters, their charm, and their enveloping atmosphere. The main story of *Friar Bacon* concerns itself with the exploits of two rival magicians, each trying to outdo the other in wizardry. With this pair is associated a low comedy element largely focusing upon Bacon's stupid scholar Miles and upon a Devil, who finally runs off with the magician on his back. Alongside these characters move Edward, Prince of Wales, and Lacy, Earl of Lincoln, both in love with the lowborn Margaret. We have accordingly three different worlds mingled together—the world of wizardry, the world of aristocratic life, and the rustic world. Instead of remaining separate, as so often they had done in preceding plays, these have been merged into one through the superimposition upon them of a harmonizing mood, somewhat akin to that which Lyly had spread over his comedies but less delicate and visionary. The same method is to be seen in *James IV*. Here the Kings of England and of Scotland, surrounded by a group of courtiers, meet in the same play with Bohan, a melancholy Scot, and Oboram, or Oberon, King of the Fairies; here, too, is introduced a story of romantic love, with Dorothea, the best-drawn heroine in sixteenth-century drama outside Shakespeare's plays, as the main figure. The whole is fused into a unity by Greene's humour; realism and idealism are interfused.

The indebtedness of Shakespeare to Greene is by no means confined to his romantic patterns. Greene did much to expand the resources of poetic dialogue. Although deeply influenced by Marlowe's example, he modified the model he found in *Tamburlaine* and made it more supple. Sometimes his rhythms remind us of Shakespeare's, as in

> Why? Thinks King Henry's son that Margaret's love
> Hangs in the uncertain balance of proud time?

Sometimes lines such as

> Poring upon dark Hecate's principles

strike out interesting variants upon the blank-verse norm. And throughout there is an adaptation of this measure to dramatic requirements, less rhetorical, less lyrical, and more varied than Marlowe's.

Other dramatists in diverse ways exploited the romantic forms, frequently following Greene's method in choosing some 'historical' framework for their adventures, occasionally falling back upon the employment of dramatic devices inherited from the time of the interludes, and once or twice suggesting lines of further advance. Three plays may be briefly used to illustrate this. In *John of Bordeaux* we have a piece obviously in the Greene style, introducing an 'historical' plot in which the central character, John, takes service with Frederick, the German Emperor; his adventures are associated with the magic wrought by two wizard rivals, Bacon and Vandermast; low comedy is provided by Perce, Bacon's man. Apparently the audiences of the period did not weary in seeing the same dramatic elements served up to them again and again. Nor were they averse to watching plays which utilized methods inherited from former years. *A Knack to Know a Knave* has its historical setting in the reign of King Edgar, and its magician (here a thoroughly worthy character) in Bishop Dunstan; but its romantic atmosphere is coloured by the mood which produced the old moralities. We hear much of the sins of the age, the evil courtiers, the cozening knaves, the grasping farmers; and in the midst of the ordinarily named persons we actually encounter the abstract figure of Honesty as well as a Devil, who bears off a wicked Bailiff to Hell. How easily at this period the old and the new could co-exist may be seen when we turn from such a drama to George Peele's *Old Wives' Tale*, wherein the romantic material is handled in a fresh manner. The central concept of this humorous whimsy is a clever one. Antic, Frolic, and Fantastic enter lost at night in the depths of a forest. Old Clunch, lantern in hand, encounters them and takes them to his cottage. There, after a simple rustic repast, his wife Madge starts to tell them a fairy-tale. And suddenly the persons of this tale assume bodily form and enact their story before the cottagers. The adroit development of the play-within-the-play device, the fusing of the actual world and the world of the romantic imagination, its enrichment with sly satirical touches, makes this a dramatic piece still not without real interest, and in spirit it seems removed by decades from the contemporary *Knack to Know a Knave*.

This was the realm which the young Shakespeare entered with his *Two Gentlemen of Verona* and his *Love's Labour's Lost*, and in entering it he became its master. It is obvious that he took over much from his predecessors and fellows; there is no difficulty in tracing the episodes and devices he borrowed from Munday and Greene and the rest. Nevertheless, he wrought the romantic comedy into a new shape. Not for a moment was he tempted to follow the pattern set by others, and to place his romantic stories within a vaguely historical setting. Instead of exhibiting his romance against a misty background of the English past, he deliberately elected to 'distance' his plots by taking them abroad to Italy and elsewhere. Instead of heaping adventure upon adventure, he tended to keep his plots limited to the telling of a fairly simple story. Instead of submerging himself completely in the realm of the impossible, he sought to make the impossible seem real, he used his low comedy persons to comment upon the extravagances of romantic passion. Stepping into this world of the imagination, he was careful to see that his feet came down on firm ground. *The Two Gentlemen of Verona* is by no means a great comedy, and no doubt the first version of *Love's*

Labour's Lost lacked the witty effervescence of the play which has come down to us; but already Shakespeare was indicating the course his particular treatment of the romantic material was to take.

4. THE FINAL ACHIEVEMENTS OF ELIZABETHAN DRAMA

During the seasons of 1592 and 1593 the plague descended cruelly upon London, and for the greater part of that time the theatres had to be closed. When regular performances started again it was evident that the time of apprenticeship had gone and that mature mastery had been gained. Crude plays there must have been in plenty, hastily written to satisfy the continual demands of the several stages now active in the metropolis, but in most of those which have been preserved a new assurance and a firm confidence became apparent.

In general, we receive the impression that the spectators of the century's last decade were less interested in tragedy than in other dramatic offerings. Apart from *Julius Cæsar* at the very end of the period, Shakespeare wrote only a single play of this kind, *Romeo and Juliet* (1595), and this work might well be regarded rather as a romantic comedy which has taken a wrong turning than as a 'tragedy' in the stricter sense of the term. Perhaps contemporaries saw it as such; when it was printed in 1597 it appeared as "An excellent conceited tragedie," and the use of the epithet, "conceited," which was otherwise exclusively used to describe comic dramas, is revealing. *Romeo and Juliet*, of course, is a triumph, but it stands apart, not only from all the rest of Shakespeare's tragic works, but also from all other tragedies which have been preserved from these years. It stems neither from *Tamburlaine* nor from *The Spanish Tragedy*; it does not lead to *Hamlet* or *Macbeth*; although it presents a tale of woe, it is kin rather to *Much Ado About Nothing*.

If we may judge from such plays as are extant we may hazard the conjecture that the comparatively few tragedies produced were not of prime importance, and that they belonged to two categories. If *Alphonsus, Emperor of Germany* comes, as seems likely, from this period it may serve to illustrate one of these. Marlowe and Kyd here meet together in a plot which shows us a monster of vice, Alphonsus, proceeding by poison, dagger-thrust, and intrigue to destroy those who stand in his way. To the arousing of wonder at this image of sheer wickedness has been added the fascination of the revenge motif and both contribute a display of horror-incidents calculated to make the spectators' spines run cold. The other category has greater interest in that it introduced something entirely new. Some time just before 1592 an anonymous author presented in *Arden of Feversham* a 'tragedy' based on an almost-contemporary middle-class murder—that of a Mr Arden sordidly done to death by his wife Alice. Already, in his three first plays, Marlowe had shattered the ancient principle which had insisted that tragedy could deal only with princely characters. Tamburlaine certainly became a monarch, but he started as a Scythian shepherd; Faustus was an ordinary German scholar; Barabas was a Jewish merchant. These persons, however, he had invested with his own enthusiastic dream of grandeur, so that in spite of their humble origins they did not depart overmuch from the splendour attached to formal tragedy's kings. The author of *Arden of Feversham* takes the final and perhaps in a sense the logical step of making the hero of his play humble in every respect. There is no ecstatic, wondering lyricism in this play; the dialogue, even when not expressed in prose, clearly aims at making the action seem as 'realistic' as possible.

From the titles of a number of lost plays produced within the decade, we know that other authors also experimented in the style of domestic tragedy, and these experiments, since they point the way towards dramatic forms characteristic of the modern stage, are obviously of considerable significance. It may, however, be doubted whether they made really great appeal in their own time. It would appear that Elizabethan audiences found more joy in plays less drearily realistic, and in particular they found their demands met more effectively in the chronicle histories and in various forms of romantic drama. Shakespeare himself, having completed one tetralogy covering the reigns of Henry VI and Richard III, now turned to write another dealing with Richard II, Henry IV, and Henry V. *Richard II (c.*

1595) was moulded as a tragedy, with no comic relief, its action depending almost entirely upon the actions of two contrasting figures, the pettish but imaginative king and the unimaginative but practical Bolingbroke. Then came the two parts of *Henry IV* (1597), built upon an entirely different plan. Instead of dwelling exclusively in palaces and conversing with courtiers and quarrelling lords, we are here asked to spend much of our time in an Eastcheap tavern and to enjoy the company of a John Falstaff, one of Shakespeare's most vital creations even although in his relations with the young Prince he takes the place of the Vice in the old moralities. And finally the set of four plays was completed by the patriotic *Henry V* (1599) with its far-flung tale of military conquest lightened through the presence of two groups of humorous characters, Nym, Bardolph, and Pistol and the representatives of Wales, England, Scotland, and Ireland. Even if we neglect *King John* (c. 1595), wherein for some reason Shakespeare deviated from the theme animating his two tetralogies and reverted to a much earlier reign, we must acknowledge that this vast historical canvas, executed with such skill and diversity, revealing both abstract principles and living persons, testifies as much to Shakespeare's greatness as do his tragedies and comedies.

Other playwrights during these years eagerly ransacked the chronicles, seeking for material in diverse reigns, and still others experimented with what might be called the biographical chronicle play. Munday penned a *Sir Thomas More* (c. 1595)—a play of special significance, not only for its own sake, but also because the extant manuscript contains additions which many scholars believe to be in Shakespeare's own hand. Munday, associated with three collaborators, was also concerned with another drama, *Sir John Oldcastle* (1599–1600), which likewise has Shakespearian affiliations, although of a different kind. In *Henry IV* the character of Falstaff had originally been called Oldcastle, and it seems that some descendants of that historical person registered complaints which induced Shakespeare and his company to rename the comic knight and to present a half-hearted apology in the epilogue to the second part of the play: "Oldcastle," said Shakespeare, "died a martyr, and this is not the man." In all probability, these irate descendants sought even further vindication of their ancestor, encouraging the preparation of the *Oldcastle* play, confessedly written as a rebuttal of Shakespeare's work; announced as a "true and honourable history," it aimed to show that Sir John was "no pampered glutton" but "a valiant martyr and a virtuous peer."

These were all serious essays in the interpretation of historical events recorded in the chronicles; commoner perhaps were other plays in which the events were imaginatively embroidered and treated in a manner more cavalier. Typical of such works are the two parts of *Robert Earl of Huntingdon* (1598), penned by Munday in collaboration with Henry Chettle. This two-part drama exploits the popular interest in the legendary Robin Hood and moulds the 'historical' material to its special requirements. Worthy of note here is the skilful manner in which the playwrights have appropriately wrought their scenes into a kind of play-within-the-play, a device, eminently in keeping with the folk-lore stories, that no doubt was partly responsible for the success of the work when it was put on the stage by the Lord Admiral's men. This success may well have been so great as to have encouraged Shakespeare to write a rival attraction for his company, the Lord Chamberlain's; there is indeed some reason for believing that his excursion into the greenwood of *As You Like It* (1599) and even, perhaps, the very title of that play were occasioned by the popularity of Munday's and Chettle's effort.

As You Like It leads us into Shakespeare's romantic comedy world, a world enriched by *A Midsummer Night's Dream* (*c.* 1595), *The Merchant of Venice* (*c.* 1596), and *Much Ado About Nothing* (*c.* 1598). In these plays Shakespeare has passed far beyond the achievements of Lyly and Greene. His architectural planning is now masterly, his language vibrant and assured, his sense of character deepened, his mingling of romantic idealism and of practical good sense wrought into a single harmony. Above all, there appears in these works an appreciation of the contrast between appearance and reality, between being and seeming, made still more profound by an imaginative likening of the stage to the world of men. "These things," says Demetrius in *A Midsummer Night's Dream*,

> seem small and undistinguishable,
> Like far-off mountains turned into clouds,

and Hermia answers him,

> Methinks I see these things with parted eye
> When everything seems double.

At times the dream becomes the only reality; at times reality is
changed into the dream; and, as for the plays in which this
vision is expressed,

> The best in this kind are but shadows, and the worst
> are no worse if imagination amend them.

It is important to stress the fact that nowhere else in the entire
range of the drama of the time can we find anything similar to
this. Shakespeare had many mighty contemporaries; in his youth,
and even later, he was often content to base his efforts upon their
accomplishments; sometimes we are able to catch glimpses of
him in the process of writing plays in rivalry with them; yet his
achievement remains distinct. The individual vision inspiring his
scenes, the adroit weaving together of the variegated strands in
A Midsummer Night's Dream, the fusing of the almost incom-
patible elements in The Merchant of Venice, the subtle admixture of the ludicrous and the serious, the artificial and the real,
in Much Ado—all demonstrate that his eminence depends upon
his ability not merely to do better what others were doing but
essentially to grasp something far beyond their reach.

The contrast between him and them becomes clear when we
transfer our gaze from his comedies to other works which caught
the attention of the contemporary public. William Haughton's
Englishmen for my Money; or, A Woman will have her Will
(1598), for example, certainly gathered crowds in the year when
Much Ado was probably performed. We may admit that it
exhibits dramatic skill, but in the end we are forced to the conclusion that basically it consists of no more than a pleasant, shallow display of love, intrigue, and disguise informed by a strong
patriotic sentiment. The piece no doubt proved effective in the
stage action, with its story of three girls designed by their miserly
father for a Frenchman, a Dutchman, and an Italian, and suc-

ceeding by a series of tricks in gaining the hands of their English lovers; but beyond its story it has nothing of value to offer. Occasionally we encounter something a little deeper, such as Thomas Dekker's *Old Fortunatus* (1599) and *The Shoemakers' Holiday* (1599), yet even these do not touch the fringe of Shakespeare's magic gown. The former cleverly mingles its mortals with creatures of the imagination and its dialogue is poetically delicate —and still never approaches the quality of his comedies. *The Shoemakers' Holiday*, with its love affairs, its merry Simon Eyre, and its humorous Rodger and Firk, may be accepted as one of the most charming romantic plays of the period; yet we are forced to acknowledge that its charm rests rather on the surface than penetrates within.

III

The Jacobean and Caroline Drama

1. AUDIENCES AND THEATRES

POLITICALLY, one age ended and a new age began in the year 1603, when Elizabeth, after her long reign of over four decades, finally passed away, and when James VI of Scotland made his slow progress southward to assume the crown of England as James I. So far as the theatre is concerned, however, the break between the old and the new came several years earlier, at the very end of the sixteenth century. If the true start of the Elizabethan drama can be marked by the erection of The Theatre in 1576, its conclusion may be associated with the opening of the Globe in 1599 and of the Fortune in 1600. At the very time that these two great houses were being built to accommodate the Lord Chamberlain's Men and the Admiral's Men, the children's companies, which had been quiescent since Lyly's days, suddenly entered the professional field. In 1596 James Burbage purchased part of the buildings which before had been Blackfriars monastery, converted them into a playhouse, and let this to two impresarios who brought there the Children of the Chapel. The venture was an immediate success from its beginning in 1599 or 1600, and within a few months Shakespeare was referring in *Hamlet* to the "aery of children, little eyases, that cry out on the top of question, and are most tyrannically clapped for't"; these little players, he observed, "are now the fashion"; they have "carried away" Hercules and his load (the emblem of the Globe theatre), and the adult players are forced to take to the road. Thus was the 'private' playhouse, roofed in, more comfortable in its appointments and more expensive than the 'public' playhouses, firmly established in London. One or two later structures modelled on The Theatre, the Globe, and the Fortune were erected, but the stages more characteristic of the early seventeenth century were those inspired by Blackfriars. About 1608 the Lord Chamberlain's Men themselves took over that theatre from the children and made it their principal home, while other companies followed their lead by presenting their repertories at the Cockpit or Phœnix in Drury Lane (1616), Salisbury Court (1629), and similar private playhouses. So far as we can tell, the transference of plays from the public theatre's platform to the smaller private theatre's stage did not involve any fundamental alteration in the methods of performance; nevertheless, since the private playhouse was indoors, artificial lighting was for the first time introduced, and, as the years went by, opportunity was found for experimentation in the use of scenery. The theatre, even if it remained closely tied to Elizabethan traditions, was moving in the direction of its modern form.

The success of the private theatres was due largely to changing social movements and moods. During the last five years of Elizabeth's reign many men were anxious, disturbed, and worried. No one was quite sure what would happen on her death, and the Wars of the Roses remained as a persistent memory. In addition, the Essex affair had spread a gloom over England. To those who were opposed to him it revealed dangers which might lie ahead; to those thousands on whom he had cast his strange spell his execution aroused bitterness and dismay. Thus a darker spirit prevailed from about 1598 to 1603 than had been evident in the years immediately following the defeat of the Armada in 1588 and the exultation consequent upon that event. When James I came to the throne he brought a new atmosphere to the Court; numerous hangers-on travelled down with him from Scotland, he was inclined to lavish honours upon favourites, he loved banquets and revelry; as a result the Court party slowly became estranged from the mass of serious-thinking folk. In these circumstances, those who belonged to the 'high' English Church, and who were prepared to give support to the idea of the divine

The Swan Theatre

Two Elizabethan Stages

right of kings, formed a body of opinion completely opposed to the continually growing and hardening school of thought which embraced the tenets of puritanism and stood for the power of Parliament. James, dying in 1625, handed on an ill legacy to his son, Charles I; and Charles, although personally dignified and worthy, helped to increase the cleavage in the nation. He angered the Parliamentarians; he married a princess who was a devoted Catholic; and in his Court Catholic gallants were freely welcomed. The end came in 1640, when civil war broke out, and shortly afterwards the King went to his execution.

The opposition of the Puritans to the theatre and the gradual spread of their doctrines necessarily meant a decrease in the play-going public; and at the same time other movements contributed towards a change in the theatrical world. During the last years of Elizabeth's reign the mood of the age encouraged the arising to prominence of a group of angry young men who sought to express themselves through satire and who aimed at a 'realistic' drama dealing with social errors and vices. Although their activities had started within the public playhouses, they soon found that the private theatres suited them best. Their public was not a general one; they appealed mainly to intellectuals; and the 'little theatre' offered them more opportunities than could be secured in the Globe or the Fortune. The private playhouses, of course, were not 'private' in the modern sense, restricted to a subscription audience, but their seats were expensive, and economically they established an élite body of spectators distinct from the larger and more widely representative bodies of men and women who attended the shows in the 'public' playhouses. This was the beginning, and the vogue of the private theatres increased as the years went on, so that when we reach the final period of Charles' reign we might be prepared to say that the drama had become the almost exclusive delight of the king's courtiers. The very fact that one of the very first acts of the victorious Parliamentarians was to suppress theatrical performances altogether clearly indicates how closely the stage had become identified in the public mind with the despised and detested Cavaliers.

From one point of view the drama produced from the beginning of the century until the closing of the theatres may be regarded as a single unity. If we cast our minds back forty years from 1599, when Shakespeare's *Julius Cæsar* was being presented at the Globe, we find ourselves in the midst of the moral interludes; in technique and in spirit the two worlds are entirely different. If, on the other hand, we cast our minds forward forty years we discover that we are in the company of a playwright such as James Shirley, whose works, however much they may reflect a changed environment, are technically and to a large extent spiritually akin to the plays being written in 1600. Nevertheless, it is also necessary to look upon the theatre of these forty years from another point of view whereby it becomes divided into three sections: the first may conveniently be styled the early Jacobean, even although it embraces the last few years of Elizabeth's reign; extending to about 1610, this gives place to the second, which may be called the late Jacobean; and finally there is the Caroline, covering the period from 1625 on to 1640. The one fades into the other, yet each has its distinctive qualities.

2. SATIRICAL AND CITIZEN COMEDY

The prevailing atmosphere in the playhouse from 1587 on to about 1598 was, as we have seen, romantic, but already within that decade signs of a movement towards realism were not wanting. *Arden of Feversham* carried tragedy into a middle-class milieu, and its counterpart in comedy is to be found in Henry Porter's clever *Two Angry Women of Abington* (1598), in which we are shown a couple of bourgeois families involved in strife and blundering their way through the confusions of a night's darkness. In neither of these, however, was the realistic method purposeful. What characterizes the years immediately following is the determined effort on the part of the angry young men to use the anti-romantic method with the object of presenting social criticism, generally satiric in spirit.

In the development of the new form of comedy, one man, Ben Jonson, stands out pre-eminent. Shakespeare's company, the Lord Chamberlain's, put in the first version of his *Every Man in his Humour* in 1598, but he soon found more fitting audiences and actors in the private playhouse. *Every Man in his Humour* was followed by *Every Man Out of his Humour* (1599), *Cynthia's Revels* (c. 1600), *Poetaster* (1601), *Volpone* (1606), *Epicoene; or, The Silent Woman* (1609), *The Alchemist* (1610), and the slightly later *Bartholomew Fair* (1614). Through these, Jonson became one of the most talked-about dramatists of the time; and although some contemporaries raised their eyebrows, the publication of his plays as *Works* in 1616 was a testimony to the position he had won for himself. No previous playwright had had the distinction of having a collected edition of his writings for the stage, and not one had dared to suggest that these writings were worthy of such a high-sounding title.

By no means all of Jonson's plays are realistic in form; indeed the first version of *Every Man in his Humour* had an Italian setting. They are all, however, animated by one spirit, and in general they make use of similar methods. Fundamentally, his objective is clearly set forth in the prologue to his first play. There he protests that, although he seeks for audience approval, he is not prepared to sacrifice his integrity by serving "the ill customs of the age." He is not willing to follow his romantic predecessors and contemporaries by making

> a child, now swaddled, to proceed
> Man, and then shoot up, in one beard and weed,
> Past threescore years; or, with three rusty swords
> And help of some few foot-and-half-foot words,
> Fight over York and Lancaster's long jars.

The contemptuous allusion to Shakespeare's chronicle histories is patent. Instead, Jonson

> rather prays you will be pleased to see
> One such to-day as other plays should be—
> Where neither chorus wafts you o'er the seas,
> Nor creaking throne comes down the boys to please,
> Nor nimble squib is seen, to make afeard
> The gentlewomen, nor rolled bullet heard
> To say, it thunders, nor tempestuous drum
> Rumbles to tell you when the storm doth come.

He wants

> deeds and language such as men do use,
> And persons such as comedy would choose
> When she would show an image of the times.

Obviously, Jonson is thoroughly opposed to romantic comedy and historical chronicles, objecting to these on two grounds— first, because they are what we moderns would call 'escapist,' and secondly because they lack classically precise form and indulge in cheap theatrical effects. He seeks to correct both faults by reverting to the tightly wrought pattern of Latin drama, and by making his comedies comment upon the errors of his age. In order to carry out his purpose, moreover, he adopts a special approach in his presentation of characters. The word "humour" appears in the title of his first play, and familiarly his form of comedy is now called "the comedy of humours." To appreciate the significance of the term we must turn to the widely prevailing contemporary medical belief that in man there were four basic 'humours' or 'moistures' (the word 'humour' being akin to our modern 'humid'). In the well-balanced individual these humours existed in due proportions, so that an even harmony ensued; but in many men one humour, or two humours in conjunction, attained such force as to destroy the operation of the others, the result leading towards disease. This medical concept Jonson applies to character, and once more he himself has succinctly explained his objectives:

> in every human body
> The choler, melancholy, phlegm, and blood,
> By reason that they flow continually
> In some one part and are not continent,
> Receive the name of humours. Now thus far
> It may, by metaphor, apply itself
> Unto the general disposition—
> As when some one peculiar quality
> Doth so possess a man that it doth draw
> All his affects, his spirits and his powers,
> In their confluctions, all to run one way—
> This may be truly said to be a humour.

In effect, therefore, Jonson endeavours, for the purpose of presenting his satirical picture of society, to put upon the stage, not individuals, but types—the testy old father, the curmudgeonly miser, the bombastically boasting soldier, the jealous husband.

Jonson's satirical style possesses both strength and weakness. Unquestionably he had power both in the architectural planning of his plays and in the vigour with which he set his typical persons on the stage; his dialogue has sting and wit and at times deadly accuracy. Nevertheless, this author, whom many contemporaries were inclined to rate more highly than Shakespeare, now has his plays but seldom produced on the stage; and, even when an *Every Man in his Humour* or a *Volpone* is granted a rare revival, it fails to appeal. Partly the reason for this may be found in the author's topicality; any writer who regards the drama as offering him an opportunity for social comment tends to limit the possibility of enduring popularity. Beyond this, however, we must go if we wish to assess Jonson's worth correctly. He is a magnificent satirist, but his satire is not accompanied by any positive vision, and it tends to become personal in a double sense. He could see errors and vices clearly in the society of his age; what he could not show was any picture of a better world. He lashed out at boastfulness and arrogance, and these were precisely the qualities of his own nature. He professed to take a wide impartial view of the social world, and in fact marred many of his plays by introducing petty personalities. In *Every Man Out of his Humour* the central plot, involving the outhumouring of the humorous characters and the final outhumouring of the outhumourer himself, has been excellently planned, but the fact that many of the characters, such as Clove, Carlo Buffone, and Puntarvolo, are patently caricatures of Jonson's opponents bring the scenes down to a level of self-centred petulance. Still further, in his plays there is evident but little sympathy, and as a result audiences, although they may be impressed by the vigour of his vituperation, are apt to depart unsatisfied. *Volpone* thus impresses us as a terrible indictment of human greed, duplicity, and lust; its Corbaccios and Voltores are like creatures born of a nightmare; its selfish intrigues grip our attention; but in the end, since there has been presented to us hardly any contrasting elements, we find ourselves bored, if not repelled. It is undoubtedly rather wearisome to live, even for a brief three hours, in the company of none save monsters, fools, and knaves.

Epicoene is a singularly bright comedy in the midst of the more bitter plays, and rich laughter is combined with satiric barbs both in *The Alchemist* and *Bartholomew Fair*; but with these works Jonson's truly creative work in the theatres came to an end. He did write some more comedies, but these are less adroitly constructed, and are marred by exaggeration and personal pettiness. Other dramatists, however, eagerly took up his style, adapting it to their own purposes. Already in 1597 the classically minded friend of Jonson, George Chapman, had penned a comedy with the significant title of A *Humorous Day's Mirth*, in which he showed a similar approach towards character-drawing, and for years thereafter he proceeded to contribute to the stage a number of interesting plays. Chapman's approach, however, differs from that of his companion in that he commonly mingled satiric purpose with romantic appeal. *The Gentleman Usher* (c. 1602) thus introduces the elderly, sack-loving widow Corteza, the foolish Poggio, and the pedantic Sarpego within an almost tragicomic framework of love and adventure; in *Monsieur D'Olive* (1604) the episodes which exhibit a Jonson-like gulling of the title-hero by the witty Roderique and Mugeron are set against a story of emotional grief, in which a Marcellina has vowed herself to eternal seclusion and a Count St Anne lives as a hermit mourning the loss of a dead wife; even *The Widow's Tears* (c. 1609), satirically revealing the shallowness of a woman's devotion, has been placed in a romantic environment. The settings of Chapman's plays, together with an effervescent sense of fun which makes him delight constantly in practical joking, separate his comedies from Jonson's, and it is noteworthy that the only one in which he elects to pursue a 'realistic' approach is *Eastward Ho* (1605), wherein he had as collaborators John Marston and Jonson himself. This piece, localized in London, offers us a moralizing satirical picture of the good apprentice Golding marrying his master's daughter, and of

the bad apprentice Quicksilver rioting his goods away and ending in the hands of the watch.

Chapman was Jonson's friend; Thomas Dekker, one of the
freshest and liveliest theatrical writers of the time, was his
enemy. Among the latter's earliest works, indeed, was *Satiro-
mastix; or, The Untrussing of the Humorous Poet* (1601), in
which one of the main persons, Horace, is palpably a contemptuous caricature of the author of *Poetaster*. This Horace is a
dogmatic, conceited little versifier who endeavours to write by
the aid of a kind of riming-dictionary, and the brightest scene in
the comedy is that which presents him in his study trying to
compose an ode:

> O me thy priest inspire,
> For I to thee and thine immortal name
> In—in—golden tunes—
> For I to thee and thine immortal name—
> In—sacred raptures flowing—flowing—swimming—
>   swimming—
> In sacred raptures swimming—
> Immortal name—game—dame—tame—lame—lame—
>   lame—
> Pox! hath—shame—proclaim—Oh!
> In sacred raptures flowing will proclaim—
> O me thy priest inspire!
> For I to thee and thine immortal name,
> In flowing numbers fill'd with spright and flame—
> Good! Good! In flowing numbers fill'd with spright
>   and flame. . . .

Dekker's true gifts, however, lay not in satire but in the exploitation of realistic comedy with a kind of warmth and affection.
Jonson hates; Dekker has a goodhumoured sympathy. *The Shoe-
maker's Holiday* showed this at the start of his career, and it is
equally evident in the sentimentally conceived portrait of *The
Roaring Girl; or, Moll Cutpurse* (c. 1610) more than a decade
later.

Dekker's devotion to London's streets finds a reflection in
Thomas Middleton's delineation of life in the metropolis, but
here, without Jonson's bitterness, a seamier side of existence has

been put before us. Like Chapman, Middleton started with plays placed in romantic settings—*The Old Law* (1599), *Blurt Master-Constable* (c. 1601), and *The Phœnix* (c. 1603)—but his real virtues were exhibited only when he adopted the realistic style in *A Trick to Catch the Old One* (c. 1605) and *A Mad World, My Masters* (c. 1606). In neither of these do the characters attract our attention; we are in a world of abstract types, Lucres and Hoards, and Lampreys and Moneyloves. On the other hand, the dialogue is consistently fresh and the intrigues are managed with skill. Crime and vice form the main ingredients of the plots; the scenes are bustling with vitality and life. It may be noted that the former of these two plays well illustrates another feature of the drama cultivated by the realistic writers, the opposition of youth and age, and the tendency to take youth's side. In *A Trick to Catch the Old One*, the hero is Witgood, a profligate but a merry wit, who has been cheated of his estates by his uncle, Lucre. He devises a plan: he introduces his uncle to one of his mistresses, a courtesan, pretending that she is a rich widow and that he is her favoured suitor. Thus misled, Lucre is persuaded to restore to him the titles to his lands. Plots of a similar sort were to become frequent in the following years, and Witgood's descendants were to flourish mightily. The gallants, the tavern haunters, the needy younger brothers here were given a flattering glass wherein their wit could constantly triumph over age's severity and greed.

3. THE FLOURISHING OF TRAGEDY

The most interesting and exciting thing about this period is the fact that the new mood which encouraged satire and realistic-sentimental scenes also had the power to stimulate what we now recognize was the greatest development of tragedy since the time of the ancient Athenians. As we have seen, the tragic stage did not flourish luxuriantly after the days of Marlowe and Kyd; the decade between 1589 and 1599 found its desires expressed more aptly in romantic comedy and the chronicle-history play. By the latter year, however, the well of the English chronicles had been drawn nearly dry. Every reign since that of Edward I up to the close of the sixteenth century had had its dramatic treatment after the production of Shakespeare's *Henry V*. It is true that Elizabeth's death made it possible for playwrights to deal with the early Tudor period, which during her lifetime they dared not touch, and that several of them eagerly seized on this opportunity. Thomas Dekker and others thus collaborated in a *Sir Thomas Wyatt* (c. 1604), dealing with the pathetic fate of Lady Jane Grey; Samuel Rowley, in *When you see me, you know me* (1604), penned a play on Henry VIII; Thomas Heywood capped this with the two parts of *If you know not me, you know nobody* (1604), in which he dealt with "the troubles of Queen Elizabeth"; and Shakespeare, at the very close of his career, presented his nostalgic *Henry VIII* (1613). Fundamentally, however, there was not much more that could be accomplished in this kind of play, and gradually it disappeared. When John Ford wrote his belated *Perkin Warbeck* in 1633 he was forced to acknowledge that the history play type had long since gone "out of fashion."

Despite the rise of the realistic school, too, the romantic comedy succeeded in retaining its popularity, and Shakespeare was not alone in seeking to infuse into it a spirit which might meet the desires of a new age. His *Twelfth Night* (c. 1600), although perhaps invested with a melancholy not present in his earlier comedies, remained pure romance; but already in *The Merchant of Venice* (1596), with many of its scenes set on the Rialto, and in *Much Ado About Nothing* (c. 1598), with its theme of desertion and threatened death, he had started to make the content of his comedies deeper, and in *Measure for Measure* (1604) and *All's Well that Ends Well* (c. 1602) he was definitely reflecting in his own way the mood which was animating Jonson's efforts. The reflection becomes even clearer when we turn to the strange *Troilus and Cressida* (1602), which contemporaries found impossible to classify, and which in its scenes obviously expresses a sense of unease and perplexity. The change in content and mood has induced us to separate these works from the earlier comedies, and to classify them as "the dark comedies" or as "the problem plays," and, treating them so, we realize that they are among the most interesting of all Shakespeare's writings. At the same time, we are forced to admit that they are dramatically unsatisfactory precisely because an attempt has been made to force more into the romantic form than it is capable of assimilating. All's Well has never appealed on the stage; even in the best productions of Measure for Measure audiences find it difficult to harmonize the almost tragic intensity of the Angelo story with the twists, tricks, and turns of the romantic plot; and, although Troilus and Cressida has made some appeal to modern spectators, its puzzling contrasts have failed to give complete satisfaction.

Others besides Shakespeare similarly sought to utilize the romantic style for new purposes, and their plays too produce the same impression. One example may serve for many. In 1602 or 1603 Middleton wrote his The Phœnix, selecting just such an imaginative setting as was appropriate for a comedy of romance, the court of an only vaguely identified Duke of Ferrara. Within this framework, however, he places a series of episodes in which artificial intrigue is mingled with social satire. Phœnix, the young prince, who has been ordered to travel abroad, remains at home in disguise for the purpose of revealing the ill practices of Lussurioso, Infesto, and other evil lords; a worthy matron Castiza is sold by her husband to one of these lords; a young girl is assigned to the care of her uncle, Falso, who steals her money and incestuously seeks to seduce her; Falso's three servants, Latronello, Fucato, and Furtivo, are aided by their master to rob the poor, and his daughter, the wife of a Jeweller, maintains a dissolute Knight as her lover; Tangle, a rascally lawyer, delights in ruining his clients by encouraging them to indulge in lawsuits. Two things are manifest here: the incompatibility of the romantic framework for the exploitation of social satire and the tendency to revert to the methods employed in the old moralities. The Phœnix has many features of interest, but as a play it fails.

Fortunately, to Shakespeare and several of his companions evidently came a realization that what they might wish to accomplish in this new social and theatrical atmosphere demanded the adopting of a dramatic form other than that of the romantic comedy. In the year 1599 Shakespeare presented his Julius Cæsar and John Marston brought forward the two parts of his peculiar Antonio and Mellida. The former ushers in the great

series of Jacobean tragedies, and the latter, although by no means
a masterpiece, is a work of very great value for an understanding
of the changing temper of the period. In the first part of *Antonio
and Mellida* Marston offers us a 'satirical' romantic comedy akin
in style to *The Phœnix*. Antonio and his father, Andrugio, Duke
of Genoa, have been defeated by Piero, Duke of Venice, and a
price is on their heads. Disguised as an Amazon, Antonio penetrates into Piero's court and steals his beloved mistress Mellida
away. Adventure follows adventure until at the end Piero suddenly abandons his jealous rage and welcomes the banished son
and father. We are here on familiar ground. The second part of
the play, however, starts abruptly with a completely changed
atmosphere. Piero enters "unbrac't, his arms bare, smear'd in
blood, a poniard in one hand bloody, and a torch in the other";
revenge and murder become the theme of the action; Andrugio is
slain and appears in ghostly form to his son; Piero finally perishes
at Antonio's hand in the midst of a court masque. The atmosphere of romantic comedy has gone and a new kind of tragic
spirit has taken its place. Marston's work is in many respects
ridiculous, yet it may serve as an image of the time. In the first
part of *Antonio and Mellida* he has adopted the romantic comedy
style, and has tried to fit it to other ends than those for which
it was originally calculated; in the second part he has gone right
back to the style of *The Spanish Tragedy* and frankly embraced
a tragic form. Still further, in the particular form he has selected,
he points steadily in the direction of *Hamlet*.

Hamlet must have appeared on the stage two years later, in
1601; *Othello*, *Macbeth*, and *King Lear* followed between 1603
and 1606; *Antony and Cleopatra*, *Coriolanus*, and *Timon of
Athens* must have been written almost immediately thereafter.
In these, Shakespeare, who had been losing his grip in endeavouring to expand the scope of the romantic comedy, manifestly
found what he required; and the success of the four plays from
Hamlet to *King Lear* shows clearly that he was giving his public
what at that time they wanted. After the passage of many years
the spirits of Marlowe and Kyd were revived, fused with one
another, and endowed with fresh strength. The former's intensity and sense of grandeur were granted new dramatic force; not

only was the theme of *The Spanish Tragedy* reflected in the theme of *Hamlet* but, throughout, the qualities which had given distinction to Kyd's work were taken over and refashioned. The bitterness, uncertainty, and melancholic sentiment of the period here was provided with such a fitting form of expression as to give these tragedies enduring existence. The expanded romantic comedy could provide little beyond an unsatisfactory amalgam of discordant elements; the realistic comedy, even in the hands of a master like Jonson, could hardly rise beyond the topical and the temporary; in Shakespeare's tragedies the immediate present was enlarged into the eternal.

In saying this, however, we must be careful to observe that the last three tragedies, the so-called 'Roman' plays, are of a kind different from their predecessors. Not only are they distinct from the others in dealing with classical themes, they are cast in another form. From *Hamlet* to *King Lear* we have the impression that Shakespeare's supreme aim is to produce work calculated for the stage; the dramatist is completely in control. From *Antony* to *Timon* we are inclined to feel that the poet is overmastering the playwright. Even if allowances are made for the apparent fact that *Timon* was left unfinished, its basic concept is a poetic rather than a dramatic one; *Coriolanus* may be recognized as a masterly achievement without accepting it as a thoroughly satisfactory play; and *Antony and Cleopatra* undoubtedly makes a deeper impact in the reading of its text than in the witnessing of its scenes on the stage.

It is unnecessary in any general survey of the drama to devote further comment to plays so well known as these, but it is of importance to fit them in to the wider pattern of the contemporary theatre. Many other among Shakespeare's fellow-playwrights from Jonson downward essayed the tragic form during this decade. Not a single one of them produced any play worthy of being set alongside his; none was able to reach the complex impression he gives of living characters, of inevitable movement from proposition to final conclusion, of integrated individual, political, and metaphysical action, of complete mastery in the handling of diverse material. At the same time, the tragic form, evidently closely bound up with the demands of the period, did yield a series of dramas which, even when not evoking a thoroughly harmonious poetic vision, made notable contributions to the theatre. There were, of course, numerous failures of contrasting kinds. Jonson's own *Sejanus* (1603) and *Catiline* (1611), although ambitious and carefully wrought, have practically no dramatic value, and they may stand as representative of several other kindred works inspired rather by a scholarly dream than by theatrical fervour. At the opposite extreme are plays such as Henry Chettle's *The Tragedy of Hoffman; or, A Revenge for a Father* (c. 1602) and the anonymous and undatable *Alphonsus, Emperor of Germany*, wherein theatricality runs riot. In the former, lurid incident follows lurid incident as the gloomy hero, seeking to avenge his father's murder, proceeds to assassinate his enemies and himself perishes at the close because he has allowed "fickle beauty and a woman's fraud" to deflect him from his main purpose. In the latter, Alphonsus, a monster of vice, moves from crime to crime until he is caught by one of his intended victims, forced to deny God, and then stabbed to the heart.

Obviously, contemporary audiences derived some delight from crude pieces of this sort, enjoying the thrill which comes from contemplation of intense evil and the pleasure of watching complex intrigue plots. They were also prepared, however, to welcome tragedies of deeper intent. George Chapman, for example, offered to them a series of dramas which, although replete with sensational scenes, were inspired by a philosophic concept. In 1604 appeared his *Bussy D'Ambois*, based on contemporary events in the French Court and presenting a strong-willed, aggresssive hero cast in an almost Marlovian mould. Boldly the story of his adventures is told, with scenes of fighting, devil-conjuring, ghostly visitations, letters signed in blood; it might all have seemed ridiculous had Chapman not been able to convince us that basically his object is to set upon the stage the image of one kind of great man, the individual who determines to be a law unto himself and will bow to neither God nor man. The ghost of the dead Bussy dominates over a second companion piece, *The Revenge of Bussy D'Ambois* (c. 1610), in which the dead Bussy's brother Clermont, a calmer, deeper, and more balanced character, is driven to seek a revenge against which his instincts are opposed. Another two-part play, *The Conspiracy and Tragedy of Byron* (*c.* 1605), traces the career and final defeat of a second ambitious and trampling hero, the dramatic picture of a man possessed of the virtues and weaknesses of the recently executed Earl of Essex—to whom, indeed, Chapman specifically likens him. Finally, in *The Tragedy of Chabot Admiral of France* (*c.* 1613) these essays in political tragedy are brought to a close with the treatment of a noble-minded although low-born servant of a king who moves forward faithfully amid others' corruption until his master's ill-founded suspicion breaks his heart.

A vastly different purpose animates the plays of John Webster, whose *The White Devil* (*c.* 1610) and *The Duchess of Malfi* (*c.* 1614) are among the few non-Shakespearian tragedies of this time to preserve their fame and even to witness occasional revival on the stage. Both inhabit a world of intense evil. The first concentrates upon a woman, Vittoria Corombona, who might be accepted almost as the female counterpart of the Marlovian hero —prepared to indulge in any crime in order to achieve her ambitious ends. The second shows a noble Duchess caught in the toils of men cruel and ambitious, tormented in spirit and in body, done wretchedly to death. Webster's was a peculiar half-genius. In some respects he exhibits the true dramatist's skill in the handling of his scenes; and hardly any could match him in the conjuring up of dark, macabre situations illuminated by a poetic imagination ever dwelling on the thought of death. Yet neither of these plays gives us full satisfaction; the vision flags at times, vanishes for a space or loses itself in perplexed confusion. Perhaps he is the playwright who comes nearest to Shakespeare in his power of character delineation but his tragedies rather serve to illuminate Shakespeare's magnificent balance than to vie with his.

Webster's world of evil appears in a variant form in *The Revenger's Tragedy* (1607) and *The Atheist's Tragedy; or, The Honest Man's Revenge* (*c.* 1608), the latter certainly and the former probably written by Cyril Tourneur. The first of these offers us a cynically melodramatic plot, introduced by the hero, Vindice, who, with the skull of his murdered mistress in his hand, soliloquizes on the wickedness of his enemies and on his determination to achieve their ruin. The action moves with lugubrious inevitability towards a scene in which an amorous Duke is confronted, in a darkened room, with the dummy figure of a woman on the top of which is placed the skull, smeared with corrosive poison. The Duke is induced to salute the 'lady,' falls writhing to the ground, and is stamped to death. It might well be thought that such a play could have no value, and indeed we may readily confess that it is almost unrevivable in the theatre; yet the nervous tension of its dialogue and the poetic virulence of its longer speeches gives it a quality of strength matched in no other tragedy of the time. Vindice's apostrophe to "the skull of his love dressed up in tires":

> Does every proud and self-affecting dame
> Camphire her face for this? And grieve her Maker
> In sinful baths of milk, when many an infant starves
> For her superfluous outside, all for this?
> Who now bids twenty pounds a night, prepares
> Music, perfumes and sweetmeats? All are hush'd.
> Thou mayest lie chaste now. It were fine, methinks,
> To have thee seen at revels, forgetful feasts,
> And unclean brothels—sure, 'twould fright the sinner
> And make him a good coward, put a reveller
> Out of his antic amble,
> And cloy an epicure with empty dishes.
> Here might a scornful and ambitious woman
> Look through and through herself. See, ladies, with
>   false forms
> You deceive men, but cannot deceive worms—

in itself reveals the strange, extraordinary passion breathed into the play. In contrast with *The Revenger's Tragedy*, *The Atheist's Tragedy* brings forward a hero who, although confronted by an enemy as confirmed in his wickedness as any Jacobean villain, deliberately rejects the idea of executing his own vengeance and leaves God to punish the evil-doer. The fact that this hero's name is Charlemont suggests a close connexion between this play and Chapman's *Revenge of Bussy D'Ambois*, with its not dissimilar portrait of Clermont. The revenge theme, we must remember, appealed to this age not only because it offered opportunities for thrilling dramatic situations but also because it raised fundamental philosophical and religious issues.

Amid all these various experiments in the writing of tragedy one other must be noted. *Arden of Feversham* in 1591 had essayed an absolutely novel dramatic form, that of the domestic drama, and during the late Elizabethan and early Jacobean periods several attempts were made to follow its example. Eight years later, in 1599, Shakespeare's company produced an anonymous play called *A Warning for Fair Women*, dealing with the story of a murder that had occurred in 1573, which carried the naturalistic style a stage farther. Although some of its scenes are almost melodramatically absurd, others, such as that where the children sit down to play by the door and that wherein the husband, Sanders, angers his wife by refusing to give her money for the settlement of a milliner's bills and thus in effect seals his own doom, demonstrate that the anonymous author was seeking for what we now should call a "documentary" effect, and that he possessed at least some skill in recording common speech and characters. Perhaps, however, the greatest interest of this piece is its illuminating introduction—a debate, carried on by Tragedy, History, and Comedy, which casts considerable light on contemporary interpretations of these three dramatic kinds. Tragedy's presentation of Sanders' murder is, in effect, a reply to Comedy's satirical description of prevailingly romantic tragic styles; these, she declares, show

> How some damn'd tyrant, to obtain a crown,
> Stabs, hangs, impoisons, smothers, cutteth throats;
> And then a Chorus, too, comes howling in
> And tells us of the worrying of a cat,
> Then of a filthy whining ghost,
> Lapped in some foul sheet or a leather pilch,
> Comes screaming like a pig half-stick'd
> And cries 'Vindicta! Revenge! Revenge!'
> With that a little rosin flasheth forth,
> Like smoke out of a tobacco-pipe or a boy's squib.
> Then comes in two or three like to drovers,
> With tailors' bodkins stabbing one another.
> Is this not trim? Is not here goodly things?

We might almost say that this domestic drama aimed at creating for contemporaries a 'progressive theatre'; the kitchen sink had hardly been created then, but the 'kitchen-sink' kind of play was being adumbrated.

Others followed this lead. *A Yorkshire Tragedy* (c. 1606) is a potted play evidently intended to form part of a composite *All's One; or, Four Plays in One*, and, although crude, is remarkable for the fierce intensity which invests the central figure of the husband who destroys his family in a wild fit of passion. At the opposite extreme, so far as length is concerned, come the two parts of Dekker's *The Honest Whore* (1604–5), a work which might almost be taken as anticipating the modern 'domestic drama' not tragically conceived but intent on dealing with a 'problem.' True, the setting, instead of being a bourgeois English home, is romantic, but the entire atmosphere of the scenes belongs to contemporary London. The sub-plot is comic, concentrating upon the patient, pacifistic citizen Candido, whose wife seeks many means to make him angry. This serves as a contrast and comment on the main story which, amid a fair amount of intrigue, focuses attention upon a courtesan, Bellafronte, who meets the pure-minded Hippolito, is deeply moved by his words of reproof, and is completely converted. Particularly interesting is the method which Dekker has employed in dealing with the second part of his play—virtually a reversal of the first, wherein we see Hippolito suddenly gripped by lustful thoughts, pursuing Bellafronte, now married to an honest man, and being rejected by her. We are, of course, far removed here from the world of *Arden of Feversham*; indeed, some of the dialogue, with its scalding fury, comes close in spirit to Tourneur's, while the humorous scenes remind us of the citizen comedies of the period; nevertheless, despite those qualities and despite its romantic framework, *The Honest Whore* obviously springs from a concept animating the writers of realistic tragedy.

One particular play from this group is still remembered and occasionally even revived—Thomas Heywood's *A Woman Killed with Kindness* (1603); and the praise it has received is well deserved. In it, Heywood has done several things. His play is a 'tragedy,' with a theme akin to those of *Arden of Feversham* and

A *Warning for Fair Women*, but, instead of simply exhibiting a domestic murder, it mingles a story of death with the presentation of a problem, enriching the treatment of this problem by deliberately avoiding violent sensational incident. Secondly, it binds together two entirely different plots in such a manner as to make them complementary. And, finally, it succeeds in putting upon the stage real-life scenes wherein, when occasion demands, the language can be made to soar beyond the commonplace. The first of the two plots introduces us to a couple of friends, Sir Francis Acton and Sir Charles Mountford, who go hunting, and suddenly fall into a violent quarrel over a triviality; Mountford flies into a passion and kills two of Acton's men, thus ruining himself; Acton plans a personal vengeance but is deflected from his purpose when he falls in love with Mountford's sister. This serves as background for the other, and main, plot, which opens on the picture of a happy contented domestic interior; John Frankford and his wife are devoted to each other; the former befriends a man named Wendoll and brings him to his house; there, in spite of all their attempts to quench their infatuation, the wife and Wendoll become lovers; Frankford's old servant Nicholas divines the truth and tells his master; at first the husband, blind with rage, plans to murder the pair, but calmer thoughts prevent him; he sends off his Anne to live in seclusion at a lonely manor, and when she, dying of shame and a broken heart, begs him to come to her, he acquiesces, and she passes away pardoned. The treatment of the two stories clearly reflects an imaginatively individual approach, and the language gives strength and colour to the situations and characters. As Frankford, for example, looks upon the guilty lovers in their bed, Heywood is able to find for him a form of expression at once 'realistic' and 'poetic':

> O God, O God! that it were possible
> To undo things done, to call back yesterday,
> That time could turn up his swift sandy glass
> To untell the days and to redeem these hours!
> Or that the sun
> Could, rising from the west, draw his coach backward,
> Take from the account of time so many minutes,

Till he had all these seasons call'd again,
Those minutes and those actions done in them,
Even from her first offence, that I might take her
As spotless as an angel in my arms!
But O! I talk of things impossible,
And cast beyond the moon. God give me patience,
For I will in to wake them.

Years later, some time in the twenties of the century, Heywood
wrote another play which, although removed from it in time,
deserves to be taken along with A Woman Killed with Kindness.
In The English Traveller the story once more is that of an erring
wife, but here the emphasis is laid upon the man who falls in
love with her. Geraldine, a fine, sensitive young gentleman,
returns from foreign travel and goes to the home of an elder
friend, Wincott. There he meets and becomes devoted to Wincott's wife, who returns his love. The pair, however, vow that
they will not betray the husband, and pledge eternal, chaste
affection, at least until the wife is free. Geraldine, in order not
to risk temptation and to avoid possible scandal, absents himself
from the house; but the wife, against her better nature, finds herself drawn into a sordid affair with an evil-minded Dalavill.
Like Anne Frankford, she dies repentant after her unfaithfulness
has been discovered. In this and in his earlier play Heywood
demonstrates that he is not interested in sin as such; he is interested in the reflection of that sin in the minds of others. Frankford is more carefully studied than Mrs Frankford; Geraldine is a
more carefully executed portrait than is the erring wife. This
approach to his dramatic material gives Heywood a special position of his own in a period when most of his companions were
inclined, Tourneur-like, to concentrate on the exhibition of evil
for its own sake.

Since The English Traveller has been mentioned here, one
other later play, A Fair Quarrel (c. 1616) by Middleton and
Rowley, may be dealt with, since in spirit, if not in plot, it might
be regarded as a kind of companion-piece to Heywood's dramas.
Here also two contrasting plots have been interrelated. The first
tells of a girl Jane, secretly married to Fitzallen, whom her
money-seeking father plans for a rich fool, Chough. The father,

by a legal trick, gets Fitzallen put into prison; she finds herself with child, and when she goes secretly to a doctor she is confronted by that medico's amorous advances. Rebuffed, the doctor reveals her condition to Chough, who promptly rejects the thought of marrying her; and the father is forced, in desperation, to bring Fitzallen out of bondage. The second plot has an entirely different theme. Captain Ager quarrels violently with his friend, a Colonel. Lady Ager, his mother, tries vainly to stop a duel by falsely pretending that she had been unfaithful to her husband; her efforts, however, are in vain, the duel is fought, and the Colonel falls, seriously wounded. The affair brings calm to his passionate spirit, and he not only seeks the Captain's pardon but makes him his heir. The entire play is written with distinction, and the characters come alive; at the same time, its realistic approach definitely veers at moments towards the sentimental. A *Fair Quarrel* cannot justly be styled sentimental as a whole, but, excellent as it is, it betrays signs of the almost inevitable trend of the domestic drama towards the mawkish and the artificial.

The impulse which inspired, directed, and partly created Shakespeare's tragedies continued to exert its power over the theatre during the latter part of James' reign. Although it is easy to trace signs of debility, the appearance of numbers of plays worthy of remembrance and the evolution of new dramatic forms testify to the fact that its formative strength had not yet been lost.

Three or four playwrights may be taken to illustrate the course being taken in the tragic sphere. First come those two men, Francis Beaumont and John Fletcher, who gave their names to a dramatic style destined to prove almost as influential as the styles of Shakespeare and Jonson. In 1616 the *Works* of Ben Jonson, completed by a second volume in 1640, had ushered in a novelty—the collected edition of an author's writings for the stage. In 1623 this was followed by the *Comedies, Histories, and Tragedies* of Shakespeare. The only other corresponding publication during this period was the folio issued in 1647 as *Comedies and Tragedies written by Francis Beaumont and John Fletcher Gentlemen*. In fact, however, the title of this last work was a misnomer; with only a few of the plays was Beaumont associated;

Fletcher wrote some of them unaided and others in collaboration with several other authors; a number of the pieces were penned probably without either Beaumont's or Fletcher's participation. This fact needs to be appreciated for our purposes, but the question of authorship may be put aside and the term 'Beaumont and Fletcher' used, not to suggest that these two men were responsible for the plays concerned, but simply to designate a dramatic style illustrated generally in the 1647 compilation.

The Maid's Tragedy (c. 1611) exhibits their tragic form at its best. The plot is simple. Amintor is married by his King's command to Evadne, and discovers on his wedding night that she is in fact the unashamed mistress of the monarch. Thoughts of revenge surge in upon him, only to be barred by the contemplation of that divinity which hedges in a king. Evadne, however, is stirred to repentance, murders her royal lover, and is swept into fresh despair by seeing the horror that her act has aroused in Amintor's mind. There is a powerful imagination at work here, but the play fails to hold us as it should have done; and perhaps this is due mainly to the fact that the focus of attention has been directed rather to the central 'problem' than to the characters. At times we may feel that, despite the intensity of the passions, The Maid's Tragedy comes closer to the spirit of the later romantic tragi-comedy than it does, say, to Othello. Constantly, in other 'Beaumont and Fletcher' tragic dramas, the romance material and attitudes enter in, while at the same time stress tends to be placed more on patterned theme than on the persons presented. In Cupid's Revenge (c. 1612) we are not interested in the characters; all attention is devoted to watching the development of a story which tells how the god Cupid, angered at the lack of devotion accorded to his shrine, descends to earth and causes havoc. Thierry and Theodoret (c. 1617) exists rather for its sensational presentation of a terrible mother and her two wretched sons than for any real attempt to make these persons live. Indeed, in the 'Beaumont and Fletcher' plays we can see clearly how the individualization of characters, which had given force and distinction to earlier dramas, was being submerged by the tendency to rely upon stock types. A king becomes merely a monarch, good or bad according to the requirements of the plot; a heroine is made all innocent, a hero all noble; a faithful friend takes shape almost as though he were the personification of Loyalty in a morality. Some of these 'Beaumont and Fletcher' tragedies have interest, but fundamentally they are theatrical rather than dramatic; they are invested with no driving sense of purpose, but aim only at catching immediate audience favour.

Considerably different is the work of Philip Massinger, but in many of his efforts, even though he seeks to win approval by the introduction of sensational incident, we feel a lack of excitement, of subtlety, of inner penetration—with the result that their conclusions leave us relatively unmoved. There may be a terrible villain in The Duke of Milan (c. 1622), but he is made to protest too much; Sforza may be a great lover, but the rhetoric given to him tends to make his love seem more like lust. Further indications of weakness are apparent in The Unnatural Combat (c. 1623), wherein a number of genuinely effective scenes are rendered nugatory by the emphasis on melodramatic effects (including the final destruction of a character by lightning) and especially by the concealing of certain basic information until the final act, so that a sudden surprise may be sprung on the spectators. If these plays demonstrate some of Massinger's weaknesses The Virgin Martyr (1620) and The Roman Actor (1626) illustrate his strength. The former, essaying the hard task of creating tragic passion out of Christian faith, succeeds in giving life to its central character, Dorothea; while the latter in the person of the actor Paris achieves a kind of dignified grandeur.

A consideration of these tragedies as a whole suggests that Massinger was unfitted to write genuinely effective tragedy because he lacked intensity of vision and deep sensitivity. Both of these qualities find expression in two of Middleton's plays, The Changeling (1622) and Women beware Women (1621), although unfortunately the vigour of the former is vitiated by the combination of the main plot with another plot wholly inappropriate and that of the latter by a plethora of romantic intrigue. The Changeling, like Macbeth, shows crime being born of crime. Beatrice, in order to escape marrying a man she does not love, engages a court hanger-on, De Flores, to get rid of the unwanted suitor. The murder is effected; De Flores is offered money but contemptuously demands a greater and more intimate reward. Beatrice proudly draws his attention to the distance between her noble blood and his—but his reply inexorably brings her down to reality:

> Look but into your conscience; read me there;
> 'Tis a true book; you'll find me there your equal.

What gives this tragedy distinction is what follows upon this. Beatrice gives herself with loathing to De Flores, but gradually the evil which she has let loose penetrates into her soul. Not only does she become willing to proceed with further murder in a sorry attempt to conceal her first crime, she even comes to dote on the villainous De Flores whom originally she had despised and used only as a tool. The atmosphere of *Women beware Women* is akin to this, but as we struggle our way through its complicated plot we realize the quality that is wanting in Middleton's tragic world: the figures he puts upon the stage are all voluptuaries, knaves, lechers, and as a result the unrelieved blackness, instead of making a deep impression, palls upon us.

4. THE CULT OF TRAGICOMEDY AND SOCIAL COMEDY

For the most part, the tragedies written at this time, whatever their poetic virtues, were merely developments of forms established during the years preceding; but the late Jacobean theatres did succeed within other fields in evolving types of drama which either had not previously been exploited or had only vaguely been adumbrated. Of these, two are of special importance.

In 1608 appeared a play, *Pericles*, which immediately caught the attention of the public. Unfortunately, its text, as printed the following year, is so mutilated as to make it impossible to determine its provenance exactly, but certainly Shakespeare was responsible, if not for the whole, at least for a number of its acts. Its structure offers several points of interest; it is wrought in the form of a dramatized story, the poet Gower coming forward as Prologue and Chorus, narrating some of the events and introducing those parts acted out on the boards; and, in keeping with this device, the plot itself is executed on a large, wide canvas, showing a hero, sorely plagued by fortune and man, eventually arriving at a haven of rest. Although there are clear connexions between this work and Elizabethan romantic comedies, the differences are equally obvious. A spirit of wonder is conjured up; at times an element of mysteriousness carries the action towards the symbolic; the realm of romance is being exhibited in a new way.

The mood evoked here colours Shakespeare's next three plays —with the exception of *Henry VIII*, his last writings—*Cymbeline* (c. 1609), *The Winter's Tale* (c. 1610), and *The Tempest* (1611). The long, spun-out plots of the first two; the visions and the scenes of wonder; the stress on the word 'tale,' associated with the narrative method used at the beginning of *The Tempest*; the hints of symbolism, accentuated by the employment of such names as Marina, Perdita, and Miranda for the heroines; the quality of the poetic style; the theme of the lost one fortunately found again—all these features bind the four plays together in a single group. To explain their appearance various suggestions have been offered: to some they seem the aftermath of Shakespeare's tragic passions, 'reconciliation' following upon torment; by others they are thought to have originated from the fact that in 1608 or 1609 Shakespeare's fellow-actors took over a new kind of playhouse, the 'private' Blackfriars; still others would seek to argue that he was here applying himself to the exploitation of a new sort of tragicomedy initiated by Beaumont and Fletcher. Although we shall probably never be able to answer the question directly, it is necessary to observe that there is no evidence to suppose that these were any other than Globe theatre dramas and indeed that such evidence as we do possess connects them rather with the public than with the private stage; while, still further, the facts available to us suggest that, instead of Beaumont and Fletcher influencing Shakespeare, their associated efforts owed their being to his example. No doubt Shakespeare freely borrowed from others, but there is no need to assume that throughout his career he was incapable of thinking and inventing for himself.

In any case, a vast chasm yawns between the Beaumont and Fletcher tragicomedies and Shakespeare's. His are deep and theirs are shallow; his manifest a profound imaginative vision, whereas even the best of theirs aim simply at theatrical effect; rarely do theirs present any save stock characters and assuredly none worthy of being considered alongside the living persons created by his imagination. *Philaster* (c. 1610), frequently evoked in this connexion, provides us with little more than a skilfully told story of a hero, Philaster, who has some dangerous political and pathetic amorous adventures; its incidents are controlled, not by thought of the persons involved in them, but by a desire to keep the audience constantly alert. This theatricality in the Beaumont and Fletcher tragicomedies went so far as to originate a relatively new dramatic pattern—that which offered to spectators an action which seemed inevitably destined for a tragic end but which was suddenly twisted to a happy conclusion through the introduction of a surprise. In *A King and No King* (1611), for example, we are shown a young monarch gripped by an incestuous passion for his sister and apparently heading for inexorable ruin; then, unexpectedly, the final act of the play reveals a triple fact hitherto concealed—that the girl is not his sister, that he is not the king, and that she is really the queen. Occasionally, as in the tragic *Bonduca* (c. 1612), these authors could for a moment escape from their prevailing desire to pander to a weakening public taste, but as a rule theatricalism rules—a refined theatricalism, no doubt, when we compare it with the cruder efforts of some minor Elizabethan playwrights, yet artificial as theirs. Scene after scene is devised to provide contrast and surprise; never for a moment are we allowed repose. *The Custom of the Country* (c. 1620) introduces at the start a hero Arnoldo newly married to Zenocia; the lord of the country demands that she should be sent on her wedding night to his apartments; the couple flee by boat, accompanied by Arnoldo's brother; Zenocia is captured by pirates; Arnoldo arouses lustful passions in the breast of an Hippolyta; she tries to poison Zenocia and ruin the hero, but incredibly repents in time to avoid disaster; the brother apparently kills a stranger in a street brawl and is protected by this stranger's mother; later he is obliged to take service in a male brothel; the supposedly slain man is found to be alive; and all ends happily.

Dozens of such plays, some very poor, some reasonably interesting, poured from the pens of Fletcher and his collaborators.
The Sea Voyage (1622), like *The Tempest*, bears us to a distant
island, but its inhabitants, a group of Amazons, are used merely
as an excuse for the introduction of amorous affairs romantically
strange. Sometimes, as in *The Maid in the Mill* (1623), comic
intrigue modifies the romantic; sometimes, as in *The Two Noble
Kinsmen* (1613), in which some believe Shakespeare to have
been Fletcher's collaborator, pathetic sentiment predominates.
In most of them, at least a few episodes offer features of interest;
most of them are adroitly constructed and Fletcher's easy, witty
poetic style gives quality to their dialogue; but fundamentally
these were plays for a time and not for all time. They appealed to
the audiences of courtiers who flocked to Blackfriars and occasionally to the Globe, but the tastes of these spectators were
becoming jaded. They could, from time to time, accept the sensationalism of some revenge play, especially if it brought in novel
incidents; they could also give their plaudits to a cleverly
wrought tragicomedy which offered them pleasing surprises;
nevertheless, they were rapidly losing the power of appreciating
the serious drama in any of its forms.

The result of this is that, even when we look beyond the
'Beaumont and Fletcher' plays, we find ourselves confronted by
patent artificiality. Massinger was a worthy playwright; he
knew how to construct a drama effectively, and he possessed a
strong, if rhetorical, poetic style. Although these qualities are
present in *The Bondman* (1623), they cannot conceal the fact
that not a single one of the characters has other than a theatrical
existence; although the theme of *The Renegado* (1624), dealing
with a Christian induced to abandon his faith, promises an interesting and forceful play, the author finds himself prepared to
vitiate his work by indulging in one of the usual happy-ending
twists at the end; in *The Maid of Honour* (1621), which also
promises well, we are confronted only by a pathetic lover,
Adorni, a comic Signor Sylli, a noble innocent heroine, Camiola,
a commonplace headstrong king, Roberto, and a lustful woman,
Aurelia—stock persons all. The significance of this becomes
patent when we reflect that Massinger was unquestionably one

of the most serious-minded, ambitious, and accomplished playwrights of his time; if he failed we may have a measure for
estimating the extent of the general decline, not only in tragedy,
but also in the tragicomic sphere.

During this second part of James' reign, even while artificial
tragicomedy won applause, the audiences of young gallants also
favoured the development and expansion of a kind of comedy
which shadowed forth the comedies of manners so characteristic
of the later years of the century.

Jonson, as we have seen, first consciously aimed at the establishment of plays opposed to the romantically inspired works
which had been so popular before 1600, and his influence was in
all probability the most potent force in encouraging various other
dramatists, between the beginning of the century and 1610, to
exploit London's citizen world. This provided the foundation. In
Middleton's A Trick to Catch the Old One something further was
suggested. In that play the hero was a gay young spark, im-
poverished but able by the exercise of his wit to win money for
himself. It was this type of hero who was taken over and elaborated by Fletcher and his associates. In focusing attention on
these witty young men, Fletcher once more displayed his keen
awareness of what would please the public of these years. He
recognized that the private theatres were largely supported by
youthful courtiers, inns-of-court men, and their companions; in
the clever, audacious heroes of these comedies the spectators were
offered an idealized picture of themselves, and at the same time
they were regaled with the polished witty conversation towards
which they aspired in their own society. Many a gallant took
his place in the playhouse, notebook in hand, ready "to write
down what again" he might "repeat at some great table, to deserve" his "meat." Wit indeed had now become "the word in
fashion"—so much so that the audiences sought for it not only
in the dialogue but also in the prologues to plays. The use of the
prologue, of course, had for a long time been common; we may
even trace it back to the time of the medieval mysteries; but in
the past it had generally been employed merely to explain the
contents or objectives of the drama to which it was attached.
In Romeo and Juliet, for example, the opening verses simply out-

line the main course of the action, while those which preface
Henry V are designed to apologize for setting such great events
as the battle of Agincourt upon a bare platform. Now, in James'
latter years, the prologue was "advanced above the fabric of the
whole work," and the position which it came to occupy in the
minds of the audience is shown by the fact that not infrequently
dislike of the author's preliminary verses occasioned condemnation of the piece which followed.

This emphasis upon wit led, too, to the growth of a critical
spirit in the auditorium such as had not been usual before;

> He that can
> Talk loud and high is held the witty man;

such a man

> censures freely, rules the box, and strikes
> With his court nod consent to what he likes.

In the theatres there were many

> deep-grounded, understanding men
> That sit to censure plays, yet know not when
> Or why to like;

the authors recognized that

> Some in a humorous squeamishness will say
> They come only to hear, not see, the play;
> Others to see it only; there have been,
> And are good store, that come but to be seen,
> Not see nor hear the play.

It was in this milieu that the youthful, well-born Fletcher won
his success by transferring witty conversation to the stage.
Many among the plays with which he was associated were
romantically set, but whether supposed to take place in a vague
France or Italy or amid London surroundings they brought to the
spectators the spritely immodest libertine whom they could
admire, or the eccentric character at whom they could laugh, or
the cleverly conceived plot from which they could derive intellectual delight. In *The Woman's Prize; or, The Tamer Tam'd*
(c. 1611) they derived merriment from watching a Petruchio

subjugated by his second wife, an English girl; they were pleased to see the careless, roguish Valentine win a lively widow in *Wit without Money* (c. 1614); they laughed at the foolish dapper La Writt, in *The Little French Lawyer* (c. 1619), who fondly imagines he has become a valiant duellist; and above all they derived joy from watching a Witty-pate Oldcraft (*Wit at Several Weapons*, 1609) gaily cheating those less intellectually alert but richer than himself. One particular comedy, *The Wild-Goose Chase* (1621), suggests what later was to be fashioned out of Fletcher's example. Although this play is different in many respects from the Restoration comedies of manners, it definitely anticipates them in others; the merry heroine Oriana, who indulges in a series of tricks to win her elusive Mirabel, together with her sisters, Rosalura and Lillia-Bianca, with their lovers, the blunt Belleur and the witty Pinac, clearly suggest the social circle dealt with by Etherege and his companions. It was not by chance that Farquhar selected this comedy as the basis for his own comedy of manners, *The Inconstant*.

5. CAVALIER SPECTATORS AND THEIR TASTES

In moving from the Jacobean to the Caroline drama, once more it is essential to consider the typical audiences and the playhouses to which they flocked. Fundamentally, the gentlemen and their ladies who supported the actors were the same as those who dominated the theatre in James' time; yet there were several important differences. In 1625 the Civil War was not far off; the Puritans were growing in power and severity; the Cavaliers more and more were becoming self-consciously aware of themselves as a social unit dependent upon the Court; and, as the Puritans proceeded to attack the stage in such vituperative terms as appear in William Prynne's *Histriomastix* (1633), these Cavaliers replied by making the playhouse a kind of appendage of Whitehall.

Their interests, therefore, assumed predominance, and they induced the actors to move on from the hitherto prevailing Elizabethan methods of production towards a new style which may be regarded as the basis of the modern theatre. The courtly spectators had been familiar for many years with the elaborate royal masques developed from the collaboration of Ben Jonson and the architect-designer Inigo Jones. The first of these had come in 1605—*The Masque of Blackness*; and James, who delighted in such shows, encouraged not only Jonson but other poets as well to devise similar spectacular pieces; organizations associated with the Court party, such as the Inns of Court, followed suit, and various wealthy nobles sought, in their own mansions, to emulate the practice of the palace. Throughout the reigns of James and Charles these spectacular aristocratic entertainments followed one another in magnificent procession.

Although the masque itself remains outside the range of the drama proper, its influence on comedy and tragedy alike during the Jacobean period may easily be traced. Undoubtedly, Shakespeare's last plays were partly inspired at least by the idea of the masque, and numerous stage writings, both comic and serious, adopted the device of introducing into their action short masque-like interludes. Until about 1625, however, the influence was indirect rather than direct; the professional stage still remained for the most part a bare platform backed by a façade, and scenery (in the modern sense) was virtually unknown. During Charles' reign there are numerous signs of change. No doubt most plays were given in the older manner, but with the still closer association of court and playhouse several attempts were made towards the reproduction in the professional houses of effects akin to those with which many of the spectators were familiar at Court. When we hear that in the performance of Thomas Nabbes' *Hannibal and Scipio* (1635) that

> The places sometimes chang'd too for the scene,
> Which is translated as the music plays
> Betwixt the acts,

and when we find that Heywood's *Love's Mistress* (1635), after being given three times before royalty, was presented publicly at the Phœnix, we realize that we stand upon the threshold of a new theatre. In his preface to this last-mentioned work, Heywood specifically gives praise to Inigo Jones,

> who to every act, nay almost to every scene, by his excellent inventions gave such an extraordinary lustre, upon every occa-

sion changing the stage to the admiration of all the spectators that, as I must ingeniously confess, it was above my apprehension to conceive, so to their Sacred Majesties and the rest of the auditory it gave so general a content that I presume they never parted from any object, presented in that kind, better pleased or more plenally satisfied.

The days when poet and player alone were of account had begun to vanish.

Apart from this practical impress which the Cavalier spectators were making upon the theatre, two other things must be noted. At Court, especially under the tutelage of Queen Henrietta Maria, there was an active cult of the Platonic romance which was then so fashionable in Paris, and encouragement was being given to young courtiers of literary pretensions to practice writing in this style for the stage. Up to this time, nearly all plays had been written by authors who remained well outside aristocratic circles—the Shakespeares, the Chapmans, the Dekkers, the Heywoods. Fletcher, it is true, was gently connected, but he did not himself walk the Court's corridors or lounge in its anterooms, and most of his collaborators came from humble environments. Now, during the reign of Charles, the Cavalier poet makes his appearance, and in the main his endeavour was to flatter royal taste by cultivating a kind of drama, much influenced by the Platonic romances, which was bound to remain caviare to the general.

All of this, naturally, does not mean that suddenly the older styles disappeared, to be supplanted by new forms; what it implies is that during these fifteen years the stage oriented itself more and more towards the Cavalier audience, slowly changing shape and, without completely severing its connexion with the Elizabethan tradition, prophesied an entirely different kind of theatre to come.

While the strictly 'Cavalier' playwrights—such as Lodowick Carlell, with the two parts of his *The Passionate Lovers* (1638) and the corresponding parts of his *Arviragus and Philicia* (1636) —hardly need examination in a survey such as this, three writers of tragic and tragicomic plays deserve attention both for the manner in which they illustrate the changing styles and for the merit of some of their own achievements. The first of these is James Shirley, who might be taken as representative of dramatists attempting to carry on the earlier tradition. *The Traitor* (1631) and *The Cardinal* (1641), the one set in Italy and the other in France, so inflate the tragedy of revenge and villainy as to make their scenes, despite the author's poetic passion, become absurd. Extravagance has here been substituted for intensity, and the result is often ludicrous: when one of the characters, stabbed and dying by the side of his enemy, cries out:

> Now must I follow:
> I'll fight with him in t'other world,

we recognize how 'literary' and artificial are Shirley's concep-tions. Almost the final words of the play come from the lips of one among the few survivors: "Here is a heap of tragedies"; but the very excess of blood prevents us from receiving the impres-sion which the author desired. "By these you see," he made one of his persons say,

> There is no stay in proud mortality;

but the crop of murders leaves us strangely cold. When, simi-larly, a Duchess remarks in *The Cardinal*:

> He says he loves me dearly and has promised
> To make me well again, but I'm afraid
> One time or other he will give me poison,

a laugh rather than a thrilling shudder might well be the audience's response. The older kind of tragic expression clearly had lost its potency.

John Ford sought another path. Gifted with a subtle and imagi-native sensitivity, and at the same time an avid student of such writings as Burton's *Anatomy of Melancholy*, he sought to create what might be called 'psychological' tragedy. *The Lover's Melancholy* (1628) in its very title reflects the general trend of his work. This, a tragicomedy, does not possess much value, but *The Broken Heart* (1629) and *'Tis Pity She's a Whore* (c. 1627) have been accorded a considerable amount of romantic praise. The former lingers fondly upon thwarted love, strained emotions,

Proscenium Arch and Scene I for "The Queen of Arragon"

CXXX.

Ludas Scenicus.

A Stage-Play.

A Seventeenth-century Stage   129

and bizarre situations. While we would assuredly be willing to admit that Ford is a true poet and that certain scenes, such as that in which Calantha learns of the death of lover, friend, and father, are effective in the reading, it is impossible to accept this work as a masterly dramatic achievement, and the very nature of his persons' names indicates how 'literary' is Ford's approach; Ithocles, he explains to us, is "The Honour of Loveliness," Orgilus is "The Angry One," Calantha is "The Flower of Beauty," Penthea is "Complaint." Symbolic titling may be proper in such a play as The Tempest; Ford's employment of it here betrays the falsity of his tragic attitude. Perhaps 'Tis Pity exhibits greater power, yet its action must leave us with a sense of dissatisfaction. Ford had every right, if he so wished, to take as his theme the story of incestuous passion between a brother, Giovanni, and a sister, Annabella; but we are uneasily oppressed by the manner of his treatment of the situation; at times it almost seems as though he had deliberately chosen this, not because it fired his imagination, but because the exploitation of a relationship normally taboo would excite the jaded attention of his listeners. This means that, instead of intensity being generated by a poetic vision, intensity is being aimed at through the nature of the plot itself.

Finally, a glance at least must be devoted to the writings of an author far less gifted as a poet but much more significant for the position he occupied in the mid-century theatrical world, Sir William D'Avenant. This man, who before 1640 was a favoured courtier and the privileged master of a playhouse company, was to be one of the first to stimulate a revival of dramatic activity after Oliver Cromwell's power had gone; and to a certain extent he was to prove the moving force in the development of the characteristic "love and honour" drama of the Restoration period. In his first independent efforts, Albovine (1628) and The Cruel Brother (1627), he had shown himself a crude exponent of the gloomy and murderous tragedy, where lust, ambition, rapine, and violence are pervasive. When, however, in 1634 he gave the significant title of Love and Honour to a rumbustious tragicomedy, when, the following year, he called another play The Platonic Lovers, and when, in 1638, he made Eumena of The Fair

Favourite a king's platonic 'mistress,' it was as though he were setting up a great signpost pointing directly and accurately towards John Dryden some thirty years ahead. His Theander and Eurithea are not far removed from Almanzor and Almahide.

All through this period tragicomedy flourished, and its styles were various. *The Spanish Gipsy* (c. 1623) by Middleton and Rowley mingles, rather charmingly, the story of a licentious Roderigo who deflowers Clara, but later, repentance-struck, marries her, and a second story which shows us the banished Alvarez and his delightful daughter Pretiosa living disguised in a gipsy camp. Sudden flights of lyrical utterance, passages of rhetorical sentiment, complex intrigue, and scenes coarsely designed to catch the attention of the public characterize most of the romantic comedies and tragicomedies with which James Shirley supplied the stage from *The Brothers* (1626) onward, through *The Grateful Servant* (1629) and *Changes; or, Love in a Maze* (1632), to *The Young Admiral*, *The Gamester*, and *The Bird in a Cage* in 1633. Robert Davenport comes forward with his fairly successful *City Night-Cap* (1624) in which a double plot is presented, one part showing a pathologically jealous husband who actually suborns a friend to tempt his wife, and the other dealing with an overtrusting Lodovico, who allows all liberty to his priggish and riggish spouse. And, during the final years of Charles' reign, such plays as William Habington's *The Queen of Arragon* (1640), Thomas Rawlins' *The Rebellion* (c. 1636), Sir William Berkeley's *The Lost Lady* (1637), and Thomas Randolph's *The Royal Slave* (1636) illustrate the cultivation of pathos, sentimentalism, and extravagant incident which, dear to the tastes of the Court, were to exert considerable influence on the stage when the theatres reopened on the restoration of the monarchy. With these, too, may be associated the related experiments in pastoral style. About the year 1608 Fletcher had tried his youthful hand at a *Faithful Shepherdess*, but apart from this work the earlier decades had largely avoided pastoral subject-matter. Now, during these years just before the outbreak of the Civil War, numerous poets turned to it—Jonson with *The Sad Shepherd* (c. 1637), Shirley with *The Arcadia* (printed 1640), Randolph with *Amyntas* (c. 1630), Rutter with

The Shepherds' Holiday (c. 1634)—none of them, however, succeeding in producing any dramatic achievement truly memorable.

Considerably more of positive value may be found in the extension and elaboration of the realistic comedy which had originally been established at the beginning of the century, and which obviously was in harmony with the tastes of the Cavalier audiences. Some authors, such as Philip Massinger, pursued the Jonsonian course, and by no means without distinction. Indeed, this playwright's *A New Way to pay Old Debts* (c. 1625) stands out among early seventeenth-century dramas as one of the truly enduring theatrical successes. Not only did it remain steadily in the playhouse repertory up to the nineteenth century, it has also witnessed a number of revivals within our own period. In the terrible portrait of the "cruel extortioner" Sir Giles Overreach, Massinger displayed his ability to take a 'humour' cast in Jonson's mould and to give it living quality. One might almost say that in this character the dramatic methods of Jonson and Shakespeare have been fused; in it appear both the concentration upon a type embodying qualities designed to illustrate a social evil and a vitalizing power which makes the type seem to have individual existence. Another later comedy of Massinger's, *The City Madam* (1632), has something of the same force. Although none of its persons possess the vitality invested in Overreach, this bitter picture of a rich merchant's household, with its selfishly ambitious Lady Frugal and its hypocritical Luke, exhibits genuine theatrical virtues.

Somewhat similar in purpose are the plays of William Rowley. *A New Wonder, A Woman never vexed* probably appeared about the same time as *A New Way to pay Old Debts* and, like Massinger's play, deals seriously and morally with social problems of the time. Although vaguely set in an historical atmosphere, its characters and situations are manifestly contemporary, telling the story of Old Foster, a self-righteous merchant, who casts off his brother Stephen, a spendthrift with a good heart, and even disinherits his own son Robert for attempting to aid him; in the end, the father himself, in difficulties, is succoured by the son and the brother, and comes to a deeper understanding of human values.

Once more in this play the double influence of Jonson and Shakespeare is apparent.

Numerous comedies of this time reflect kindred qualities, and some of them are worthy of remembrance. Most of the plays, however, which retain interest for us to-day were individual efforts, single successes by minor authors; apart from Massinger, the only two playwrights who attract attention for the body of their dramatic writings are Richard Brome and James Shirley, each of whom possessed the ability to establish a characteristic style. The former began his career as a follower of Jonson; he had been, in fact, Jonson's servant, and his early efforts were blessed and aided by his master. Even if we are forced to decide that he was not a great poet or writer, it must be admitted that he had a real talent for the stage, a talent which enabled him to pen a number of pieces which won success in their own time and a few of which remained popular well into the eighteenth century. Two features in his dramatic offerings deserve note; first, he was able to modify the Jonsonian 'humours' comedy so that it approached the later comedy of manners; and, secondly, he exploited the musical element in his plays so that they vaguely pointed the way towards the ballad-opera of later years. To illustrate this *The Northern Lass* (c. 1629) and *A Jovial Crew; or, The Merry Beggars* (1641) may be taken as examples. The former presents a novelty in the introduction of the dialect-speaking heroine, Constance, a girl who comes to London, falls in love with Sir Philip Luckless, and, before she succeeds in gaining his hand, finds herself involved in a world of marriage-hunters, fools, and would-be wits—the whole of the action being diversified by a free use of songs and masques. The atmosphere of *The Northern Lass* is carried a stage farther in *A Jovial Crew*, a piece which has the double interest of having been the last play performed before the theatres were closed in 1641 and of enjoying a later wide success when, in the eighteenth century, it was transformed into a ballad opera. Charmingly Brome tells his story of the worthy old squire Oldrent who, after his steward Springlove leaves him to join a company of beggars, discovers to his joy that this Springlove is in reality his son by a beggar-woman. The story, however, really does not matter; for Brome, and for us, the quality of the piece rests in the imaginatively conceived scenes within the beggars' camp.

Brome's writings show one way in which the Jonsonian comedy was being extended; another is revealed in the plays of Shirley. Already in *The School of Compliment*, produced in the year when Charles I came to the throne, Shirley had indicated the path he was to follow. Although this comedy does not possess much value, introducing neither an effective plot nor vital characters, its presentation of a fantastic 'school' in which young gallants are instructed in the art of delivering highly flowered compliments clearly demonstrates that the author's attention was being devoted, not to social errors and evils, but to what may be called the manners of the age. It is this orientation which gives distinction to *The Witty Fair One* (1628), *Hyde Park* (1632), and *The Lady of Pleasure* (1635). All of these depend on their scenes of wit and social polish; all display a new, anti-romantic attitude towards the relationship between men and women. "Come," says the hero of *The Witty Fair One* to the heroine, "remember you are imperfect creatures without a man; be not you a goddess; I know you are mortal, and had rather make you my companion than my idol; this is no flattery now." The Petrarchan sonneteer has gone, as has the deity he worshipped; we have stepped into another world. As the theatres shut their doors in 1641 their productions have come close to the spirit of the productions which were to be characteristic of the days when these doors were officially opened again after 1660. Shirley's comedy of manners, Brome's modifications of the Jonsonian style, D'Avenant's themes of love and honour, had laid the foundations for what was to come.

IV

Restoration Drama

1. DRAMA UNDER THE PURITANS

THE theatres were officially closed by Commonwealth ordinance in 1642; theoretically there was no further acting in England until the restoration of Charles II. Appearances, however, are often deceptive, and we have evidence that in various ways the theatrical tradition established during the early years of the seventeenth century was carried on to the years after 1660.

There is no question but that the Puritan authorities were anxious to put a stop to all sorts of amusement, innocent and otherwise; but there is equally no question but that the actors and spectators frequently evaded the vigilance of the soldiery and presented their shows in defiance of authority. Acting in the Commonwealth period was of two kinds: at the old theatres with performances by some of the players of Caroline days, and at theatres, booths, inns, halls, by bands of actors who put before the spectators 'drolls' or farces, usually derived from already existing plays. Thus, for example, the more rudely comic portions of *A Midsummer Night's Dream* were extracted and performed under the title of *Bottom the Weaver*. Of these 'drolls' two collections are extant, one entitled *The Wits*, published in 1662, and the other *The Stroler's Pacquet Open'd*, issued in 1742. This 'droll' tradition is an important one, for it ran its course by the side of the regular theatre tradition right on to the close of

the eighteenth century. Nor does the acting of 'drolls' exhaust
the theatrical activities of the Commonwealth period. Regular
plays too were frequently to be seen on the boards. Whenever
the actors could gather an audience together in one of the several
half-dismantled playhouses they would, no doubt in most un-
seemly haste, hurry through some Beaumont and Fletcher or
Shakespeare drama. Sometimes these performances were inter-
rupted by the rude entrance of the Puritan soldiers, and then the
affair was reported in the primitive newspapers of the time; more
often than not the players must have got off unscathed, all record
of the performance being lost irretrievably. There are many
extant accounts of acting during these years, and those accounts,
we must presume, are but roughly indicative of a fairly constant
series of irregular performances both in London and in the
provinces. The continuity of tradition was thus in two distinct
ways being preserved.

Nor were these the only means by which the earlier Caroline
theatre was connected with the later. After Cromwell came to
power, some actors formed themselves into a company and set off
for Germany under the leadership of one George Jolly, who was
later to associate himself with William Beeston, formerly master
or governor of the King's company of child players at Salisbury
Court. His repertory must have been composed of well-known
Elizabethan, Jacobean, and Caroline plays, and the acting traditions of earlier days must have been carried on by his activities
over the eighteen years of theatre suppression. William Beeston
himself forms another link. This man, whom Dryden called the
"Chronicle of the Stage," was the son of Christopher Beeston,
who had known Shakespeare in the opening years of the seventeenth century. It is likely that William Beeston, owner in 1660
of the Salisbury Court playhouse and associated with D'Avenant
in the latter's theatrical undertakings, played the part of a
maestro to the younger players. These acting links are completed in Sir William D'Avenant, one who was intimately associated with the theatre in the days of Charles I and who became
leader of a patent company under Charles II. His own operatic
endeavours in The Siege of Rhodes and other similar pieces performed during the last years of the Commonwealth period pro-

vide a pleasant little oasis of licensed acting in the midst of an otherwise arid desert.

Many of those who were not of the severest Puritanical convictions looked back to the theatrical glories of days gone by and kept alive in their hearts the love of acting. The various links we have already glanced at serve to show the binding together of the theatre tradition so far as actual performances and methods of acting are concerned; but the tradition of the written play was also preserved in several distinct ways. Many of the actors found their regular sources of income taken away from them, and they were forced to dispose of that which in earlier days they had jealously guarded. In the early seventeenth century some players seem to have believed that a drama unprinted was more likely to be popular in the theatre than a drama published. Accordingly they held in their tiring-rooms stacks of manuscripts which they refused to sell to the 'stationers.' Only in times of distress—as, for instance, during the periods when the playhouses were shut because of the Plague—did they reluctantly dispose of their treasures. There, are, of course, obvious exceptions. Heminge and Condell issued in 1623 many then unpublished works of Shakespeare, apparently as a kind of last service to their deceased friend; Jonson evidently looked upon his plays as his own property and had his *Works* printed in 1616; but some of the various dramas were regarded as the possessions of those companies by whom they had first been produced. During the Commonwealth period many of these plays were released by the actors. Apart from numerous separate comedies and tragedies these years gave us the rich array of the Beaumont and Fletcher dramas, published in 1647, as a large folio volume. That this publication would have been impossible without a corresponding reading public is a necessary assumption; there were many in England who, remembering pleasant days spent in the theatres, turned from the stage to the study and perused there their favourite tragedies and comedies of Shakespeare, of 'Beaumont and Fletcher,' or of Shirley.

2. THE RESTORATION THEATRE

In 1660 Charles II returned to his throne amid the rejoicings of a nation wearied of the excessive restrictions of the Commonwealth era, and his band of devoted Cavaliers, who had shared his exile with him, joined with the many people in England eager for a return of earlier Caroline traditions. No sooner was Charles on his throne than bodies of actors were formed into companies. George Jolly hurried back from Germany; William Beeston hastily opened up the Salisbury Court theatre; Killigrew gathered together the remnants of the old King's men; D'Avenant collected a body of young actors, untrained, but eager for histrionic glory. The King, however, was anxious to keep the affairs of the theatre in his own hands, and within a few months of his accession he had issued orders and patents by which the number of companies was limited to two, one under Killigrew and another under D'Avenant. These two companies settled down to a comfortable monopoly, the first at the various Theatres Royal, the second at the Duke's houses in Lincoln's Inn Fields and in Dorset Garden. In 1682 both were amalgamated into one, and remained so until the year 1695 saw the secession of a number of the best actors. The first point we note, then, is this, that for thirteen years one theatre supplied all the needs of London, and that for the other twenty-seven years to the end of the century only two theatres were running. When we remember that a smaller London of thirty or forty years previously had been able to support as many as six theatres running concurrently it becomes obvious that some great change had come over the playgoing public. That change is really the culmination of the gradual movement we have seen growing in the early years of the century: the theatre has degenerated completely into a thing of the Court; the middle classes for the most part keep away. A few of the unaristocratic people of the time, such as Pepys, may have attended the playhouses during these years, but such people were those who sought for Court preferment or who aped in one way or another the manners and tastes of the Cavaliers. All we know of the theatre in these times proves conclusively that the typical audience was composed of the courtiers, their ladies, the gallants, and the 'wits,' with a sprinkling of the riff-raff of the town. The playhouse had become the rather riotous haunt of the upper classes, and, as a consequence, the plays written for that playhouse were distinctly calculated by the authors to appeal to a courtly and Cavalier audience. It is this that explains both the rise of the heroic tragedy and the elaboration of the comedy of manners. The one appealed to artificial aristocratic sentiments on the subject of honour; the other reflected the morally careless but intellectually brilliant atmospheres of the boudoirs and the taverns.

At the same time, the playhouses changed their shape. In three particular ways the Restoration theatre differed from the Elizabethan. Save for the first few years after 1660, when some of the still-existing playhouses were utilized by the actors, the old open-air 'public' theatre disappeared. The new theatres were, with one early exception, roofed in, and consequently lit by artificial light. Moreover, the first new premises occupied by the players were not of the square inn-yard type, but were converted tennis-courts, oblong in shape. It is obvious that in houses of this sort the Elizabethan platform stage would have been out of the question; on the other hand, tradition pointed to a stage surrounded by the audience. A compromise was effected whereby a proscenium arch, unknown in the early seventeenth century save in the masques at Court, cut off part of the theatre, and an 'apron' in the form of a semicircle jutted out into the midst of the pit. There is here the union of two mutually opposing systems of staging. Intimacy with the audience could still be secured by the players when they moved to the forward portion of the stage, and yet there remained the possibility of scenic display in the back portion of the house. We shall expect to find, therefore, and do find, that technically the plays written for this theatre show many anomalies. They are transition plays, at one and the same time looking back to the earlier platform stage with its free conventions, and looking forward to the development of a new theatre. For the first few years it is natural that the dramatists should not have learned how to write for the altered stage; their plays are cast in the Elizabethan form. Gradually, however, the exigencies of the changed conditions made themselves felt; play-

wrights realized the needs of the actors, and their plays, because
of the influence of the scenery, became more co-ordinate and less
scattered in subject-matter than the plays written in Shakespeare's time. Only in the spectacular productions of the period
do we discover shifting of locality such as appears, for example,
in *Antony and Cleopatra* or in *King Lear*.

The presence of this scenery, added to the fact that lighting of
a primitive sort accompanied all plays, led to the loss of one important Elizabethan convention. We have already seen how
Shakespeare and his fellows were forced, because of the absence
of scenery and because the plays were performed in daylight, to
explain to the audience where their actors were supposed to be
and at what time the action was supposed to take place. In the
Restoration theatre such information given to the audience
would have been superfluous, and consequently as we study the
drama of this period we can see how, gradually, more and more
was left to the scene designer and to the machinist; more, that is
to say, was left to the eye and less to the ear. While this made
for greater concentration in the plays themselves and prevented
minor dramatists from wandering into would-be poetical disqui-
sitions on Nature's loveliness, it took away to a certain extent
from the poetic quality inherent in the dramas of earlier years;
the element of verbal splendour was subdued.

The third point which is to be noted concerning the Restoration theatre is the introduction of actresses. In the former years
all the players were men or boys. The pleasure-loving Charles II,
however, had seen many performances by women during his
exile abroad, and he evidently decided that the introduction of
actresses here would be a good thing. Cynically enough he pretended he was instituting the innovation in the interests of
morality. Probably no one believed him but on the other hand
no one objected, and a woman first appeared on the English stage
to speak the prologue to *Othello* and play the part of Desdemona.
Just at first the number of women capable of fulfilling their tasks
must have been small, and boys continued occasionally to take
feminine rôles, but by 1670 the new conditions had been fully
established. Not only was a Betterton and a Mohun praised, but
a Nell Gwyn, a Moll Davis, a Mrs Barry, a Mrs Bracegirdle, and

a Mrs Oldfield. It is unnecessary here to point out the many changes, good and bad, which these women brought into the theatre, but one consequence demands special comment. For the most part, the early seventeenth-century writers were diffident about bringing women into their plays. There is a Rosalind and a Celia in *As You Like It*, but they are vastly outnumbered by their men companions. There are only two women in *Hamlet*, three in *Othello*, two in *Macbeth*, three in *King Lear*. With the advent of actresses, on the other hand, it became more and more necessary to provide suitable parts for the Nell Gwyns and the Mrs Bracegirdles. When D'Avenant (if he indeed be guilty) came to alter *Macbeth* he saw the necessity of enlarging the rôles of both Lady Macbeth and Lady Macduff; and when the same author in collaboration with Dryden sought to improve *The Tempest* the two authors provided Miranda with a sister and Ariel with a spirit mate. This tendency, noticeable in the adaptations of Shakespeare, is visible everywhere in the original plays of the time.

In all respects the Restoration stage was pursuing a new path, even if it could not quite shake off memories of the old.

3. LOVE AND HONOUR DRAMA

The period of the Restoration is remarkable for the development of several distinct species of drama which were destined to become the typical forms of theatrical activity or to give rise to equally typical cognate forms in the following century. These types of drama, of which the heroic tragedy, the comedy of manners, the opera, and the farce are the chief, all display a union of diverse forces. Each, regarded from one point of view, is the lineal descendant of some species of pre-Restoration drama, yet each is coloured and modified by the influence of contemporary Continental theatrical literature. The heroic tragedy may thus be considered, from one point of view, as merely a further elaboration of those romantic plays which were first made popular by Beaumont and Fletcher. D'Avenant knew of the contest between Love and Honour, and the exaggerated, flamboyant language apparent in the writings of Dryden and Settle was anticipated by more than one dramatist of the early seventeenth century. On the other hand, we have the testimony of Roger Boyle, Earl of Orrery, who was the first to attempt the introduction of the heroic style into England, that the employment of rime in place of blank verse in these heroic plays was due to the influence of France, exerted through the enthusiasm of the King. Nor was it only in outer form that the Restoration dramatists modified their styles to accord with the prevailing tastes in Paris. The heroic drama, with its grandiloquent sentiments and air of exaggeration, is to be regarded as the representative in the theatre of the mood and atmosphere of the heroic poem, a form of literature which, popularized by men such as Chamberlayne and D'Avenant, had come from France in the middle of the century. The comedy of manners, likewise, is an admixture of similar ingredients. Its source lies in Jonson's comedy of 'humours' and Fletcher's comedy of intrigue. Everywhere we can trace in its form the older strains altered a trifle to suit the tastes of a later age. The witty, debonair, callous, philandering air of Congreve's muse is thus born of the sterner and more satiric muse of Jonson. Yet much of what we know now as the comedy of manners would have remained unwritten, or would have been written in a different style, had the English theatre not possessed Molière for a guide and a model. The same analysis of forces holds good, also, for farce and opera. Farcical elements enough are apparent in sixteenth- and seventeenth-century comedies, and the later farce of the Restoration and Georgian eras owes a great deal of its vitality to older examples. The first afterpiece, however, and the first true English farce—Otway's The Cheats of Scapin (1676)— was but an adaptation from the French, and many other similar pieces produced in the last decades of the seventeenth century and in the years that followed were either alterations of French farcical works or farcical renderings of true comedies originally written by Molière and his companions. In the same way, too, the Restoration opera, made glorious by the music of Purcell, was a purely native development, even although it might not have come into being had it not been for the operatic efforts of

Renaissance Italy and the cognate efforts of contemporary France. It cannot be too often asserted that, despite the immense change which had come over the English theatre with the advent of Charles II, the substratum of all the dramatic activities during the latter half of the seventeenth century was, in the main, English. The great wave which had risen to a surge with Shakespeare was still eddying along the shore, slightly disturbed but not clearly altered in its course by neighbouring cross-currents.

In the realm of the serious drama the first two decades of Charles' reign are characterized by the cult of the heroic play, sometimes carried to a 'tragic' conclusion, sometimes given a reasonably happy ending. Instead of continuing the use of blank verse as the normal instrument for the dialogue, the authors of these works deliberately chose to employ rimed couplets, their selection of this medium no doubt being dictated by the realization that the blank verse which had been proper for the Shakesperian period no longer was in harmony with the changing speech-patterns of the later age, and that this blank-verse medium had, in the hands of Fletcher and his fellows, lost much of its original precision and vigour. The plots and situations, too, were different. Bold but artificial expression of emotions were dominant in these plays; violent ranting and inflammatory speeches ruled; and virtually the only conflict admitted was that between love and honour. In 1671 the Duke of Buckingham wrote a burlesque of the heroic play in *The Rehearsal*, and it must be confessed that the serious dramas of the time exhibit situations just as absurd as those he presented in his satirical scenes. Even the delightful soliloquy of Prince Prettiman over his boots, the one symbolizing honour and the other love, which closes with his hobbling from the stage with the one on and the other off, can be paralleled by equally ridiculous scenes in plays intended by their authors to arouse awe and admiration.

Among these authors, John Dryden is the greatest, and perhaps the first. If he did not invent the heroic play, at least he was responsible for giving it impetus; and when, in 1677, he recanted and bid his long-loved mistress, rime, adieu, most of his companions followed his lead. Starting with *The Indian Queen*

(1664), written in collaboration with Sir Robert Howard, he led the van of the love-and-honour playwrights, producing before 1675 *The Indian Emperor; or, The Conquest of Mexico by the Spaniards* (1665), *Tyrannick Love; or, The Royal Martyr* (1669), *The Conquest of Granada by the Spaniards* (1670), and *Aureng-Zebe* (1675), besides the rimed 'opera' wrought out of Milton's *Paradise Lost* and entitled *The Age of Innocence* (printed 1677). All the five heroic plays are built upon a set plan. There is in each a hero of superhuman prowess and boundless pride; there is a heroine of unsurpassed constancy and beauty; in the minds of several of the characters there is an inner conflict between love and honour; there is a stirring story of fighting and martial enthusiasm. All of this is expressed in couplet form, the artificiality of the medium corresponding to the artificiality of the situations and the persons. Shakespearian echoes can be found here, but the language as a whole bears the same relation to Shakespeare's as a bad gramophone record bears to the voice of a skilled singer. The tones are exaggerated and made harsh; there is the continual drone of metallic rimes; instead of imaginative vitality there is only mechanical accomplishment.

In saying this, however, we must bear in mind Dryden's basic objective. In these plays, as in his non-dramatic poetry, he was impelled by the desire to establish something fresh. During the Caroline period the impulse which had produced Shakespeare was rapidly losing its power, was becoming decadent, was often descending to absurdity. Against this the Restoration period reacted and sought for a new clarity and precision. In prose and verse alike the need was for logic, clearness, direct utterance; and thus the substitution of heroic couplets for the older blank verse may be looked upon as a particular manifestation of a general movement of change. At the same time, we must consider for what it was suited and what it could not hope to express. Fundamentally inspired by an intellectual concept, it inevitably failed completely in the attempt to delineate the passions, but for rhetorical utterance it was admirably adapted. This may be exemplified from a single passage in *The Conquest of Granada*. Almanzor enters, intent upon seeing his mistress, and is confronted by the ghost of his mother; his words obviously are totally inadequate to summon forth the desired atmosphere of awe and wonder:

> *Almanzor.* A hollow wind comes whistling through that door,
> And a cold shiv'ring seizes me all o'er:
> My teeth, too, chatter with a sudden fright.
> These are the raptures of too fierce delight,
> The combat of the tyrants, Hope and Fear,
> Which hearts, for want of field-room, cannot bear.
> I grow impatient: this or that's the room.
> I'll meet her: now, methinks I hear her come.
> > [*He goes to the door. The Ghost of his Mother meets*
> > *him. He starts back. The Ghost stands in the door.*
> Well may'st thou make thy boast, whate'er thou art;
> Thou art the first e'er made Almanzor start.
> My legs—
> Shall bear me to thee in their own despite:
> I'll rush into the covert of thy night,
> And pull thee backward by the shroud to light.
> Or else I'll squeeze thee like a bladder there,
> And make thee groan thyself away to air.
> > [*The Ghost retires.*
> So! Art thou gone? Thou canst no conquest boast.
> I thought what was the courage of a ghost.

This, of course, is sheerly ridiculous; but then there follows another speech uttered by the ghost which aims, not at arousing emotion, but at making a logical statement:

> *Ghost.* I am the ghost of her who gave thee birth,
> The airy shadow of her mould'ring earth.
> Love of thy father me through seas did guide;
> On seas I bore thee, and on seas I died.
> I died; and for my winding sheet a wave
> I had, and all the ocean for my grave.
> But when my soul to bliss did upward move,
> I wander'd round the crystal walls above,
> But found th'eternal fence so steeply high
> I flagg'd and flutter'd down, and could not fly.
> Then, from the battlements of the heav'nly tower,
> A watchman angel bid me wait this hour,
> And told me I had yet a task assign'd,

To warn that little pledge I left behind,
And to divert him, ere it were too late,
From crimes unknown and errors of his fate.

The first passage is foolish; the second rises to assured dignity and effectiveness.

Alongside of Dryden roared and ranted a goodly company of heroic dramatists, most of them but of little account. Elkanah Settle, with his wretched *Cambyses, King of Persia* (1671) and his not much better *The Empress of Morocco* (1673), hardly deserves more sympathetic treatment than Dryden meted out to him in his satiric verses. John Crowne's work is almost equally negligible. *The Destruction of Jerusalem by Titus Vespasian* (1677) is his most accomplished effort in this style, but even it follows long after *The Conquest of Granada*. Among all the rout of heroic rimesters barely three stand forward with a display of occasionally noteworthy scenes.

Roger Boyle, Earl of Orrery, warrants attention both because he was one of the first to experiment in the heroic form and because he pursued a path somewhat different from that taken by Dryden. The latter, adhering to the line of native dramatic development, produced plays which may be considered the descendants, if descendants far-off and considerably removed, of the Shakespearian tragedy. Orrery is more deeply influenced by the rimed tragedy of France. His atmosphere has a decided chill, an attempt at classical restraint, which marks him out as the follower of Corneille and Racine rather than of the Elizabethans. Somewhat surprisingly, however, in some of his plays he reverted, in his choice of subject-matter, to the long-forgotten chronicle-history tradition. If in *Mustapha, Son of Solyman the Magnificent* (1665) and in *Tryphon* (1668) he adopted those Eastern themes so popular with the heroic writers, in *The History of Henry the Fifth* (1664) and in *The Black Prince* (1667) he took up the chronicle-history tradition abandoned by almost all dramatists in the Caroline period. It is assuredly true that his treatment of these native historical themes is totally unhistorical and that it owes nothing to sixteenth-century example, yet the very fact that Orrery thought of English history at a time when grotesque visions of Peru and Persia and

Egypt prevailed shows that he had a mind of his own, and his practice no doubt had some influence upon later dramatists who turned for inspiration to the historical events of their native land.

Of different importance is Nathaniel Lee, the Bedlamite. This man, who first appeared on the dramatic horizon in the full flush of heroicism with his *Nero, Emperor of Rome* (1674) and who continued to provide the theatre with rimed and blank-verse pieces until 1689, was one of those unhappy creatures who, born with an undue share of enthusiasm and passion into a world of intellect and reason, eventually found relief only in madness. He is akin to Cowper and Smart and Blake, light flashing from his brain in lurid intervals, gleaming all the more brightly because of the surrounding gloom. The follies of Lee's rhapsodies are patent, yet we can discern beneath the absurdities of *Sophonisba; or, Hannibal's Overthrow* (1675), of *Gloriana; or, the Court of Augustus Cæsar* (1676), and of *Theodosius; or, The Force of Love* (1680) elements which call for praise. Formless and hysterical though his plays may be as a whole, his power of creating individually impressive scenes demands due recognition.

The only other heroic writer who calls for attention here is Thomas Otway, who, before he penned his two minor masterpieces, gave a rimed *Alcibiades* (1675) and *Don Carlos, Prince of Spain* (1676) to the theatre. Both are marked by surer touches than may be found anywhere in the period save in the plays of Dryden. *Alcibiades* has many foolish scenes, but even in it there is strength of utterance; and *Don Carlos* is one of the best among these heroic dramas, with a theme less exaggerated than is usual in the type, and passions not artificialized out of all likeness to human emotions. Otway shows himself here, at the very opening of his career, and working in a peculiarly difficult and circumscribed dramatic sphere, possessed of a quality which later he was to refine and deepen in *The Orphan; or, The Unhappy Marriage* (1680) and in *Venice Preserv'd; or, A Plot Discover'd* (1682).

4. THE RETURN TO SHAKESPEARE

These two dramas introduce us to a dramatic development certainly influenced by, but essentially distinct from, that of the heroic play, and that development unquestionably was due to a new appreciation of Shakespeare. In 1677 Dryden had written his *All for Love* confessedly in imitation of Shakespeare's style, and two years later Otway turned from his heroic writings to pen an adaptation of *Romeo and Juliet* as *The History and Fall of Caius Marius*. Thus, even although *The Orphan* may seem rather to look forward towards the later sentimental style rather than to look back towards Shakespeare, the force which inspired its composition was evidently an admiration of what the Elizabethans had achieved and a wish to recapture some of their power. Basically, the story told here of the fatal error by which a brother deflowers a brother's wife has been dealt with in a manner deeply influenced by Shakespearian tragedy, even although the stress upon pathetic situations has been imposed on the author by his sense of what the audiences of 1680 demanded. Even more 'Elizabethan' in form is *Venice Preserv'd*, with its contrasts between the stern yet generous Pierre, the vacillating Jaffier, and the troubled Belvidera; and the invigorating power still possessed by that form may be gauged from the fact that this tragedy of Otway's is perhaps the most interesting and effective contributed by his age.

Dryden's *All for Love* was not simply an adaptation: rather it set out to fashion the theme of *Antony and Cleopatra* into a shape harmonious with the dramatic philosophy of the late seventeenth century. Abandoning the wide passionate sweep of Shakespeare's tragedy, even while showing itself constantly inspired by its spirit, the play presents a clearly wrought and economically patterned version of the historical events and reduces the complex emotions of the lovers to a simpler form such as might be appreciated by the spectators of Dryden's time. In itself, it marks the upward reach of that author's power, and its long popularity on the stage during years when the original *Antony and Cleopatra* could not successfully be put upon the boards is a testimony to its excellence within its own kind.

Dryden's other tragedies, however, have hardly the same strength and fervour. *Amboyna* (1673) is a crude drama written purely as a piece of propaganda against the Dutch; *Troilus and Cressida; or, Truth found too late* (1679) is merely a re-treatment of Shakespeare's peculiar tragicomedy; while *Don Sebastian, King of Portugal* (1689) and *Cleomenes, the Spartan Hero* (1692) return to heroic sentiments, even although these heroic sentiments are couched in blank verse instead of rime. Altogether Dryden's efforts in this realm are disappointing. Except for *All for Love*, his best work was cast in the form of the heroic drama, a type of theatrical literature which, however absurd at times, best suited his talents.

As tragedy developed after 1679 several marked tendencies become apparent, tendencies which are inherent in *All for Love* and *The Orphan*. The first is pseudo-classicism, leading towards strictness of form, including the retention of the three unities, and towards chill of dialogue and simplification of plot. The other, which takes diverse forms, is the movement towards pathos and pity. These two tendencies dominated practically the whole of tragic productivity from the last decades of the seventeenth century on to the latter part of the eighteenth. The pseudo-classical school, at least that part of the pseudo-classical school which held most strictly to the 'rules' of propriety and of good conduct, hardly obtained a secure footing in the seventeenth century itself, and even in the Augustan age proper (from the reign of Anne to the last quarter of the eighteenth century) it failed to produce anything of intrinsic value. These dull dramas were duly mounted and revived, but none proved genuinely popular, unless we assume that the success of Addison's *Cato* (1714) was due entirely to its own merits, and had nothing in it savouring of political prejudice. If the more extreme pseudo-classicists, however, had little hold during the Restoration period, the rules so cherished by them penetrated through all the realms of drama and came to influence greatly both comedy and tragedy.

In reaction to this, although frequently it took a course parallel to, and even joined paths with, the pseudo-classical movement, we find the development of pathetic and pitiful sentiments and scenes. This tendency has already become apparent in *The*

Orphan, has been noted, indeed, several decades previously in some dramas of the period 1610–40. Now, however, it flourished most abundantly. Love and honour themes had led men to stress more deeply than in Elizabethan days the subject of amorous passion, so that by the end of the seventeenth century hardly any tragedy was penned which did not introduce as a main theme a tale of love. Instead of the deep emotions, varied and diverse, which marked the tragedies of Shakespeare we now find constant plaints and passages of amorous bombast in the sincerity of which we cannot believe. In accordance with this change of atmosphere went an alteration of tragic plan. In Elizabethan times tragedy had been predominantly masculine; the hero formed the centre and keynote of the play; on him all attention was focused. With the entrance of love into the theatrical arena the heroine rapidly came to take a more prominent place. Her progress, however, was hindered in the days of pure heroics by the presence of martial prowess from which—for few heroines were Amazons—she was banished. The advent of pathos, on the other hand, distinctly favoured the heroine, who came more and more to usurp the prominent position, until towards the end of the century we reach the 'she-tragedy,' where the hero has almost completely vanished, and a woman figure dominates the entire action of the drama. This final culmination was not attained until the eighteenth century, when Rowe fully established the type, but the tendency can clearly be traced in the preceding decades. The most important predecessor of Rowe in this sphere was John Banks, who, starting with a couple of heroic dramas—*The Rival Kings; or, The Loves of Oroondates and Statira* (1677) and *The Destruction of Troy* (1678)—passed from those to pen a series of pathetic plays on historical themes, *The Unhappy Favourite; or, The Earl of Essex* (1681), *Virtue Betray'd: or, Anna Bullen* (1682), *The Island Queens; or, The Death of Mary, Queen of Scotland* (printed 1684), and *The Innocent Usurper; or, The Death of the Lady Jane Gray* (printed 1694). The titles of these tragedies clearly show their general scope. None is remarkable in itself, although Banks was a more capable writer than is usually supposed, but their historical value is great. Several of these works remained long on the stage; Rowe cer-

tainly was acquainted with them; so that Banks became one of
the most potent forces in the development of eighteenth-century
tragedy. It is not too much to say that in several dramatic schools
his influence, direct and indirect, for forty or fifty years after his
death was second only to that of Shakespeare himself.

5. OPERA AND SPECTACLE

These heroic, pathetic, and other movements all combined with
a general operatic tendency. Scenery had, as we have seen,
come into general use in this period, and along with this
advent of scenery we have noted the tendency towards
exaggeration and artificiality of plot and character. The age
still retained that enthusiasm for music which was so marked
a feature of the Elizabethan period, and this enthusiasm for
music, added to the other movements indicated above, readily
made way for the elaboration of the opera. To trace this development accurately it is here necessary to return to the dramatic
work of Sir William D'Avenant, who is not only one of the in-
augurators of the heroic drama but also the popularizer of the
operatic form in England. It has been already noted that he was
the only person authorized during the Commonwealth régime
to arrange theatrical performances, and no doubt he was enabled
to do so only by convincing the authorities that his performances
were not of plays, but of musical entertainments. *The Siege of
Rhodes* (1656), along with *The Cruelty of the Spaniards in Peru*
(1658) and *The History of Sir Francis Drake* (1658), was indeed
a musical entertainment of this sort, written in rime and designed, on the lines of Italian opera, to be sung in recitative
and aria; and it stamped its impress both upon the heroic drama
and upon opera. The new scenes, the accompaniment of the
orchestra, the pleasant airs, all attracted the attention of playgoers, and before a few decades had passed other writers were
striving along the same path.

The first approach towards the opera in the Restoration period
proper was in the direction of Shakespearian adaptation. *The
Tempest*, after a considerable amount of sophisticated alteration
and addition, was made operatic by Dryden and Shadwell;

Macbeth similarly was operatized by an unknown author, who has been conjecturally identified with D'Avenant. The adaptations proved popular, as is witnessed by the numerous references, scathing as well as flattering, to the new fashion. That popularity inevitably led towards the composition of original operas of an even more ornate cast. Dryden, always ready to adopt a current novelty likely of success, penned his *Albion and Albanius* (1685) and his *King Arthur; or, The British Worthy* (1691). D'Urfey, Settle, and others vied with one another in producing similar works, each more gorgeous and full of telling incidents and novelties than the last. These operas, it may be observed, were all on the English plan, and were commonly designated by the title 'dramatic' to distinguish them from the 'Italian,' the cardinal difference between the two types resting in the presence or absence of recitative. All the dialogue of the dramatic opera is spoken; such operas were in fact spectacular plays with many incidental songs and full accompaniments of instrumental music. The Italian operas, on the other hand, designed wholly for singing, permitted no spoken dialogue unless in occasional scenes of a comic character. With the aid of Purcell, the former type held the field all through the Restoration period, but by the beginning of the century following efforts, eventually successful, were made to supplant the English style by the continental.

The approach was made at first through translation. Two theatrical workers, MacSwiny and Motteux, seem to have been chiefly instrumental in preparing for the stage the first two operas of this type, *Arsinoe* (1705) and *Camilla* (1706). The singers in these were all English, and the original music was adapted to the conditions under which the works were produced. Soon, however, it was found that the stock of English vocalists was limited; every one praised the voices of Italy; and accordingly high sums were offered by the managers to tempt away from the Continent a few of the more noted singers. Even yet the production of operas in the Italian tongue was delayed, the managers adopting the expedient of making the English singers perform in English and the Italians in Italian. The confusions and absurd situations which arose from this convention may be found chronicled satirically by Addison in several well-known

Spectator papers. Such a compromise could not endure for long, so that we are not surprised to find within a few years the appearance of Italian operas in all their original glory. Once established upon the stage, these operas definitely held their position. Handel came to England and aided in arousing still more enthusiasm for the type; hardly a year passed by without the production of several new works; the Italian opera became the fashionable haunt of society, and in its own way aided in the weakening of native dramatic work.

The advent of the Italian opera had several well-marked influences upon the English stage. The dramatic operas were rapidly cast into the background. *The Tempest* and *The Prophetess* still were held in the repertories as stock pieces, but few new works of the same class were written. While the older successes still retained something of their charm, the form was clearly felt to be old-fashioned, and those authors who tried to write something which might rival the Italian works penned their verses in recitative and aria. Beyond this, however, the new fashion placed its mark upon the age. The success of the opera-house frequently caused a corresponding failure of the other theatres. Upper-class society in the eighteenth century was often plagued with the curse of indigence, and the high prices charged for opera subscriptions left many without the means of patronizing regular plays. The many complaints which were uttered against the novelty were not by any means ill founded.

6. COMEDIES OF HUMOURS AND OF INTRIGUE

Tragedy and opera gave no real masterpiece to the theatre in this age, and the reason is not far to seek. The men of the Restoration period were searching for truth, not in the realm of passion and 'enthusiasm,' but in that of common sense and reason. The rich music of the Elizabethan playwrights and the bizarre stanzas of the metaphysical poets were alike displaced in favour of the heroic couplet, a verse-form which demanded for its successful execution little beyond a good ear, a sense of proportion, and a lively intellect. With the appearance of this reign of common sense, moreover, a new prose was discovered, a prose fitted for the enunciation of logical thoughts and witty fancies. More and more men turned to this prose as a medium in which to express their desires, so that comedy, that species of drama which alone permitted of prose dialogue, became the dramatic form most capable of expressing the temper and spirit of the age. The Restoration period could produce no tragic dramatist ranking higher than Otway and Dryden; but it produced some of the finest comic writers in the history of the English theatre.

The characteristic style of comedy developed during these years was the comedy of manners, but in thinking of the contributions in this style made by Etherege, Wycherley, Congreve, Vanbrugh, and Farquhar, it is important to remember that the 'manners' form was rivalled by many another which proved as popular, if not more popular, with contemporary audiences.

Among these types the old comedy of humours took a prominent place. Jonson was still acclaimed chief of comic dramatists, and his intellectualism made full appeal to an age weary of degenerate imagination. There were some who placed him, because of his art, higher than Shakespeare; and even Dryden, much as he revered Shakespeare's name, did not dare to place the one above the other. The influence of Jonson on the period is twofold. We find, in the first place, a number of comedies obviously modelled directly upon his style; and, besides these we discover many dramas which, while not prevailingly Jonsonian in essence, betray clearly the influence of his work in dialogue, scene, or character. Even the masters of the comedies of manners frequently showed that they had learned part of their art at least from the early seventeenth-century playwright .

Among Jonson's stricter disciples Thomas Shadwell is without doubt the chief. No man more insisted on Jonson's greatness; no man attempted more to carry on his dramatic method, and it must be admitted that he was no mean descendant of his master. His style, certainly, is rough, lacking refinement and careful polish, but he had a true flair for the theatre and a considerable skill in the depicting of humorous types. In a sense he is the truest mirror of the age that we possess. Congreve may show more brilliantly the fine wit of the time, but his very brilliance takes away from the reality of the portrait; Shadwell, rising to

less exalted heights, displays more accurately the ordinary existence of his time. Of his eighteen dramas three or four stand
forward as deserving of particular attention—the early *Sullen
Lovers* (1668), *The Humorists* (1670), *Epsom Wells* (1672), *The
Virtuoso* (1676), *The Squire of Alsatia* (1688), and *Bury Fair*
(1689). In each of these we meet with a lively story of contemporary life, an array of eccentric and extravagant humours, and
a somewhat loose love-plot. In each the scenes are presented to us
with gusto and the life of the age is keenly observed. *The Sullen
Lovers* puts recognizable caricatures of individuals on the stage;
Epsom Wells gives a racy picture of the world of sport and
dalliance; *The Virtuoso* ridicules the amateur antiquarians and
scientists; in *The Squire of Alsatia* the author penetrates into the
underworld. Spread out before us here is a kind of Restoration
'documentary.'

Others besides Shadwell followed the Jonsonian line. Sir
Robert Howard, brother-in-law of Dryden, won success with *The
Committee* (1662), a moderately good-humoured attack upon
Puritan hypocrisy, well-written and vivacious, with characters
not too heavily exaggerated and containing one particularly
popular figure in Teg, or Teague, a loyal Irish servant and ancestor of many similar types in later years. With Howard may
be mentioned the rougher and more plebeian John Lacy, who in
The Old Troop; or, Monsieur Raggou (1663), contributed another
anti-Puritan satire to the theatre. Beside this play Lacy has left
us an adaptation of Shakespeare in *Sauny the Scot; or, The
Taming of the Shrew* (1667), one of Molière in *The Dumb
Lady; or, The Farrier made Physician* (1669), and a more original
work in *Sir Hercules Buffoon; or, The Poetical Squire* (1684). All
of these are marked by the same features, a tendency to follow Jonson in the depicting of grotesque humours, a certain
roughness and vulgarity of texture, and a decided propen-
sity towards farce. This last characteristic of Lacy's plays may
be due to the fact that he himself was an actor, and consequently
was fully alive to all the possibilities inherent in stage action for
the summoning forth of laughter. A companion of Lacy in the
fields of farcical 'humours' is John Wilson, whose *The Cheats*
(1663) has an amusing plot and some fairly ludicrous dialogue,

although it is marred, like most of these Jonsonian works, by coarseness and lack of delicacy in style and in treatment.

These comedies of 'humours,' even from the first, were by way of being a trifle out of date. Dryden was acting more in accordance with the changing tendencies of the age when, in his comedies, he strove to unite the strength of Jonson, the courtly spirit of Beaumont and Fletcher, and the new air of intellectual wit. Had Dryden possessed more of the debonair, outwardly brilliant, but not necessarily profound, temperament of Etherege and of his successors he might have succeeded in founding the comedy of manners. As it is, his undercurrent of emotion, his lack of fine wit, his inability to throw himself completely into the thoughtless follies and amusements of his time, prevented him from capturing the precise note of the 'manners' school. He stands as a link between the earlier and the later, incapable of casting off his enthusiasm for the Elizabethan drama, yet not content merely to reproduce, as Wilson and Lacy strove to do, the exact style of the earlier period. His first comedy, The Wild Gallant (1663), comes closest to previous models, the inspiration for it having been obviously derived from Jonson's dramas; but even here the Restoration author showed that he felt the needs of his own age. In painting the portraits of Lady Constant and Loveby he displayed clearly enough his consciousness that the Stuart society for whom he was writing demanded something more than the rough satire which Jonson had thrown into his early seventeenth-century plays. The Wild Gallant is not a good comedy, but it certainly shows the main features of Dryden's style, features he was to delineate with much greater skill in his later plays. In the comic scenes of Secret Love; or, The Maiden Queen (1667), with their gay intrigues, he introduced something finer. The air of careless abandon, the hilarious wit, the setting free of all conventional restraint—all features of his earliest play —are here crystallized in the two figures, Celadon and Florimel, who will always remain monuments of his power and genius. This pair reappear, in variant form, as Wildblood and Jacintha in An Evening's Love; or, The Mock Astrologer (1668), Palamede and Doralice in Marriage A-la-mode (1672), Ascanio and Hippolita in The Assignation; or, Love in a Nunnery (1672), Mercury and Phædra in *Amphitryon; or, The Two Socia's* (1690), but without surpassing the gaiety and witty abandon of the original couple. In these plays Dryden shows plainly his position in the development of the comic theatre. He owes a debt to Jonson, chiefly in his minor characters; he owes, too, a debt to Beaumont and Fletcher, his main plots being framed on the style of the comedy of intrigue; above all, he strikes out on a path of his own in striving to delineate something of the new spirit of the age. In thus fusing together many diverse elements Dryden did a great service to the English theatre, but the very fact that he did so has to a certain extent taken from his posthumous fame. His comedies, fine as they are and excellently fitted for stage representation, have not that individual flavour which distinguishes the works of Etherege and of Congreve. There is, too, one other thing which makes them less acceptable to modern readers. Congreve dwells almost wholly in the world of the intellect; his amours are not of passion, not of the heart, but of the head. Dryden, as has been noted, still retained something of the Elizabethan age in him, and as a consequence his scenes of licence may strike us as being often less palatable than similar scenes in the comedies of 'manners.'

Few of the many other dramatists who patronized comedy during these years can be dealt with here. Most of the ordinary works written for the theatres are dull and uninteresting and demand no special attention. There are, however, a few particular writers who deserve at least brief mention. Of these Mrs Aphra Behn is the first. As Shadwell is the representative of the comedy of 'humours' in this period, she is the chief representative of the comedy of intrigue. Her dramatic career started in 1670 with the appearance of a tragicomedy, *The Forc'd Marriage; or, The Jealous Bridegroom*, but her chief activities in later years were to be confined to the realms of comedy proper. Her most popular success was *The Rover; or, The Banish't Cavaliers* (1677; second part, 1681), but besides this she has several plays well worth reading, especially *The Dutch Lover* (1673), *The Town-Fop; or, Sir Timothy Tawdrey* (1676), *Sir Patient Fancy* (1678), and *The City-Heiress; or, Sir Timothy Treat-all* (1682). There is little of wit in these plays, but there is an amount of intrigue cleverly worked out, and a decided skill in comic portraiture. Vivacity is her chief merit; a bustling movement dominates all her works. This species of comedy of intrigue, made popular by the Spanish tastes of the Court, was adopted by a few other writers, such as John Crowne in *Sir Courtly Nice; or, It Cannot Be* (1685), but it was not taken up again by any author with the same enthusiasm until the appearance of Mrs Centlivre in the eighteenth century.

In the midst of all this varied comic writing, one form deserves attention, not because of any intrinsic value, but because of its influence on the history of the theatre in following years. Although farcical elements may be found in many earlier plays, this was the period when farce evolved as an independent dramatic type. In the year 1676 Thomas Otway produced a tragedy called *Titus and Berenice* and, when this was published, it appeared along "with a Farce call'd *The Cheats of Scapin*." Within a few seasons after that Nahum Tate was delighting audiences with *A Duke and No Duke* (1684), apparently winning such success that he was persuaded in 1693 to add a preface to the printed text giving "an account of the *personæ* and *larvæ* of the ancient theatre" and providing a critical defence of the newly established dramatic type. Farce had thus, within little more than a decade, fully set itself on the boards and had presented its case for formal acceptance alongside the time-honoured genres of tragedy and comedy.

For the most part the earliest farcical experiments were derivative, taking shape either as crude adaptations of already-existing comedies or as versions of those Italian-French *commedia dell'arte* performances which at that time were being introduced to the public. *The Cheats of Scapin* clearly has its source indicated by its title; *A Duke and No Duke* is a version of a comedy written by Cockain in imitation of the Italian style; Edward Ravenscroft's *Scaramouch a Philosopher, Harlequin a School-boy, Bravo, Merchant and Magician* (1677) was specifically described as "after the Italian manner"; while the same author's *The Anatomist; or, The Sham Doctor* (1696) was a reworking of a French comedy, and Tate's *Cuckold's Haven; or, An Alderman No Conjuror* (1685) clearly was derived from a selection of scenes from Jonson's *Eastward Ho* and *The Devil is an Ass*. The original source of farce, therefore, may be seen as two-fold—one impulse coming from the Italian-French comedians and the other being little more than an elaboration of the tradition which had been responsible for the 'drolls' presented at the fairs.

Very soon, however, it was to expand beyond this limited sphere, and during the eighteenth century it came to be one of the most popular and staple elements in the theatre's repertory. As such, these early experiments, even if they have nothing of value to offer, clearly need to be remembered.

6. THE COMEDY OF MANNERS

They need to be remembered particularly because their popularity was extended during the very years when the comedy of manners reached its finest form. These two types of play stand at diametrically opposite poles, the one aiming to arouse rude laughter by absurd incident, crude humour, and physical gesture, the other laying all stress upon polish and wit and sprightliness. A complete picture of the playhouses during this period cannot be gained unless we bear in mind that the same spectators who encouraged the farcical displays also gave support to a form of comedy far more intellectually brilliant than anything which the English stage had so far witnessed.

The comedy of manners, as its name implies, concentrates upon the depiction of men and women living in a social world ruled by convention. Its 'manners' are not simply the behaviour of humanity in general but the affectations and cultured veneer of a highly developed and self-conscious group. In the White-hall which was ruled over by Charles II, intellectual refinement, epigrammatic wit, and easy dalliance had been made the prime qualities sought after by the gallants and their mistresses, and it is these qualities which are reflected in the 'manners' comedy. Already during the very first years after the playhouses were reopened in 1660 Dryden had given a foretaste of what was to come, but by his nature he was unfitted to enter completely into this new world. Although the typical comedy of manners gives delight by showing the contrast between natural man and man as conditioned by the social code, at the same time it tends to tone down and to intellectualize ordinary emotions. The young, reckless, careless, cynical hero may be induced by the operation of love to follow his mistress into the horrors of a lonely country house far removed from the dear delights of the Town; a confirmed bachelor, anxious to retain his freedom, he may be led to put his head in the marriage noose, and his equally freedom-loving sweetheart may in the end be persuaded to dwindle into a wife; but basically the natural emotions are kept in the background for purposes of contrast; the foreground is reserved for the exercise of the intellect. Dryden, in presenting his Celadons and Florimels, unquestionably was anticipating the fashionable pairs who were to follow them, but he himself was sufficiently 'Elizabethan' to prove unable to adopt a strictly intellectual approach. In his early comedies the emotional element refuses to be subdued.

Others besides Dryden made some contributions towards the new comic form, and of course, as we have already seen, even before 1640 dramatists such as Shirley were beginning to give it shape, but for its first clear outline we have to wait until the debonair Sir George Etherege applied himself to the stage, starting with *The Comical Revenge; or, Love in a Tub* in 1664 and following that with *She wou'd if she cou'd* (1668) and *The Man of Mode; or, Sir Fopling Flutter* (1676). In the first of these he almost completely failed to develop a characteristic style. Somewhat similar to Dryden's *Secret Love, The Comical Revenge* is an unintegrated piece in which scenes cast in rimed couplets alternate with others in dallying prose. Had this been his only contribution to the theatre, Etherege's name would not now be remembered. The four years which elapsed between the appearance of this work and *She wou'd if she cou'd*, however, wrought in him a mighty dramatic change. In this his second play the realm of fine gentlemen and witty ladies is presented in a new light; the shape and form of Restoration society is evoked in all its scenes; the dialogue succeeds in reflecting the very tones of contemporary civil conversation. And the eight further years between this comedy and *The Man of Mode* show an advance almost equally great. Although *She wou'd if she cou'd* unquestionably established the Restoration comic style, it still lacked final distinction; that distinction came with the putting upon the stage of Dorimant, the fashionable hero, of Harriet, the clear-eyed lady on whom his wandering eyes fix their gaze, and of Sir Fopling Flutter, the beau who carries fine manners to excess and who thus becomes a figure of ridicule.

By the early seventies, the influence of *She wou'd if she cou'd* was inspiring several playwrights to pen scenes in imitation of its style, and before *The Man of Mode* appeared, William Wycherly produced three plays—*Love in a Wood; or, St James's Park* (1671), *The Gentleman Dancing-Master* (1672) and *The Country-Wife* (1675)—which made notable contributions to this comic form. All three revel in a world of fops and fools and gallants; all are concerned with the eternal love-chase; in all there is a sure handling of character and of situation.

In these three works Wycherley gave himself wholeheartedly to the spirit which had animated Etherege, but deep within himself this author concealed a sense of moral purpose of which his predecessor was impenitently innocent. A Puritan with the veneer of a Restoration gentleman, Wycherley has been called; and the description seems admirably to fit. He adopted the current modes of contemporary society, but he was in the end unable to prevent the assertion of his native self and to avoid a bitterly satirical attack upon the very vices with which he had gaily amused himself in his first plays. Thus in 1676 came his *The Plain-Dealer*, in which the hero is no longer an easy careless libertine, but a gentleman whose very name, Manly, puts him in opposition to the elegant Dorimants of the time. One might have thought that a play of this sort would have been a failure on the Restoration stage; in fact, it was Wycherley's greatest triumph, and that triumph is a witness not only to the author's dramatic power but also to the widely varying interests of the contemporary public.

If Wycherley in *The Plain-Dealer* seems to be shattering the fabric of the comic style established by Etherege, William Congreve carries it to still further achievements. Certainly untroubled by any puritanical reflections, this author at once differs from, and bases his dramatic work upon, the creator of *The*

Man of Mode. He has not Etherege's firm command of plot-material, but he possesses an airiness of fancy and a pointed delicacy of style which goes beyond his. In Congreve's dialogue the words and phrases pirouette and bow, pierce with rapier flash, laugh and flirt and dally. All is subordinated to brilliance of wit and modulations of style. Four plays he contributed to the stage —*The Old Bachelor* (1693), *The Double Dealer* (1693), *Love for Love* (1695), and *The Way of the World* (1700)—and these in their variety illustrate how delicate was the balance necessary for the full expression of the new comic spirit and how easily that balance could be disturbed. The first play, although confused in plot and including some characters which seem somewhat out of place, was a decided success, presenting something finer, more scintillating, than anything which had gone before: no previous writer had succeeded in offering to the public a comedy so rich in racy, cultured, easy, debonair conversation. *The Double Dealer*, on the other hand, was, by comparison, a failure—and the failure seems due to the fact that here Congreve permitted an emotional quality to disturb the play of his wit. In *Love for Love* there is a return to the mood of *The Old Bachelor*, but again a disturbing element intrudes—not because of the intrusion of emotional scenes, but because Congreve has been led to bring in some characters and situations of what might be called a 'realistic' kind. Fundamentally, his genius depended upon the creation of a world which, although it might seem to be a mirror of existing life, was a refinement and not a copy of reality; and as a result the episodes involving Miss Prue and Tattle, so far from extending the comedy's range, almost destroy its essential spirit. Only perhaps in *The Way of the World* was Congreve able to reach complete perfection. Here there is no false note. Millamant sails gloriously through its scenes, affected and fascinating; from her the servants, the fools, the lovers, the wits all seem to take something of the air of modish triviality which makes her so delightful. We may say that the plot of the play is no plot, only a series of often impossible and confusing incidents designed to afford the author opportunity for regaling us with his streams of conceited metaphors and the bewildering flights of his fancy; but in fact we do not want more than Con-

greve has given us; his power lay, not in the fashioning of dramatic incident, but in his mastery of wit and in his command of
dancing words. The melodies charm our ears:

Mirabell. Do you lock yourself up from me to make my search
more curious? Or is this pretty artifice contrived to signify that
here the chase must end and my pursuit be crowned, for you can
fly no further?

Millamant. Vanity! No, I'll fly and be followed to the last
moment: though I am upon the very verge of matrimony, I expect
you should solicit me as much as if I were wavering at the grate
of a monastery, with one foot over the threshold. I'll be solicited
to the very last—nay and afterwards.

Mirabell. What? After the last?

Millamant. O, I should think I was poor and had nothing to
bestow if I were reduced to an inglorious ease, and freed from the
agreeable fatigues of the solicitation.

Mirabell. But do you not know that when favours are conferred
upon instant and tedious solicitation that they diminish in their
value, and that both the giver loses the grace and the receiver
lessens his pleasure?

Millamant. It may be in things of common application, but
never, sure, in love. O, I hate a lover that can dare to think he
draws a moment's air independent on the bounty of his mistress.
There is not so impudent a thing in nature as the saucy look of an
assured man, confident of success. The pedantic arrogance of a very
husband has not so pragmatical an air. Ah! I'll never marry unless
I am first made sure of my will and pleasure.

Two years before the theatre audiences listened to these words,
however, a chill blast had been blown over the stage. In 1698 a
stern Nonconformist clergyman, Jeremy Collier by name, had
startled actors, authors, and spectators with a work entitled *A
Short View of the Immorality and Prophaneness of the English
Stage.* Within the next few months the presses were busy printing
pamphlets written by those who sought to rebut its arguments
and by those who for moral or religious reasons were anxious to
reform or to overthrow the playhouse. In many respects the
attack was justified, even although many of Collier's own arguments verge upon the absurd; and the truth which underlay his
attack is made amply apparent in the replies of the poets

arraigned at the bar of Nonconformist justice. Dryden, who had been specially singled out, magnanimously, as was his way, confessed his errors, and without whining for mercy expressed regret that his pen had been guilty of vices he heartily deplored; others, not willing to acknowledge faults in their writings, endeavoured to distract public attention by referring to the sect of which Collier was a member and by concentrating upon the more trivial of his strictures. His main contentions remained for the most part unanswered.

It was, however, these main contentions which made their impact upon the readers of the *Short View*. By this time a new mood had taken the place of that which had dominated the Whitehall of Charles II. His successor, James II, had been driven from the throne because of his Catholic affiliations, and William had brought to England a spirit different from that which had hitherto prevailed. An outward veneer of moral sentiment was beginning to curb the excesses of the gay gallants, and the upper middle classes, which had stood apart from aristocratic society, now were coming to enter into its previously closed circle, leavening with their influence its codes of behaviour.

Everything conspired together, and the comedy of manners, licentious, vain, worldly, found itself under attack. The days of Congreve, the days of thoughtless, brilliant, careless wit, were virtually over, and the old free grace was never completely to be recaptured. For a time comedy strove to preserve something of its old abandon, but its light soon flickered out, quenched by the rising tide of sentimentalism.

Among those who aided in keeping alive something of the spirit of the Congrevian comedy were George Farquhar and Sir John Vanbrugh, men whose careers stretched from a period contemporaneous with the Collier attack on to the middle of the reign of Queen Anne. Farquhar's first play, *Love and a Bottle*, was produced in 1698, his last, *The Beaux' Stratagem*, in 1707; Vanbrugh's *The Relapse; or, Virtue in Danger* appeared in 1696, his last farces in the early years of the eighteenth century. The careers of both these men are alike, and, taken together, they indicate the general trend of theatrical tastes. Both commenced in the seventeenth century with largely 'immoral' comedies, full of wit and striving to capture the fine grace that had distinguished the Stuart Court; both, as they progressed, showed with frequent touches of satire and cynicism a descent to farce and sentimentalism. Not that the two had precisely similar natures. Farquhar is at one and the same time nearer to the spirit of Congreve and more foppish than Vanbrugh. He has, in *The Constant Couple* (1699), in *The Inconstant* (1702), and in *The Beaux' Stratagem*, caught something of the true 'manners' style. His plots are more carefully elaborated than are those of Congreve, but he retains at least a reflection of the Congreve wit. In *The Twin Rivals* (1702) and in *The Recruiting Officer* (1706), on the other hand, he displays clearly the impress of the newer age. The first is deeply tinged with a hypocritical sentimentalism, and the second has a realistic touch quite alien to the comedy of manners. Vanbrugh is much more robust than Farquhar, and that robustness removes him from the ranks of Congreve, leading him to draw comedy down from the high levels it had held to the lower depths of farce. More than any other writer of this kind of play, he relies upon action for comic effect. The plots of his comedies are designed, not, as Congreve's were, for the expression of fancies of the mind, but for the elaboration of comic situations. This tendency is not so noticeable in his early works, *The Relapse*, *The Provok'd Wife* (1697), and *Æsop* (1696–97), nor is it especially apparent in *The Confederacy* (1705) or in *The Mistake* (1705), but it is abundantly evident in *Squire Trelooby* (1704), a collaborative farce made out of Molière's *Monsieur de Pourceaugnac*, and in *The Country House* (1698), another farce taken from Dancourt. Like Farquhar, too, Vanbrugh turned to a type of sentimentalism, evidently insincere, in *The False Friend* (1702). The truth is that men of Farquhar's and Vanbrugh's calibre did not know where to stand. They had lost freedom of action in the conflicting moods of the time. Spectators, perhaps, were just as pleasure-loving as they had been in the days of Charles II, but there were now societies for the reformation of manners, and statutes against oaths, and other dreadful things to be feared. The efforts in the older style were therefore, bound to be only half-hearted, or, if indulged in boldly, were sure to be followed by a succeeding moment of painful reflection.

V

Drama in the Eighteenth Century

1. THE CHANGING PLAYHOUSE WORLD

WHILE no strict frontier line can be drawn between the seventeenth and the eighteenth centuries, the year 1700 may be taken as marking the division between the old and the new. It is certainly true that signs of change were becoming apparent during the years 1690–99 and perhaps they can be traced even earlier, but the season which witnessed *The Way of the World* saw the last of the Restoration comedies, and those seasons which immediately followed looked upon a series of plays clearly written in a different mood and in a different style.

In considering the eighteenth century as a whole, several theatrical developments attract our attention. First come three related movements—the growth of a new audience, the enlarging of the 'patent' theatres, and the springing up of the 'minor' playhouses. It has already been noted that from 1682 on to 1695 one single theatre met London's needs, and even so we encounter numerous complaints among the actors that spectators were not numerous enough to fill the auditorium. In 1695, however, Betterton headed a group of dissentient players and once more set up a second house, operating under the authority of the 'patent' which had temporarily lapsed thirteen years before. In itself, this action of his may be taken as a sign that conditions were altering: the playgoing public was beginning slowly to expand. That expansion, in turn, was largely dependent upon the altering structure of society. In Charles' days, as we have

seen, the theatre belonged essentially to the Court; hardly any
middle-class spectators were to be found entering its doors. As the
century drew towards its close, however, it becomes evident that
the old tightly knit aristocratic society was beginning to disin-
tegrate; many of the older families were finding themselves in
financial difficulties, while at the same time numerous merchant
families, having made themselves affluent, were showing a desire
to enter into the circle of society; and as a result marriages of
convenience started to break down the former barriers. Naturally, in these circumstances the newcomers were led to take an
interest in the diversions which had delighted the aristocratic
world, and thus the potential playgoing public was enlarged.

This enlargement continued all through the century, with the
consequence that the playhouse, instead of being reserved for a
privileged few, was invested with an upper-middle-class atmosphere; and for the new body of spectators accommodation had
to be found. The opening of a second theatre in 1695 met the
needs for a time, but very soon even two houses were found
inadequate to cope with the growing demands. Two things
thereupon happened. The 'patent' theatres were periodically re-
constructed so as to provide more seating space, and numerous
'minor' playhouses were built and operated outside the 'patent'
authority. In 1737 the notorious Licensing Act sought to curb
their activities, but in diverse and devious ways they succeeded
in carrying on their work—work which on occasion proved even
more popular and of more value than that of Drury Lane and
Covent Garden: it was at one 'minor' theatre that *The Beggar's
Opera* was presented, and on the boards of another 'minor'
theatre the great David Garrick first made his appearance in
London.

The entry of the middle classes into the playhouse world is
important not only because they added to the potential number
of playgoers. Undoubtedly members of those families which had
been successful in becoming related through marriage to the
people of quality tended to accept the conventions of society, yet
they inevitably brought with them some of their inherited
bourgeois, and occasionally Puritan, tenets and tastes. Thus the
union of the two led towards the creation of an audience at once

less homogeneous than that which had been characteristic of the Restoration theatre and lacking in what might almost be called the harmonized generality of the audiences in Elizabethan times. Society still enjoyed the licence of the comedy of manners; Shadwell, Dryden, Etherege, Wycherley, and Congreve still held the stage: but the new groups of spectators, with their more serious predilections, also delighted in moralizations, in sentimentally conceived situations, in scenes of pathos. As we watch the development of eighteenth-century drama we see a constant struggle silently proceeding between the force of intellectual dalliance and the more solemn objectives of the mercantile world, until during the sixties and seventies victory finally was gained by the sentimentalists.

London still remained the theatrical focus from the beginning of the century to its end, but the enlargement of the audience in the metropolis is paralleled by an interesting growth of playhouse activities elsewhere as well. Touring players, of course, had been numerous in the sixteenth and early seventeenth centuries, and, although they do not seem to have had much success in Restoration times, they still pursued their traditional circuits during Charles' reign. After the year 1700 we begin, however, to see their position becoming more secure and their influence spreading more widely. Hitherto they had had no permanent homes, producing their plays wherever they could find some empty hall or barn; now, during the eighteenth century, they began to erect their own playhouses, some of them even graced with the title of Theatre Royal, and a few companies were given sufficient local support to persuade them to abandon their laboursome tours and settle down as permanent stock troupes. For the most part, their repertories consisted of London successes, and consequently they offered little to the drama of the age, but they rapidly came to be the schools wherein stage aspirants gained their training. David Garrick first practised on their stages, and it was from one of these provincial theatres that Mrs Siddons and her brother came to startle London with their performances.

In all these ways, the eighteenth-century playhouse established its own traditions, traditions which were to be passed on to the nineteenth century and even to the present day.

2. PSEUDO-CLASSIC AND PATHETIC TRAGEDY

In the realm of tragedy the eighteenth century inherited three or four traditions—that which may be styled heroic, that which led towards renewed appreciation of Shakespeare, the pathetic style (often in the form of English historical plays) as expressed by Banks and Otway, and the gradual development of pseudo-classical theory and practice. Of these, in the seventeenth century, the last-mentioned was infinitely the weakest. All the more chill pseudo-classical dramas written and produced before 1700 were unsuccessful; audiences still admired the bombast of Dryden, the pathos of Otway, the natural warmth of the Shake-sperian style. In the eighteenth century, however, pseudo-classical theory became more and more predominant. Addison, Pope, Steele, and a host of lesser men, including Dennis and Gildon, aided in establishing firmly that strict set of laws which bound poetry for well over half a century and which still exercised its influence in the days of Byron. According to these rules imitation of the 'Ancients' was the best that a modern author could do. His plays must preserve the three unities of time, place, and action. He must not permit more than a certain number of characters to appear in his work. He must, above all, endeavour always to secure decency, propriety, order, and common sense. Intellectual rhetoric rather than passionate rhapsody must be aimed at. These rules dominated almost all the poetic and dramatic activity of the reigns of Anne and the early Georges, but dominated it as a force from without. Some writers may have found the pseudo-classic theory well to their tastes, but the spectators still looked for something more inspiring, something more bombastic, than they could discover in the chill of the classical tragedy. We find, therefore, in this period a constant struggle proceeding between the pseudo-classicists and those who preferred other styles. The heroic tragedy continued to exert its charm on the audience; imitations of Shakespeare constantly made their appearance; Otway ruled over a large body of dramatists and of spectators. The lack of a central purpose, however, told heavily on the fortunes of the tragic stage. Few playwrights seemed to know their own aims, and the majority compromised by observing the unities, filling their plays with pathos, and adding a seasoning of heroic ardour and of Shakespearian echoes. The result, as might be imagined, is a mass of uninteresting dramas unrelieved by any true features or marks of genius.

It was not for want of courage or for want of patience that the pseudo-classicists failed to reform entirely the tastes of their age. Again and again they returned to the attack, but few were successful in their endeavours. In the early years of the century Dennis and Gildon made serious attempts to enlist favour on their side, and failed; so did Dr Johnson in his *Irene* (1749), and managed to secure some small applause for his effort only through the good services of his erstwhile pupil, David Garrick. Barely three or four of these dramas were popular, and all lack true energy and tragic fervour. The first which definitely established itself upon the stage was *The Distrest Mother* (1712), written by Ambrose Philips, Pope's rival in pastoral poetry. This play was an adaptation from Racine, distinguished by a few passages of effective dialogue and introducing two characters delineated in a not uninteresting manner—yet still remaining an alien growth.

The year following the appearance of *The Distrest Mother* Joseph Addison saw the production at Drury Lane of his *Cato*, a play at once accepted by his friends and associates as a masterpiece. Even although now it has long been forgotten, we may admit that the praise accorded to it was by no means unjustified. If any play of this kind merited acclaim certainly *Cato* deserved it. What could be done within the pseudo-classic form Addison has done, and our only legitimate criticism may be directed to the style of drama to which it belongs. Instead of absurdly making a love-theme the centre of an intellectual tragedy, as had been the practice among his predecessors, Addison took as his hero the philosopher Cato, a character whose nature and problems could obviously be revealed more appropriately through the medium of rhetorical dialogue than could the natures and problems of violently passionate lovers and their mistresses. Addison thus displayed his acumen in boldly striving to find a theme suited to the restricted sphere within which he chose to work.

Few other writers of the period, however, realized the reason of his success. His companions continued to devote their scenes to love affairs, introducing weeping Andromaches and dismal Hecubas. Just for a moment, towards the middle of the century, it looked as though this style of play was to receive a fresh impetus from the pen of James Thomson, author of the widely popular *Seasons*, but the promise offered was by far greater than the actual achievement. In *Sophonisba* (1730) this dramatist appeared, like Addison, to divine what was demanded in the classically influenced rhetorical drama; instead of presenting his heroine as inspired wholly by amorous emotions, he strove to show her as dominated by patriotic sentiment, intent above all in a desire to benefit her native land. Something of the same approach, too, distinguished his treatment of *Agamemnon* (1738). After writing these two dramas, Thomson then turned to subject-matter of a different kind in *Edward and Eleonora* (printed 1739) and *Tancred and Sigismunda* (1745), but the titles of both indicate that, while historical interest attaches to their groping towards the choice of themes outside the realm of Greek legend, Thomson was reverting to the methods of his predecessors.

During the latter part of the century this kind of tragic endeavour offered nothing of any worth, and soon the type was to be overwhelmed by the onrush of spectacular melodrama better suited, with its flagrant rant, to the tastes of a public already animated by the rise of romantic, and at times revolutionary, sentiment.

Relics of the heroic drama were numerous during these years. Even a writer such as Gildon, despite his strict critical views, could seek to emulate Dryden's bombastic flights. No single play of this sort, however, can be found to exhibit any real quality. Joseph Trapp's *Abra-Mule; or, Love and Empire* (1704) contains one or two striking passages, but its characters are hopelessly stereotyped and the language rarely rises above mediocre competence. Benjamin Martyn's *Timoleon* (1730) as well as David Mallet's *Eurydice* (1731) and *Mustapha* (1739) may similarly be lifted out of the rout, but even these possess no great virtue. At most, a few occasional effective scenes give them a merit denied to their companions.

The school of pathos has a little more of worth to offer. No doubt none of the dramatists who elected this style have left any plays with enduring qualities, but precisely because they limited their aims they were enabled to produce something which can be accorded at least limited praise. Prominent in this field during the early part of the century was Nicholas Rowe, a disciple of Otway and Banks, and to a certain extent an ancestor of George Lillo. In his works there are echoes of the heroic style, touches which remind us of Shakespearian tragedy and a general structure deeply influenced by pseudo-classical theory: nevertheless, despite these diverse elements, they were clearly designed with the principal object of evoking pity rather than awe. His first drama, *The Ambitious Stepmother* (1700), confessedly inspired by Otway's style, may hardly be regarded as more than an apprentice piece, and not much may be said in favour of the 'heroically' designed *Tamerlane* (1701), but *The Fair Penitent* (1703), *The Tragedy of Jane Shore* (1714), and *The Tragedy of the Lady Jane Gray* (1715) all possess an individual quality which rightly established their author at the head of the Augustan tragic writers. Each is a 'she-tragedy,' with a heroine instead of a hero as the central character; each is so wrought as to throw main stress upon pathetic situations and scenes. Rowe exhibits undoubted skill in the exploitation of pitifully distressing emotions; his persons come fitfully to life; and he has the gift of writing pleasant if not very powerful blank-verse dialogue. Taken as a whole, his dramas, whatever their weaknesses and defects, are among the best serious plays of their time.

The selection of English and related historical themes provided impetus for a cognate species of drama, often with echoes of Shakespeare and Otway, during succeeding years. Mrs Haywood attempted a tragedy on the subject of *Frederick, Duke of Brunswick-Lunenburgh* (1729); Ambrose Philips wrote *The Briton* (1722) and *Humfrey, Duke of Gloucester* (1723); Aaron Hill followed the fashion in *Elfrid; or, The Fair Inconstant* (1710) and in *King Henry the Fifth; or, The Conquest of France by the English* (1723), as did Henry Brooke in *Gustavus Vasa* (1739), William Havard in *King Charles the First* (1737), William Shirley in *Edward the Black Prince; or, The Battle of Poictiers* (1749), and John St John in *Mary Queen of Scots* (1789). These plays for various reasons appealed more to contemporary audiences than the stricter 'classical' essays. Often they introduced patriotic sentiments; their plots and characters were for the most part nearer to the spectators than those which dealt with ancient legendary persons; they frequently permitted the introduction of at least some bustle and action. Yet not one is anything more now than a mere title; not one succeeded in holding the stage for more than a few performances.

Their failure unquestionably has to be attributed to the style in which the authors worked, and this may be illustrated from the solitary play of this kind which did have the power to arouse a certain amount of excitement in its own time and which was remembered beyond the period of its original production. In 1756 John Home's *Douglas* was presented to an Edinburgh audience, and the house was stimulated to a frenzy of excitement. Here, said some men, was the triumph of a Scots Shakespeare. In the following year the drama was offered to the Covent Garden public, and, although the reception was not so fervent, its qualities were esteemed, and it became accepted as a stock-piece, frequently revived. In many respects this work of Home's seemed to be providing exactly what was needed by the time; the spirit of romanticism was then begining to stir, and at a time when the way was being prepared for Percy's *Reliques* and Chatterton's 'medieval' experiments, the choice of the plot-material in *Douglas* might well have been thought likely to bring about a revival of the serious poetic drama. Just as soon, however, as we turn to the text, we realize that this could not be. Indeed, we need go no farther than that speech of 'The Stranger' which endured as a recitation piece up to within living memory:

> My name is Norval. On the Grampian hills
> My father feeds his flocks; a frugal swain,
> Whose constant cares were to increase his store
> And keep his only son, myself, at home.
> For I had heard of battles, and I long'd
> To follow in the field some warlike lord,
> And heaven soon granted what my sire denied.
> This moon which rose last night, round as my shield,
> Had not yet fill'd her horns, when, by her light,
> A band of fierce barbarians, from the hills,

Rush'd like a torrent down upon the vale,
Sweeping our flocks and herds. The shepherds fled
For safety and for succour. I alone,
With bended bow and quiver full of arrows,
Hover'd about the enemy and mark'd
The road he took, then hasted to my friends,
Whom with a troop of fifty chosen men
I met advancing. The pursuit I led
Till we o'ertook the spoil-encumber'd foe.
We fought and conquered.

As a passage for parlour declamation this is all very well, but clearly the language is stilted and rhetorical. There could be no hope for the creation of successful serious drama within this style.

3. THE BALLAD-OPERA AND PANTOMIME

The spectacular and operatic tendencies in the Restoration period have already been briefly noted, and a glance has been cast at the development of the Italian opera in the eighteenth century itself. This spectacular and operatic movement may seem somewhat at variance with the chastening influences dealt with summarily in the preceding chapter; but it is to be interpreted as the expression of popular taste moving against the restrictions of the severer among the poets and critics. The men and women of the time obviously liked show; music appealed to them, and dancing. After listening in bored silence to the ceaseless drone of the heavier tragedy they flocked for recreation to the opera, or applauded vigorously the singers, instrumentalists, and dancers who gave *intermezzi* before and after, and occasionally in the midst of, regular performances in the theatres. To appreciate aright the theatrical movements of the age the opera must be intimately related to the chiller form of tragedy, and out of the two a picture of the period must be wrought.

Four popular species of entertainment must here be noted— the operatic, the spectacular, the terpsichorean, and the mimic. From Restoration days (and even in Elizabethan times) dancing formed a popular part of dramatic performances. Many plays ended with a dance, and we know how such an actress as Moll Davis charmed her public. To satisfy the craving for these dances theatrical managers in the late seventeenth century called in the services of dancing-masters from Paris, and these dancing-masters soon became a recognized feature of the theatres. We learn the names of many of them from the newspaper advertisements of the early eighteenth century, and we can see from the prominence given to them there what a position they occupied in the minds of the spectators. At first their performances were limited in scope, but soon came in the taste for mimic dancing, where a story was told silently by means of expressive movement. It is here we reach the beginnings of pantomime, a form of theatrical presentation which owed much to the activities of various French and Italian troupes which from season to season brought their wares to London audiences. From the very start of its existence, the *commedia dell'arte* had encouraged the display of gesture and action on the stage, and, since French and Italian dialogue could be understood by only a few English spectators, naturally it was the physical skill of the foreign comedians rather than any of their dialogue which made appeal in the London theatres. Not surprisingly, therefore, when the time came for native experiments in a related style, the English managers encouraged the development of wordless performances in which music, dance, mimed action, comic business, lavish scenery, and machinists' tricks held the spectators' attention. Thus the typical English pantomime came into being, delighting the public, and gradually extending its fantastic empire.

Although these pantomimes cannot be said to have driven ordinary drama from the stage, since they were for the most part performed along with, and not instead of, regular comedies and tragedies, nevertheless their establishment and later expansion wrought considerable changes in the typical theatre repertories. In the first place, they aided in helping forward the disintegration of true dramatic taste; unquestionably they lowered the general power of appreciation on the part of the audience. Secondly, they established fully the reign of the afterpiece. The afterpiece, as we have noted, was inaugurated in England with the appearance of Otway's *The Cheats of Scapin*, and in the first years of the eighteenth century it was fairly common for a tragedy or a comedy to be given along with a one-act farce. Still, the appearance of these farces was only sporadic; they were not rendered necessary appendages to the ordinary plays. With the success of the pantomime, however, the public came to demand some light refreshment when the heavier meal of tragedy or sentimental comedy was over, and, if a pantomime was not shown, some short ballad-opera or farce was positively called for. There seemed nothing extraordinary to the audience in their listening to Lear's agony at 7.30 and laughing hilariously at pantomime or farcical afterpiece at 8. And there was a further result. The pantomime not only aided in the degeneration of taste and in the establishment of the afterpiece, but it also led dramatists who might otherwise have contributed serious work to the theatre to indulge in the lesser forms of dramatic endeavour. A one-act farce paid better than a full-length tragedy; the trivial words for an operatic pantomime were well rewarded. Farce, then, came to occupy the minds of the playwrights, and many men such as Lewis Theobald, editor of Shakespeare and a capable scholar, turned to pen the foolish ditties which pleased the spectators in the pantomimic displays.

The reign of pantomime is ultimately associated with the reign of the ballad-opera. In origin the ballad-opera—or ballad-farce, as it was frequently called—was at once a burlesque and a rival of the Italian opera. It aimed at capturing some of the attention paid to the Italian type, and it employed for effect many satirical attacks upon the follies that were inherent in that form. Nor would the ballad-opera have had its success if the ground had not already been prepared by the musical enthusiasts. Men had now become accustomed to hearing a story sung; they were delighted when they heard their favourite ditties, native popular and Italian, provided with new and witty words and set in a plot which (being told in English) they could understand and (being comic) they could enjoy.

The ballad-opera was invented, almost by chance, by the erratic John Gay. Already, in some earlier dramatic essays, he had shown that his tastes lay within the field of the extravagant and the satirical. The Mohocks, described as a "tragicomical farce" when it was printed in 1712, was designed to make fun of diverse contemporary vices and stupidities, and the peculiar play entitled *The What D'Ye Call It* (1715) indicates in its very title the mixed style in which Gay delighted. Only when he came to write *The Beggar's Opera*, however, did he reach success, and that success was immediate and lasting. When this musical piece was given at the little Lincoln's Inn Fields Theatre in 1728 the whole of fashionable London flocked to see it; its month-long run set up a long-remembered record. Its triumph was due both to the novelty of the form and to Gay's own skill. In effect he gave to audiences of the time something which might be called the fantasy of rationalism. Shakespeare, in his *Midsummer Night's Dream*, with its dim-wood setting, its antique background, its mingling of fairies, lovers, and artisans, offers us emotional fantasy; in *The Beggar's Opera* the time of action is contemporary, the characters are rogues and vagabonds, but by jesting and exaggerating Gay has created a fantastic new world of his own: "Where is my dear husband?" cries Polly:

> Was a rope ever intended for his neck? O, let me throw my arms about it, and throttle thee with love! Why dost thou turn away from me? 'Tis thy Polly. 'Tis thy wife.
> *Macheath.* Was there ever such an unfortunate rascal as I am!
> *Lucy.* Was there ever such a villain?
> *Polly.* O, Macheath, was it for this we parted? Taken! Imprisoned! Tried! Hanged! Cruel reflection! I'll stay with thee till death; no force shall tear thy dear wife from thee now. What means my love? Not one kind word! Not one kind look! Think what thy Polly suffers to see thee in this condition.
> > Thus when the swallow, seeking prey,
> >   Within the sash is closely pent,
> > His consort, with bemoaning lay,
> >   Without sits pining for th' event.
> > Her chatt'ring lovers all around her skim;
> > She heeds them not, poor bird, her soul's with him.

Lucy and Polly quarrel over the wretched man:

> *Lucy.* Art thou then married to another? Hast thou two wives, monster?
> *Macheath.* If women's tongues can cease for an answer, hear me.

Lucy. I won't. Flesh and blood can't bear my usage.
Polly. Shall I not claim my own? Justice bids me speak.
Macheath. How happy could I be with either,
          Were t'other dear charmer away!
          But while you thus tease me together
          To neither a word will I say.

We, who have seen The Beggar's Opera give delight to audiences two hundred years after its original performance, can well imagine the excitement aroused by its production in 1728.

Unfortunately, Gay was not able to repeat his triumph. The sequel to The Beggar's Opera, which he called Polly, was printed in 1729 but, because the authorities discerned, or pretended to discern, revolutionary sentiments in it, did not appear on the stage until many years later, in 1777. Not so skilfully wrought as its predecessor, it fails to capture its spirit; the realistic elements are not made so consistently fanciful and wayward, and the style lacks the easy abandon so characteristic of the other. Nor does Gay's later attempt in the same form, the burlesque Achilles (1733), merit any great attention.

Other authors, however, applied themselves with enthusiasm to the kind of drama which he had invented. In diverse shapes the ballad-opera pursued its course, dozens of authors eagerly striving to rival Gay in his newly won popularity and affluence, but only a few of their pieces have any distinctive features. Sometimes, as in Henry Carey's The Dragon of Wantley (1737) and its sequel Margery; or, A Worse Plague than the Dragon (1738), burlesque scenes predominated; sometimes, as in Colley Cibber's Damon and Phillida (1729) and John Hippisley's Flora (1729), they assumed a pastoral shape. A few were successful, but most of them died after their initial runs. Among them all, the only one worthy of praise is the much later Duenna, which Sheridan produced in 1775. Here the characters are cleverly delineated; the lyrics are pretty and melodious; the dialogue is rarely dull and often illuminated by flashes of wit. In fact, however, The Duenna brings us to a form of dramatic entertainment which should be considered separately from that of the ballad-opera. This play and others, such as Isaac Bickerstaffe's The Maid of the

Mill (1765) and *Lionel and Clarissa* (1768) really belong to the category of comic opera, and, although Gay's success of 1728 cannot be dissociated from Sheridan's of 1775, the two remain in several ways distinct.

After penning *The Beggar's Opera*, Gay, as we have seen, wrote *Achilles*, and this piece reminds us of the connexion between the ballad-opera and burlesque. Even if many of the eighteenth-century burlesques are not musical the impulse which gave them birth is akin to the impulse which encouraged the other. In 1728, the very year of Gay's triumph, Henry Fielding presented his first play, *Love in Several Masques*, and it is probable that the example of *The Beggar's Opera* induced him, two years later, to bring forward his tragic burlesque, *Tom Thumb*, later reworked and renamed *The Tragedy of Tragedies*. Following the objective of Buckingham's *The Rehearsal*, this gaily attacks contemporary follies—the absurd situations, the flatness of language, the stereotyped characters in the tragedies of the age. Witty and penetrating, it remained long popular both in its original form and in a later 'ballad-opera' version. Among his many plays, Fielding has several other pieces inspired by the same literary-satirical purpose, *The Covent Garden Tragedy* (1732), *Pasquin* (1736), *Tumble-down Dick; or, Phæton in the Suds* (1736), and *The Historical Register for the Year 1736* (1737). All are animated by a keen sense of contemporary audience tastes, and a reading of their scenes gives us a vivid picture of what was happening to the stage during these years. In *Pasquin*, for example, Fustian, a rather stupid tragic poet, is shown in the theatre with his companion, the critic Sneerwell, watching a rehearsal of his new play. A battle-scene has been put on the boards and the curtain falls. Says the playwright, preening himself:

> There, there, pretty well; I think, Mr Sneerwell, we have made a shift to make out a good sort of a battle at last.
> *Sneer.* Indeed I cannot say I ever saw a better—
> *Fust.* You don't seem, Mr Sneerwell, to relish this battle greatly.
> *Sneer.* I cannot profess myself the greatest admirer of this part of tragedy; and I own my imagination can better conceive the idea of a battle from a skilful relation of it than from such a representa-

tion; for my mind is not able to enlarge the stage into a vast plain, nor multiply half a score into several thousands.

Fust. Oh! your humble servant; but if we write to please you and half a dozen others, who will pay the charges of the house? Sir, if the audience will be contented with a battle or two, instead of all the raree-fine shows exhibited to them in what they call entertainments——

Sneer. Pray, Mr Fustian, how came they to give the name of entertainments to their pantomimical farces?

Fust. Faith, Sir, out of their peculiar modesty; intimating that after the audience have been tired with the dull Works of Shakespeare, Jonson, Vanbrugh, and others, they are to be entertain'd with one of these pantomimes, of which the master of the playhouse, two or three painters, and half a score dancing-masters are the compilers. What these entertainments are, I need not inform you who have seen 'em; but I have often wond'red how it was possible for any creature of human understanding, after having been diverted for three hours with the productions of a great genius, to sit for three more, and see a set of people running about the stage after one another, without speaking one syllable, and playing several juggling tricks . . . and for this, Sir, the town does not only pay additional prices, but lose several parts of their best authors, which are cut out to make room for the said farces.

Sneer. It's very true, and I have heard a hundred say the same thing, who never fail'd being present at them.

Fust. And while that happens they will force any entertainment upon the town they please, in spite of its teeth [GHOST OF COMMON-SENSE *rises*]. Oons, and the devil, madam! What's the meaning of this? You have left out a scene; was ever such an absurdity, as for your ghost to appear before you are kill'd?

Ghost. I ask pardon, Sir, in the hurry of the battle I forgot to come and kill myself.

Fust. Well, let me wipe the flour off your face then; and now if you please rehearse the scene. Take care you don't make this mistake any more tho'; for it would inevitably damn the play, if you should. Go to the corner of the scene, and come in as if you had lost the battle.

Ghost. Behold the ghost of Common-Sense appears.

Fust. 'Sdeath, madam, I tell you you are no ghost,
You are not kill'd.

Ghost. Deserted and forlorn, where shall I fly?
The battle's lost, and so are all my friends.   [*Enter a* POET.

Poet. Madam, not so, still have you one friend left.
Ghost. Why, what art thou?
Poet. Madam, I am a poet.
Ghost. Whoe'er thou art, if thou'rt a friend to misery,
Know Common-Sense disclaims thee.
Poet. I have been damn'd
Because I was your foe, and yet I still
Courted your friendship with my utmost art.
Ghost. Fool, thou wert damn'd because thou didst pretend
Thyself my friend; for hadst thou boldly dar'd,
Like *Hurlothrombo*, to deny me quite;
Or, like an opera or pantomime,
Profest the cause of ignorance in public,
Thou might'st have met with thy desir'd success.
But men can't bear even a pretence to me.
Poet. Then take a ticket for my benefit night.
Ghost. I will do more, for Common-Sense will stay
Quite from your house, so may you not be damn'd.
Poet. Ha! Say'st thou? By my soul a better play
Ne'er came upon a stage; but since you dare
Contemn me thus, I'll dedicate my play
To Ignorance, and call her Common-Sense.
Yes, I will dress her in your pomp, and swear
That Ignorance knows more than all the World.

No better commentary than this could be found on the typical theatrical affairs of the time, for, however satirically exaggerated, it bears upon it the weight of truth.

The burlesque form, partly because of Fielding's own endeavours, proved highly popular in the middle of the eighteenth century, but few of the pieces rises above mediocrity. One of the best of the early examples is Henry Carey's *The Tragedy of Chrononhotonthologos: Being the most Tragical Tragedy, that ever was Tragediz'd by any Company of Tragedians* (1734) with its famous first lines:

> SCENE, *An Antichamber in the Palace.*
> [*Enter* RIGDUM-FUNNIDOS, *and* ALDIBORONTIPHOSCO-
> PHORNIO.

Rigdum-Funnidos. Aldiborontiphoscophornio!
Where left you Chrononhotonthologos?

This, however, is a short piece, and indulges not in witty satire, but merely in extravagance. Much more subtle is R. B. Sheridan's *The Critic; or, A Tragedy Rehearsed* (1779), which contains the well-known character of Puff, who has reduced the gentle art of advertisement to regular rule and scientific method. To Sneer, who questions him on the point, he cries:

> O lud, Sir! you are very ignorant, I am afraid. Yes, Sir—PUFFING is of various sorts—the principal are, The PUFF DIRECT—the PUFF PRELIMINARY—the PUFF COLLATERAL—the PUFF COLLUSIVE, and the PUFF OBLIQUE, or PUFF by IMPLICATION.—These all assume, as circumstances require, the various forms of LETTER TO THE EDITOR—OCCASIONAL ANECDOTE—IMPARTIAL CRITIQUE—OBSERVATION FROM CORRESPONDENT—or ADVERTISEMENT FROM THE PARTY.
>
> *Sneer.* The puff direct, I can conceive——
>
> *Puff.* O yes, that's simple enough. For instance—A new comedy or farce is to be produced at one of the theatres (though, by the by, they don't bring out half what they ought to do). The author, suppose Mr Smatter, or Mr Dapper—or any particular friend of mine—very well; the day before it is to be performed, I write an account of the manner in which it was received—I have the plot from the author,—and only add—Characters strongly drawn— highly coloured—hand of a master—fund of genuine humour— mine of invention—neat dialogue—attic salt! Then for the performance—Mr Dodd was astonishingly great in the character of Sir Harry! That universal and judicious actor, Mr Palmer, perhaps never appeared to more advantage than in the Colonel;—but it is not in the power of language to do justice to Mr King! Indeed he more than merited those repeated bursts of applause which he drew from a most brilliant and judicious audience! As to the scenery—The miraculous powers of Mr De Loutherbourg's pencil are universally acknowledged!—In short, we are at a loss which to admire most,—the unrivalled genius of the author, the great attention and liberality of the managers—the wonderful abilities of the painter, or the incredible exertions of all the performers!——
>
> *Sneer.* That's pretty well indeed, Sir.
>
> *Puff.* O cool—quite cool—to what I sometimes do.

These quotations serve to point out the evils, and to show the virtues, of the time.

4. THE GROWTH OF SENTIMENTALISM

In the sphere of tragedy the age's chief weakness lay in the lack of a clear orientation, and the same may be said for the sphere of comedy. The comedy of manners, which had produced Etherege, Wycherley, and Congreve, was rapidly degenerating when Farquhar and Vanbrugh took it over. A few other dramatists, such as Charles Burnaby and Mrs Centlivre, tried to keep its spirit alive; but it had lost its original force, and could never again assume quite the same delicately careless and polished tone which it had exhibited during the earlier years.

In place of the wit and the pointed conversational sallies, the expression of moral sentiment was becoming the chief object of many playwrights. Sometimes they were not prepared to go beyond the enunciation of well-intentioned platitudes; sometimes they proceeded farther towards the expounding of social concepts and the delivering of 'messages'; sometimes, during later years, they indulged in the presentation of humanitarian views and in encouraging pity for the 'distressed.'

In considering this development in drama, we must look at it from two points of view. On the one hand, we are bound to deplore the effect it had upon the spirit of comedy and the weight of ridiculously lachrymose scenes which it imposed upon the theatre. On the other hand, we are compelled to acknowledge that, for good or evil, it did open up several novel possibilities for the playwrights—indeed, that it gave birth to an entirely new sort of play which may be regarded as the ancestor of the typical dramatic works of our time. We may regret that there could never appear another Etherege or another Congreve blissfully ignorant of any moral obligations, but we must at the same time admit that the new humanitarianism, the recognition of social problems, the endeavour to make the theatre express in its own way the many social issues confronting the members of the audience, were an inevitable reaction to what had gone before. With Congreve the moving power of the old comedy, in reaching its culmination, had vanished, while the serious dramas, heroic and other, had but little to offer to the public which might be related to their own lives. The new middle-class spectators wished to see their interests reflected on the stage; in the 'tragedies' they found themselves in an alien and artificial realm which did not have even the merit of excitement, and in the comedies they moved uneasily amid scenes of gallantry which inwardly they tended to condemn. What they sought for, and what the sentimental dramatists gave them, was an intermediate kind of play in which occasional comic scenes alternated with others in which serious, if facile, comments were made on the world around them.

This sentimental trend may be traced back as far as the early eighties of the seventeenth century, and it seems probable that the political interest which was aroused during the last days of Charles II, the reign of James II, and the Rebellion had something to do with the shifting of focus from gay intrigues to more serious scenes. The political disturbances caused men to give thought to problems of government and of religion, and from these they were led naturally to a consideration of the problems of social life in general. This consideration of life's problems coincided with the development of a reaction to the excesses of the Stuart Court, and together the two forces moved forward rapidly. Touches of a reflective sort crept into comedies and tragedies; men such as Thomas D'Urfey, women such as Mrs Behn, began to introduce into their plays themes which displayed their consciousness of the difficulties arising from the social conventions of the time. Even Shadwell felt the impress of the age and gave expression to it in his later productions. It must, of course, be understood that before 1700 all these trends were merely tentative and experimental, and that even towards the very end of the century nothing more had been achieved than the occasional introduction of a 'moral' note into plays the plots of which were mainly concerned with flagrant exhibitions of the love-chase. Typical is Love's Last Shift (1696) by Colley Cibber, a playwright who showed himself always eager to satisfy popular tastes. Here the best is being made of two entirely different worlds. The licentious comic characters and themes of the old comedy are freely exploited, and the author goes so far as to point out to the spectators that his hero is "lewd" throughout the course of the first four acts; when the fifth act comes, however, we are regaled with an artificially conceived conclusion in which the erring gallant is made to promise a mending of his ways. Thus were all the spectators made happy: the reformers rejoiced because virtue triumphed at the end; the pleasure-loving were willing to accept the wholly incredible conversion for the sake of the careless intrigue and loose dialogue of the preceding scenes.

During the years that followed, Cibber and others turned out dozens of similar transitional plays, the only marked development being a tendency to tone down the licentiousness and to concentrate attention in the comic situations rather upon fashionable foibles than upon intrigue. Cibber's *She wou'd and she wou'd not* (1702), *The Double Gallant; or, The Sick Lady's Cure* (1707), *The Lady's Last Stake; or, The Wife's Resentment* (1707), and *The Refusal; or, The Ladies' Philosophy* (1721) all agree in placing stress on affected, vain women and their foppish courtiers. In a sense, these plays may be taken as a kind of 'she-comedy' paralleling the contemporary 'she-tragedy.' The heroines become of more consequence than the heroes, and the general atmosphere is made more 'genteel.' Wit of the Congreve sort no longer appears in their scenes, nor is there any rich play of fancy. Instead, we are presented with all the fashionable follies, all the darling delights, of the town. The men and women are here seen changing their interests and relationships. The former tend to become mere beaux intent, not on a satire, a lampoon or a witty jest, but on ribbons and wigs; the latter, less intellectual than their Restoration sisters, spend their lives in trivialities.

Amid the plays of this kind, others of a somewhat different sort start to make their appearance, and in these the later development of sentimentalism is more clearly adumbrated. Especially important are the works of Sir Richard Steele, joint-author of *The Spectator* and the writer of a seriously reflective essay called *The Christian Hero*. Steele's inclinations, in spite of his own somewhat careless life, were all on the side of morality. He believed in domestic happiness, he believed in faithful love, he believed in the goodness of the human heart. It is not surprising, therefore, to find that in his four comedies—*The Funeral; or,*

Grief A-la-mode (1701), *The Lying Lover; or, The Ladies' Friendship* (1703), *The Tender Husband; or, The Accomplish'd Fools* (1705), and *The Conscious Lovers* (1722)—he should have endeavoured to give utterance to his own genuinely sincere reflections upon life. The first of these plays shows his hatred of hypocrisy expressed in the characters of Lady Harriot and of the honest old servant Trusty. In *The Lying Lover* his hatred of duelling is fully exemplified. The question of domestic virtue occupies his mind in *The Tender Husband*, and in *The Conscious Lovers*, his best play, he develops an emotional theme which at times tends to take us far from the comic. The hero, Bevil junior, is here presented as about to be married to Lucinda, the daughter of Sealand. He has, however, met and befriended an unknown girl named Indiana, with whom he ultimately falls in love. Unlike the rakes of earlier times, he will not endeavour to betray this girl, nor will he marry her without his father's consent. For a time it almost seems as if the play is to end unhappily, until Sealand discovers in Indiana his own daughter. The artificiality of the conclusion may perhaps call forth from modern readers a superior smile, but the dialogue is capable, the characters are well drawn, and the situations cleverly managed.

It must be obvious that such a play as *The Conscious Lovers* is moving towards a dramatic form distinct from what hitherto had been implied in the term "comedy," and it was this new form which became characteristic of the sentimental developments during the later years of the century. Comedies of a mixed kind —such as Mrs Centlivre's *The Gamester* (1705), with its attack upon gambling, and William Taverner's *The Artful Wife* (1717), with its morally reflective comments—no doubt made up the bulk of dramatic writings in this period; but the style adumbrated in Steele's final work was now destined to come into its own, and in its advance it was aided considerably by an influence from abroad. In Paris, numerous playwrights were engaged at this time in encouraging much the same trend as is to be seen on the London stage, and, although they themselves derived considerable support from what was being done contemporaneously in England, they made certain definite and significant sentimental contributions of their own. In particular, instead of simply cloaking earlier kinds of comedy with moralizations and virtuous statements, they were beginning to dream of the establishment of an entirely new dramatic genre worthy of taking its place alongside the other dramatic genres hallowed by classical precept and practice. True, the formal expression of this new critical approach did not come until Diderot and Beaumarchais propounded it in the fifties and sixties of the century, but several decades before that the concept of a new kind of drama was already in the air. Hence interest attaches to the appearance in 1732 of John Kelly's *The Married Philosopher*, the first adaptation of a French sentimental drama in English—and one which very definitely was aimed at achieving what later was to be styled the "serious comedy."

The fuller development of the sentimental play in England had to wait for some years, until two men, Hugh Kelly and Richard Cumberland, actively applied themselves to the cultivation of its mood. Of this pair, Kelly stands more closely allied than Cumberland to the older native traditions: such a play as *The School for Wives* (1773), for example, obviously has been based on the older type of 'genteel' comedy. At the same time, his concentration on the virtues of natural affection and on the evils of social conventions carries these older forms into an entirely different atmosphere. Emphasis on foibles which before had been an occasion for laughter is now supplanted by condemnation of these foibles, and as a result seriousness takes the place of laughter. In *False Delicacy* (1768), which was one of the triumphs of its age, vociferously applauded by spectators and avidly read at home, two heroines nearly ruin their lives because they are inclined to sacrifice the dictates of their hearts to society's demands, and a happy conclusion is reached only because an unconventional gallant, inspired by sentimental motives, dares to plead the cause of nature. Similarly, in *A Word to the Wise* (1770), a girl's happiness is nearly destroyed because of her father's insistence that she should marry the man of his choice, and at the end smiles follow tears only because the proposed bridegroom conceals a kindly, good-natured, and sentimental heart beneath his foppish exterior, making him prepared, magnanimously, to release his bride-to-be.

In the devising of these situations, Kelly and his companions sought to be 'realistic,' but in fact they imposed upon the stage a kind of dialogue insipid and ridiculously artificial. "O, Sir George," exclaims the heroine, when she has decided to reveal her true affections to the man she does not love,

> O, Sir George, to the greatness of your humanity let me appeal against the prepossession of your heart. You see before you a distressed young creature whose affection is already engaged and who, though she thinks herself highly honoured by your sentiments, is wholly unable to return them.
>
> *Sir George.* I am extremely sorry, madam—to have been—I say, madam—that—really I am so exceedingly disconcerted that I don't know what to say——
>
> *Miss Dormer.* O, Sir George, you have no occasion for apologies, though I have unhappily too much. But I know the nicety of your honour, and I depend upon it with security. Let me then entreat an additional act of goodness at your hands, which is absolutely necessary as well for my peace as for my father's —— this is to contrive such a method of withdrawing your addresses as will not expose me to his displeasure.

There is, then, in these plays a strange dichotomy, an attempt to cultivate the 'natural' and at the same time a hopelessly artificial approach.

Precisely the same dichotomy is apparent in Cumberland's writings. These, for the most part, rely on two dramatic devices. The first is the presentation of the reckless libertine whose faults and vices are shown to be external to his true nature. In the popular *West Indian* (1771), for instance, the hero is an inherently benevolent but rakish youth who, after having tried to seduce the heroine, eventually marries her although he is given to believe that she is poor, improbably reforms himself from all his former vices, and is rewarded materially by the discovery that his bride is, in fact, a wealthy heiress. The other trend in Cumberland's plays is his deliberate choice of characters on whom he may lavish his pity. In one play he seeks to present the Irishman, hitherto a familiar ridiculous stage booby, as endowed with a feeling heart; in another he endeavours to do the same for the stock comic stage Scotsman; and in his best-known work, *The Jew* (1794), he treats his Sheva in kindred manner. This moneylender in his hands becomes a generous-minded friend of the distressed; it is he who rescues the son of Sir Bertram from ruin; it is he who moves through the scenes as a kindly *deus ex machina*. We must certainly acclaim Cumberland's purpose in writing this play, but we cannot avoid seeing it as a tissue of artificialities; the propagandist aim induces him to make his situations mawkish, his characters unreal, and his dialogue artificially dull.

Kelly and Cumberland neither stood alone in thus elaborating the sentimental genre nor were their works the best in this kind produced during these years. As early as 1748, for example, Edward Moore wrote a well-planned play called *The Foundling*, which, although a 'comedy,' was deliberately designed to "steal the pitying tear from beauty's eye" through the treatment of a theme (that of unknown parentage) beloved by the sentimentalists from the time of Steele's *The Conscious Lovers* to that of Cumberland's *The West Indian*. A son sentimentally seeking for his father, or a maiden cast parentless upon the world, was sure to call for the free use of handkerchiefs in the eighteenth century, even although it can only occasion now an incredulous smile. So, too, at a later date Thomas Holcroft bore the sentimental play yet farther along its path. His best-known effort, *The Road to Ruin* (1792), which long remained as a popular stock-piece on the stage, introduces a hero, Harry Dornton, who is destroying himself by his love of gambling. However riotous he may be, however, he has a feeling heart, and he is cast into despair when he learns that his follies are about to bring his father to disaster. Nobly, he decides that he will sacrifice himself by proposing marriage to an ugly but rich old widow. In the nick of time, of course, all comes right, and due rewards are apportioned to the good in heart. On the surface, this play seems no more than another example of the sort of drama which had already been amply exploited by others, yet Holcroft was essentially different from Kelly and Cumberland. When the prologue-speaker comes forward to address the audience he is made to pretend that the author's original script has been lost and that thus he is forced to improvise. "The author," he says,

had mounted on the stilts of oratory and elocution—
Not but he had a smart touch or two about Poland, France, and
the—the Revolution,
Telling us that Frenchmen and Polishmen and every man is our
brother,
And that all men, ay, even poor negro men, have a right to be
free, one as well as another.
Freedom at length, said he, like a torrent is spreading and
swelling,
To sweep away pride and reach the most miserable dwelling,
To ease, happiness, art, science, wit, and genius to give birth—
Ay, to fertilize a world and renovate old earth!

In fact, these supposedly extemporized lines reveal Holcroft's real objective. He was representative of those sentimentalists who towards the end of the century were moving from the enunciation of virtuous platitudes to the inculcation of revolutionary ideas. Within the hundred years from the time when first the comedy of manners was being modified by the early reformers we have indeed made a lengthy journey.

5. COMEDY'S TEMPORARY REVIVAL

It is evident that in essence the sentimentalists looked not towards comedy but towards 'drama.' In place of laughter, they sought tears; in place of intrigue, melodramatic and distressing situations; in place of gallants and witty damsels, pathetic heroines and serious lovers. Most of their plays may have been labelled 'comedies,' but in the development of the comic they were not interested.

We must not, of course, assume that this sentimentalism completely dominated over the stage. Farce still was popular, and there were many who saw the follies of the sentimentalists' endeavour. Whitehead gave expression to a fairly common thought when, in A Trip to Scotland (1770), he satirically makes one of his characters declare that "the good company will perceive that, whatever effect the late run of sentimental comedies may have had upon their audiences, they have at least made the players men of honour"; and Cobb has a characteristic passage in The First Floor (1787):

Young Whimsey. Hey-day! What's become of the exquisite luxury of a feeling mind in relieving distress?

Furnish. It may do very well for people of fortune, but a tradesman should never indulge in luxury.

Young Whimsey. Consider, generosity is part of the business of man.

Furnish. And a d——d losing trade it is; therefore it shan't be a part of *my* business.

In diverse ways, through satire and burlesque and through practical experiment, numerous authors tried their best to keep the comic spirit alive. Samuel Foote, a prolific actor-playwright of the third quarter of the century, thus devoted himself to the penning of more or less farcical pieces enlivened by satirical stings. *The Knights* (1749), *The Orators* (1762), *The Minor* (1760), and similar pieces were designed to delight spectators through the arousing of laughter; such plays as *The Maid of Bath* (1771), with its portrait of Miss Linley, later to be the wife of Sheridan, and with its attacks on the Methodists, were written amusingly with topicalities in mind. Foote's work was rough, if vigorous, but even in its roughness it preserved something of the old spirit.

More important is George Colman, generally known as "The Elder" to distinguish him from his son, known as George Colman the Younger. Although his plays contain episodes and characters obviously influenced by the sentimental style, he consistently supported the cause of laughter and ridiculed the cult of pity. *Polly Honeycombe* (1760) is a clever satire of contemporary absurdities which anticipates both in general outline and in definite phrases Sheridan's more polished satire in *The Rivals*. Colman's opposition to the sentimental style is seen clearly enough in his selection of Fielding's novel *Tom Jones* for the plot of his more ambitious *The Jealous Wife* (1761), a comedy which, while it lacks Congreve's sparkling wit, is effectively written in the style of the comedy of manners, and the same style predominates in the excellent *Clandestine Marriage* (1766), which he penned a few years later in collaboration with David Garrick. For its portrait of Lord Ogleby alone, a portrait intimately conceived and genuinely comic in its excution, *The Clandestine*

Marriage would deserve to be remembered, but in addition to this it presents an adroitly planned action and a flow of sprightly dialogue which makes it well worthy of revival.

More sentimental touches appear in the plays of Arthur Murphy, yet he too has three comedies, *The Way to Keep Him* (1760), *All in the Wrong* (1761), and *Know Your Own Mind* (1777), in which there is an evident effort to preserve the integrity of the comic tradition. While the Cumberlands and Kellys and Holcrofts were engaged in making their distressed heroines talk in terms far removed from those of ordinary conversation, he can introduce his lively Lady Bell reciting part of a love-lyric:

> Yes, I'm in love, I own it now,
> And Cœlia has undone me;
> And yet, I swear, I can't tell how
> The pleasing plague stole on me.

What would I give to have some miserable swain talk in that style to me? 'Belinda has undone me!' Charming!

Miss Neville. A lively imagination is a blessing, and you are happy, Lady Bell.

Lady Bell. I am so. But then I am not talked of. I am losing my time.

Lady Jane. Why, you bold creature! I hate to hear you talk with so much intrepidity.

Lady Bell. Prudery, my dear sister, downright prudery! I am not for making mysteries of what all the world knows.

Lady Jane. And how do I make mysteries, pray?

Lady Bell. Why, you confident thing, I'll prove it against you.

Lady Jane. But what? What? What will you prove?

Lady Bell. That you are ready to jump out of your little wits for a husband, my demure, sober sister. Miss Neville, a poet is not more eager for the success of a new comedy, nor one of his brother poets more desirous to see it fail, than that girl is to throw herself into the arms of a man.

In a kindred manner Mrs Hannah Cowley, author of nearly a score of comedies, farces, and tragedies, strove to work in the older tradition. *A Bold Stroke for a Husband* (1783), *The Belle's Stratagem* (1780), and *A School for Greybeards* (1786) are all equally vivacious, adding to cleverly constructed intrigues reminiscent of the plays of Mrs Behn and Mrs Centlivre characters which take life on the stage; the Doricourt of the last-mentioned play, handsome, witty, and gallant, succeeds in recalling the vanished Dorimants and Mirabells of an elder age.

These comedies, which are merely a few selected from among many others, demonstrate that even the force of prevailing sentimentalism could not completely banish laughter from the play-houses. Nearly all are now neglected because of Goldsmith's and Sheridan's triumphs, but several of them gave suggestions to these two authors for their better-known works, and all deserve to be remembered for their own intrinsic merits. Oliver Goldsmith first took up the cudgels against the sentimental drama in 1759 when he published his essay on *The Present State of Polite Learning*, and a decade later, in 1768, his *The Good-natured Man* directed its barbed shafts at the style of Kelly, Cumberland, and their kin. The audience realized fully the cleverness of the work, although their tastes were too squeamish to permit them to accept without protest the 'low' scenes which Goldsmith had introduced into his play. Reading this comedy now, we may perhaps fail to discern wherein exactly Goldsmith departed from the sentimental camp. The concluding lines seem cast entirely in the spirit of the Cumberland:

> *Honeywood.* Heavens! How can I have deserved all this? How express my happiness, my gratitude! A moment like this overpays an age of apprehension.
>
> *Croaker.* Well, now I see content in every face; but Heaven send we be all better this day three months.
>
> *Sir William.* Henceforth, nephew, learn to respect yourself. He who seeks only for applause from without has all his happiness in another's keeping.
>
> *Honeywood.* Yes, Sir, I now too plainly perceive my errors—my vanity, in attempting to please all, by fearing to offend any; my meanness in approving folly, lest fools should disapprove. Henceforth, therefore, it shall be my study to reserve my pity for real distress, my friendship for true merit, and my love for her, who first taught me what it is to be happy.

Certainly this shows that Goldsmith had not completely thrown over the shackles of the style he condemned, and similar

"Red Bull" Stage

Scene in Settle's "The Empress of Morocco"

passages may be found scattered throughout the play. But when we come to the bailiff scenes in the third act Goldsmith's sly satire becomes clearly apparent. Says the minion of the law:

> Looky, Sir, I have arrested as good men as you in my time—no disparagement of you neither—men that would go forty guineas on a game of cribbage. I challenge the town to show a man in more genteeler practice than myself. . . . I love to see a gentleman with a tender heart. I don't know, but I think I have a tender heart myself. If all that I have lost by my heart was put together, it would make a—but no matter for that. . . . Humanity, Sir, is a jewel. It's better than gold. I love humanity. People may say, that we, in our way, have no humanity; but I'll shew you my humanity this moment. There's my follower here, little Flanigan, with a wife and four children; a guinea or two would be more to him, than twice as much to another. Now, as I can't shew him any humanity myself, I must beg leave you'll do it for me. . . . Sir, you're a gentleman. I see you know what to do with your money.

The Good-natured Man cannot be regarded as a truly success-ful play; the plot moves creakingly, much of the dialogue is stilted, and there are scenes which show that the author has not grasped fully the requirements of the stage. All these defects, however, are remedied in She Stoops to Conquer; or, The Mistakes of a Night (1773). This comedy, of richly deserved fame, presents a peculiar and interesting fusion of different forces. Clearly it owes part of its inspiration to the school of which Farquhar was the last true representative, but in essence it approaches more nearly to the spirit of Shakespeare's romantic comedies, which, it may be noted, were at that time winning an esteem they had not enjoyed since the early seventeenth century. In effect, the con-ception of Hardcastle, Tony Lumpkin, Diggory, and the lovers exhibits, not a witty intellectual approach, but the exercise of humour. Here are the sly smiles, the subtle sallies, the humane sensitiveness characteristic of that mood. Basically, Tony Lump-kin is born of Falstaff's company: he is a fool and yet a wit; for his follies we laugh at him and at the same time we recognize that often the laugh is turned back upon ourselves. Although the setting and the persons of the comedy seem far off from Shake-speare's Rosalinds and Orlandos, Bottoms and Dogberrys, it seems certain that in penning its scenes Goldsmith was looking back fondly over a period of nearly two hundred years.

Entirely distinct in character and in aim, save for a common objection to the sentimental style, Richard Brinsley Sheridan pursued Goldsmith's endeavour to keep laughter on the stage. His contributions to the theatre, dating from the year 1775, are of a strange variety. The comic opera called *The Duenna* (1775) has already been noted, and almost at the same time appeared *The Rivals* (1775), a comedy in which diverse influences can be seen at work. There is no suggestion of Shakespearian reminiscence here, but the impress of Jonson and of Congreve is amply apparent. The names given to many of the persons, such as Sir Lucius O'Trigger, Sir Anthony Absolute, and Lydia Languish, take us back to the comedy of 'humours,' while much of their dialogue recalls the late-seventeenth-century style. A concession to sentimental tastes may be found in the Julia-Faulkland scenes, even although the satire directed at Lydia indicates Sheridan's awareness of its falsity. The author's object patently was to keep to the level of comedy, yet farcical episodes are freely introduced. All of this suggests that as yet Sheridan had not been able to secure a determined orientation towards his work; *The Rivals*, despite the vigour of its writing and despite such inimitable portraits as that of Mrs Malaprop, does not present an integrated whole.

The School for Scandal (1777), on the other hand, is a completely harmonious masterpiece. Nothing disturbs the constant glitter of its wit, and the complicated plot is kept moving with consummate skill. Satire of the sentimental strain, expressed in the person of Joseph Surface, falls into its proper place. All is crystal clear, and never for a moment does the author deviate from his effort to follow Etherege and Congreve in the exploitation for comic ends of the manners of society.

Unfortunately, Sheridan never rose to such heights again. *The Critic; or, A Tragedy Rehearsed* (1779) is amusing and clever, but after all it is merely a burlesque; *A Trip to Scarborough* (1777), although it possesses an individual quality of its own, is but an adaptation of a play by Vanbrugh; and when we reach the melodramatic *Pizarro* of 1799 we see that the author of *The School for Scandal* has utterly forgotten the comic stage. In many respects, the writing of these two works by the same man is symbolic. In his great comedy Sheridan said almost the last word for the kind of play which was brought to perfection in *The Way of the World*; in *Pizarro* he was saying almost the first word for nineteenth-century melodrama.

6. THE DOMESTIC DRAMA

The melodrama was born out of many things, and not least out of the domestic 'tragedies' which were part of the sentimentalists' contributions to the theatre.

Domestic tragedy, as we have seen, had already been attempted in Elizabethan times, producing an *Arden of Feversham* and *A Woman Killed with Kindness*, but this type of drama soon vanished amid heroic ardours and pseudo-classic rhetoric. About the time, however, when we can discern the first glimmerings of sentimentalism, some signs appear to indicate that it was due for revival. Otway's *The Orphan* concentrates upon characters who, if aristocratic, are at least not royal; Banks, in his historical plays, tends to stress pathetic 'domestic' situations; in his *Oroonoko* (1695) Southerne makes his hero an ill-used, dark-skinned, native chieftain. In these works and in others of a similar sort which followed them two things may be observed. The first is a deliberate attempt to tone down the heroic, rhetorical style and to make it more 'ordinary.' The second is the development of the concept of 'fate'—no doubt due partly to the feeling that, in turning from regal splendours, some compensating 'tragic' element was essential, and partly to the opportunity which these 'fatal' situations offered for the display of pathetic sentiment.

During the first years of the eighteenth century we can watch the slow elaboration of this type of play. In 1704 comes the anonymous *Rival Brothers*, obviously based on *The Orphan*; barely two decades later, in 1721, Aaron Hill casts his eyes back to the early *Yorkshire Tragedy*, and in *The Fatal Extravagance* gives us the first play of its time which deals with middle-class English characters in a 'tragic' manner. These, and other, plays laid the foundation for George Lillo's *The London Merchant; or,*

The History of George Barnwell, a play which fluttered all London society when it was first produced in 1731, and which remained a stock piece for many years. Here at last was found a writer daring enough to make the hero of his tragedy a mere apprentice; here was one sufficiently bold to pen his serious dialogue in prose. It is true, of course, that this prose was not only artificial in its pattern but also strongly influenced by the blank-verse measure. The Uncle enters and soliloquizes in a manner almost identical with that which could be heard in any one of the scores of contemporary dramas dealing with more heroic persons:

> If I was superstitious, I shou'd fear some danger lurk'd unseen, or Death were nigh. A heavy melancholy clouds my spirits; my imagination is fill'd with gashly forms of dreary graves and bodies chang'd by death—when the pale lengthen'd visage attracts each weeping eye and fills the musing soul at once with grief and horror, pity and aversion. I will indulge the thought. The wise man prepares himself for death by making it familiar to his mind. When strong reflections hold the mirror near, and the living in the dead behold their future selves, how does each inordinate passion and desire cease or sicken at the view! The mind scarce moves; the blood, curdling and chill'd, creeps slowly through the veins, fix'd, still and motionless, like the solemn object of our thoughts. We are almost at present what we must be hereafter, 'till curiosity awakes the soul and sets it on inquiry.

Throughout the entire play, and not only in soliloquies, this style predominates, so that the dialogue assumes almost the quality of a burlesque. What we must remember is that in 1731 this prose of Lillo's was a novelty and that it seemed to the public of the time to be bringing 'reality' upon the stage. Audiences wept; men of letters praised the work; royalty perused it in palace boudoir; foreign playwrights hastened to adapt it and to pen imitations. Ridiculous though it may seem to us, *The London Merchant* marked the downfall of the classical tragedy, and to a large degree established the basis for the modern theatre.

This lachrymose play Lillo followed with *Fatal Curiosity*, a not ineffectively penned drama dealing with an ordinary peasant couple led by poverty to commit a terrible crime. Like *The Lon-*

don Merchant, Fatal Curiosity was translated into several languages, and its echoes for long could be heard on many stages.

Witnessing the success of Lillo, other dramatists attempted to pen similar plays of a similar character. Thus John Hewittt came forward with his Fatal Falsehood; or, Distress'd Innocence (1734) and Thomas Cooke with his peculiarly named play The Mournful Nuptials; or, Love the Cure of all Woes (printed 1739; acted as Love the Cause and Cure of Grief; or, The Innocent Murderer, 1743), but these were dull works, wanting vitality. Much more forceful was Edward Moore, who in The Gamester (1753) produced an affecting and effective domestic drama. The story is one of unrelieved misery. Beverley, the hero, is ruined through his inordinate passion for gambling. Reduced to his last few coppers, he takes his wife's jewels, and, playing recklessly, loses them. In the meantime, Lewson, the lover of Beverley's sister Charlotte, discovers the evil machinations of the hero's pretended friend Stukely. The latter, realizing that his exposure is imminent, instructs his tool Bates to murder the lover; he is assumed to be dead, and the blame is cast on Beverley, who in his misery takes poison and dies—just at the moment when he is informed that a large sum of money has been left to him. Moore's success rests in two things. First, he has given to his drama a grimly concentrated atmosphere, akin to, but stronger than, that of The London Merchant. And secondly, although he is obviously influenced by Lillo's style, he does have the ability to bring his language nearer to reality. As a contrast with the Uncle's soliloquy already quoted, Beverley's soliloquy in prison illustrates both the indebtedness to and the improvement on the speech-forms of the earlier drama:

> Why, there's an end then. I have judg'd deliberately, and the result is death. How the self-murderer's account may stand I know not. But this I know — the horrors of my soul are more than I can bear. [Offers to kneel.] Father of mercy! I cannot pray. Despair has laid his iron hand upon me and seal'd me for perdition. Conscience! Conscience! thy clamours are too loud! Here's that shall silence thee. [Takes a vial out of his pocket and looks at it.] Thou art most friendly to the miserable. Come, then, thou cordial for sick minds, come to my heart. [Drinks.] O, that the

grave wou'd bury memory as well as body! For if the soul sees and
feels the sufferings of those dear ones it leaves behind, the Ever-
lasting has no vengeance to torment it deeper. I'll think no more
on't. Reflection comes too late. Once there was a time for't, but
now 'tis past.

It is obvious that the language in these soliloquies by Lillo and
Moore savour of what we now call the 'melodramatic,' and the
melodramatic quality becomes even more apparent when we
move from the reflections uttered by men about to die to the
speeches which accompany sensational actions. In *The London
Merchant*, for example, the apprentice-hero, goaded on by the
prostitute with whom he has been associating, determines to
murder and rob his Uncle. Barnwell, we are informed in a stage
direction, "sometimes presents the pistol, and draws it back
again; at last he drops it—at which his Uncle starts and draws
his sword":

> Barnwell. O, 'tis impossible.
> Uncle. A man so near me, arm'd and mask'd!
> Barnwell. Nay, then there's no retreat.
> [*Plucks a poniard from his bosom and stabs him.*
> Uncle. O, I am slain! All-gracious Heaven, regard the prayer of
> Thy dying servant. Bless, with my choicest blessings, my dearest
> nephew; forgive my murderer; and take my fleeting soul to endless
> mercy.
> [Barnwell *throws off his mask, runs to him, and,
> kneeling by him, raises and chafes him.*
> Barnwell. Expiring saint! O, murder'd, martyr'd uncle! Lift up
> your dying eyes and view your nephew in your murderer.

We need not be surprised, therefore, that, when romanticism
came with its predilictions for 'gothick' ruins and Oriental
strangeness, the style set by Lillo and Moore should have been
incorporated within the scenes of those melodramatic plays
which flooded the stage during the first half of the nineteenth
century. Although sentimental dramas by the score were contributed to the theatre from 1750 onward, and although *The
London Merchant* and *The Gamester* were accorded considerable
acclaim, the audiences of the time were not really interested in
'tragedy.' They found greater delight in plays which presented

sinners reclaimed, distressed maidens saved, sympathy rewarded, and evil exposed—plays, too, which offered opportunities for the introduction of colour and music, which mingled thrills and laughter. All of this the melodrama gave them, and serious attempts at the writing of domestic 'tragedy' had again to wait until many decades had gone by.

VI

Drama in the Nineteenth Century

1. THE MAIN TENDENCIES OF THE TIME

AFTER the time of Sheridan and Goldsmith the drama rapidly decayed. For this several reasons may be adduced, each of which must be considered in relation to the others. Chief in importance, unquestionably, is that which concerns the size of the playhouses. In 1787 the Theatre Royal in Covent Garden was enlarged, and five years later it was rebuilt; Drury Lane about the same time witnessed a similar transformation. The results were as might have been expected. The profits of those in charge of the theatres were sometimes much larger than before, but the distance of the stage from the pit and galleries rendered subtle acting impossible and forced the performers to indulge in rant and bombast. Contemporaries were unanimous in declaiming against these lofty structures. Mrs Siddons herself, we are told, was forced to make her inflections coarser and rougher; the flash of repartee was impossible; the tender whisper or the excited aside were rendered ridiculous by the necessity which lay upon the actor to shout, if his words were to carry to the topmost galleries. Scott and Joanna Baillie, with many others, proclaimed, in the words of the latter, that "the largeness of our two regular theatres, so unfavourable for hearing clearly, has changed in a great measure the character of pieces exhibited within their walls." It is clear that in these theatres anything approaching the comedy of manners would have been impossible, that subtle tragedy would have failed to appeal, that only the roughest and rudest effects could be employed. Hence the rise and popularity of the spectacular play. Never before had scenic artists and machinists had so much to do. All kinds of gorgeous effects were devised. The dialogue ceded place to attractive scenes. Choruses which filled with sound the huge spaces of the theatres made great appeal, and melodrama with its songs, its stereotyped characters, its bold delineated plot, became the prime form of dramatic literature.

It was probably the size of these theatres which served to intensify the evils of the audience during the century's earlier decades. Society was libertine and vulgar, and the upper-class people set a tone in the playhouses which was aped by the more dissolute among the bourgeoisie. From contemporaries we learn of the number of prostitutes who thronged the foyers, of the coarse language heard on all sides, of the drunkenness and the rioting. Boaden in his *Life of Kemble* (1825) tells a characteristic story. *Coriolanus* was being performed one November evening in the year 1806, Mrs Siddons herself playing the part of Volumnia. "When," says the author, "Mrs Siddons was supplicating as Volumnia, the conqueror, her son, to spare his country; when every eye should have been riveted to the scene, every ear burning with the pure flame of patriot vehemence—at such a moment an apple was thrown upon the stage, and fell between Mrs Siddons and Mr Kemble." Kemble naturally protested vigorously and received a verbal reply "that this apple was thrown at some of the disorderly females in the boxes." Debauchery, fashionable vice, evils of all kinds centred in these houses of amusement, and the saner, soberer people who might have aided towards the elaboration of a finer drama were forced to keep themselves apart.

The size of the 'patent' theatres, the prevailing show and spectacle demanded and supplied, encouraged the cultivation of the melodramatic form; and this was intensified by the many 'minor' playhouses which sprang up during these years. At first, the 'minors' were permitted by authority to pursue their activities if they avoided spoken dialogue; and towards the close of the eighteenth century and the beginning of the nineteenth we have record of various productions in which the plots were explained to the spectators partly by the use of mime, partly by the introduction of a few songs, and partly by the display of title-boards, with, upon them, a few snatches of written dialogue—a device reminiscent of the captions accompanying the later silent films. Soon, however, these 'minors' won concessions, until there came a time when they were permitted to present three-act plays with dialogue spoken to the constant accompaniment of a musical background and with a stipulated minimum of songs. Quite clearly, these conditions operative in the realm of the 'minor' playhouses was of a sort to encourage precisely the same kind of dramatic production as was being encouraged by the different conditions operative in the larger theatres. In both the melodrama, musical, spectacular, bold in its effects, flourished.

The result of this was that many authors who might have applied themselves energetically to the stage tended to turn to other literary forms. Melodramas were crude affairs, and they could easily be turned out by hacks. These hacks, the managers found, could be satisfied with meagre monetary rewards; consequently to them they applied for their theatrical wares, sometimes indeed engaging such men, at low salaries, as 'house authors,' who guaranteed to turn out each season so many melodramas apiece. An ever-widening gulf, accordingly, yawned between the men of the letters and the playhouses. Numerous poets tried their hands at the penning of plays, but few were successful, partly because the poets had their eyes fixed on the Elizabethans, partly because the theatrical environment did not permit them, or at least encourage them, to learn their trade within the theatre itself. Most of the poetic plays have about them an air of condescension, as though their authors were conscious of their higher station, and when, often with very good reason, their offerings were rejected by the managements, it was the managements and not themselves they blamed. At the same time, numbers of such 'literary' playwrights moved a step farther, penning poems in dialogue form which, they declared, were not intended for the stage: never before were there published so many unacted, and frequently unactable, dramas.

As the century moved towards its mid-point signs of change become evident. In the year 1873 a reviewer in the *Westminster* expressed the opinion that the drama in England had by then become a defunct art, with no hope of revival; yet by the seventies, even by the sixties, we can now discern movements which ultimately were to prove the foundation of the twentieth-century stage. Already in 1843 had been passed the epoch-making Act for "regulating" the theatres. By that year Drury Lane had sunk to such depths that resort was made to shilling concerts in an effort to restore solvency, while Covent Garden had been turned into an opera-house; the drama was now almost completely in the hands of 'minor' stages precariously carrying on their activities without legal support. Obviously, such a state of affairs was ridiculous, and the Act of 1843 logically destroyed the power of the 'patents,' while, at the same time, putting the 'minors' at liberty. It is true that at first few signs of change are observable in the kind of dramatic fare offered to the public, but, as the years went by, and as new playhouses were erected, we can trace the establishment of a new theatre world. The smaller theatres which were built after the middle of the century permitted a better chance for the appreciation of both tragedy and comedy; actors no longer were forced, as in the larger houses, to mouth their lines grandiloquently, but were given the opportunity of developing subtler and more delicate styles of performance; and, above all, at least some of the new theatres were able by various means to draw back those spectators who, disgusted and alarmed by the conditions prevailing in earlier years, had abandoned their attendance at the playhouse.

Two trends here coalesced. Largely because of the influence of Queen Victoria and her Court circle, life generally was becoming more sober and respectable; and the Queen gave, as it were, a directive to her people when she started to invite prominent actors to bring their companies to Windsor, there to present command performances. For worthy middle-class men and women, therefore, there was less chance of being affronted in the theatres with flamboyant rowdyism; seated in the auditorium, they were no longer offended by coarse conversation around them or by missiles recklessly flung at players or spectators. This was the first trend. The second was the deliberate effort made by some managements to make their theatres more comfortable. Stalls were cushioned and set on carpeted floors; the 'dress-circle' was invented, and with it, for less wealthy patrons, the 'family circle.' With the coalescing of these two trends, more-over, came an alteration in the range of performances offered to the public. At the beginning of the century, doors opened early, and usually the show went merrily or dismally on to near mid-night; in one evening the spectators could see a farce, a tragedy, a pantomime, interlarded with entr'acte divertisements. When we move to the end of the century we note that most of the play-houses have completely changed their programmes; now, a single play accompanied by no more than a 'curtain-raiser' is the rule; the doors open later and close earlier; and, above all, each theatre tends to have its own speciality. The playgoer, therefore, now knew that he could attend the theatre comfortably and at a time to suit his own convenience; and he knew more or less what to expect when he made his choice of tickets.

Improvements, however, are rarely without their disadvan-tages, and two movements in particular militated against this system's encouraging the best in drama. The first of these, and the most important, was the establishment of the long run. Up to the middle of the eighteenth century, and even well into the nineteenth, runs of any length were unknown except for panto-mimes. Before 1640 the run of nine performances for Middle-ton's *The Game at Chess* was a much-talked-of record, and the month's endurance of *The Beggar's Opera* in 1728 was regarded as extraordinary. Normally, the theatres were conducted on the repertory system, with constantly changing bills; the only diver-gence from the system was in the performance of pantomimes, which, with their elaborate scenery and special effects, more and more tended to be presented frequently. With the coming of the new conditions all this tradition had to be cast aside. When a manager found that, in order to put on a really effective produc-tion, he had to devote a great deal of time and money to the re-hearsals, the designing of the scenery and costumes, the general business of the stage representation, and when he also found that the potential playgoing public was growing very much larger than it had been before, obviously he was induced to let his pro-duction run so long as it could attract an audience. This, in turn, led to something else. In the old days the theatres had their stock companies, engaged at the start of each season, and these presented all the pieces selected for performance. Now, however, with the establishment of the long run, the managements found it more profitable and artistically better to engage players for particular parts; if the piece proved popular, then these players might remain with it for months or years; if it was unsuccessful, then they had to look round for other engagements. Thus theatre economics altered drastically, and a cleavage arose between 'managers' and 'actors.' During the nineteenth century itself this cleavage did not become acute, since many of the managers were, like Henry Irving, 'actor-managers,' and thus actively concerned with the putting on of the plays; but the system wrought marked changes in the earlier years of our own century, when many managers were interested in the theatre only for the profit it might bring them, and when hundreds of actors found themselves victimized. The creation of a manager's association and the corresponding creation of an actors' association were the obvious result. Industry and trade-unionism had come upon the stage.

The effect of this alteration in the conduct of theatrical affairs was no less marked outside of London. Gradually, the dozens of Theatres Royal, each of which had had their resident companies, came into the hands of managers many of whom were merely businessmen. With the introduction and development of the railway, travelling was being made easier and more rapid, with the result that London productions could profitably be sent on lengthy tours or, more commonly, 'second companies' could be engaged to carry to the provinces the latest metropolitan successes even during their first runs. Thus many provincial managers tended to become no more than booking-agents occupied in filling in their seasons with visiting troupes; and the playhouses throughout the country no longer had the opportunity of serving as a training-ground for young actors.

Naturally, in these circumstances, there were numerous efforts designed to make adjustments likely to meet the altered needs. From 1750 onward the question of a 'dramatic school' was animatedly debated, and eventually out of this debate the Royal Academy of Dramatic Art was founded. Concurrently, the idea of a 'national theatre' was mooted, a theatre which might keep alive numerous plays which, in this era of long runs, the public no longer had the chance of seeing. No such national theatre was opened in this period, and even now nothing of the kind exists; but at least certain organizations, such as the Independent Theatre Society and the later Stage Society, were set up for the purpose of presenting plays which, although interesting, could not be expected to attract sufficient support for runs, and these organizations led, in the early twentieth century, to the establishment of numerous others with similar aims, and to the rise of the repertory playhouses.

Wherever we look we can see currents flowing which at one and the same time may be traced back to their sources in the trends associated with the work of the sentimentalists in the late eighteenth century and yet which have changed completely the theatrical landscape. A typical example is provided by playhouse illumination. During his management of Drury Lane, David Garrick had brought in an improved method of lighting the stage, capable of producing effects unknown before, and so, in essence, substituting for the older conventionalism something of a 'realistic' kind. His interest in this matter further led him to engage a scenic designer named De Loutherbourg, who spent a great deal of his time in experiments with light, and whose name is associated with a device, which he styled the "Eidophusikon," planned with the object of showing to spectators a stage set continually changing its atmospheric quality. Obviously, attempts of this kind made at a time when the only means of illumination were candles and lamps could not go very far; but just as the "flying coaches" of the late eighteenth century anticipated, in idea, the railways to come, so Garrick's and De Loutherbourg's innovations anticipated, in idea, the theatrical wonders which were soon to be made possible by the invention of gas-lighting and later of electricity. With these, entirely new instruments were put into the hands of theatre-workers; the effects of nature could be simulated with comparative ease; and, most important of all, the house lighting could be so controlled as to separate the stage world from the world of the auditorium.

All these fresh conditions made necessary a human and not a

mechanical invention—that of the 'producer,' or 'director.' Not only had the theatre become so complex as to demand the control of its various activities by one man, there was also the fact that when a play was being prepared for performance the actors were no longer members of an association trained to work together but simply a collection of individuals engaged for the occasion. For the most part, those who during the nineteenth century undertook to co-ordinate the stage action were either actor-managers such as Irving or authors such as Gilbert, but already before 1900 there are clear signs of the arising on the theatrical horizon of a new and dominating functionary, the man who did not write plays and who did not act but who devoted all his efforts to the co-ordination and direction of the pieces presented upon the stage. Those who describe the new theatre as the "directors' playhouse" are unquestionably in the right.

Several other trends during the latter years of the nineteenth century deserve at least brief mention. Particularly significant is the way in which the increasing number of playgoers stimulated the growth of theatrical criticism. Periodical reviewing of plays, of course, developed markedly before 1800, and in that period some few attempts were made at the establishment of journals specifically devoted to playhouse affairs. This trend was expanded still further within the first decades of the nineteenth century, but it is only after 1850 that we find it reaching its culmination. No previous critic had approached the power wielded by Clement Scott of the *Daily Telegraph*; in the *Era*, followed by the *Stage*, those occupied in theatrical affairs were provided with their own newspaper; and in *The Theatre* the public was offered a playhouse journal which went far beyond any of its predecessors.

Along with this went a fresh critical-historical approach towards the past. In earlier years there had been a very few men interested in exploring theatrical conditions during bygone ages, but in general their efforts did not take them far. Only during the last decades of the nineteenth century do we begin to see a really vital attention being paid to this subject. For the first time, some men began to have ideas concerning the shape of Shakespeare's Globe Theatre, and to realize that the stage as a whole had altered steadily from the time when it had originally been founded in the Middle Ages. The impact of these inquiries is well illustrated by the productions presented under the ægis of William Poel by his Elizabethan Stage Society, but its influence extended far beyond this limited range. The study of the theatre of the past aided the dramatists of the time in clarifying their concepts. They were enabled to see why such and such a convention should have been, and why it might now be abandoned or modified. They were provided with the basis for a fresh dramatic theory. Studying Shakespeare in relation to the conditions under which he worked, they could divine more accurately what elements in his writings belonged exclusively to his own age, what might offer suggestions to themselves. The antiquarian researches operated, too, on the minds of the producers. Unquestionably the heavily decorated set-pieces of the Lyceum management were most characteristic of this period, but already the issue of rich stage-decoration versus simplicity was being posed, and some men were beginning to wonder whether after all the drama had not been most effective when the stage was a bare platform, and when the imagination of the spectators was called upon to create visions of leafy forests and palace towers and gloomy dungeons. At the time, realism and spectacularism were dominant, but the questions were at least being asked.

2. THE POETIC PLAYS

The "decline of the drama" was a theme which exercised many men's minds during the period from 1790 to the time when Robertson brought forth something which seemed to betoken the awakening of a new age, and countless efforts were made to provide for the theatre a drama which should be worthier than facile melodrama and miserable farce. Practically all of these attempts, however, were doomed from the very start by the fact that they were indulged in, not, as it were, from within the theatre, but from without. A pronounced tone of superiority accompanies most of this work; instead of coming down to the level of the stage and endeavouring gradually to raise the standards of performance, the literary men persisted in standing, god-like, aloof, carefully and self-consciously lowering down their precious tragedies and dismally monotonous comedies as though these were machine-borne divinities through which alone the evil current of events might be altered. This sense of superiority, allied to a sad ignorance of theatrical conditions, marred practically all their efforts.

The general tendency of serious drama in the eighteenth century, as we have seen, had been classical. Although a certain liberalizing element had intruded because of the genuine enthusiasm, felt by nearly all, for the plays of Shakespeare, Otway, and Rowe, and although, through the hesitating imitation of these, the stricter forms of the pseudo-classic stage were sometimes abandoned—a sparkle of life gleaming fitfully in scenes otherwise mechanically conceived and hopelessly chilled by convention—over all the classic mood predominated. Besides this classical tragedy, there had appeared two forms which offered interesting features. The first was the domestic tragedy, inaugurated by Lillo; the second was a type of serious play which might be called pseudo-romantic. Home's *Douglas* belongs to this category, and several other writers essayed the same style, among them the not unimportant Robert Jephson, with his *The Law of Lombardy* (1779), a tragic rendering of the tale told in *Much Ado about Nothing*, and *The Count of Narbonne* (1781), which is based on the thrillingly 'romantic' novel of Horace Walpole, *The Castle of Otranto*. Walpole himself provided an even more startling unacted play of the type in *The Mysterious Mother* (1768).

Of these three styles of tragic drama—the classic, the domestic, and the pseudo-romantic—the first, quite naturally, did not receive much formal recognition in an age when poets were revolutionaries battling against those forces of critical restraint which had been imposed on literature by Pope and his companions. There were certainly some belated supporters, such as John Delap, who had started his career with a *Hecuba* in 1761, and who carried on his activities till the printing of *Abdalla* in 1803, and there were others who, like Byron, professed an admiration for the old literary laws, and made fitful attempts to follow them in practice. For all essential purposes, however, we may say that the rule of the Augustans was dead.

The domestic tragedy, it might have been thought, would have provided a sphere of legitimate and inspiring activity for the romantics. There was something of novelty here; there was offered the possibility of searching criticism of life; there was presented to the dramatists a field comparatively untilled which they might cultivate and sow as they desired. But, as has been seen, the poets preferred to soar to realms more fantastically conceived. They preferred the way of Home and of Jephson.

Home and Jephson had both been deeply influenced by Shakespeare's works, and this Shakespearian influence is the most marked feature of the literary drama during the early nineteenth century. Sometimes it becomes confused with the strain of German medievalism—the spectacular thrill of Kotzebue or the sensationalism of Schiller—but everywhere it is apparent. It influences the choice of theme; it induces repetition of imitated characters; it fetters the dramatists to a blank-verse style which, because no longer in its vigorous youth and harmonized to the speech of the age, strikes false, shallow, and artificial. This Shakespearian influence is deeply marked, at the very beginning of the century, in the plays of John Tobin, whose *The Honey Moon* was acted in 1805 and *The Curfew* in 1807. The plot of the former is a patchwork of ideas taken from *The Taming of the Shrew, Twelfth Night, Romeo and Juliet,* and *Henry IV,* with some suggestions filched from Fletcher's *Rule a Wife and have a Wife.* Rolando is a poor imitation of Benedick, who, for purposes of variety, is made to love, not a Beatrice, but a Viola, here called Zamora. The way in which this Shakespearian tendency was allied to a tendency in the direction of 'Gothick' romance is shown by the second play, *The Curfew.* Gloomy halls and dismal caves, bands of marauding robbers, a stock 'Baron,' appeals to superstitious sentiment, recognitions of long-lost wives and of long-lost sons—all these are introduced into this hotchpotch of romantic imaginings, and are expressed in language which seems an equal mixture of debased Shakespeare and adulterated Fletcher.

Typical, too, are the *Plays on the Passions,* issued in a series of three volumes dated 1798, 1802, and 1812, by Joanna Baillie. These are well-meaning enough, but the path of true drama cannot be paved with good intentions alone. No one now reading these long-forgotten dramas can fail to be impressed by Joanna Baillie's genuine talent. The language rarely sinks to mediocrity, and rises at times to a genuinely impassioned utterance. Yet the *Plays on the Passions* are all failures. Joanna Baillie had no real knowledge of the stage; she was merely a woman of letters condescending to show the theatre what it ought to be; she was not, as every playwright should be, honestly anxious to make herself acquainted with the many requirements of the playhouse. Beyond that, too, her tragedies have their weaknesses. The authoress has gone the wrong way to work. Shakespeare, we may believe, did not say to himself, "I shall write a play on Jealousy," and turn out *Othello*, or "I shall write a play on Pride," and turn out *Lear*. The cardinal passion of Shakespeare's dramas is dependent upon the characters and the theme; Joanna Baillie's plays have character and theme dependent on a preconceived passion. This error, it may be noted, was shared by other more distinguished poets: Coleridge's *Remorse* is a cardinal instance. Moreover, in penning their tragedies the greater dramatists do not limit themselves to one emotion. Joanna Baillie never seems to trust herself to speak of pride when her theme is jealousy, or to speak of hate when her theme is ambition. She has successfully documented men's emotions, boxed them up in nice little romantic caskets, to be opened one at a time with excessive care. Still further, her plays display marked crudities. Her love of murder as a dramatic device makes many of her situations monotonously stereotyped, and her weakness for revealing to the spectators or readers the whole development of the plot in her first act renders the later portions of her tragedies uninteresting. The only one of her plays which won any sort of success on the stage was *De Monfort* (acted 1800), and that moderate success the authoress owed apparently less to her own genius than to a wonderful piece of stage-carpentry by which the theatre was turned into a fourteenth-century church magnificently decorated.

Of the several members of the early, or 'Wordsworth,' group of romantic poets, all tried their hands at play-writing. Of these,

Robert Southey, because of the influence he exerted on the others, may first be mentioned. His dramas all belong to the early pantisocracy period, when his heart was thrilled by visions of a millennium heralded by the French Revolution. *The Fall of Robespierre*, written in collaboration with Coleridge, appeared in 1794, and *Wat Tyler* was issued surreptitiously by his enemies in 1817, when its author had long left his youthful republican sentiments and had turned to Toryism instead. Both of these are pitiful enough, and the latter reads almost as if it were a parody of sentimental, humanitarian melodrama. A trifle more successful was Samuel Taylor Coleridge in his *Remorse* (1813), a revised version of an early *Osorio* which had been sent to Sheridan as early as 1797 and impolitely refused. *Remorse* reminds us somewhat of Joanna Baillie's productions. Don Alvar is the upright hero of the play, whose life is plotted against by his evil brother, Ordonio. After a thrilling series of adventurous actions, in the course of which the honest Moor, Isidore, and Ordonio are slaughtered, Alvar throws off his disguise, and the whole ends on a moderately happy note. There is little vitality in the work, and rarely if ever do we thoroughly associate ourselves with the characters. In general atmosphere this play shows clearly the influence of German romantic dramas, the theme of two brothers, one of whom is honest and the other evil-minded, bearing a close resemblance to Schiller's popular *Robbers*.

The same defects may be traced in the pessimistic *Borderers* (written 1795–96) of William Wordsworth. This play also may be traced in inception to a Schillerian source; the crime committed with the best-intentioned motives is clearly a legacy of the German drama: but Wordsworth has nothing of Schiller's power over dramatic form. Touches of character-delineation there are in Marmaduke and Oswald, but never carried out to fullness, so that the personages of the tragedy remain without life. The plot is chaotically constructed, and the author pours forth unrestrained pages of blank verse in his most uninspired strain.

Sir Walter Scott too tried his hand at drama. His studies in German literature led him early to write his rather pedestrian rendering of *Götz von Berlichingen*, and from that he turned to more original composition in *The House of Aspen* (1829). This latter work is thoroughly in the German style, and can take rank only with the spectacular plays of *The Castle Spectre* class. Nowhere in it does the author of *Waverley* show that power which was to make him one of the greatest literary figures in Europe.

Other writers of the time fondly hoped for success in the theatrical world. Charles Lamb, who furnished Coleridge with the prologue for *Remorse*, attempted a tragedy in *John Woodvil*, to which was given originally the title of *Pride's Cure* (written 1799; printed 1802). This tragedy, which Lamb submitted unthanked to Kemble, again displays well the weakness of the poetic drama of the time. Poetry there is in it, with, as might have been expected, numerous reminiscences of the Elizabethan dramatists, but of co-ordinated central power it has none, and the characterization is, at best, mere sketchy patchwork.

When we come to the later, or 'Byron,' group of romantic authors there is an equal attention paid to drama. Byron himself left a series of dramas, some of which were acted; Shelley gave us *The Cenci* and *Prometheus Unbound*; Keats penned his *Otho the Great*.

Of Keats' effort, executed in collaboration with Armitage Brown, not much need be said. It was apparently composed in the year 1819, and actually was accepted for production at Drury Lane, although never produced. The Gothick story is not interesting, and the characterization is weak. Conrad, the villain, reunited in friendship to Otho, weds his sister, Auranthe, to the latter's son, Ludolph. The maiden, however, has, in order to shield her own stained honour, slandered an innocent Erminia; complications ensue, and eventually Auranthe dies, while Ludolph goes mad. The purposes of the characters do not always seem plain, and the verse, contrary to what might have been expected, is of a somewhat lumbering nature. Here, decidedly, Keats displays none of his genius.

Shelley's *The Cenci* (1819) deserves more careful notice. It is certainly true that this is one of the most striking tragedies among the many poetic plays of the century, but we must guard against overrating it because of the general level of dramatic mediocrity. Assuredly we may find in it many defects, defects due to the lyrical tendencies of the author and to his lack of theatrical knowledge. Many passages seem to be dramatically unnecessary, and at times the wealth of language makes the action drag. Even beyond this we may question whether *The Cenci* actually succeeds in its aim. Beatrice Cenci is obviously the central figure, but, in reading as on the stage, she somehow fails to convince us. Her uncompromising denial of complicity in the murder of her father seems to us not in harmony with her character as displayed in the first acts and at the end of the play; and, although we can find an explanation for the heroine's conduct, that explanation is one not likely to occur to ordinary spectators or to appear theatrically appropriate.

Among the various poets of this period Lord Byron comes nearest to success in the world of drama. His plays possess greater power and reveal a surer knowledge of theatrical technique than those of his companions, and their range, extending from *Manfred* (1817), continuing through *Marino Faliero, Sardanapalus, The Two Foscari,* and *Cain* (all 1821), to *Werner* (1830) is very wide. All of these reveal the presence of a creative spirit at once more in touch with ordinary life and more dramatically intense than may be found in any of the other poets. The Romantic writers habitually put themselves forward in their dramas, but not Coleridge, Shelley, or Keats could have been a tragic hero. Byron, however, is shaped in the mould from which Marlowe's heroes were formed. Like Faustus and Tamburlaine, Byron had his aspirations; he was a lonely figure setting himself up against the world. The creator of *Childe Harold* and of *Don Juan* might well have been thought to have in him the stuff of which great drama is made, and in fact his plays are not without their own value. *Manfred,* although theatrically the weakest of his works, exhibits to the full his appreciation of grandiose ambitions, his misanthropic hatred, and his appreciation of nature's solitary spaces. In *Werner; or, The Inheritance* we can see more clearly the German influence at work; dedicated to Goethe, it bears the stamp both of that author's *Götz von Berlichingen* and of Schiller's *Die Räuber*. Siegendorf, disguised as Werner, is set against his arch-enemy Stralenheim, who is murdered by young Ulric,

Werner's son; an innocent soldier is accused of the crime, and, in searching to reach the truth, Werner is eventually led to recognize that the guilt lies immediately with his own son, and, ultimately, with the pride and passion which he had inspired in that son's heart. The story, although improbably melodramatic, has been wrought out in not ineffective scenes. *Sardanapalus*, too, with its complex hero, effeminate yet capable of heroic action, and its skilfully drawn heroine, displays real dramatic ability. Even in this play, however, as in the others, we feel something lacking. The imaginative concept is greater than the ability to give it theatrical expression, and the total effect is vitiated by the constant stress upon a few 'passions' which, unrelieved by contrasting elements, become in the end drearily monotonous.

Apart from the major poets of the early nineteenth century there were several other writers who endeavoured to convince the audiences of their worth and who were successively hailed by the critics as prophets of a new age. Of these Charles Robert Maturin won transitory fame with his *Bertram* (1816), produced by Kean at the solicitation of Lord Byron. This play, as well as the showy *Manuel* (1817) and *Fredolfo* (1819), is marked by a keen sense of word-beauty, but the excessive sentimentality and pathos introduced into every scene render all these works of minor dramatic importance. So, too, failed Richard Lalor Sheil, who tried to capture the stage by storm, heaping excess upon excess in wild confusion. *Adelaide* (1814) is a typically German-type play which deals with the subject of the French Revolution, and *The Apostate* (1817) is full of grandiloquent passages which occasionally rise to tragic heights, but which more often sink to bathos. Sometimes this author comes as near as any of his contemporaries to the securing of a truly dramatic note, yet none of his plays, with their admixture of Elizabethan, romantic, and 'Germanic' elements, can make any stir in our hearts to-day.

Henry Hart Milman was another of these. His *Fazio* (1816) was designed as an "attempt at reviving our old national drama with greater simplicity of plot," but it fails in its effort through its rather rambling blank verse and its want of intensity. The plot is a peculiar one, concerned mainly with the alchemist Fazio, in whose house Bartolo, an old miser, dies. The former seizes the latter's bag of gold and then pretends he has found the philosophers' stone. In a fit of jealousy, his wife Bianca accuses him of being guilty of Bartolo's murder; he is arrested and hanged while she dies of remorse. As is evident, the theme is hardly one fitted for tragic treatment. For the subject-matter of his *Ivan* (1816) William Sotheby went to Russia. This is a poorly wrought drama of palace intrigue and of would-be philosophical sentiment—typical, in its lack of co-ordinated impression, of so many tragedies of the time. More effective proved the few tragedies of Mary Russell Mitford, *Julian* (1823), *The Foscari* (1826), and *Rienzi* (1828). All of these possess individuality and a few effective scenes, but again they exist in a literary-imaginative world far removed from that of the contemporary stage.

For a time it seemed as though one writer were to succeed in drawing the literary drama out of the general rut of mediocrity or incompetence, but when we now look back on the plays of this author—James Sheridan Knowles—we realize that he too had nothing fresh to give to the theatre of his period. More than most of his companions, he was prepared to utilize devices calculated to make his scenes attract audience attention; he had sufficiently lofty ideals of a critical kind to keep him steady in his aim; he had grasped something of the middle-class demands of the contemporary audiences. An examination of his plays, however, shows that, with all this, he had nothing fundamentally novel to present. *Virginius* (1820) is merely a bourgeois rendering of a classic story; *William Tell* (1825) is only a superior melodrama; *The Wife: A Tale of Mantua* (1833) is hopelessly artificial in its romantic fashion, with long-lost loves miraculously revealed in time-honoured fashion. Some interestingly drawn characters he has to offer, but, like his fellow poetic dramatists, his plots and his objectives seem artificial and forced.

The attempts thus made in the first few years of the century were energetically followed by various writers of later decades. Walter Savage Landor, not with much dramatic skill, early essayed tragedy in *Count Julian* (1812), and again, a quarter of a century after, in *Andrea of Hungary* and *Giovanna of Naples* (1839) and in *The Siege of Ancona* (1846). No more significant

were the various plays written by his brother, Robert Eyres
Landor. Thomas Noon Talfourd came closer to the theatre with
his *Ion* (1836), a play hailed by many as the long-awaited drama
destined to lead men towards a new world. This work, however,
cannot hold our attention now. The characters are chilly conceived, and the language drags monotonously on, stilted and
artificial, leading to soliloquies such as the following:

> *Ion.* Distrust me not.—Benignant Powers, I thank ye!
> [*Exit.*
>
> *Adrastus.* Yet stay—he's gone—his spell is on me yet;
> What have I promised him? To meet the men
> Who from my living head would strip the crown,
> And sit in judgment on me?—I must do it—
> Yet shall my band be ready to o'erawe
> The course of liberal speech, and if it rise
> So as too loudly to offend my ear,
> Strike the rash brawler dead!—What idle dream
> Of long-past days had melted me? It fades—
> It vanishes—I am again a King!

No more ardent vitality could he infuse into romantic themes;
his later *Glencoe, or, The Fate of the Macdonalds* (1840), although its theme is unclassical and based on a fairly recent historical event, presents characters just as lifeless set in an equally
frigid artificial pattern.

Variously these literary authors played with their romantic or
classic visions; their blank verse meandered through 'classic' or
Shakespearian meadows; but nowhere can we find here the
vividity of pulsating dramatic expression. The great poets succeeded no better than their lesser fellows. Thus Robert Browning,
who at first might be deemed gifted with just such qualities as
befitted a genuine dramatist, failed with the rest. Here, it might
have been thought, was one at least who loved not merely to
elaborate melodious cadences on which the ear soon surfeits or
to persist in dull repetitions of Shakespearian phraseology; here
was one with a knowledge of men, a dominant will, and a love
of reality; here was one who in his mid-career created his famous
gallery of "Men and Women." Undoubtedly Browning was
better qualified than most of these poets to pen successful dramas,

but several things prevented him from achieving anything truly vital. His love of the soliloquy, admirably suited for the 'dramatic lyrics,' does not meet the demands of the stage. His attraction towards the odd, the peculiar, the extraordinary, tends to become boring when exploited throughout the length of a play.

Browning's introduction to the theatre was auspicious; he was especially requested by Macready to prepare a play for him. *Strafford*, his answer to the request, was dutifully produced in 1837 but soon had to be put aside. Despite its force, the dialogue of this work is over-rhetorical and the characters have no movement in them. The chaotic splendour of *Sordello* intervened between *Strafford* and Browning's next efforts, *King Victor and King Charles* (1842) and *The Return of the Druses* (1843). The former may be regarded as one of the poet's nearest approaches to dramatic success. Confining himself to four characters, he has been able here to concentrate and vitalize his scenes; the resolute and occasionally treacherous Victor, his son Charles, perplexed and at odds with himself, the latter's noble wife Polyena, and the politician D'Ormea are all impressively planned. The latter deals, not ineffectively, with a Syrian race, the Druses, living under the domination of the Templars. These men, goaded into rebellion by the tyranny of the old Prefect, accept Djabal as a god reincarnated to free them from oppression, and as a result they reject the efforts of Loys, an honest member of his order, to release them from their bondage. Conflict arises in Loys' mind through his love of Anael, the betrothed of Djabal, and this conflict gives interest to his character, while the study of Djabal himself, the born leader who, in order to secure his end, pretends to divine attributes, is executed not without skill. In neither play, however, did the age find what it was seeking. Plot and treatment in both are bold and imaginative, yet theatrical vigour is lacking and the dialogue is marred by obscurities; and these defects are even more apparent in the later *Blot in the 'Scutcheon* (1843) and *Colombe's Birthday* (1844; acted 1853).

Browning, then, in spite of those qualities in him which might have prognosticated genuine achievement in the dramatic form, failed in his attempt; and if he failed, we need not wonder that others gave even less than he to the stage. Thomas Lovell Beddoes, certainly, had a true eye for the needs of the time. "The man," he said, "who is to awaken the drama must be a bold, trampling fellow.... With the greatest reverence for all the antiquities of the drama I still think that we had better beget than revive—attempt to give the literature of this age an idio-syncrasy and spirit of its own." What he produced, however, was only *Death's Jest Book* (completed in its first form 1826; printed 1850) with its macabre visions, its violently passionate blank verse, and its lyrics, all reminiscent of the Jacobean Webster and Tourneur. So, too, Jeremiah Wells' much-praised *Joseph and His Brethren*, originally published in 1824 and frequently revised up to 1879, owes its being to a literary and not to a dramatic impulse. Even the more theatrical plays of Richard Henry Horne—*Cosmo de Medici* (1837), *The Death of Marlowe* (1837), *Gregory VII* (1840), and *Judas Iscariot* (1848)—although imaginative in conception and written in a style more apt for stage presentation, betray the general weaknesses evident in all the poetic plays of the period. They give nothing new to the play-house; they are but imitations of earlier dramatic activity; they are out of touch with their age.

During the last quarter of the century many men were induced to see Lord Tennyson as the man likely to re-establish a vital poetic drama, but no more than the others was he able to put new life into the form. With the support of the Kendals and of Irving, he managed to get a hearing from the public, but the reception of his tragedies was polite, formal, and dictated rather by respect for his non-dramatic writings than by any real enthusiasm. Audiences found, as we now find, that *Queen Mary* (1876) is dull in spite of its promising theme, that *Harold* (printed 1877) is planned and written without enthusiasm, and that *Becket* (printed 1879, revised by Irving 1893), although including some interesting scenes, has no forceful dramatic drive.

Without question, we must give esteem to the general aim which induced all these poets to devote themselves to the stage— the desire to invest the drama with poetic fire and thus to revive the glories of the Shakespearian period. Yet, at the same time, we are compelled to admit that not one of them had the quality necessary for bringing this laudable purpose to fulfilment.

3. MELODRAMAS, FARCES, AND EXTRAVAGANZAS

For the energy, the theatrical sense, and the air of excitement so completely lacking in the serious poetic dramas of this period we have to turn to the entirely different world of the melodrama and its lighter associates.

Already, the playhouse conditions which led to the cultivation of the melodramatic style have been briefly outlined, and these conditions were responsible for the particular shape which such plays assumed in the English theatre during the first decades of the nineteenth century. Some attention, too, has been paid to the dramatic influences, continental and native, which were incorporated into its form. This general background, however, requires now some further sketching in.

One of the potent forces which led to the establishment of the melodrama at the turn of the century was the impact of the contemporary German theatre, and here we must take note of the peculiar fact that the same plays which had made such a deep impress upon the poets also stimulated the hack-writers whom they despised. During the decade from 1790 to 1800 the publishing-houses were busily engaged in printing translations of German dramas; most of these were never put on the stage, but the extraordinary number of editions which many of them reached indicates how avidly they were being read. Nothing quite like this strange furore had been witnessed in earlier years, and the explanation seems to rest in the wide appeal, for intellectuals and for others, which they made upon the public generally. There can be no doubt that several of the German dramas, written by men of high distinction, Lessing, Goethe, and Schiller, were works of genuine importance; *Die Räuber* was a notable achievement, and even Goethe's youthful *Götz von Berlichingen* was framed in a richly imaginative form. We need not wonder that they aroused excitement in the hearts of the romantic poets and that they were taken as models by them. On the other hand, the structure of these plays has a decidedly 'melodramatic' quality; here are ruined castles, the trappings of 'Gothicism,' the outlaws, the noble heroes, the distressed heroines, the sensational thrills—all of them capable of captivating those less literary and less exalted in their aspirations. Moreover, among the German plays introduced to the notice of the English public were many written by men who certainly did not possess the power of the greater masters, and among these August von Kotzebue won most esteem. In several respects, Kotzebue was an accomplished playwright; he knew the stage well, and in some of his works, such as *Menschenhass und Reue* and *Falsche Scham*, he showed that his purposes were serious, if sentimental; but at the same time his writings descend far more than the others towards the 'melodramatic' style. For many English readers at that period the newly discovered German drama meant Kotzebue rather than Schiller and Goethe. From the time when, in 1786, James Johnstone prepared the first rendering of a German drama—*The Disbanded Officer*, adapted from Lessing's *Minna von Barnhelm*—the chief theatrical influence of these plays was in the direction of increased sentimentalism, the employment of stock, stereotyped characters, the introduction of sensational scenes, and, generally, the exploitation of 'Gothick' material, or of material of an exotic kind which, in its strangeness, was apt to create a kindred mood in the minds of the public.

Meanwhile, in the midst of this, a fresh current was flowing from the Parisian playhouses. There, Guilbert de Pixérécourt was setting himself up as the Gallic counterpart of Kotzebue, and when Holcroft, in 1802, presented a version of his *Cœlina, ou l'enfant du mystère* as *A Tale of Mystery*, he brought forward a play which is commonly regarded as the first true melodrama on the English stage. We must, however, always bear in mind that the French and German influences were not running against native English traditions and that their force was due, not so much to their novelty, as to the fact that they were expressing in a more emphatic form a dramatic trend which is amply evident in the repertories of the eighteenth-century London playhouses. The sentimental hero of Steele's *The Conscious Lovers* is the direct ancestor of the hero, eager to rescue innocence in distress, who appears in such a play as Thomas Morton's *Speed the*

Plough (1800), a work which hovers on the borderline between serious comedy and frank melodrama; the line of development from Home's *The Fatal Discovery* to James Boaden's *Fontainville Forest* (1794) is easy to trace. In this last piece the background is a ruined Gothic abbey set in the fifteenth century, and in it the poverty-stricken Lamotte has taken refuge; hearing a cry of terror, he rescues the distressed Adeline; later, driven to despair by hunger, he waylays the Marquis of Montault, and this nobleman, when Lamotte's identity is discovered, threatens to have him arrested unless he persuades Adeline to become the Marquis' mistress; shortly afterwards, the villain finds that the heroine is none other than the daughter of his own brother, whom long since he had murdered; his crime revealed, he commits suicide and the good are saved. All the paraphernalia dear to the romantic melodramatists are here—the ancient abbey, the highway robbery dictated by abject hunger, a ghost in a darkened room, the long-concealed murder startlingly exposed— and all this in 1794, before ever Pixérécourt and Kotzebue were made familiar to English audiences.

These were the situations which captured the English playhouses at the beginning of the century and continued to exert their hold upon them until towards its very close. In their hundreds came these melodramatic plays, and clearly the mould from which they derived was virtually the same for them all. This being so, the selection of a few examples here will serve to illustrate their commonly expressed style. In 1796 *The Iron Chest* by George Colman the Younger, based on William Godwin's novel *Caleb Williams*, provides a specimen of the plays transitional between the later sentimental pieces and the melodrama proper. In this exciting work, Sir Edward Mortimer, headkeeper of the New Forest, is the central figure, a man who shortly before had been tried for murder and acquitted. The noble Wilford discovers that he was, in fact, guilty, and the villain, thinking to get rid of him, accuses him of robbery. Since Wilford is the hero, however, and since heroes always win out in the end, a document strangely preserved in an iron chest is made to reveal Sir Edward's crime. Closely akin in plan and execution is William Dimond's *The Foundling of the Forest*, pro-

duced more than a decade later, in 1809. Here the villain is a
Baron Longueville, who, loving Geraldine, daughter of De Valmont, seeks to murder Florian, a foundling. His plot fails; and in
the meantime it is discovered that De Valmont's long-lost wife
still lives. Bertrand, Longueville's tool, is smitten with conscience, and through his means it is further discovered that the
foundling is, in reality, De Valmont's son. Again a story of criminal purpose and of distressed virtue triumphant at the end.

Nearly all the settings for these early melodramas were
medieval or Oriental, and many exploited supernatural effects.
Writers such as "Monk" Lewis, with his *The Castle Spectre* of
1797 and with his *Adelmorn the Outlaw* of 1801, ran the entire
gamut of eerie and sensational incident. The title of the former
play is sufficiently indicative of its central theme, and a short
passage from the latter gives an illustration of Lewis' style. Ulric
is the villain, intent upon slaying the innocent Adelmorn; Lodowick is the comic honest man, companioned by Hugo, a minstrel,
and Innogen is the distressed heroine. Ulric, confronted by the
forces of the good, is bidden to swear his innocence and he starts
to obey:

> *Ulric.* As I have hopes of happiness hereafter, by all that is holy
> in Heaven, by all that is fearful in Hell, I swear that——
> > [*As he proceeds, the* GHOST *rises slowly with a flaming*
> > *dagger in his hand, and stands opposite to* ULRIC, *who*
> > *stops and remains gazing upon him for some time*
> > *without motion.*
> *Sigismond.* Why stop you?
> *Ulric* [*motionless*]. My Lord!
> *Sigismond.* What gaze you at?
> *Ulric.* My Lord!
> *Sigismond.* Proceed.
> *Ulric.* He cannot be a witness in his own cause.
> *Sigismond.* Who?
> *Ulric.* He! He! My uncle! See you not my dagger? Flames curl
> round it! Lo he points to his bleeding bosom! But 'tis false—'tis
> false! The wound I gave him was not half so deep!
> > [*All utter a cry of mingled joy and horror.*
> *Innogen* [*wild with joy*]. Heard ye that? Heard ye that? O,
> father, heard ye that?   [*Embracing* SIGISMOND.

Adelmorn. They are Ulric's lips, but the voice is Heaven's!

Ulric. Look off me! I cannot bear thy glance! Flames shoot from thine eyeballs, and fire my brain! O, look off me!

Sigismond. Mark how passion shakes him.

Ulric [*frantic*]. Thy grave was deep: why hast thou left it? To save thy darling? To drag me to the block prepared for him? This prevents it! [*Drawing his dagger, and rushing towards the* GHOST, *who till now has remained fixed like a statue, but on his approach raises his arm with a terrible look and motions to stab him.* ULRIC *utters a cry of horror.*] Mercy! I am guilty, but not fit to die!

[*He falls on the ground, while the* GHOST *sinks.*]

The same atmosphere still breathes in Edward Fitzball's *The Flying Dutchman; or, The Phantom Ship*, produced fifteen years later, in 1827. Here we find ourselves in the 'Devil's Cave';

An overhanging rock, leading into the cave—a grotesque rock in the centre resembling an antique table, and massy book, closed. Music. LESTELLE *discovered, supporting herself against the rock in an attitude of distress.* VANDERDECKEN *comes down, with a torch and points to the magic book.*

Lestelle. Thine, earthly or unearthly, never! Terrible being, thou mayst indeed trample on my mortal frame, but the soul of Lestelle is far above thy malice.

[*Music. He is angry. He takes her hand, and, approaching the book, it flies open and displays hieroglyphics.* LESTELLE *screams and sinks at the base of the rock. Footsteps heard without.* VANDERDECKEN *listens.*

Mowdrey [*calling*]. Lestelle! I am here! You are safe! [*He descends and sees* VANDERDECKEN.] Ah, wretch, is it thou! Tremble!

[*Music.* VANDERDECKEN *laughs, then draws a sword. A terrific fight.* MOWDREY, *after repeatedly stabbing his opponent in vain, is taken up by* VANDERDECKEN *and furiously thrown down.*

Vanderdecken. Mortal, die! [*Thunder.*] Ah, what have I done? [*He displays bodily agony.*] I have spoken. [*Music.*] The spell which admits my stay on earth is destroyed with my silence. I must begone to my phantom ship again, to the deep and howling waters. But ye, the victims of my love and fury, yours is a dreadful fate—a hundred years here, in torpid life, to lie entombed till my return. Behold!   [*Points to the book. A chord.*

Scene in Addison's "Cato"

A Water Melodrama at Sadler's Wells Theatre

Such was the melodrama during the early years of the nineteenth century; but, even while we note the fundamental characteristics of all specimens of this genre, it is equally important to observe that the genre itself had sufficient vitality to enable it to accommodate within itself new themes corresponding to changing tastes. Very soon the constant seeking for fresh plots led the authors to the flourishing world of contemporary fiction. Sir Walter Scott, they found, had many stories which, when stripped down to the bone, could be easily adapted to melodramatic requirements. Thus in *Rob Roy* they found the stock bandit of sympathetic heart; they found there a hero in young Osbaldistone; they found a graceful heroine (with the usual secret) in Diana Vernon, and a thorough villain in Rashleigh Osbaldistone. Since there was no dramatic copyright in those days, the melodramatists were free to use this heaven-sent material as much as they desired. Hearts of Midlothian throbbed on every stage.

Partly through this delving into the world of fiction, partly because of changing tastes in the age, an alteration in the choice of melodramatic themes becomes apparent during the thirties and forties of the century. Having ransacked Scott, the 'minor' playwrights quite naturally looked back to the fiction-writers of the preceding years. They tried their hand at Fielding and Smollett, and discovered in Defoe an author who, because of his love of action, well suited their purposes. But when one of them had turned, say, *Moll Flanders* into a play, and when others followed with kindred picaresque themes (such as B. N. Webster with his *Paul Clifford, the Highwayman of 1770* (1832)) it was found that a nearer approach towards contemporary life was possible here than had been possible in the romantic or bizarre stories hitherto utilized. Through these adaptations the way was paved for the introduction to the stage of the 'naturalistic' melodrama, a form which was given fresh impetus through the dramatization of Dickens' novels. These, full of action, character, and exciting incident, were avidly seized on. His proof-sheets were snatched as they came wet from the press; as many as half a dozen separate dramatic versions of one of his novels were produced within a week of its publication. Through such plays the public became accustomed to see depicted before them, in the now time-honoured melodramatic way, scenes of a familiar cast; they sobbed over little Nell and outrageously hissed poor Scrooge, discovering a novel and added excitement because little Nell was nearer to them than a shadowy Adeline and Scrooge a more potent villain than a nebulous Marquis of Montault.

From this it was but a step to the sentimental depiction of all kinds of life—mostly lower-class life—known to the spectators. Usually—for action and thrill were demanded as essentials—the themes had some background of crime, war, or rebellion, and, as the century advanced, more and more ingenuity was displayed in treating themes likely to appeal to the popular audiences. Dickens having been fully exploited, actual contemporary murders were put upon the stage; there Sweeny Todd recommitted his crimes and Maria Marten nightly pursued her dismal career. The introduction of this domestic melodrama, allied to the effects produced by the truly epoch-making Theatre Act of 1843, soon brought something new. When the minor dramatists turned from the Middle Ages, the East, and the realm of the supernatural to the common themes of daily existence, quite naturally they began to lose some of their artificiality of style and proceeded to think of ways suited for the securing of naturalistic impressions. Sometimes they seemed unable to imagine any means better than the introduction on the stage of familiar objects—street-lamps, hansom-cabs, and, later, actual weapons used for their crimes by the criminals who were chosen as the protagonists of their plays; but gradually an appreciation of subtler methods dawned on their minds, and their technique was improved. Fuller 'realism,' of course, could not be developed out of the melodramatic style, but in these plays a step at least was being taken towards the dramatists of 1890–1920. The importance of these early experiments must not be ignored, and, even although we may now deplore the too-long-enduring sway of realism in the theatre, we can honestly welcome this nineteenth-century movement which followed the dull scenes and chill rhetoric of the classic and romantic literary drama.

The melodramatic works of such men as Tom Taylor and Charles Reade thus possess a strength lacking in earlier examples of this kind. Sometimes, it is true—for example in *Two Loves and*

a Life (1854), written by these two authors in collaboration—
they might choose themes of a romantic sort; this drama thus
deals with the rising of 1745 and shows how Ruth, having aided
the Duke of Cumberland, succeeds in saving the unfortunate
hero, Gervase, from execution. Most characteristic, however, of
their style are their melodramas written on domestic themes.
Taylor's *Still Waters Run Deep* (1855) and *The Ticket-of-leave
Man* (1863) turn to the contemporary criminal world, and treat
its scenes with a distinction lacking in earlier melodramatic
efforts. Even Henry Arthur Jones could patronize this form and
in *The Silver King* (1882) produce a melodrama which, in spite
of many artificialities, has a genuine interest and vitality.

While the melodrama thus pursued an independent course,
various developments are to be observed from about the year
1840 onward, tending towards a corresponding popularization of
the literary drama. Already in 1838 Lord Lytton had brought
The Lady of Lyons before the public, and in 1841 appeared Dion
Boucicault's *London Assurance*. Each of these is important in its
own way. Through Lytton's effort the literary authors were
taught how to make their works more suited for ordinary con-
sumption. *The Lady of Lyons* is a play written by an author
intent on achieving something more than the melodramatic hacks
of earlier years had aimed at, yet from their ephemeral writings
it derived its inspiration. Lytton's later comedy of *Money* (1840)
is even more positive in its significance. Here a theme of immediate interest has been chosen. The audience in the mid-
nineteenth-century theatre was largely middle-class, and this
story of 'money' proved that Lytton, unlike the other literary
dramatists, was aware of the fact that these spectators were
clamouring for a comedy and a tragedy expressive of their own
conditions. Many of Boucicault's plays too deal with social life
of the period. *London Assurance* aims at depicting the manners
of the metropolis, and *The School for Scheming* (1847) embraces
within its sphere the fashions of the aristocracy, the ambitions of
the merchant classes, the virtues of the poor. Boucicault is a sen-
timentalist; his dialogue often sounds to us now stilted and artificial; but he had a true sense of the theatre. These early works of
his are by no means to be despised, and his later efforts in which

his genuine sense of humour is ably allied to his appreciation of theatric thrill, were quite justifiably esteemed in his own time. *The Colleen Bawn* (1860), *Arrah-na-Pogue; or, The Wicklow Wedding* (1864), *The Shaughraun* (1874), *The O'Dowd* (1873), and *Fin Maccoul* (1887) may merit critical condemnation, but they still possess a virtue of their own.

While these movements were in progress in the spheres of melodrama and of sentimental comedy, the purely comic theatre, save for one exception, continued to languish. Vapid comic opera and stupid farce for the most part held the boards. The audiences could not appreciate fine wit; rude, primitive, and often coarse physical action took the place of flashing epigram and dazzling metaphor. The exception, however, is important. The early nineteenth-century audiences were not always ignorant of the essential foolishness of the spectacles in which they took delight, and alongside of sensational melodrama flourished the burlesque. This burlesque in itself has not provided the theatre with any great masterpieces; the innumerable travesties of *Hamlet* or of contemporary serious dramas are mostly dull and monotonous; yet the burlesque style contributed in its own way to the development of a form of play essentially characteristic of the age and destined to aid in the drama's later development. To this form of play is usually given the name "extravaganza," and for its popularization in England we have to thank chiefly the prolific James Robinson Planché, a writer who started his career with *Amoroso, King of Little Britain* in 1818 and continued writing until the second half of the century. His extravaganzas abound in puns; his style is sometimes crude; his ideas are often weak and trivial—but one thing he did achieve. He showed how the romantic love of the wonderful could be turned from an impossible Orientalism and from a medieval atmosphere of ridiculous proportions to a sphere of genuine creativeness. The imaginative quality of the fairy-tale joins in his work with the light touch of burlesque and satire. *Olympic Revels; or, Prometheus and Pandora* (1831), with its clever mingling of spectacularism, delicate topical allusions, and parody of classical legend might well serve as typical of his achievements. Planché himself tells us that he was responsible for altering the methods of costuming in these burlesque pieces; before his time it had been the custom to dress the characters in as crude and 'vulgar' garments as might be, whereas he demanded for his fairy extravaganzas as rich and as 'historically accurate' dresses as he could devise. This record might, indeed, be regarded as a motto for all his work; he introduced delicacy and refinement into a dramatic form which before had been but coarsely crude.

The extravaganza thus established by him proved popular, and other authors followed in his footsteps. Robert Brough was one of his earliest successors with his *Camaralzaman and Badoura; or, The Peri who loved a Prince* (1848), and he, in turn, passed on the style to H. J. Byron, who cultivated it enthusiastically in the seventies. Its chief importance rests in the fact that the extravaganza proved the basis for the writings of W. S. Gilbert.

To define the Savoy Operas is impossible; they exist on a plane of their own, and, although they belong to the extravaganza tradition and although they have exerted a considerable influence on later English comedy, it is impossible to class them justly either with the one or the other. Gilbert's dramatic career had started in the seventies, when, in the variety of different styles he attempted, he indicated the many qualities which later went to make up the spirit of his later and more accomplished work. His main tendencies were cynical, witty, and satirical, with a decided leaning towards parody and burlesque; but to these he added a strangely poetic fancy and a delicate, whimsical humour. Gilbert can see the opposite side of the picture as the romantic poets could not see it, yet he retains something of their fervour; he can be as intellectually witty as any man, yet there always exists in his work that sense of topsy-turvyism which reminds us of the atmosphere of Shakespeare's comedy of humour.

Something of these qualities is apparent already in *The Palace of Truth* (1870) in which King Phanor's enchanted palace, where all entering must speak the truth, forms the setting. There the cold Princess Zeolide becomes hysterically passionate; the gushing Prince Philamir there grows *blasé* and chill; there the sardonically bitter Aristæus becomes a genial philosopher. Gilbert's fancy is well exemplified in the scenes where the coquettish

Azema tries to entrap first Philamir and then Chrystal, truthfully
revealing as she does so all the artifices of the coquette's trade.
Pygmalion and Galatea (1871) is more serious, revealing the
generally concealed element of sadness which was another in-
gredient in Gilbert's writing, and this receives even more emphatic expression in *Broken Hearts* (1875); while at the very
same time *Tom Cobb* (1875) merrily proceeds with its farcical
absurdities. The truth is that Gilbert was a genius unique in kind.
In his laughter lurks an element of bitterness; in his parody a
note of reverence; in his irresponsible topsy-turvyism a serious
purpose. Those who flock to *The Mikado* (1885) or to *The Pirates
of Penzance* (1879) or to *Patience* (1881) may for the most part
lose sight of the bitterness and the seriousness of aim, but,
although his first object was to raise a laugh or to charm by a
song, he desired that the laugh and the song should bear the sting
of a satirical touch. Even such a delightfully fantastic opera as
Patience exhibits this. The cult of the sunflower and the velvet
breeches has now long passed away, but it was a cult in the last
decades of the nineteenth century. Gilbert's satire of it reminds
us of the satire of Restoration times, even as his wit sometimes
has a flavour of Congreve's style.

In Gilbert the nineteenth century produced one of its most
interesting dramatists; and, however original his genius may
have been, he arose out of the ranks not of the poets who were
would-be playwrights but of the despised compilers of melodramas, burlesques, and farcical skits. No better illustration
could be formed to demonstrate the vitality of the one group and
the theatrical sterility of the other.

4. THE DRAMATIC REVIVAL

Between the years 1845 and 1865, a young man, then quite
obscure, was busily engaged in penning a series of melodramas,
farces, and comediettas no different in kind from those which
contemporaneously were being turned out in scores by the bevy
of lesser theatrical authors of the period. *The Battle of Life*
(1847), *The Haunted Man* (1849), *The Star of the North* (1855),
The Muleteer of Toledo (1856), *The Half-Caste; or,The Poisoned*

Pearl (1856)—these followed each other rapidly, most of them being composed for production at outlying playhouses such as the popular Grecian and Surrey. Only one play, and that written at the close of his twenty-years activity, seemed somewhat more ambitious than the rest, *David Garrick*, a comedy-drama which, after opening in Birmingham, appeared at the Haymarket in 1864.

In 1865, however, Liverpool audiences saw the first performances of *Society*, and six months later, when it was presented at the Prince of Wales' Theatre, its author, Tom Robertson, was basking in the sunshine of success. Encouraged by the reception of this comedy, he proceeded to compose several works with similar laconic titles—*Ours* (1866), *Caste* (1867), *Play* (1868), *Home* (1869), *School* (1869), *War* (1871), and others—thus establishing a new kind of domestic drama which some contemporaries came to style the "teacup-and-saucer" theatre. As one critic observed, Robertson's aim was to urge the public to bring their "fireside concerns" to the playhouse, and this he sought to do by making his plots and characters and settings as realistic as he possibly could. He delighted his audiences by revealing on the stage, not the old conventional painted flats in which doors, for example, were merely canvas-frames with the knobs indicated by the scenic-artist's brush, but more solidly built scenery in which the doors had real knobs to be grasped by the hands of the actors. By visual as well as by other means he wished to suggest to the spectators that they were looking upon reality.

Realism, of course, is a relative term, and nowadays Robertson's efforts seem sentimental and artificial. Nevertheless, we must acknowledge two things, that he carried this realism as far as the audiences of his time could permit and that he was able to incorporate into these plays a quality which still succeeds in giving them an appealing charm to readers and spectators who have passed far beyond the world for which they were originally intended. One of Robertson's chief virtues was that he set out to bring life into the theatre, abandoning the distressed maidens and black villains and impossibly noble heroes, and that, in doing so, he strove to avoid any doctrinaire approach. Although his basic creed is essentially Victorian, he takes a wide view of the world around him. The loudness of the profiteer, Mr Chodd, in *Society* is no more an object of attack than the egocentric meanness of Lady Ptarmigant; the brutality of Eccles in *Caste* is not stressed more than the thoughtlessness of Captain Hawtree and the thoroughly obnoxious pretensions of the Marchioness. Robertson had no particular axe to grind.

In style, too, he struck a new note. Although many passages in his plays continue to exploit the stilted artificialities which we associate with the earlier sentimental dramas, in others he shows that he is trying his best to make his characters speak in their natural tones. As an example, we may take the scene in *Caste* when George D'Alroy shocks his mother, the Marchioness, by telling her that he is married to Esther Eccles:

> *George.* Stay, mother. [MARCHIONESS *turns slightly away.*] Before you go [GEORGE *has raised* ESTHER *from sofa in both arms*] let me present to you Mrs George D'Alroy. *My wife!*
> *Marchioness.* Married!
> *George.* Married.
>> [*The* MARCHIONESS *sinks into an easy-chair.* GEORGE *replaces* ESTHER *on sofa, but still retains her hand. Three hesitating taps at door are heard.* GEORGE *crosses to door, opens it, discovers* ECCLES, *who enters.* GEORGE *drops down back of* MARCHIONESS'S *chair.*
> *Eccles.* They told us to come up. When your man came, Polly was out, so I thought I should do instead. [*Calling at door.*] Come up, Sam.
>> [*Enter* SAM *in his Sunday clothes, with short cane and smoking a cheroot. He nods and grins.* POLLY *points to* MARCHIONESS. SAM *takes cheroot from his mouth and quickly removes his hat.*
> Sam had just called, so we three—Sam and I and your man—all came in the 'ansom cab together. Didn't we, Sam?
>> [ECCLES *and* SAM *go over to the girls, and* ECCLES *drops down to front of table, smilingly.*
> *Marchioness* [*with glasses up, to* GEORGE]. Who is this?
> *George.* My wife's father.
> *Marchioness.* What is he?
> *George.* A—nothing.
> *Eccles.* I am one of nature's noblemen. Happy to see you, my

lady. [*Turning to her.*] Now my daughters have told me who you are—[GEORGE *turns his back in an agony as* ECCLES *crosses to* MARCHIONESS]—we old folks, fathers and mothers of the young couples, ought to make friends. [*Holding out his dirty hand.*]

Marchioness [*shrinking back*]. Go away! [ECCLES *goes back to table again, disgusted.*] What's his name?

George. Eccles.

Marchioness. Eccles! Eccles! There never was an Eccles. He don't exist.

Eccles. Don't he, though. What d'ye call this?

> [*Goes up again to back of table as* SAM *drops down. He is just going to take a decanter, when* SAM *stops him.*]

Marchioness. No Eccles was ever born!

George. He takes the liberty of breathing notwithstanding. [*Aside.*] And I wish he wouldn't!

Marchioness. And who is the little man? Is he also Eccles?

> [SAM *looks round.* POLLY *gets up close to him, and looks with defiant glance at the* MARCHIONESS.]

George. No.

Marchioness. Thank goodness! What then?

George. His name is Gerridge.

Marchioness. Gerridge! It breaks one's teeth. Why is he here?

George. He is making love to Polly, my wife's sister.

Marchioness. And what is he?

George. A gasman.

Marchioness. He looks it. [GEORGE *goes up to* ESTHER.] And what is she—the—the sister?

> [ECCLES, *who has been casting longing eyes at the decanter, edges towards it, and when he thinks no one is noticing, fills wine-glass.*]

Polly [*asserting herself indignantly*]. I'm in the ballet at the Theatre Royal, Lambeth. So was Esther. We're not ashamed of what we are! We have no cause to be.

This excerpt from *Caste*, a fair specimen of Robertson's dialogue, may perhaps arouse a smile, but before we start to ridicule it we should remember that the fate of 'realistic' dialogue is that, however close it may appear at one time to the speech of the day, within a few years it has become 'dated.' The most 'realistic' dramas of our present years cannot escape that fate. Robertson's lines deserve to be read with this thought in mind, and we should admit that, when the play is revived to-day, these lines prove both speakable and, although definitely old-fashioned, acceptable to an audience. One other thing deserves notice in this excerpt. The very full stage directions show how keenly aware Robertson was of the necessity of binding together words and action and of the inability of ordinary words to convey what he wished to say. From even such a short specimen it is clear that he is conscious of the constant problem facing the realistic playwright and that he is here anticipating the trend, evident in numerous twentieth-century dramas, towards falling back upon gesture and stage-movement when words fail.

Robertson himself did not carry his work very far, but his influence is deeply marked on the theatre of the seventies. For the most part, it is true, the plays which stemmed from his endeavour tended to be even more sentimental and artificial in their conception than his; at the same time we can well see how his writings were calling others' attention to the possibility of dealing, not simply with sensational or intrigue plots, but with what we may call themes. Thus, for example, the prolific H. J. Byron, most of whose theatrical activities had been in the field of farce and burlesque, turned in 1868 to write *Cyril's Success*, not an important piece certainly, but one wherein he honestly tried to pen a 'problem' drama in which the domestic happiness of a popular novelist is nearly ruined by the acclaim with which his books are greeted by the public. Some years later, in 1875, he followed this with a not ineffective study of artistic jealousy between husband and wife, *Married in Haste*.

The sentimental strain evident in Robertson's writings was most patently carried on by James Albery, whose once enormously popular *Two Roses* (1870) was the harbinger of a long line of soft and pretty comedy-dramas. Sydney Grundy in general followed the same line. A *Pair of Spectacles* (1890), based on a French play, is made into a rather mawkish commentary on contemporary social life; *A Fool's Paradise* (1887) might have become an interesting domestic study had its scenes exhibited sincerity and seriousness of purpose; *Sowing the Wind* (1893), although it deals with the problem of the illegitimate child, treats its theme so delicately and with such refinement that it completely fails to make any real impact upon us. Perhaps the spirit of Grundy's theatre is symbolized in the title of his best-known work, A *Bunch of Violets* (1894).

To the end of his life this dramatist remained bitterly opposed to another strain in dramatic writing which also, ultimately, may be traced back to Robertson's example. During the years immediately following the appearance of *War*, two young men had started, like Robertson himself, to provide the stage with a number of relatively unimportant farces and melodramas; both were destined, again like him, to stand out as dramatic innovators in their later works. The first was an actor named Arthur Wing Pinero, who came forward as a dramatist in 1877 with a trivial sketch, £200 *a Year*. A few years later, in *The Squire* of 1881, some discerning critics found promising qualities, but *Sweet Lavender*, seven years after that, suggested that at best he might merely be another Grundy. Looking back, however, we can see how in the writing of these plays he was training himself for what was to come; technically, he profited greatly from the composition of such farces as *The Magistrate* (1885), *The Schoolmistress* (1886), and *Dandy Dick* (1887), and we realize now that *Sweet Lavender* was simply a trial essay, leading the way towards the first of his more serious efforts, *The Weaker Sex* (1888). In this he outlines the story of a man who, having broken with the woman he loves, emigrates to America, there grows rich, returns nostalgically home, and becomes pathetically infatuated by the daughter of his one-time sweetheart. This play was followed by *The Profligate* (1889), and that by the triumphant *The Second Mrs Tanqueray* (1893), a drama widely hailed as the true herald of an important dramatic revival.

Through this play Pinero was at once accepted as a master-playwright, and he retained a position of eminence up to the close of the first decade in the present century. During these years he wrote numerous works in diverse styles, extending from such a delightful comedy as *Trelawny of the "Wells"* (1898), in which he presented an imaginative picture of the young Tom Robertson, on to the more serious dramas, *The Notorious Mrs Ebbsmith* (1895), *Iris* (1901), and *Mid-Channel* (1909), on which his reputation is chiefly founded. Although he continued his theatrical career until as late as 1932, when A Cold June was produced, by 1910 he was beginning to seem old-fashioned, and other writers with newer ideas were carrying the stage beyond his reach.

Pinero's serious plays are distinguished, in the first place, by excellence in construction, and through this he taught much to his successors even although we now recognize that the excellence itself is often mechanically rigid. Secondly, he improved upon earlier efforts at the development of realistic dialogue, providing dialogue for his scenes which at once preserved the flavour of actual conversation and gave that conversation an atmosphere of theatrical excitement. These were his virtues. His principal failure lay in his inability to fulfil the promise of his themes. He essays to deal with the stuff of tragedy and yet rarely deals with his material in a tragic manner. His characters do not come truly alive, generally they are obscured by the idea or problem which he selects as the core of his drama, and instead of intensity of emotion he relies upon pathos. In him we see the playwright who has the desire to create a modern realistic tragedy but who in essence cannot pass beyond the sentimental.

This sentimental strain is most clearly marked, of course, in his earlier works, such as The Weaker Sex and The Times (1891), but it is equally present, although somewhat concealed, in The Second Mrs Tanqueray. This story of a man (Aubrey Tanqueray) who marries a woman (Paula) whom he loves but whose past he knows to have been deeply stained is well worked out, and some of the subsidiary characters, such as the daughter Ellean and the good-hearted friend Cayley Drummle, have vitality; yet we cannot accept it now with anything akin to the enthusiasm which was accorded to it in 1893. To us it must seem no more than a very skilful, and for its time worthy, theatrical piece in which the author succeeds in doing what he was best fitted to accomplish—the creation of a dramatic form in which social conventions are opposed to natural instincts, and in which a certain shallowness in emotional power is covered up by undoubted skill in the invention of situation. The combination of the pathetic and the spuriously theatric is to be seen even more clearly in

The Notorious Mrs Ebbsmith, a work which attempts to be a study of character but which depends on such 'curtains' as that at the close, when the free-thinking heroine, after flinging a Bible into the fire, "utters a loud cry," and "thrusting her arm into the fire drags out the book." Similar weaknesses are to be discerned in *Iris* and even in *Mid-Channel*, although in these we may decide that the characters are treated with a greater firmness and sureness of touch.

Whatever failings Sir Arthur Pinero exhibits, however, he must be acclaimed a master of his craft and unquestionably one of the most important figures in the dramatic revival which came at the start of our own period. His sentimentalism and often conventional treatment of character cannot take from his significance as a pioneer who helped to build a foundation for the twentieth-century realistic theatre and who pointed out to others the virtues of the play of ideas.

By his side, at the end of the nineteenth century, stood a second young man eager to enrich and expand this kind of drama. During the seventies, when Pinero was first introducing himself to the theatre, Henry Arthur Jones began similarly to experiment in the writing of farces, comediettas, and melodramas. These reached their culmination in *The Silver King* of 1882, a sensational play which, although conceived in melodramatic terms, includes some powerfully written scenes and some excellently handled situations. Two years afterwards came *Saints and Sinners*, and here Jones showed clearly his true objectives. Its background is a middle-class environment in a provincial town, and its chief persons are Hoggard, a ruthless small-business man, and Prabble, a mean little grocer of low mentality and hypocritical godliness. Opposed to them is Letty, daughter of Pastor Fletcher, symbolic of ideals and desires beyond those of the sordid world in which he lives. In its development the play takes a double course. On the one hand, we are presented with a set of everyday problems, the hatred of the petty shopkeeper at the larger Co-operative Stores, the meaninglessness of conventional puritanism, the rapacity and poverty of soul in middle-class provincial society. On the other, we are treated to a somewhat melodramatic story in which Letty is betrayed by a high-born villain, one Captain Fanshawe. Letty dies, but not before there is a scene of pathos in which her true lover, George Kinsmill, has returned to utter his most generous of sentiments. The two moods are but ill combined; and yet the fact that Jones is here dealing with subject-matter which goes considerably beyond Pinero's favourite theme of the woman with a past inclines us to accept *Saints and Sinners* as a more remarkable play in 1884 than *The Profligate* was in 1889. And Jones was to show that his choice of material in this his first important drama was not a thing of chance. The later *Judah* also concentrated upon the problems of man's spiritual life; the unsuccessful but poetically conceived *The Tempter* (1893) expanded this field of inquiry; and Jones' two masterpieces, *The Triumph of the Philistines* (1895) and *Michael and his Lost Angel* (1896), were firmly set on this foundation. Jones realized that if the drama were to advance it must get beyond themes of sex to depict, in the largest sense, man's religious faith and spiritual life.

This does not mean, however, that Jones restricted himself to a single kind of play and plot. Between *The Tempter* and *The Triumph of the Philistines*, for example, appeared *The Masqueraders* (1894), which deals with the all-consuming and altruistic love of a hero (David Remon) for a thoughtless woman (Dulcie Larondie). It is at the same time worthy of note that in Jones' depiction of passion there is considerably greater intensity than can be found in Pinero's treatment of emotional themes; the latter rarely, if ever, reaches further than the pathetically sentimental, whereas the former, even although he cannot escape the cloying atmosphere of sentimentalism, does manage to invest his situations with an almost heroic fervour. David Remon's consuming devotion is paralleled by that of Dr Carey for Edana Hine in *The Physician* (1897), and the same intensity gives quality, although in another form, to *Mrs Dane's Defence* (1900). This last play well illustrates something else which Jones contributed to the drama of his time. Pinero's strength rests ultimately in his constructional skill; Jones' strength rests in his nervously and theatrically written dialogue. The scene in which Sir Daniel Carteret divines the secret of Mrs Dane's past, with its sustained tension and its consistently held dramatic interest, amply displays the author's keen sense of the theatre and his power as a writer. The examination starts quietly:

Sir Daniel. Then we'll consider that episode closed, and we'll make a fresh start.

Mrs Dane. Yes, ask me anything you please. I'm only too anxious to help you in getting at the truth.

Sir Daniel. That ought not to be very difficult. [*Seats himself in revolving chair at writing table, takes a pen and occasionally makes notes of her answers.*] Now Felicia Hindemarsh was your cousin?

Mrs Dane: Yes.

Sir Daniel. Her father was the vicar of Tawhampton?

Mrs Dane. Yes.

Sir Daniel. And your other cousin—Annie Allen?

Mrs Dane. I had no other cousin. When you asked what my cousin's first name was I couldn't say 'Felicia Hindemarsh,' so I gave the first name I could think of.

Gradually the tension increases:

Sir Daniel. When Felicia Hindemarsh left Tawhampton, where did she go?

Mrs Dane. I don't quite know.

Sir Daniel. But you had letters from her. Where did they come from?

Mrs Dane. Let me think—it was some seaside place I think.

[*Pause.*

Sir Daniel. You don't remember?

Mrs Dane. No. I'm getting so terribly muddled, I don't know what I'm saying. I—I—you frighten me.

Sir Daniel. I frighten you?

[*His manner throughout has been calm and kind but very firm.*

Mrs Dane. Yes. I know you're very kind, and that I've nothing to fear, but I feel—I feel as if I were being thumb-screwed, and if you ask me one more question I must shriek out for help. [*A little pause.*] I'm sure it would be better for me to go and write it all out when I'm alone [*making a movement to go*]. Don't you think so?

Sir Daniel [*arresting her with a gesture*]. No.

Gradually the tense atmosphere grows still more tense, and the dialogue moves into a new pace:

Sir Daniel. When was the last time you saw Felicia Hindemarsh?

Mrs Dane. After the fearful scandal in Vienna she wrote to me in Montreal. She was desperate and begged us to shelter her. We had been like sisters, and I wrote to her to come out to us, and we would give her a home.

Sir Daniel. And you did?

Mrs Dane. Yes, till her death.

Sir Daniel. When was that?

Mrs Dane. About a year ago.

Sir Daniel. Where?

Mrs Dane. At Montreal.

Sir Daniel. She lived with you in Montreal—as Felicia Hindemarsh?

Mrs Dane. No; we called her Mrs Allen.

Sir Daniel. Give me the names and addresses of those people who knew you in Montreal as Mrs Dane, and her as Mrs Allen.

Mrs Dane. I'll write them out. Let me bring it to you this evening. What are you going to do with it?

Sir Daniel. I'm going to prove that you are Lucy Dane—*if you are Lucy Dane.*   [*She looks at him.*

Sir Daniel. Does Risby know who you are?

Mrs Dane. What do you mean?

Sir Daniel. Does Risby know who you are?

Mrs Dane. Yes—he knows that I am Mrs Dane.

Sir Daniel. The cousin of Felicia Hindemarsh.

Mrs Dane [*after a pause*]. Yes.

Sir Daniel. You told Risby, a mere acquaintance, that Felicia Hindemarsh was your cousin, and you didn't tell Lionel, you didn't tell me?

Mrs Dane. I—I—[*She looks at him*] I—oh—I'll answer you no more. Believe what you please of me! I want no more of your help! Let me go!

Sir Daniel [*stopping her*]. How much does Risby know?

Mrs Dane. Don't I tell you he knows I am Mrs Dane?

Sir Daniel. Woman, you're lying!

Mrs Dane [*flashes out on him*]. How dare you? How dare you?
                              [*Stands confronting him.*

Sir Daniel [*looking straight at her*]. I say you're lying! You are Felicia Hindemarsh!

This passage, which in the theatre becomes truly effective, well demonstrates Jones' skill and perception, yet at the same time we cannot escape observing that it exists within a play which hardly justifies its passion. Mrs Dane's past contained nothing that is strikingly terrible, even allowing for the social conventions of 1900, and there is no dramatic necessity for her sentimental return to her son in the last act or for the pretty-pretty touch of Janet's kiss.

In many respects Jones failed as Pinero failed. He has real seriousness of purpose; he was always very much in earnest; but his power as a playwright was marred by sudden descents into facile sentimentalism, while his very sense of the theatre often bore him into situations which, impressive in themselves, were ill-harmonized with the basic purposes of the plays in which they appeared. In addition to this, he showed little ability to move with the times. Although Pinero exhibits less strength than he did, the plays written between *The Second Mrs Tanqueray* and *Mid-Channel* show an awareness of changing styles and a determination to modify earlier conceptions in order to meet later audience demands. Although Jones was a skilled craftsman, one who thought seriously about the drama and one who laid a firm basis for his successors, he seemed, after 1896, to lose touch with his surroundings and become merely a relic of the past.

While these two men were vivifying the stage of the nineties by their 'problem' plays, there was a corresponding resuscitation of the comic theatre. Pinero himself, as we have seen, won success with several farces, and these display both sparkle and humour; despite his seriousness, Jones, in *The Liars* (1897), exploited a kind of laughter which had been heard but rarely in the English playhouses since the times of Goldsmith and Sheridan—not the loud outburst of merriment occasioned by farcical situations or overt jests, but the mellowed delight which results from intellectual enjoyment. In its scenes the spirit of the comedy of manners clearly is being revived.

In the main, however, it was other playwrights who gave the strongest lead to comedy during the last years of the century; and of these two are pre-eminent. The first, George Bernard Shaw, although he had written at least half a score of plays before 1900, remained in that time but little known, either for his social dramas, such as *Widowers' Houses* (1892) and *Mrs Warren's Profession* (1892), or for his more 'pleasant' works, such as *Arms and the Man* (1894), *Candida* (1895), *The Devil's Disciple* (1897), and *Cæsar and Cleopatra* (1899). This being so, his contributions to the stage may be reserved for later treatment. The other, however, Oscar Wilde, captured the London public by storm. If we omit his feeble serious pieces—*Vera; or, The Nihilists* (printed 1880), *The Duchess of Padua* (printed 1883), and *Salomé* (printed 1893)—we have from his pen four plays of genuine significance—*Lady Windermere's Fan* (1892), *A Woman of No Importance* (1893), *An Ideal Husband* (1895), and *The Importance of Being Earnest* (1895).

On the surface, the first three of these seem to be merely extensions of the now-extended sentimental drama. *Lady Windermere's Fan* thus tells the story of the high-spirited and proud heroine who gives her name to the title of the piece. Although she is not aware of it, she is the daughter of a Mrs Erlynne, a woman of sullied life who, unknown to the wife, has been blackmailing Lord Windermere. Gossip starts to buzz, and, when Mrs Erlynne forces Windermere to invite her to a party in his house, Lady Windermere, after having threatened to strike the interloper with her fan if she dares to make her appearance, decides to abandon her husband and go to a man who had professed himself to be in love with her. Mrs Erlynne discovers what has happened, hurries off to this man's rooms, and succeeds in persuading the wife to leave. Unfortunately, a group of gay and somewhat inebriated aristocrats enter and, finding Lady Windermere's fan on a chair, begin to jest about her attachment to their companion. At this, Mrs Erlynne, nobly deciding to sacrifice herself, steps forward and claims it. In similar manner, *A Woman of No Importance* and *An Ideal Husband* are founded on situations sentimental and sometimes pathetic. Wilde's strange half-genius, however, has enabled him to invest these situations with a spirit which carries us back to Congreve. Sentimentalism killed the comedy of manners in the eighteenth century, but Wilde had the skill to combine the would-be serious with the constant volleying of paradoxes and swift verbal sallies; and in doing this he unquestionably opened up new paths for comedy.

The gaiety, the paradoxical twists, and the verbal sallies find, of course, a more harmonious setting in the fantastic *Importance of Being Earnest*, a play in which artificiality is exploited for artificiality's sake, in which the absurd assumes complete command and yet in which the seemingly irresponsible quips have delicately pointed barbs. Two maidens meet:

Cecily. Pray let me introduce myself to you. My name is Cecily Cardew.

Gwendolyn. Cecily Cardew? [*Moving to her and shaking hands*]. What a very sweet name! Something tells me that we are going to be great friends. I like you already more than I can say. My first impressions of people are never wrong.

Cecily. How nice of you to like me so much after we have known each other such a comparatively short time. Pray sit down.

Gwendolyn [*still standing up*]. I may call you Cecily, may I not?

Cecily. With pleasure.

Gwendolyn. And you will always call me Gwendolyn, won't you?

Cecily. If you wish.

Gwendolyn. Then that is all quite settled, is it not?

Cecily. I hope so.   [*A pause. They both sit down together.*

Gwendolyn. Perhaps this might be a favourable opportunity for my mentioning who I am. My father is Lord Bracknell. You have never heard of papa, I suppose?

Cecily. I don't think so.

Gwendolyn. Outside the family circle, papa, I am glad to say, is entirely unknown. I think that is quite as it should be. The home seems to me to be the proper sphere for the man. And certainly once a man begins to neglect his domestic duties he becomes painfully effeminate, does he not? And I don't like that. It makes men so very attractive. Mamma, whose views on education are remarkably strict, has brought me up to be extremely short-sighted; it is part of her system. So do you mind my looking at you through my glasses?

Cecily. Oh, not at all, Gwendolyn. I am very fond of being looked at.

Gwendolyn [*after examining* CECILY *carefully through a lorgnette*]. You are here on a short visit, I suppose.

Cecily. Oh, no. I live here.

Gwendolyn [*severely*]. Really? Your mother, no doubt, or some female relative of advanced years, resides here also?

Cecily. Oh, no. I have no mother, nor, in fact, any relations.

Gwendolyn. Indeed?

Cecily. My dear guardian, with the assistance of Miss Prism, has the arduous task of looking after me.

Gwendolyn. Your guardian?

Cecily. Yes, I am Mr Worthing's ward.

Gwendolyn. Oh! it is strange he never mentioned to me that he had a ward. How secretive of him! He grows more interesting hourly. I am not sure, however, that the news inspires me with feelings of unmixed delight. [*Rising and going to her.*] I am very fond of you, Cecily; I have liked you ever since I met you. But I am bound to state that now that I know that you are Mr Worthing's ward, I cannot help expressing a wish you were—well, just a little older than you seem to be—and not quite so very alluring in appearance. In fact, if I may speak candidly——

Cecily. Pray do. I think that whenever one has anything unpleasant to say, one should always be quite candid.

Gwendolyn. Well, to speak with perfect candour, Cecily, I wish that you were fully forty-two, and more than usually plain for your age. Ernest has a strong upright nature. He is the very soul of truth and honour. Disloyalty would be as impossible for him as deception. But even men of the noblest possible character are extremely susceptible to the influence of the physical charms of others. Modern, no less than ancient, history, supplies us with many most painful examples of what I refer to. If it were not so, indeed, history would be quite unreadable.

Cecily. I beg your pardon, Gwendolyn, did you say Ernest?

Gwendolyn. Yes.

Cecily. Oh, it is not Mr Ernest Worthing who is my guardian. It is his brother—his elder brother.

Gwendolyn [*sitting down again*]. Ernest never mentioned to me that he had a brother.

Cecily. I am sorry to say they have not been on good terms for a long time.

Gwendolyn. Ah! that accounts for it. And now that I think of it I have never heard any man mention his brother. The subject seems distasteful to most men. Cecily, you have lifted a load from my mind. I was growing almost anxious. It would have been terrible if any cloud had come across a friendship like ours, would it not? Of course you are quite, quite sure that it is not Mr Ernest Worthing who is your guardian?

Cecily. Quite sure. [*A pause.*] In fact, I am going to be his.

Gwendolyn [*encouragingly*]. I beg your pardon?

Cecily [*rather shy and confidingly*]. Dearest Gwendolyn, there is no reason why I should make a secret of it to you. Our little country newspaper is sure to chronicle the fact next week. Mr Ernest Worthing and I are engaged to be married.

Gwendolyn [*quite politely, rising*]. My darling Cecily, I think there must be some slight error. Mr Ernest Worthing is engaged to me. The announcement will appear in the *Morning Post* on Saturday at the latest.

Cecily [*very politely, rising*]. I am afraid you must be under some misconception. Ernest proposed to me exactly ten minutes ago.   [*Shows diary.*

Gwendolyn [*examines diary through her lorgnette carefully*]. It is certainly very curious, for he asked me to be his wife yesterday afternoon at 5.30. If you would care to verify the incident, pray do so. [*Produces diary of her own.*] I never travel without my diary. One should always have something sensational to read in the train. I am sorry, dear Cecily, if it is any disappointment to you, but I am afraid I have the prior claim.

Cecily. It would distress me more than I can tell you, dear Gwendolyn, if it caused you any mental or physical anguish, but I feel bound to point out that since Ernest proposed to you he clearly has changed his mind.

Gwendolyn [*meditatively*]. If the poor fellow has been entrapped into any foolish promise I shall consider it my duty to rescue him at once, and with a firm hand.

Cecily [*thoughtfully and sadly*]. Whatever unfortunate entanglement my dear boy has got into, I will never reproach him with it after we are married.

Gwendolyn. Do you allude to me, Miss Cardew, as an entanglement? You are presumptuous. On an occasion of this kind it becomes more than a moral duty to speak one's mind. It becomes a pleasure.

Cecily. Do you suggest, Miss Fairfax, that I entrapped Ernest into an engagement? How dare you? This is no time for wearing the shallow mask of manners. When I see a spade I call it a spade.

Gwendolyn [*satirically*]. I am glad to say that I have never seen a spade. It is obvious that our social spheres have been widely different.

Thus the last years of the nineteenth century closed with a revival of both wit and woe in the theatre. The play of ideas, dealing with social problems, had arisen out of the sentimental experiments of earlier years; where the poetic dramatists had all failed, younger literary men were now engaged in evolving a new theatrical form out of farce, extravaganza, and melodrama; the public was being regaled with a fresh kind of serious realistic dialogue and an exploitation of artificiality for gaily jesting purposes. Here the foundation of the modern stage was firmly built.

VII

Drama in the Twentieth Century

1. CONFLICTING TRENDS

IF WE search for one single epithet to apply to the modern stage we are forced in the end to select the adjective "eclectic." No era offers such a motley array of complex and confusing trends. During the Elizabethan, the Restoration, and other periods there was, no doubt, considerable diversity in influences from without and in the flow of native theatrical currents, but when we compare these with corresponding conditions in the period between 1900 and 1962 they must indeed appear simple and orderly. This means that, while it is entirely proper to look at the drama of these sixty-odd years as a unit, recognizing that a clear line can be drawn from the plays which were being produced during the reign of Edward VII on to those now being performed during the reign of Elizabeth II, we must be alert to observe the series of dramatic waves which, within the six decades, constantly disturbed and at times even redirected the main currents.

In order fully to appreciate the growth of the theatre from 1900 onward there must be borne in mind many things which here can only summarily be mentioned. Fundamental is the fact that the twentieth century witnessed the final culmination of the stage's commercialism and, as an answer to that commercialization, the rise of the repertory playhouses, all ultimately taking their inspiration from the devoted work of Annie Horniman at the Abbey Theatre in Dublin (1903) and at the Gaiety Theatre in Manchester (1907). Alongside of this development within the dramatic playhouse itself, we have to give due weight to several associated movements. These were the years when the music-hall soared into prominence, and, although the majority of music-hall turns were not concerned with drama as such, the fairly regular performances of short sketches incorporated into their multiple bills contributed to the popularity of the one-act play—a popularity which was fostered also by other forces. Among these was the very considerable extension of the amateur companies. Amateurs, of course, had been active on the stage from medieval times, but only in the twentieth century did they come to take their work seriously and aided in the encouragement of young playwrights. Partly this was due to the establishment of amateur companies intent not merely upon amusing themselves but also upon presenting dramas which for one reason or another had hardly any chance of being given professional public performances; these companies were, in effect, an adjunct to the 'theatre clubs' which, from the time of the Stage Society onward, put on new plays and old for matinée or Sunday productions before their members. Partly, however, the amateur companies took shape as an adjunct to the repertory movement as a whole. In 1919 Nugent Monck thus established the Norwich Players and created an Elizabethan-type stage in the Maddermarket Theatre; shortly before, in 1911, the People's Theatre at Newcastle was founded; out of the originally amateur touring group called the Pilgrim Players grew Sir Barry Jackson's Birmingham Repertory Theatre. The significance of these amateur activities was recognized by Geoffrey Whitworth, who, in 1919, founded the British Drama League for the purpose of aiding their efforts and encouraging their more serious endeavours. The Scottish Community Drama Association was established with a similar objective for the territories north of the border. For the first time since the days of the mystery plays the amateurs began to make real contributions to the stage as a whole.

At the same time, other developments operated on the theatre from without. Just before 1914 the silent cinema was beginning to make its impact on the public, and soon luxurious 'picture palaces' sprang up all over the country, rapidly destroying the last remnants of the old Theatre Royal tradition. Then in the thirties came the popularity of the sound films, dominant until in turn they were confronted by the rivalry of television.

The music-halls and films were, to a certain extent, responsible for the tremendous vogue of 'revues' during the middle years of this period, and the revues themselves contributed much to the growth of new styles of musical drama, many of them originating abroad in New York and elsewhere. These musical dramas and revues clearly cannot be appropriately discussed within the limits of this particular volume, but any attempt to secure an adequate picture of the theatre as a whole during the twentieth century has to take them also fully into account.

Perhaps at no time has the English theatre shown such a keen, eager, and informed interest in current dramatic movements outside its own national boundaries. Certainly, the Elizabethans knew something about sixteenth-century Italian drama, Racine and Molière were known in the Renaissance period; Schiller and Kotzebue made their impact at the close of the eighteenth century; throughout the nineteenth century French plays were freely adapted to English requirements. All of this, however, was to a large extent a hit-or-miss affair. Only in the twentieth century do we encounter a determined effort to know everything about what was going on abroad. Translations of foreign works proliferated, while dozens of books and articles were devoted to the current fortunes of the theatre in many countries. Thus playwrights such as Strindberg, Chekhov, Toller, came to mean for English dramatic authors more than Molière and Racine had meant for the men of the Restoration; we are concerned now, not merely with the adapting of some particular plays chosen at random, but with an attempt to explore fundamental dramatic attitudes. This has meant that throughout the twentieth century, from the time when Ibsen was relatively new to the time when Brecht became the nonpareil, the advance guard of English intellectuals has been engaged in a continual series of discoveries, most of them arousing immediate excitement and then being tossed aside. Concurrently, an equally eager attention has come to be paid to the production styles of Stanislavski, of Meyerhold, of this man and that, and often individual performances showed, and still show, unintegrated elements caught from divers sources and bound loosely together.

Needless to say, the stage of this period was deeply coloured by the historical events and by the scientific trends which have so markedly disrupted and altered our lives. Two world wars could not but leave their impress on the theatres. At the same time, the curious fact must be observed that neither the 1914–18 nor the 1939–45 war made any such break in dramatic development as we might have expected. Even although the earlier conflict encouraged the managers to turn to lighter and frothier plays, and even although the bombings of the later years for a time caused some of the playhouses to close, we cannot see any definite distinction between the dramatic writing before 1914 and immediately after 1918 or between 1939 and immediately after 1945. While, therefore, the incidence of the two wars must be taken duly into account, we must refrain from speaking of "pre-war" and "post-war," in so far as the stage is concerned, as though those terms applied to two distinct styles. Much more impact has, in fact, been made by the growth of scientific thought and practice, although the impact itself is intangible rather than capable of positive elucidation. Unquestionably, both the earlier and the later realism must be associated with this, while the mood expressed in many plays written between 1955 and 1962 can be traced back to a combination of forces— the establishment of a lounge-suited scientific priesthood without any god to worship, the ironic contrast between washing-machines and nuclear bombs, and that other ironic contrast between man's conquest of a little space outside his own planet and the illimitable, unconquerable, even unimaginable expanse of eternity.

Obviously, in the midst of this welter of frequently conflicting influences and conditions, it is impossible to speak of any prevailing modern style in dramatic composition. It is true that, both early and late, there has been a tendency in certain quarters to draw a distinction between the 'non-commercial' and the 'commercial' drama, with the implication, expressed or suggested, that only in the former area was virtue to be found. Before we are tempted to acquiesce in such a proposition, however, a moment of cautionary pause is advisable. While it may be acknowledged that the early repertory playhouses stimulated several young playwrights who had failed to secure a hearing in London's West End and that within recent years some much-talked-about dramas have been presented by non-commercial theatres, an objective survey of dramatic fare in the twentieth century amply proves that the commercial houses have been responsible for presenting to the public many of the theatrical works which give distinction to this age, and that no hard and fast line can be drawn between the one group of writings and the other.

In looking at the dramatic achievements of the period as a whole, all we can do is to draw attention to a few general tendencies. One of these is the definite establishment of the prose realistic play, sometimes concerned with the personal relationships of the characters, sometimes seeking to present theatrical images of wider social forces, often with particular stress upon 'ideas.' In saying, this, however, it is necessary to emphasize once more that 'realism' in the theatre is a relative term, and that even now, at a time when the realistic endeavour has been pursuing its course through many generations, there is still active debate as to what the term truly implies.

In addition to this observation, it is also essential to note that throughout these fifty years there have been constant efforts on the part of many dramatists to plead for, and to experiment in, plays constructed according to different patterns. The fantastic, the symbolic, the poetic, all have co-existed alongside the 'naturalistic' and the 'realistic'—and in so far as the poetic is concerned we are forced to admit that several of the dramas written in this style during recent years have come closer to genuine success than any of the verse plays penned between the seventeenth century and our own time.

Some of the authors of the more 'imaginative' dramas, and particularly those who have written their dialogue in verse forms, have endeavoured to look back towards the time-honoured genre of tragedy; but their efforts in this direction have been sporadic and frequently uncertain, with the result that we may regard the cultivation of the middle range of drama as one of the age's characteristics. Whereas in the past the majority of theatrical works were specifically designated according to the 'kinds' to which they belonged, the majority of twentieth-century dramas are called nothing but "plays," occasionally mingling together the laughable and the serious, but most commonly (at least in the earlier decades) pursuing a sombre path quite distinct from tragedy's passionate intensity. Comedies and farces, of course, have abounded during these years, but tragedy has virtually vanished.

In theme the playwrights of this time have tended to cultivate two areas, those of social and sexual revolt. The word "modern" was being freely bandied about in the earlier years of the century and that has been caught up in to-day's trite use of the word "contemporary"; numerous play-titles, such as *The New Morality, The New Sin, The Younger Generation, The Young Idea*—tell their own story. This trend has led towards two things. First, in certain circles there are signs that dramatic worth is being regarded as of less importance than the social attitude adopted by a particular author, and, in addition, there is an inclination to speak of plays, not in terms of good and bad, but in terms of "modern" and "old." Secondly, the revolt against Victorian conventions, against parental authority, against romantic love, against all sorts of conditions, has led towards the employment of shock tactics. In itself such a movement is by no means reprehensible, but the trouble about shock tactics is that, as we proceed, the shocks have continually to be made greater and greater; even so, over the passage of years audiences are likely to become so familiar with the device that it ceases to have its intended effect and that in the end it may arouse only feelings of boredom. Some few decades ago Shaw was startling his public by introducing the word "bloody" into his dialogue; within recent years his successors have been taking delight in exploiting words rather more extreme, in bringing upon the stage characters unable to control their natural functions or eager to talk about their bowels. The difference lies not in the dramatists' objectives but in the nature of their subject-matter; and we are forced to observe that the impact of that first, relatively innocuous "bloody" was far greater than the entire mass of shock effects which have been included in later plays.

Perhaps all of this has something to do with what, in the end, is the chief characteristic of this theatrical age. In 1900 the London playgoing public was an extensive one, and the theatres in the provinces were flourishing; to-day the metropolis, having mightily expanded and now attracting hundreds of thousands of visitors from outside, still has a reasonably flourishing West End; yet there can be no doubt but that the playgoing public has, as a whole, materially declined and that, in spite of the activities of the repertory playhouses, there has been a marked falling-off of interest in the theatre throughout the provinces. For such decline many things no doubt are responsible. Just before 1914 the silent pictures were beginning to attract the public away from the stage; during the thirties the sound-films came into their own; and within the past ten or fifteen years television has swept over the country. We need not attempt to deny that these rival attractions have had much to do with the difficulties which many theatres encounter in gathering audiences sufficient to cover their costs. At the same time, it may be suggested that in many ways the element of revolt within the drama of the period has been partly responsible. From the close of Victoria's reign until now scores of playwrights have shown themselves intent upon the instructional element in their writings, and constantly this instructional element has been presented, not by implication, but blatantly and directly; as a result, the quality of entertainment has declined. Playgoers, however, normally go to the theatre in order to be entertained; they are prepared to be moved by genuinely tragic events, to be caught up in an absorbing plot, to be charmed by scintillating dialogue, to have their laughter aroused by comic concepts; what irks them is dullness and sermonizing. The trouble with the stage during the modern period has been that a cleavage has developed between entertainment and instruction, leading to two kinds of performance almost akin to the 'legitimate' and 'illegitimate' productions of the nineteenth century—those which, devoid of any deeper significance, aim only at thrill or vacuous laughter and those which subordinate the giving of pleasure to an intellectual and often political end. In view of this, it is perhaps not surprising that audiences have declined. The thoughtless entertainment can be obtained more easily and more cheaply from the offerings of cinema and television, and the more serious plays lack intensity and excitement. The "crisis in the theatre" about which there has been much talk all through these six decades is a crisis which depends upon things within the playhouse as well as upon external conditions.

2. THE REALISTIC SOCIAL DRAMA

In attempting to survey the theatre during the course of the twentieth century the perplexing variety of influences and styles, as we have seen, renders very difficult the grouping of the numerous playwrights who have made significant contributions to the stage; but perhaps a general picture can effectively be composed by focusing attention upon the three principal areas of endeavour already mentioned—the 'problem' plays stemming from the native tradition set by Pinero and Jones, enriched by increasing awareness of the work of Ibsen and Ibsen's followers, the plays which seek to pursue a more imaginative and 'poetic' objective, and those which, in diverse ways, essay the path of comedy. Within each of these, the divergent styles of individual authors are, perhaps, more widely displayed than were the styles of individual authors in the past, and consequently there is less opportunity of separating the one from the other than there is, for example, in considering comedy and heroic drama during the Restoration period, or even in relating the seventeenth-century comedy of manners to other kinds of the comic within that period; but perhaps sufficient kinship in approach exists to warrant examination of their plays in accordance with these 'schools.'

During the opening decades of the century the social drama takes first place. In 1906 appeared *The Silver Box*, and with this play John Galsworthy immediately established himself as a dramatic force, donning the mantle which had been worn by Pinero and Jones but settling it in a different way upon his shoulders. Here there is a study neither of an unfortunate lady who falls foul of society's conventions nor of religious hypocrites;

rather are we confronted with a drama which strives to gain
theatrical effect from social situation rather than from character.
For his motto the author has taken the old adage, "one law for
the rich and one for the poor." Jack Barthwick, the rich man's
son, behaves just as badly as the wretched Jones; the former
escapes without punishment, the latter goes to prison. Circumstance, not human will, determines it so; this is the rule of
society. Every one realizes the truth: in the police-court scene,
when the magistrate tells Jones that he is "a nuisance to the
community," Jack leans over to his father, exclaiming, "Dad!
that's what you said to me." With care, Galsworthy avoids the
condemning of the individual persons; the invisible social structure becomes the hero of his play, and what emerges from its
totality is a sense of inevitable waste.

This first experiment of Galsworthy's was followed by many
others in which the same general objective was exemplified—
Strife (1909), *Justice* (1910), *The Pigeon* (1912), *The Eldest Son*
(1912), *The Fugitive* (1913), *The Mob* (1914), *The Skin Game*
(1920), and *Loyalties* (1922). In *Strife* he does not make either
Anthony, director of the company, or Roberts, leader of the
workers, a man who governs events. Both no doubt have iron
wills; both are determined to fight to the bitter end; but they are
not drawn in individualistic heroic terms. The one takes his
strength from what may be called the capitalist faith, the other
from the faith of the rebels. Fundamentally, each is incapable
of acting otherwise than he does, and the conclusion of the drama
gains poignancy from the realization that, after all the distress
which has been caused by their conflict, the terms by which
the strife is ended are precisely those which had been proposed
at the beginning. "A woman dead; and the two best men both
broken!" says Harness:

> Tench [*staring at Harness—suddenly excited*]. D'you know,
> Sir—these terms, they're the *very same* we drew up together, you
> and I, and put to both sides before the fight began? All this—all
> this—and—and what for?
> Harness [*in a slow grim voice*]. That's where the fun comes in!
>   [UNDERWOOD, *without turning from the door, makes a
>   gesture of assent.*

In *Justice* it is not the miserable Falder's fate which impresses us, it is the waste occasioned by the mighty turning of Justice's wheels, and a precisely similar mood is evoked in *The Mob*. *The Pigeon*, *The Eldest Son*, *The Fugitive*, and *Loyalties* are all alike in making the faiths of man his masters. In one the plot deals with vagabondage, in another with standards of morality, in another with woman's position in life, in another with racial pride and social convention; in them all the abstract yet potent forces dominate, not the individuals who are driven on by these forces.

For his dramatic task Galsworthy possessed certain sterling qualities. He had a profoundly humanitarian outlook upon life, and he strove to the best of his ability to adopt an objective attitude; he was slow to condemn individuals and preferred to balance vices and virtues; in general, he was not sentimental in his approach and only rarely did he rely upon pathos for the effect of his scenes; he had an excellent sense of dramatic architecture and, although his emphasis did not rest upon individuals, he had the power to give a living quality to the persons with whom he dealt. His failure to create greater things than he actually was able to accomplish may be attributed rather to the kind of drama he elected to write than to any weakness of his own. Basically, he was intent upon forging domestic or social 'tragedies' in which, instead of concentrating attention upon the tremendous figures set forth by a Shakespeare, he might give dramatic expression to these invisible forces holding mankind in their grip. His characters are ordinary, commonplace men and women even when they are the 'best' of their kind; his stress is not upon them but upon Strife, Justice, Loyalties; even when he concentrates upon the hero of *Old English* (1924) we feel that the stature of the man derives rather from the environment which has shaped him than from within himself. There was a time when it seemed as though, in pursuing his course, Galsworthy was indeed on the threshold of a new kind of tragic theatre adapted to suit the demands of an age different in outlook and in circumstances from the ancient Athenian and the Elizabethan. Now, however, we must confess that he did not succeed in reaching his goal, and that, in general, the prose realistic stage must perforce abandon

all hope of approaching the range of tragedy. Tragedy requires
a metaphysical vision, not an attitude economic and material; and
for its expression the intensity and penetration of verse are well-
nigh essential. Tragedy bases itself upon emotion; ordinary prose
dialogue inevitably fails when it essays to explore the passions.
This failure finds clear demonstration in Galsworthy's plays
through his employment of one particular device. In *Justice* the
silent scene of Falder's cell which so startled audiences in 1910
had every excuse, since the author's object could be achieved
only by a visual presentation of the prisoner in his complete seg-
regation from his fellows; but the many silent scenes or episodes
in others of his dramas, instead of effectively expressing by action
what could not be given in words, are in fact confessions of the
total inadequacy of the prose medium. Because he cannot discover words within this medium to convey the emotions he
wishes to stimulate, his plays tend to close upon stage directions.
In *The Fugitive* we read:

> The blond and dark gentlemen have slipped from the room; and
> out of the supper party's distant laughter comes suddenly a long
> shrill: "Gone away!" And the sound of the horn playing the seven
> last notes of the old song: "This day a stag must die!" From the
> last note of all the sound flies up to an octave higher, sweet and
> thin, like a spirit passing, till it is drowned once more in laughter.
> The YOUNG MAN has covered his eyes with his hands; ARNAUD is
> crossing himself fervently; the LANGUID LORD stands gazing, with
> one of the dropped gardenias twisted in his fingers; and the woman,
> bending over CLARE, kisses her forehead.

In *The Mob* it is:

> Then begins a scared swaying out towards the window. Some one
> turns out the lights, and in the darkness the crowd fast melts
> away. The body of MORE lies in the gleam from a single Chinese
> lantern. Muttering the words: "Poor devil! He kept his end up
> anyway!" the CHIEF STUDENT picks from the floor a little aban-
> doned Union Jack and lays it on MORE'S breast. Then he, too,
> turns, and rushes out.
> And the body of MORE lies in the streak of light; and the noises
> in the street continue to rise.

And in A *Family Man*:

> While he is doing this the door from the hall is opened quietly, and MRS BUILDER enters without his hearing her. She has a work-bag in her hand. She moves slowly to the table, and stands looking at him. Then going up to the curtains she mechanically adjusts them, and still keeping her eyes on BUILDER, comes down to the table and pours out his usual glass of whisky toddy. BUILDER, who has become conscious of her presence, turns in his chair as she hands it to him. He sits a moment motionless, then takes it from her, and squeezes her hand. MRS BUILDER goes silently to her usual chair below the fire, and taking out some knitting begins to knit. BUILDER makes an effort to speak, does not succeed, and sits drawing at his pipe.

"Builder makes an effort to speak, does not succeed"—this statement in itself might be taken as a motto expressing the dramatic impotence of the realistic prose medium; it is not Galsworthy's fault that he cannot convey in words the emotion intended to be aroused by these scenes; the fault lies in the form itself, and all the playwrights who have adopted it have been compelled to bow to its limitations.

Of these playwrights there were many during the early years of the century. Harley Granville-Barker began somewhat earlier than Galsworthy, his first play, *The Weather Hen*, written in collaboration with Berte Thomas, having ben produced in 1899, and his first important work, *The Marrying of Ann Leete*, in 1901. *The Voysey Inheritance* followed in 1905, *Waste* in 1907, and *The Madras House* in 1910. In each of these a dominant social problem has been taken for the theme, but Granville-Barker differs from Galsworthy in his attempt to analyse the sentiments and passions of his characters. Where Galsworthy's mind is intent mainly upon the problem itself, Granville-Barker always displays an interest in the inner life of his persons. Perhaps, when we consider his *Prunella* (1904, written with Laurence Housman) and *The Harlequinade* (1913, written with Dion Clayton Calthrop), we might almost be prepared to believe that, had he been born at a different period, he might most happily have found expression for his talents in the writing of poetic plays. This inner quality in his work is indicated even in the early *Marrying of Ann Leete*, especially if we compare its treatment with Bernard Shaw's handling of virtually the same concept. The life force, of which Shaw speaks so often, is enshrined in the hearts of George and Ann Leete, who look with disgust upon the convention and hypocrisy surrounding the social culture of the time. In contrast with them we are introduced to Lady Cottesham, an elder sister, whose marriage of convenience has brought nothing but misery and soul-barrenness. The two younger people strike out against the domination of convention. George is the first to find a will of his own. Stepping from the highbred and somewhat vulgar surroundings in which he has been reared, he actually makes himself a rival to John Abud, the gardener, for the love of Dolly Crowe, a common farmer's girl. He is successful in his wooing, and, in the midst of universal execration, he marries her. Ann, meanwhile, feels the spirit of revolt burning in her breast. She is destined to wed the vacuous Lord John Carp, and it seems as if she will be dragged into a loveless marriage such as will please her father, when suddenly her whole being is illuminated. John Abud comes to bring the news that George's wife has brought a child into the world. What happens nobody can tell, but light flashes into Ann's heart, and, forgetful of the eminently desirable Lord John Carp, forgetful of parental wishes, she scandalizes every one by requesting the gardener to marry her. She has found her mate and she is freed.

This play, as is evident, has about it a touch of fancifulness, Granville-Barker's first essay in depicting "the secret life." At moments we might imagine that we are wandering in the dim-set garden of Prunella's dream-house, even while the settings and the characters are placed within an exact historical environment. In *The Voysey Inheritance* once more we come upon a theme similar to one of Shaw's. *Mrs Warren's Profession* deals fundamentally with the same problem as that which Edward Voysey had to face. He is an idealist, and he hates his father's business and business methods. When his father dies and he is left with an inheritance which seems to him little else than misery, he is confronted with a difficulty similar to that which confronted Vivie Warren. Granville-Barker's play emphasizes—not with one mighty sledge-hammer stroke, but by a series of mallet tappings

—the sense of crushing, belittling imprisonment which he, along
with other dramatists, felt in the life of his day, the seeming
futility of higher ideals, the desire for freedom, the passionate
spirit of revolt. The answer which he gives to his problem, however, takes the form of a compromise. Beatrice Voysey has battled
out her own way to seeming liberty and has succeeded only in
hardening her feelings, in making coarse her inner nature. In the
struggle her soul has been seared. Obviously the author's real
sentiments are given to Alice Maitland, who, standing beside and
comforting the broken Edward Voysey, pleads for no extreme
course. She sees as plainly as the others the misery and the
squalor and the crass barrenness around, but, unlike the rest, she
divines, clear-sightedly, that society will take its toll of any who
strive too ardently against it. The solution, therefore, has about it
an element of infinite sadness.

In Waste, perhaps, Granville-Barker draws nearest to Galsworthy. The problem is that of the woman with no motherly
instincts faced by the philoprogenitive man. Fascinated by the
outward beauty of Amy O'Connell, Henry Trebell, a brilliant
young politician, falls in love with her. She is to have a child, but,
unable to face the duties of motherhood, seeks illicitly to destroy
it. The operation proves fatal both to herself and to her unborn
baby. Meanwhile her action brings disaster to Trebell. He is on
the eve of great political advancement, but Amy's folly causes
him to be socially ostracized. He is faced by cold looks, and his
advance is stopped. The loss of the child of whom he had thought
so much, and the blow to his political career, prove fatal to him.
He sinks into despondency and despair, and in a moment of
extreme misery commits suicide. While, however, in some ways
the play reminds us of Galsworthy's style, in many respects it is
wholly antagonistic to it. Galsworthy has little interest in sex
themes as such; and in this play there is little or no appearance
of these social forces which Galsworthy made his heroes. Fundamentally, it is a domestic drama with Trebell as an individual
hero. It is he who dominates the entirety of the action.

The Madras House is a much more complex play than any of
the others, involving a greater number of prominent types in its
folds. The Huxtable household at Denmark Hill introduces us to

the slightly rebellious Julia and Jane, the more rebellious Philip, the conventional Mrs Huxtable, the miserable Mrs Madras, and the socially impossible Constantine. Nor is this the only field of action. Another sphere of interest is concerned with the firm of Roberts and Huxtable, with its prim Miss Chancellor and its rebellious Miss Yates, typical of a whole world of life independent of Denmark Hill, yet fatally linked to it. *The Madras House*, along with *The Voysey Inheritance*, is an indictment of certain spheres of modern life, and the indictment should, as Granville-Barker wished, cause us to think and ponder. The free independence of a Constantine Madras may win for its possessor a certain modified liberty, but that liberty after all, is selfish. The higher idealism of a Philip can do naught against the deeply entrenched and heavily fortified forces of social custom and of social prejudice. Here some of Galsworthy's invisible presences come to tinge the drama with their darkened shapes.

Apart from translations of some Spanish and other dramas, Granville-Barker's last important play was *The Secret Life* (1923), and its title, together with its strange mixture of naturalistic and enigmatically symbolic dialogue, serves to show us that his theatre, although intimately bound to the characteristic dramatic development of the period, is in fact a thing of its own. From one point of view he may be seen as one who has carried the realistic style much farther than Galsworthy and others were doing; his plays seem, even more than the others, to be excerpts from life. The curtain rises, and we might think we were actually and not fictionally in the drawing-rooms of upper-middle-class society. Yet from another point of view we realize that the impression is an impression merely. Granville-Barker did not possess the genius of a Chekhov, but independently he was aiming in the direction taken by the Russian master. Galsworthy belongs to the tradition which produced *The Pillars of Society*, Granville-Barker comes nearer to that which gave us *The Seagull*.

With this in our minds, it may be proper here to consider some of the early writings of John Masefield before passing to a brief survey of other dramatists of the realistic school. Masefield is a poet, yet the power of the new school was sufficiently strong to persuade him, in his two most important plays, to abandon verse and deal with 'ordinary' characters. Of these two works, *The Tragedy of Nan* (1908) is unquestionably the one which deserves the greater attention, both because of its intrinsic value and because of the light it throws upon this whole area of endeavour. Masefield's title is specific: he seeks to compose a 'tragedy' and at the same time he selects for his central figure a common rustic girl with the familiar name of Nan. She herself is the child of a man who, before the action of the play begins, had been hanged for stealing a sheep. Stained by this disgrace, she lives a social outcast in the house of her uncle, Pargetter. She falls in love with the sensual, selfish Dick Gurvil, but her imagined happiness is shattered by the persons with whom she is surrounded—the ego-centred lover, the wearisomely weak Pargetter, the cruel Mrs Pargetter—so that eventually she takes her own life amid the waters of the Severn bore. It is particularly interesting here to observe that deliberately Masefield has set his action in the past, thus giving a slight touch of strangeness to his story, that he has associated this action, not with the ordinary in nature, but with the extraordinary, and that in the introduction of the old Gaffer, with his half-crazed mutterings, he has sought to find an opportunity for the employment of speech which goes beyond the range of the conversational. In all of this he is indirectly giving judgment: the tragic spirit needs for its flourishing something out of the common both in general atmosphere and in dialogue. And in all of this, too, there is a lesson: despite the excellencies of Masefield's scenes and the fine simplicity with which he has handled his story, *The Tragedy of Nan* has not been able to retain its hold upon us. It seemed a masterpiece in 1908, but now its weaknesses are only too apparent. When we read or listen to the Gaffer's speeches, it is not their force but their inadequacy that impresses us:

> *Gaffer.* The salmon-fishers'll lose their nets to-night. The tide'll sweep them away. O, I've known it. It takes the nets up miles. Miles. They find 'em high up. Beyond Glorster. Beyond 'Artpury. Girt golden flay-flowers over 'em. And apple-trees a-growing over 'em. Apples of red and apples of gold. They fall into the water. The water be still there, where the apples fall. The nets 'ave apples in them.

Nan. And fish, gaffer?
Gaffer. Strange fish. Strange fish out of the sea.
Nan. Yes. Strange fish indeed, gaffer. A strange fish in the nets to-morrow. A dumb thing. Knocking agen the bridges. Something white. Something white in the water.

The intensity and the wonder of tragedy cannot be found here, and once more we recognize that it is not the author but the form in which he works which is responsible.

Neither *The Campden Wonder* (1907) nor *Mrs Harrison* (1906) calls for individual attention, but the later *Melloney Holtspur* (1923) merits consideration. Just as in the earlier play Masefield distanced the action and strove to find an opportunity for speech out of the familiar run, so here he has turned to the supernatural. And again the failure, together with its cause, is patent. The setting is contemporary, concentrating on the love of Lenda Copshrews and Bunny Mento, and this 'real' story is bound up with the ghost-forms of Melloney Holtspur and her faithless sweetheart Lonny. Although the introduction of the supernatural had given grandeur to many tragedies of former times, its introduction into this environment has no power over us. We can neither believe in these ghosts nor credit the association of the spirit-world with a world of Copshrews and Bunnys. Masefield's strength finds ample expression in the dialogue, but he is a poet struggling against, and not with, the current.

Many other playwrights of these years pursued the various styles established by the authors whose works have been briefly examined—Pinero's pathos, Jones' broader problems, Galsworthy's social forces, Granville-Barker's inner sentiments, Masefield's tragic search, all of these may be seen reflected in the plays of their contemporaries and immediate successors. Alfred Sutro thus mingles something of Pinero's interests with those of Jones. In *John Glayde's Honour* (1907) his story concentrates upon a strong businessman who discovers that his wife's affections are being alienated by an attractive artist; in *The Builder of Bridges* (1908) the theme is that of a great engineer who falls in love with a girl although he is aware that her first object in approaching him was to catch him in her snare. The general style is Pinero's, the treatment of the strong, silent lover is Jones'.

A more individual approach was that made by St John Hankin, who, before his early death in 1909, produced four interesting plays, *The Two Mr Wetherbys* (1903), *The Return of the Prodigal* (1905), *The Cassilis Engagement* (1907), and *The Last of the De Mullins* (1908). In these he has for the most part avoided the 'tragic' attitude, and insofar we feel that he was engaged in an endeavour more in accord with the realistic dramatic form. Fundamentally, Hankin's writings are plays of ideas. He has a greater interest in man as a social animal than as an individual; he has no light to throw on separate men and women; his stage figures seem to be rather invented by his intellect than created out of his imaginative perceptions; at the same time he possesses a keen awareness of society's foibles and errors. Always he appears to stand cynically aloof, the man who thinks (although not deeply) and not the man who feels; and perhaps resultant from this his pictures of life often seem to be manufactured instead of faithfully observed.

The contrived nature of his situations finds illustration in *The Two Mr Wetherbys*, which depends upon an almost mathematically conceived contrast between the 'good' Mr Wetherby living a conventional existence with a wife who proposes to leave him and whom he seeks to keep, and the 'bad' Mr Wetherby living an unconventional existence and somewhat embarrassed, after he has long broken his matrimonial ties, when his wife proposes to return. Something of the same contrast forms the basic design of *The Return of the Prodigal*—the cynical rascal who, having squandered his patrimony, returns impenitent to the parental home and the worthy but eminently dull-minded brother whose inadequacies are revealed when set against the prodigal's amoral charm. Indeed, this design even appears in Hankin's best play, *The Cassilis Engagement*, although there its lines are more subtly drawn. Young Geoffrey Cassilis shocks his mother by announcing that he has become engaged to a lower-class girl, Ethel Borridge; instead of trying to persuade him to break this off, Lady Cassilis insists on inviting the fiancée and her atrociously vulgar mother to a lengthy stay in the country. Inevitably, Geoffrey begins to realize his mistake, but his sense of honour prevents him from taking any action; happily for him, however, Ethel finds herself unutterably desolate in this rural life away from the city's bright lights, and she casts him off. The play is interesting, but its construction is so exact that its artificiality cannot be ignored. All has been sacrificed to the idea, and even the best passages of dialogue are intellectually keyed to that idea's elucidation. Here, for instance, is a middle-aged, sensible roué speaking to Ethel:

> *Warrington.* What does Mrs Borridge do?
> *Ethel.* Lady Marchmont looks after her. I believe she gets a kind of pleasure in leading her on and watching her make a fool of herself. Old cat! And mother sees nothing. She's as pleased with herself as possible. She's actually made Lady Marchmont promise to come and stay with us in London!
> *Warrington.* Bravo, Mrs Borridge!
> *Ethel.* So I sit here in the drawing-room with a book or the newspaper and I'm bored! Bored!
> *Warrington.* And Geoffrey?
> *Ethel.* He doesn't seem to notice. If I say anything to him about it he just says I'm not *well*! He's very kind and tries to find things to amuse me, but it's a strain. And so it goes on day after day. Heigh ho! [*A short silence.*
> *Warrington.* Well, my dear, I admire your courage.
> *Ethel* [*surprised*]. What do you mean?
> *Warrington.* A lifetime of this! Year in year out. Till you can yawn yourself decently into your grave.

The common fault of the play of ideas is to permit the dialogue to include no single sentence which does not help to advance the intellectual concept. Even in Hankin's more ambitious, and in a sense more mature, *The Last of the De Mullins* the same almost painful planning is evident. The soul-destroying forces of social tradition are hammered home by the contrast between the conventionally minded Hesther, who, living at home, has lost all vitality and spirit, and the unconventional Janet, who has cast off the fetters even to the extent of having borne an illegitimate child. The dreary picture which Hankin has drawn for us, instead of vividly impressing itself on our minds, appears blurred and lacking in all power to stimulate.

Constantly, in these realistic dramas, we encounter the peculiar clash between the attempt to record the speech and actions of real life and the imposition on incidents and characters of the authors' intellectually contrived structure. Hankin lacked human sympathy, and perhaps we are not surprised to find this duality in his plays; but it is by no means confined to his works. Elizabeth Baker (Mrs J. E. Allaway), for instance, possesses a sensitivity and perception which Hankin lacks, yet her *Chains* (1909) exhibits as much contrivance as his plays. Here the milieu is lower middle-class—the little suburban household of Charley Wilson, his moderately contented, unimaginative wife Lily, and their lodger Tennant. This lodger, tired of life in London, is about to set off for Australia, and his few belongings have been packed for the journey. Suddenly, and to himself unexpectedly, Wilson finds himself set aglow by Tennant's decision: he feels that he is fettered, that he must seek escape. He decides to depart—and at this moment he is told that his wife expects a baby. The gates leading to freedom are closed; nothing remains but the drab surroundings and the continual daily grind at the dingy office-desk. Although this study has some perceptive intensity, its drabness well illustrates that theatrical movement during the early years of the century which played a not inconsiderable part in alienating playgoers from the stage. Akin to it in spirit is a later drama of Elizabeth Baker, *The Price of Thomas Scott* (1913), which deals with a puritanical fanatic who finds that some property he has sold was, in fact, bought by a company financing the erection of a dancing-hall. Here, too, the authoress shows her power of evoking character and her skill in organizing her scenes, but the drama must inevitably leave us with a feeling of uninspiring gloom. This was one of the "Manchester Repertory" plays, the school of dramatic writing which was being regarded by many intellectuals of the time as their Mecca; but, looking back, we can see that, despite its vigour and even excitement, the direction of this Repertory Theatre was, to a certain extent, helping to channel general interest away from the theatre instead of stimulating it.

The stress in Elizabeth Baker's work is upon circumstance and locality, and in this emphasis she was accompanied by many others. Githa Sowerby's *Rutherford and Son* (1912), for example, outwardly suggests that the authoress's chief objective lay in the presenting of characters, but as we examine the play we see that in fact the background assumes more importance for her than the inadequately penned men and women she has sketched in in front of it. The plot centres upon the glass factory which is John Rutherford's only love; for it he has hardened his soul. His sons drift away from him; he can understand neither the clergyman Richard nor the weak-willed John; when Janet, his daughter, stoops to have an affair with the works' foreman his anger blazes forth and she is banished from his house. And in the end he is beaten by his own lack of sympathy. His son John had married a girl, Mary, of sensitive feelings and acute intellect; when she is deserted by her husband, she comes to the Rutherford home, bringing her little son with her. The old man yearns to take the child and bring him up as his successor, but the playwright will permit no easy sentimental conclusion. Instead, Mary coldly forces her father-in-law to make a deal with her: she insists that the boy shall be under her care for ten years, and only then will she allow him to succeed to the management of the works. The play is well planned, and, although there is a piling on of the agony, the situations and the dialogue have an air of authenticity; what it lacks is dramatic excitement.

Somewhat akin to Elizabeth Baker in approach is Stanley Houghton. *The Younger Generation* (1910), like *The Price of Thomas Scott*, takes provincial puritanism for its theme. Here the central figure is a man name Kennion, a well-meaning parent who regards as sin anything which deviates from his own narrow code of behaviour. Shocked and wrathful when his son Arthur comes rolling back home, dead-drunk, one evening, he is forced, by a number of contrived situations, to admit that his own youthful life had not been without its wild oats. The play fails because the author has no steadily informing dramatic purpose controlling its action. At least *Chains* had been built out of one single dominant concept; *The Younger Generation* exemplifies those many 'modern' plays in which cynicism, melodramatic device, and even farcical episodes are mingled with unfortunate effect into the loosely designed structure of what, for convenience, was called a "play." *Hindle Wakes* (1912), which also deals

with the same subject of youthful revolt, is a more satisfactory
piece of work precisely because it directs its focus with greater
theatrical effectiveness. Alan Jeffcote, son of a highly moral
factory-owner, goes off for a week-end with a girl, Fanny Haw-
thorn; for him the escapade is a 'lark,' for her it is a gesture of
defiance directed against her dull, uninspiring surroundings.
Both the parents of the boy and those of the girl agree that the
two must marry, and Alan, a marrowless creature, is forced to
comply. To the horror of all, however, Fanny refuses point-blank.

> *Alan* [*shocked*]. Fanny! Is that all you cared for me?
> *Fanny.* How much more did you care for me?
> *Alan.* But it's not the same. I'm a man.
> *Fanny.* You're a man, and I was your little fancy. Well, I'm a
> woman, and *you* were *my* little fancy. You wouldn't prevent a
> woman enjoying herself as well as a man, if she takes it into her
> head?
> *Alan.* But do you mean to say that you didn't care any more for
> me than a fellow cares for any girl he happens to pick up?
> *Fanny.* Yes. Are you shocked?
> *Alan.* It's a bit thick; it is really!
> *Fanny.* You're a beauty to talk!
> *Alan.* It sounds so jolly immoral. I never thought of a girl look-
> ing at a chap like that! I made sure you wanted to marry me if
> you got the chance.

The trouble with this play, and of many others of its kind, is
that, whatever the author's skill in construction and his desire
to create character, we get the impression that the whole work
has been geared towards an intellectual, and not towards a
dramatic, objective. The conversation between Alan and Fanny,
in effect, has not been directed towards enlarging our awareness
of this pair; it is merely the conclusion to what might well have
taken shape as a social pamphlet.

And, in observing this, we are compelled to note also that the
topics dealt with in these pamphlet-dramas were curiously repeti-
tive and lacking in subtlety. Houghton's two pieces were concerned with the revolt of the younger generation; this is the theme
which, again and again and again, with wearisome echoes, we encounter in the plays of the time. Sometimes the treatment assumes

a simple domestic tone, as in Houghton's hands; sometimes it is given interesting variations, as in the *Milestones* (1912) of Arnold Bennett and Edward Knoblock; but the concept is always the same—and playgoers are apt to become bored if an identical record is played and replayed to them scratchily under different names. The 'idea,' instead of an emotional concept, is being taken by the dramatists as their moving force, and as a result, no matter how realistic their settings and dialogue may be, an impression of artificiality and 'stageyness' becomes manifest. *Change* (1913), the once widely discussed drama by John Oswald Francis, is just such another as *Milestones*; the 'idea' governing, although not animating, Basil Macdonald Hastings' *The New Sin* (1912) is that one has no right to continue living when one's decease may bring some joy and profit to others; the subject of the double moral code provides Cosmo Hamilton's *The Blindness of Virtue* (1912) with its treatise topic.

As we look back on these plays now, we cannot fail to be struck by the curious limitations restricting their sphere of dramatic observation and by the uninspired quality of their dialogue. Most of them are competently written; but competence is not enough. In most of them the authors demonstrate that they have learned the trick of recording current conversational speech forms; but these speech forms, being dull, stereotyped, and lacking in vitality, produce an atmosphere of insipidity and monotonous reiteration.

Such basic defects, or inhibitions, become amply apparent when we turn to the plays of a similar style being produced in contemporary Ireland, both north and south. Naturally, the contrast is most evident when we turn to consider the works stimulated by the establishment of the Abbey Theatre, in Dublin; but it is patent even from a glance at the Belfast dramas written by St John Ervine. In his early writings Ervine's method is strictly realistic; but he succeeds, precisely because he is an Ulsterman, in varying his themes and in presenting a richer language texture than the English dramatists, bound by an environment wherein speech had lost its peasant flavour, could ever achieve. *Mixed Marriage* (1911) may be taken as an illustration. In this play the struggle between master and man has been broadened by its association with the struggle between Catholic and Protestant. John Rainey, an Orangeman, speaks in favour of a strike which he knows is largely engineered by Catholics, but his inrooted sympathies are intensified when he discovers that his son Hugh has become engaged to a Catholic girl, Nora Murray. In a melodramatic conclusion, a riot breaks out, the soldiery arrive, and, of course, the innocent Nora falls, killed by a stray bullet. In one sense, the play is as artificially planned as dozens of contemporary English realistic plays were planned, but there is a greater complexity here, the evoking of intense passions, and the deepening of these passions by a more vivid speech than the majority of English plays could offer.

Even more effective is *Jane Clegg* (1913), another lower-middle-class drama in which an array of miserable creatures is presented to us, from the vicious and weak-willed husband and his evil genius, Munce, the "bookie," to the drearily tiresome old grandmother. In the midst of these, however, rises the figure of Jane Clegg, animated by a force beyond theirs. No idle dreamer of things impossible, no fettered woman craving for independence and adventure, she is a stern realist, staring life fully in the face, and rising to impressive moral stature in the presence of disaster. She watches her husband's fall; she looks through him and sees the meanness and the littleness of his character; and, in doing so, she comes to realize her duty. In sending this weak, depraved, cringing creature from her house she is doing the only thing possible. In that moment she assumes something which almost attains tragic tension.

With equal dramatic force Ervine has painted for us the 'tragedy' of *John Ferguson* (1915), another tale of middle-class life. The hero is a hard man, yet with a human understanding and a depth of sympathy in his nature. To save his daughter, Hannah, from a loveless marriage with James Cæsar he allows his farm to be taken from him. The strain is tremendous, but he rises superior to it, winning new strength from his losing yet victorious battle against fate. Meanwhile fresh misery has come upon him. His own daughter has been seduced by his greatest enemy, Witherow. Cæsar, weak though he is, plucks up courage to say that he will murder the villain, and goes out one night gun in hand for that purpose. In the morning he comes back, frightened and cringing, crying out that his will failed him in the darkness. But the seducer has in fact been murdered, and Cæsar is arrested. Money has come from Hannah's brother in America, and it seems as if, in spite of the terror of the preceding days, peace of a sort will come to John Ferguson's troubled spirit, when his son Andrew, who had hitherto kept silence, suddenly announces that it was he who had killed Witherow, that he cannot allow the innocent Cæsar to go to his death for him. Ferguson, after a moment of terrible doubt, agrees, and Hannah and Andrew pass out into the open bound on the terrible mission of confession.

All of these are impressive dramas, and the strength which they drew from their environment becomes apparent when we consider them in relation to such realistic peasant dramas as were called to birth by the establishment of the Irish Literary Theatre in 1899 and the setting up of the Abbey Theatre in 1903. Certainly, this Dublin stage, under the leadership of W. B. Yeats, J. M. Synge, and Lady Gregory, found its most characteristic expression in plays which, although rooted in the Irish soil, were irradiated by an imaginative approach, but some of the authors who attached themselves to it were clearly intent in doing for their own surroundings what was being done by realists elsewhere.

Out of this world came the solitary drama which, during these years, may be thought worthy of being considered as a realistic tragedy, *Riders to the Sea* (1904). The author of this play, J. M. Synge, had been wasting his time in Paris when, in 1897, Yeats encouraged him to return to Ireland. There Synge settled down amid the barren stretches of moorland and mountain on the extreme western coast; wandering over the stretches of heather and listening to the ceaseless roar of the Atlantic, he found himself seized by the concept of Nature's might; he listened to the intonations of the lonely peasants inhabiting that region, and there he discovered the basis for a new kind of dramatic speech. Out of this experience grew *Riders to the Sea*, a play grand in its majestic simplicity. The scene is a lonely sea-coast cottage. Outside the ocean roars hungrily for its toll of human lives. Within,

Maurya sits remembering with bitterness its greedy tax-gathering, remembers the father and the grandfather and the four strong sons who have perished in the wild waste of seething waters. To her one son alone is left, and he will go to the horse-fair far off on the mainland. Maurya knows what that will mean; it will mean that men will carry in to her a dead son, snatched lifeless from the waves. So it comes to pass, and darkness settles down on the lonely cottage. The sea has claimed Maurya's all.

We are here in the presence of elemental things. The sea becomes a living force, a demon hungering after men; the figures in the cottage, weak as they may be in face of the physical power of the ocean, reach greatness in their courage and grandeur. The drama is strong in its primeval intensity, the weakening force of civilization far off, distant, and unheard. The universality, the strength, the majesty, of this little work cannot too highly be praised, but these would not have taken such a hold upon us had Synge not gained a new medium in which to express his innermost feelings:

> Maurya [raising her head and speaking as if she did not see the people around her]. They're all gone now, and there isn't anything more the sea can do to me.... I'll have no call now to be up and crying and praying when the wind breaks from the south, and you can hear the surf is in the east, and the surf is in the west, making a great stir with the two noises, and they hitting one on the other. I'll have no call now to be going down and getting Holy Water in the dark nights after Samhain, and I won't care what way the sea is when the other women will be keening. [To Nora] Give me the Holy Water, Nora; there's a small sup still on the dresser.
>
> [NORA gives it to her.
>
> Maurya [drops MICHAEL'S clothes across BARTLEY'S feet, and sprinkles the Holy Water over him]. It isn't that I haven't prayed for you, Bartley, to the Almighty God. It isn't that I haven't said prayers in the dark night till you wouldn't know what I'd be saying; but it's a great rest I'll have now, and it's time, surely. It's a great rest I'll have now, and great sleeping in the long nights after Samhain, if it's only a bit of wet flour we do have to eat, and maybe a fish that would be stinking.
>
> [She kneels down again, crossing herself, and saying prayers under her breath.

Cathleen [*to an old man*]. Maybe yourself and Eamon would make a coffin when the sun rises. We have fine white boards herself bought, God help her, thinking Michael would be found, and I have a new cake you can eat while you'll be working.

The Old Man [*looking at the boards*]. Are there nails with them?

Cathleen. There are not, Colum; we didn't think of the nails.

Another Man. It's a great wonder she wouldn't think of the nails, and all the coffins she's seen made already.

Cathleen. It's getting old she is, and broken.

> [MAURYA *stands up again very slowly and spreads out the pieces of* MICHAEL'S *clothes beside the body, sprinkling them with the last of the Holy Water.*

Nora [*in a whisper to* CATHLEEN]. She's quiet now and easy; but the day Michael was drowned you could hear her crying out from this to the spring well. It's fonder she was of Michael, and would anyone have thought that?

Cathleen [*slowly and clearly*]. An old woman will be soon tired with anything she will do, and isn't it nine days herself is after crying and keening, and making great sorrow in the house?

Maurya [*puts the empty cup mouth downward on the table, and lays her hands together on* BARTLEY'S *feet*]. They're all together this time, and the end is come. May the Almighty God have mercy on Bartley's soul, and on Michael's soul, and on the souls of Sheamus and Patch, and Stephen and Shawn [*bending her head*]; and may He have mercy on my soul, Nora, and on the soul of every one is left living in the world.

> [*She pauses, and the keen rises a little more loudly from the women, then sinks away.*

Maurya [*continuing*]. Michael has a clean burial in the far north, by the grace of the Almighty God. Bartley will have a fine coffin out of the white boards, and a deep grave surely. What more can we want than that? No man at all can be living for ever, and we must be satisfied.

> [*She kneels down again, and the curtain falls slowly.*

Riders to the Sea, because of its limited scope, cannot be compared to the greater tragedies of the past, but it approaches them in spirit, achieving this communion because of the setting of the human characters against nature's stern power and because the language, based on a rich and still imaginatively vital

peasant speech, has the strength to soar, harmonizing with the
emotions evoked and giving them their expressive form. Noting
these qualities, we appreciate why the ordinary realistic drama,
inevitably for the most part restricted to urban environments,
has no hope of reaching tragic levels.

About the same time as Synge was thus engaged in drawing
strength from the Irish peasants struggling for their livelihood
on the western coast and on the Aran Islands, T. C. Murray
joined him in his effort to give dramatic shape to the realities of
Irish peasant life. *Maurice Harte* (1912) deals with thwarted
ambitions and misplaced hopes. Mrs Harte has determined that
her son Maurice shall become a priest. A well-meaning and intel-
ligent lad, but one by no means fitted for a clerical life, he tries
to persuade his mother that he cannot enter the Church, but like
a harsh shepherd she drives him back. Anxious to please her, he
studies hard, but the mental toil and stress tell on him; his mind
gives way under the agony of his seething thoughts, and he is
brought back to his home a lunatic. A similar conflict between
the old and the young provides the theme for *Birthright* (1910).
Hugh Morissey is Bat's eldest son, but the father cannot understand why he is not willing to devote himself, without any other
thoughts, to the constant labour of the farm. The younger son
Shane, a dull fellow, is just about to be sent off to America, and
his trunk stands ready packed, with his name boldly painted on
it. Hugh goes out with friends to a hurley match and to a following party, and in his absence a series of accidents occur. The
merrymaking of the players startles Bat's horse so that it
stumbles, breaks its leg, and has to be shot; a sow suddenly requires treatment and attention. Worn out with toil and watching, Bat, in terrible accents, orders Shane to substitute Hugh's
name on the trunk. On his return, Hugh finds what has been
done, accuses his brother of employing underhand tactics to get
him away from the farm, and finally makes an attack upon him.
Within a few minutes he himself is lying dead on the ground.
Although both these plays have force and intensity, neither
comes even near *Riders to the Sea* in spirit; they are sensational
where it is almost calmly inevitable; their dialogue, while effective in its own way, fails to draw from the peasant speech those

elements which Synge fashioned into a richer form of expression.

In *The Land* (1905) Padraic Colum likewise essayed to deal with the conflict between the old and the new generations, although in a less sensational manner. Murtagh Cosgar's only thoughts are of the soil which he has broken, tamed, and made fertile; his son, Matt, inspired by his sweetheart, Ellen Douras, dreams only of gay cities and the busy hum of men. What these two young people will find remains unknown, but they are eager to leave the lonely cry of the curlew, the circling flight of the plover, the lowing of the cattle for a world of imagination beyond. Off they go to America, and the ageing Cosgar is left lonely and broken. In two other plays, *The Fiddler's House* (1907; a revised version of *The Broken Soil*, 1903) and *Thomas Muskerry* (1910), Colum has tried to diversify the ordinary realistic themes by introducing characters who, because of their profession, go a little beyond the commonplace. The central figure in the first is Conn Hourican, an old fiddler and ballad-maker, who has been tended for some years by his daughter Maire. Suddenly the old man's mind begins to dream again of the horse-fairs and the tap-rooms and the excitement of the crowds, until at length Maire, although she knows that this will mean the end of their quiet life, silently hands him his fiddle and prepares to set off with him to the "feis" at Ardagh. Conn Hourican's place is taken in the other play by a blind piper Myles Gorman, whose tunes are heard as the brutal and hard-hearted Thomas Muskerry dies on a pauper's bed.

This series of realistic dramas, English and Irish, which were produced during the early years of the present century seemed at the time to be opening up a brave new world for the stage. There was a breath of real excitement in the air, and for that excitement there was real justification. Not for long years had the theatre succeeded in evoking any play so distinguished as *Riders to the Sea*, and even although it was recognized that most of the other 'tragically' inclined dramas being contributed to the stage were, in fact, devoid of the essential tragic qualities, many enthusiasts believed that out of these efforts a new kind of tragedy, adjusted to modern conditions, would be born. Books and articles lauding this sudden rebirth tumbled forth in the dozens. For those interested in the drama this was indeed a period of intellectual fervour.

Now, however, we can take a more objective view. Without doubt, Galsworthy and the various 'repertory' playwrights, Ervine and Murray, achieved much, and their plays still have real, although diminished, value. On the other hand, two things seem to be clear. The first is that the common trend of the sterner realists during those years towards the 'tragic' theme generally led them to the melodramatic and sensational. This means that the more such dramatists strove to create a new modern 'tragedy' the more they struggled against the dramatic form which they had made their own. They had been successful in depicting reality and in making their characters speak in life-like terms; and the imposition upon their realistically recorded scenes of a would-be 'tragic' concept could result only in creating an impression of artificiality: even Synge in his *Riders to the Sea* could call forth the tragic impression only within the scope of a short play. A second thing which has now become clear is that the achievement of these dramatists in moulding a realistic form of dialogue left the realistic form without the excitement which had attended it in earlier years. For audiences which had not listened to dialogue passing beyond that offered by Pinero and Jones the lines uttered by characters in the plays of Ervine and Houghton had all the virtue of novelty. But novelty soon palls, and, although the prose realistic form had come to stay, after about 1920 it had lost its primal power to stimulate.

The result of this was that, as it proceeded, the ordinary realistic drama tended to become less tense, to mingle comic episodes with serious, and to cultivate a general approach which, quite properly, steered indeterminately between 'comedy' and 'tragedy.' Concurrently, a recrudescence of the sentimental mood in the handling of both situations and characters frequently became apparent. In *A Bill of Divorcement* (1921) Clemence Dane managed, by technical skill and adroit dialogue, to produce an effective drama which concentrates upon the problem of a husband's insanity and its impress on wife and daughter; but most of her plays, despite their undoubted brilliance, show but little of enduring power, and, as in *Mariners* (written 1925–26; U.S.A., 1927), they reveal the sentimental touch particularly in those scenes wherein the presentation of an intellectual 'idea' or 'problem' intrudes upon the dramatic action. Even those playwrights, like Charles McEvoy and Ernest George, who more obviously followed on from the realists of the century's first years exhibit this tendency. The former's *The Likes of Her* (1923) and the latter's *Down Our Street* (1929) are both excellent studies of East End London life, yet it is obvious to us now that they are infused with a sentimentally conceived objective which was not immediately apparent to their original audiences.

Among the playwrights who elected to pursue the ordinary realistic path, John Van Druten won considerable distinction in the twenties and thirties. In 1928 *Young Woodley* took London by storm, and we must agree that the critical praise and the general popularity accorded to it were fully warranted. The play is well planned, with its neat, clear-cut characterization and its crisp situations, with its easily-written naturalistic dialogue. At the same time, it must be admitted that it is backward- and not forward-looking. In Van Druten's work there is vigour, skill, keen theatrical sense; at times, as in *Diversion* (1928), there is the ability to present emotional situations with dramatic impact; as in *London Wall* (1931), the naturalistic style is handled with consummate adroitness. Nevertheless, few of these plays, from the dramatization of Rebecca West's *The Return of the Soldier* (1928) down to *Old Acquaintance* (1940), seem to have the likelihood of any life beyond that of their original productions. The treatment of *London Wall* is sentimental; the characters in *There's Always Juliet* (1931), are all stock types who can do nothing but chat; *Somebody Knows* (1932) is only a psychological thriller.

Not less skilful is R. C. Sherriff, but again, despite his numerous successes, the enduring qualities are absent, and what once may have seemed forceful and bold now assumes the tinge of the sentimental. At one time almost every critic was acclaiming *Journey's End* (1928) as the masterpiece of the century, but twenty years later it had become little more than a memory or

something against which younger writers felt that they had violently to react. So, too, in another war play, *The Conquering
Hero* (1923; acted 1924) by Allan Monkhouse and in the same
author's industrial-strife drama, *First Blood* (1925), we sense how
difficult it was for the writers of these years to go beyond what
their predecessors had achieved in this particular dramatic style.
In the former play Monkhouse's characters are deeply and
vividly incised, and his general concept has been boldly
imagined; yet if it were revived to-day, many of its scenes would
seem artificial. *First Blood* is boldly planned, but its juxtaposition
of the 'men,' represented by Jack Livsey and Tom Eden, and of
the 'masters,' represented by Sir Samuel Stott, appears to us
merely an imitation of the situation in *Strife*, while the death of
Phyllis at the close reminds us of Nora's death by a stray bullet
at the conclusion of *Mixed Marriage*; and whereas Galsworthy
and Ervine escaped the sentimental because they were imagining
these situations virtually for the first time, both situations are
coloured, in Monkhouse's play, by that mood.

Play after play conceived in this strain was presented during
the twenties and thirties, many of them winning temporary
esteem but few with the power to hold later attention. Among
the war plays H. B. Trevelyan's *The Dark Angel* (1928) has some
effective scenes, but its overall plan suggests intellectual contrivance. In a prologue, the romantic Kitty is shown spending
the night with Hilary Trent and pledging him eternal devotion.
We then pass over several years, and find Kitty, believing Hilary
dead and yet dutifully clinging to his memory, discovering a new
devotion for Gerald Shannon. At this very moment, Hilary,
blinded, makes a reappearance and magnanimously releases her
from her oath. Closely akin in form, W. Chetham Strode's
Sometimes Even Now (1933) traces the career from 1915 to 1932
of a girl who has borne a child to a soldier killed in the war. Of
greater distinction, perhaps because it deals with a male cast,
is J. R. Ackerley's finely controlled *The Prisoners of War* (1925)
in which, interestingly, emphasis upon action is substituted by
emphasis upon character. Mordaunt Shairp has taken a somewhat similar course in his psychological study, *The Offence*
(1925), and in his essay in abnormal sex relations, *The Green*

Bay Tree (1933); Edward Percy pens his striking dialect drama, *If Four Walls Told* (1922); Halcott Glover, in *The Second Round* (1923) and *God's Amateur* (1928), seeks to give to the realistic form a greater complexity; pathos and sentimental emotions are deliberately exploited by H. M. Harwood in *Cynara* (1930; written in collaboration with R. Gore-Brown) and in *The Old Folks at Home* (1933), by Gertrude Jennings in *Family Affairs* (1934), and by C. L. Anthony (Dodie Smith) in *Autumn Crocus* (1931) and *Dear Octopus* (1938); and these playwrights are accompanied by numerous other authors, such as Hermon Ould with *The Light Comedian* (1928), Aimée and Philip Stuart with *The Cat's Cradle* (1926) and *Clara Gibbings* (1928), and E. M. Delafield with *To See Ourselves* (1930).

If the sentimental mood dominates in many of these plays others show a distinct bias towards the melodramatic—for, as has been seen, the realists are often driven, in an endeavour to give a dramatic interest to their drab themes, to fall back upon exploitation of the sensational. *Love on the Dole* (1935) by Walter Greenwood and Ronald Gow exhibits this quality, and it is clearly marked in the plays of Emlyn Williams—*Night Must Fall* (1935), *The Corn is Green* (1938), onward to *The Morning Star* (1941), *The Druid's Rest* (1943), and *The Wind of Heaven* (1945). Melodramatic episode is piled on melodramatic episode in W. S. Maugham's *For Services Rendered* (1932); much the same quality enters into A. J. Cronin's *Jupiter Laughs* (1940) and into Keith Winter's *The Rats of Norway* (1933) *The Shining Hour* (1934), and *Old Music* (1937).

Occasionally, we meet with plays which suggest that an attempt is being made to distil some fresh virtue from the realistic form, but it is hard to discern any which effect a stimulating shift in orientation. C. K. Munro thus experiments in *The Rumour* (1922) with a kind of cinematic technique without, however, achieving more than a temporary success. In *Touch Wood* (1934) Dodie Smith seeks, in her exploration of love affairs at the New Caledonian Hotel in the Scots Highlands, to enrich the psychological content of the realistic drama, but again without making deep impact on the stage. Although perhaps Ronald Mackenzie's early death robbed the theatre of a highly promis-

ing talent, the plays he has left us hardly justify the high praise
once given to them. *Musical Chairs* (1931), interestingly set in
contemporary Poland, despite its subtleties, is concerned with
the old theme of the conflict between the amoral artist and the
practical man, and in such a figure as that of the American
Samuel Pagett the author shows that, like many of his fellows, he
is prepared to fall back upon caricature in the midst of a supposedly realistic environment. Coincidences and melodramatic
devices take seriously from the impression intended to be created
in *The Maitlands* (1934).

3. THE COMIC, THE FANTASTIC, AND THE HISTORICAL

Fortunately, such essays in the more serious kind of realistic play
were accompanied throughout these decades by lively essays in
the sphere of comedy; indeed, this period witnessed not only a
renaissance of the comedy of manners but also the creation of
certain comic styles distinct from those which had been familiar
in the past, virtual innovations.

No one can deny that the dramatist who stands as a kind of
angular and erratically poised colossus over the whole theatre
world from the last years of the nineteenth century on to 1940
and even beyond is George Bernard Shaw. True, Shaw started as
an Ibsen-idolator, as an exponent of realism and as a determined
inculcator of the play of ideas. *Widowers' Houses* in 1892 was
an attack directed at the evils of the slums; *Mrs Warren's Profession* in 1898 similarly was aimed to expose the evils of prostitu-
tion. There can be no doubt but that in these and other dramas
he was concerned with using the stage as a platform for social
propaganda. Nevertheless, even at the very beginning of his
career, when he was most influenced by the continental realistic
playwrights, he was constantly engaged in penning scenes which
were not only different from those in most of the dramas which
we have just been considering but were in fact utterly opposed to
them.

Shaw's essential qualities have recently been defined by a critic
as "Augustan and Anglo-Irish," and the definition in itself indi-

cates an awareness of the distinct position which he occupied in the theatre of his time. The term "Augustan" reminds us that, whatever he may have said about his own work, he deliberately deviated from the realistic-naturalistic cult so solemnly followed by his more serious companions. His dialogue does not reproduce the tones, the rhythms, and the vocabulary of ordinary speech; it is a highly polished instrument which most closely resembles the piercing and polished periods of Swift and some other prose-writers of his time. A close examination of his sentences will show how he has built his own characteristic form of utterance upon their stylistic devices, just as it will also show with what care he has selected words which by their mere sounds as well as by their meanings are designed to make his concepts clearly per-ceptible and, still more importantly, to render his dialogue dramatically effective. Similarly, the term "Anglo-Irish" may be taken to indicate that in his plays reside qualities, often contra-dictory, which give them a force quite outside that aimed at by the ordinary realistic playwrights.

This demands some further comment. The best way of con-sidering Shaw would appear to be to think of him not as one single author but as three authors working in collaboration. One of these might be described as the social propagandist, the man who would like to make each of his dramas a clearly wrought essay on some problem leading towards a carefully conceived con-clusion; the second might be described also as a man of ideas but in a different sense of that term, the man who derives just such delight in contemplating ideas for their own sakes as another creative author might take in contemplating human characters, the man who has the power and the desire to give as effective expression to these ideas as is given by the ordinary dramatist to the persons whom he brings on the stage, the man, indeed, whom Shaw himself has depicted in the Aubrey of *Too True to Be Good* (1932). And, finally, the third collaborator might be described as an almost impish creature constantly bubbling over with a sense of fun which he constantly seeks to express in dramatic terms. Out of the operation of these three arise the Shavian comedies. If we restrict ourselves to viewing him as a dramatist of ideas in the narrow sense of the phrase we shall be doing wrong to what he characteristically had to offer; if we object that his dramatic persons do not live we shall be closing our eyes to what was one of his prime virtues, the ability to make ideas live; and, obviously, if we consider merely the exhibition of his pregnant sense of fun we shall be denying the deeper qualities in his dramatic work.

So far as the social ideas are concerned, the Shavian feature which is most obvious and which has attracted most attention is the way in which his agile mind by twists and turns has given to each of his problems an original answer. It must, of course, be acknowledged that some of those answers are not of very much use: to a certain extent, his action in leaving money in his will for the devising of a better alphabet is kin to the conclusions in some at least of his plays. Nevertheless, the originality of his approach means that his dramas of ideas have at least the delight of the odd and the unexpected. Another dramatist writing a drama on the theme of *Widowers' Houses* would have had much to say concerning the cruelty and callousness of landlords, and he would have depressed us with realistically reported scenes of slum life; Shaw dismisses the landlords and irradiates his action with plentiful scenes of mirth. Another dramatist engaged on the theme of *Mrs Warren's Profession* would have offered us much of pathos, plenty of sentimentalism; Shaw gaily declares that sentimentalism itself lies at the root of the evil. In *Arms and the Man* (1894) the chocolate soldier becomes the hero; in *Candida* (1895) the heroine elects to stay with the weaker man, not the almost effeminate æsthetic young poet but the vigorous and self-opinionated preacher; Napoleon in *The Man of Destiny* (1897) is shown as an ordinary captain, easily attracted by a pair of bold eyes, Cleopatra in *Cæsar and Cleopatra* (1899) as a kittenish girl tyrannized over by an old nurse, and Cæsar as an often-puzzled gentleman; the woman is revealed as the huntress in *Man and Superman* (1903) and Don Juan-Tanner as her poor victim. In this last, and perhaps best-known, Shavian drama we might have expected the gentle, respectable and poetically minded Octavius to be the heroine's choice, but it is the revolutionary freethinker who has been marked out despite all his protests:

Octavius. I cannot write without inspiration. And nobody can give me that except Ann.

Tanner. Well, hadn't you better get it from her at a safe distance? Petrarch didn't see half as much of Laura, nor Dante of Beatrice, as you see of Ann now; and yet they wrote first-rate poetry—at least, so I'm told. They never exposed their idolatry to the test of domestic familiarity; and it lasted them to their graves. Marry Ann; and at the end of a week you'll find no more inspiration in her than in a plate of muffins.

Octavius. You think I shall tire of her!

Tanner. Not at all: you don't get tired of muffins. But you don't find inspiration in them; and you won't in her when she ceases to be a poet's dream and becomes a solid eleven-stone wife. You'll be forced to dream about somebody else; and then there will be a row.

Octavius. This sort of talk is no use, Jack. You don't understand. You have never been in love.

Tanner. I! I have never been out of it. Why, I am in love even with Ann. But I am neither the slave of love or its dupe. Go to the bee, thou poet: consider her ways and be wise. By Heaven, Tavy, if women could do without our work, and we ate their children's bread instead of making it, they would kill us as the spider kills her mate or as the bees kill the drone. And they would be right if we were good for nothing but love.

In the end Tanner is captured. Ann marries him even as he protests solemnly that he is not a happy man. Nor is the play without its fantastic elements. Tanner and Straker are captured by some brigands as they motor over the mountains, and in the evening, as we listen to Mendoza's nonsensical rimes:

> O wert thou, Louisa,
> The wife of Mendoza,
> Mendoza's Louisa, Louisa Mendoza,
> How blest were the life of Louisa's Mendoza!
> How painless his longing of love for Louisa!

we fall asleep, and dream of a place where there is "no sky, no peaks, no light, no sound, no time nor space, utter void." We are in hell, conversing with Don Juan (who is startlingly like Jack Tanner), the statue which caused his death, and the devil. Don Juan is the embodiment of the intellectual philosophy of life. Reason for him is predominant:

That is why intellect is so unpopular. But to Life, the force behind the Man, intellect is a necessity, because without it he blunders into death. Just as Life, after ages of struggle, evolved that wonderful bodily organ the eye, so that the living organism could see where it was going and what was coming to help or threaten it, and thus avoid a thousand dangers that formerly slew it, so it is evolving to-day a mind's eye that shall see, not the physical world, but the purpose of Life, and thereby enable the individual to work for that purpose instead of thwarting and baffling it by setting up shortsighted personal aims as at present. Even as it is, only one sort of man has ever been happy, has ever been universally respected among all the conflicts of interests and illusions . . . the philosophic man: he who seeks in contemplation to discover the inner will of the world, in invention to discover the means of fulfilling that will, and in action to do that will by the so-discovered means.

Throughout the entire range of Shaw's mighty dramatic output this incisiveness and individuality of thought is never lacking. It transforms the melodramatic structure of The Devil's Disciple (1897) just as it irradiates the conflict of religion and materialism in Major Barbara (1905), the questions of medicine in The Doctor's Dilemma (1906), and the extraordinarily diverse array of issues which gave us Getting Married (1908), Androcles and the Lion (1913), Pygmalion (1913), Back to Methuselah (1919–20), St Joan (1923), on to the strange plays of his latter years.

Awareness and appreciation of the 'ideas' presented in these dramas, however, must not cause us to ignore the other qualities which give Shaw's theatrical essays their peculiar nature. It is easy to say that Shaw is not a profound exponent of human character: even with such persons as Candida and St Joan, where he came nearest to offering us stage figures of living warmth, he finds himself outstripped by many other playwrights less distinguished than himself. At first this might seem to suggest that he lacked the prime skill demanded of the dramatic author; but what we need to do is to realize that he brought something entirely new into the theatre and that, in doing so, he amply made good the lack of vital human characterization in his works. The supreme power of the dramatist ordinarily is that of being able, while preserving an overall, godlike control of his entire dramatic universe, to enter into individual characters and to make these express themselves in words which such characters in real life could never have found for themselves. Thus, for example, the continuing appeal of Shakespeare's dramas derives to a large extent from his ability to be not merely the heroes but also all the persons whom he has brought upon the stage: when Othello speaks, the author and the character have merged into one, but the author and the character likewise merge into one when Iago is uttering his lines. What Shaw possessed was the ability to make ideas and points of view his own in a similar manner; and that he himself recognized this quality in himself finds clear expression in the words which he has put into the mouth of his Aubrey—a character who must certainly be regarded as, in part at least, a self-portait. "I am a born preacher, not a pleader," says this man:

> The theory of legal procedure is that if you set two liars to expose one another, the truth will emerge. That would not suit me. I greatly dislike being contradicted; and the only place where a man is safe from contradiction is in the pulpit. I detest argument: it is unmannerly, and obscures the preacher's message. Besides, the law is too much concerned with crude facts and too little with spiritual things; and it is in spiritual things that I am interested; they alone call my gift into full play ...
> My gift is divine: it is not limited by my petty personal convictions. It is a gift of lucidity as well as of eloquence. Lucidity is one of the most precious of gifts: the gift of the teacher: the gift of explanation. I can explain anything to anybody; and I love doing it. I feel I must do it if only the doctrine is beautiful and subtle and exquisitely put together. I may feel instinctively that it is the rottenest nonsense. Still, if I can get a moving dramatic effect out of it, and preach a really splendid sermon about it, my gift takes possession of me and obliges me to sail in and do it.

If we apply this to his plays, Shaw's almost unique power finds its source. When some one of his persons is speaking, it is the idea within the man and not the man's nature which grips the dramatist's imagination, and to this character he offers his own gift of lucidity. When another person speaks, Shaw generously offers to him also his own "gift of explanation," the same lucidity and sense of conviction. This means that in his greater plays two things come together and sometimes clash—the central 'Shavian' idea and the ideas expressed with conviction and fervour by diverse persons within the drama. In *Androcles and the Lion* the 'idea' of muscular Christianity, the 'idea' of meek Christianity, the 'idea' of cultured paganism, all receive full expression, and while Ferrovius, Androcles, and the Emperor are speaking we feel that to the enunciation of the intellectual concepts of each the author has given complete power of persuasion. In *St Joan*, similarly, the 'ideas' of the various persons are all presented with vigorous force, so that each of them, considered in isolation, might appear to be alone worthy of acceptance. As a result of this, there sometimes arises in his plays a kind of dichotomy, and the dichotomy may be seen revealed in the conjunction of the plays themselves and their prefaces. As a dramatist gifted with this power of what Aubrey calls "preaching," Shaw occasionally finds himself producing a play the end impression of which does not quite agree with the central 'idea' from which he started; accordingly the accompanying preface takes shape, not simply as a background study of the material and concepts out of which the drama was born, but as a pronouncement of the central idea which had become lost in the dramatic action. We may, perhaps, see a further extension of this in the well-known epilogue to *St Joan*—not an integral part of the play but an attachment at the end put there for the purpose of stressing an 'idea' which, in fact, may be viewed as opposed to the general impression created by the dramatic action.

The third chief quality of Shaw's plays consists in their sense of fun. In the theatre there had already been developed many kinds of comedy, from farce through the presentation of humours on to the satirical and the effervescently witty, and elements taken from all of these certainly are to be found included in Shaw's style; but it is virtually impossible to discover any dramatic author before him whose characteristic approach was fundamentally based upon a delight in the ludicrous for its own sake. And this sense of fun which continually irradiates his scenes is essentially theatrical in character, testifying to the fact that, however much Shaw liked to pose as a thinker and however actively he applied himself to the study of economics and sociology, he always was and remained basically a dramatist. There may be justification for those who essay to examine Shaw's thought and philosophy; but it is not upon his philosophy that his reputation will rest. That reputation will assuredly be based upon an awareness of his dramatic virtues—his incisive prose style, his almost unique skill in making ideas walk the stage like living characters, and his cultivation of a kind of comedy distinctively his own.

From the end of the nineteenth century on through the first decades of the twentieth, the Anglo-Irish Shaw was companioned by his close neighbour and friend, the Anglo-Scots Sir James Barrie. Utterly different in temperament, in outlook upon life, and in creative style, these two men agreed in one particular respect. As a playwright, Shaw was essentially an anti-realistic; no doubt he himself would have energetically denied this, but his plays clearly demonstrate the truth of the statement; his most characteristic works, those in which we feel that he is moving with greatest ease and assurance, are set in historical or fantastic environments—*The Devil's Disciple, Arms and the Man, Cæsar and Cleopatra, St Joan, Back to Methuselah, In Good King Charles's Golden Days, Too True to Be Good*—and even in the plays with contemporary backgrounds the characters and their surroundings are invested with an atmosphere of the unreal, even of the symbolic; *Heartbreak House* (1919) by no means stands unique among his dramas. And similarly it is in the sphere of the fantastic that Barrie finds his ideal world; many of his works may apparently be set in a real environment, but even in these the author seeks every possibility of finding an escape. Apart from this, the two men share to a certain extent a common sense of the comic. Shaw's ebullient outbursts of fun seem almost boyish and adolescent compared with Barrie's more mature and gentler whimsicality; but deep down the fun and the whimsicality have roots in common. One feels that these two playwrights can often find amusement and delight in the same kinds of life's oddities.

Certainly, Barrie's sentimentalism appears to set up a great barrier between them, but even here we must be careful before we leap too rapidly towards definite conclusions. In his plays Shaw was constantly making fun of, or was more seriously attacking, sentimental attitudes; but the sentimentalism he disliked was what might be called the unconscious or stereotyped sentimental attitude which so frequently intruded, and still intrudes, into realistic plays. Barrie's sentimentalism was of an entirely different sort; it was conscious, deliberate, an attitude indulged in, not because of a surface skimming over the darker sides of life, but because of a sad contemplation of man's follies and errors. We may call this attitude escapist if we will, but it was assuredly no facile thing; it was, in fact, one result of Barrie's sad sensitivity.

Peter Pan (1904) is, of course, Barrie's best-known play, but our attention here may perhaps better be concentrated upon his other works. The Admirable Crichton (1902) exhibits his early style at its best. Here the playwright takes what seems to be a fairly normal aristocratic household, with Lord Loam the symbol of the "family" and Crichton, the impeccable butler, as the symbol of the "servants' hall." Imagine these men, says Barrie, cast on a desert island; what would happen? Lord Loam and his aristocratic relatives prove themselves completely incapable of dealing with the new situation. Crichton alone shows himself possessed of the requisite presence of mind and inventiveness: it is he who makes the camp-fire, who builds a shelter, who finds the food. And, in doing all these things, he becomes the aristocrat, and the others are forced into accepting him as the master —indeed, into developing towards him an attitude of abject devotion. Two years they stay there, and Crichton is just about to bestow his royal hand on Lady Mary when a rescue ship arrives. In London, Lord Loam naturally assumes his old position, and Crichton once more becomes the model butler. This delight in topsy-turvyism and this queerly inquiring imagination gives the core, too, to Dear Brutus (1917). Here we are introduced to a group of disgruntled people, each of whom feels that, in other circumstances, he or she would have been happy. Barrie offers them the realization of their wishes—and they find themselves exactly as they were: character, whispers the author, is the only destiny.

Somerset Maugham's "Jack Straw" at the Vaudeville Theatre 1908

Design by Paul Shelving for Kaiser's "Gas"

No doubt we may aver that the sentimentalism is overdone in many among Barrie's works; we may be inclined to smile and sneer at the introduction of the supernatural in *Mary Rose* (1920), to mock *A Kiss for Cinderella* (1916) and *Pantaloon* (1905); but we cannot deny that he brought to the theatre of his time a strangely individual quality. The delicacy of *Quality Street* (1902), the quiet smiling of *What Every Woman Knows* (1908), and the gentle ridicule of *Alice Sit-by-the-Fire* (1905), seemingly weak though they may be, rebut without undue effort all attempts to smile or laugh or gibe his dramatic contributions out of critical esteem.

The measure between Shaw's achievement and Barrie's remains, however, great, and maybe the power of the former is most clearly exemplified by the distinct kinds of impress which the two men made upon the twentieth-century theatre. No really outstanding dramatist ever has any direct followers, precisely because his style is so individually his own and his exploitation of it so complete; only the playwright of middle range has his imitators. Unquestionably Shaw set his seal upon the comedy of his age, and unquestionably we may encounter here and there scenes, episodes, devices which remind us of his; but we cannot think of any single author whom we might label a Shavian: the only Shavian is Shaw himself. This is not true for Barrie. When we turn from his works to, let us say, A. A. Milne's *Michael and Mary* (1929) we feel we might almost be reading or seeing another play by the author of *A Kiss for Cinderella*. In the second act the father clergyman thus *"goes down the stairs ... to the station ... to the lonely Bedfordshire vicarage ... saying over in his mind all that* MICHAEL *said to him, all the loving things which he meant to have said to* MICHAEL*"*—and the stage direction might have been Barrie's. Milne's play-world, like Barrie's, frequently orients its affections and attentions towards the baby, chubby and sweetly cooing. Says Mary: " 'Children, Michael? Oh, I would love to have your son. Can't I just think about him for a little?' (*She thinks about him.*)" And in *The Great Broxopp* (1923), when Broxopp has spoken of his great scheme for a new baby food he and his wife *"gaze eagerly into the future,* BROXOPP *seeing his million babies,* NANCY *seeing her*

one." Quite commonly, too, Milne concentrates his loving attention upon a heroine, wise and quiet, gifted with a sense of
humour, not unlike the heroine of *What Every Woman Knows.*
Mary in *Michael and Mary,* Nancy in *The Great Broxopp,* pass
on their mantles to the Ariadne Winter of *Ariadne; or, Business
First* (1925) and to the Jennifer of *To Have the Honour* (1924),
who, when her plain but charming husband, Michael Brown,
masquerades as Prince Michael Robolski of Neo-Slavonia, dis-
ports herself as a general's widow. Much the same lady appears
as Olivia in *Mr Pim Passes By* (1919), one of Milne's best plays,
and as Princess Ameril, affianced bride of King Hilary XXIV,
in *Portrait of a Gentleman in Slippers* (1926). *The Dover Road*
(1922) obviously has been inspired by *Dear Brutus,* and even the
more independent *The Truth about Blayds* (1921) might almost
have come from Barrie's imagination. Only in *Success* (1923),
with its almost despairing acceptance of life's crushing little-
nesses, and its sense of success "closing in," does Milne appear to
exhibit a mood distinct from that of Barrie's—and even here
we are inclined to feel that the sadness which is inherent in
all Barrie's work but which he concealed by his whimsicality
has merely come to the surface and is demanding full expression.

In considering the plays of these three authors, it may be
profitable to devote a moment's attention to a technical device
which, although it is by no means restricted to their writings,
finds rich and varied exemplification there. Already we have noted
how frequently Galsworthy closed his plays on stage directions,
and the use of stage directions by Shaw, Barrie, and Milne—not
only at the ends of acts and scenes, but persistently throughout the course of their dramas—demands special consideration,
since it is in fact a device unique to the modern stage. These
stage directions need to be related to the manner in which plays
at various times have been presented in printed form to the
public. Up to the close of the eighteenth century there existed a
limited social group actively interested in the reading of plays
and for these men and women the printing-houses produced the
quartos familiar in the seventeenth century and the octavos
which took their place in the eighteenth. Few of them, perhaps,

were models of the typographical art, but the majority were printed clearly and legibly in a form suitable for leisurely perusal and, if desired, for later binding in collections. Since the play-reading tradition was an established one among the literate, neither authors nor publishers felt the need of providing any baits, and thus in general the texts of these plays consisted for the most part merely of the stage dialogue with just such a minimum of stage directions as might make the action clear. During the nineteenth century this tradition was largely lost. With the gradual divorce of the stage from the literary world and with the consequent rise of melodrama, farce, and extravaganza, the printing of plays took a new turn: the innumerable examples of the 'minor' drama, hastily penned by hack writers, began to appear in smaller, cheaper shape, with type often so diminutive as barely to be legible. These were, in fact, not calculated for a reading public at all; they were primarily intended for actors, amateur and professional, who might wish to put them on the stage. And consequently the stage directions assumed a purely theatrical pattern, with all the abbreviations usual in the prompt-copies of the time, intelligible only to those familiar with playhouse practice: when, as frequently happened, these stage directions were lengthier than had been common in earlier years, they were concerned with strictly practical and technical matters —the construction of the sets, the costuming of the characters, the stage business demanded in the performance.

When, however, Pinero, Jones, and others at the close of the nineteenth century sought to put fresh life into the drama and to invest it once more with literary quality, they aimed, as part of their endeavour, to revive the reading as well as the seeing of plays; and, instead of having their works printed in any one of the several series of cheaply produced "acting-texts," they persuaded other publishers to issue their dramas in literary-respectable format, not in flimsy paper wrappers but properly bound. That they were successful in their efforts is proved by the willingness of the publishers to continue issuing plays in this way and also to produce collected editions of various dramatists' works: quite clearly a new reading public had arisen, and once more the drama had found its contacts with literature.

In an attempt to appeal to this reading public and for other reasons, the playwrights started to alter the nature of their stage directions. Very probably the advent of the producer had something to do with the nature of the instructions which were now provided, but when Shaw turned in his early days to pay almost as much attention to the directions as he did to the dialogue and prefaces, it would appear that his main objective was to attract the readers. The description of the set resembles that which a novelist would have provided; the costumes of the characters are similarly narrated in detail; and, in addition to the chairs and tables, the neckties and the waistcoats, the past histories of the stage persons are sketched for us. In *Man and Superman*, for example, Roebuck Ramsden is thus introduced:

> *He has not been out of doors yet to-day, so he still wears his slippers, his boots being ready for him on the hearthrug. Surmising that he has no valet, and seeing that he has no secretary with shorthand notebook and typewriter, one meditates on how little our great burgess domesticity has been disturbed by new fashions and methods, or by the enterprise of the railway and hotel companies which sell you a Saturday to Monday of life at Folkestone as a real gentleman for two guineas, first class fares both ways included.*
>
> *How old is Roebuck? The question is important on the threshold of a drama of ideas; for under such circumstances everything depends on whether his adolescence belonged to the sixties or to the eighties. He was born, as a matter of fact, in 1839, and was a Unitarian and Free Trader from his boyhood, and an Evolutionist from the publication of the Origin of Species. Consequently he has always classed himself as an advanced thinker and fearlessly outspoken reformer.*

In Shaw's hands, stage directions of this kind are complementary to the dialogue and they effectively realize their immediate objective of interesting readers in the play. In the hands of others, however, the device assumes other features, becoming both a confession of failure and a temptation. It is a confession of failure in the sense that playwrights are led to realize that the prose medium they are using does not have the power to express all they would wish to express, so that they are induced to bring into the stage directions descriptive material which ought properly to have been conveyed to the audience through the dialogue; and it is a temptation because it persuaded some authors at least to express their concepts within their stage directions and thus to avoid the more difficult and properly dramatic method of expressing them through the words of the characters. Still further, on occasion the use of this descriptive matter becomes so expanded as almost to take form more significant than the dialogue itself. Thus Barrie was led to couch a whole drama as a narrative, putting the speeches of his characters into inverted commas as though he were penning a novel, and, as in *The Old Lady Shows Her Medals* (1917), including scenes confessedly unsuited for stage performance.

Even when the device has not been carried so far, we frequently encounter paragraphs such as the following from Granville-Barker's *The Madras House*:

> PHILIP'S *wife is an epitome of all that æsthetic culture can do for a woman. More: she is the result—not of thirty-three years—but of three or four generations of refinement. She might be a race-horse! Come to think of it, it is a very wonderful thing to have raised this crop of ladyhood. Creatures, dainty in mind and body, gentle in thought and word, charming, delicate, sensitive, chaste, credulous of all good, shaming the world's ugliness and strife by the very ease and delightsomeness of their existence; fastidious— fastidious—fastidious! also in these latter years with their attractions more generally salted by the addition of learning and humour. Is not the perfect lady perhaps the most wonderful achievement of civilization, and worth the cost of her breeding, worth the toil and the helotage of all the others?*

And in Milne's *Success* we reach the final culmination of the device:

> MANNOCK *walks slowly to his desk. For a little while he sits there, holding the letter in his hand . . .*
> *Sally is dead. He has killed her. No good explaining, apologizing, whining, to a person whom you have killed. Let him be man enough to spare her that last insult. No, there's nothing to say. It was Eversley and that damned tune that got into a man's head, and made him dream . . . The sweetness of her in his dream! But that*

was twenty-five years ago. They're now dead ... But—Chancellor of the Exchequer! It will be in all the papers to-morrow. Chancellor of the Exchequer! What will the papers say? What will people say? Everybody will see it. ... Sally will see it. Will know, will understand. No, there's nothing to be said. That damned tune, that damned dream. O Sally, Sally, Sally! Don't! Don't come into my dreams again. ...

So for a little he sits, thinking. Then, with a bitter, contemptuous laugh, he tosses away his thoughts and comes back to the letter. Chancellor of the Exchequer! Briskly he dips his pen into the ink, and writes to the Prime Minister.

This brief discussion of the new kinds of stage directions may perhaps be regarded as a digression; yet it is a digression which is essential, for in a sense the development of these devices offers us not merely something new in the composition and planning of plays but also a means of understanding some of the objectives and the disadvantages of the dramatists of the period.

Shaw, Barrie, and others have shown certain dominant developments within the dramatic sphere not concerned with the grim manifestation of life's drabness; some of their plays are almost entirely comic in treatment, some are infused with sadness or seriousness of purpose, a few, like *Mary Rose* and *St Joan*, bear us into the realm of death, but all of them clearly exist in a theatrical environment distinct from that of *John Ferguson* or *Rutherford and Son*. There is constantly an escape, through comedy or imaginative fantasy, from reality conceived in strictly material terms.

Within this period, especially during the twenties and the thirties, one particularly interesting movement was that towards the re-establishment of the comedy of manners, often consciously based on an appreciation of the qualities inherent in the writings of Congreve and his companions. The Restoration comedy arose out of a society in which keen observation of life was allied to an intellectual mood of disillusion and a bitingly sardonic treatment of social follies; and that its mood appealed to early twentieth-century audiences is demonstrated by the considerable number of revivals of Restoration plays, by the publication of these plays both in popular and *de luxe* form, and by the attention which their authors attracted among the critics. It might almost be said that the rediscovery of the Elizabethan playwrights by the nineteenth-century romantics finds an almost exact parallel in the twentieth-century's rediscovery of the comedians who gave grace, brilliance, and indecorousness to the court of Charles II.

Already, of course, several years before this rediscovery of the Restoration plays, the last years of the nineteenth century had witnessed a revival of wit and a definite approach towards the establishment of an intellectual comedy. Wilde had given a lead in the composition of polished, spritely dialogue; Jones had experimented with the form of the comedy of manners in *The Liars*; and Shaw had brought his own individual style to the enrichment of the comic. The very first years of the twentieth century, so heavily occupied with the grim development of the serious realistic drama, did not fulfil this promise immediately; indeed, the stage was forced to wait for nearly two decades before there was a full realization of its possibilities. In the meantime, however, one playwright, the Irish J. M. Synge, applied himself to a different comic style, succeeding in producing several plays both excellent in themselves and destined to have considerable influence upon later comic writers. In 1903 appeared the peculiar, cynical, and imaginative little sketch called *In the Shadow of the Glen*, which takes us into the interior of a lonely little cottage where the supposedly dead body of Daniel Burke lies shrouded in a cot, while his wife Nora, only too anxious to escape from her humdrum existence, sits with the Tramp chatting, jesting, and making plans. Suddenly there is a sneeze from the death-bed; Daniel rises in a rage and sends her out of the house; presumably she will be joining the Tramp down the road. Two years later the equally cynical *The Well of the Saints* takes us to a miraculous well the waters of which can make the blind see. To it come an old beggar and his wife; the saint opens their eyes and they look upon each other's haggard, withered visage; harsh words end in blows, and they part. Darkness settles on them once more, and by chance they later stumble together. Starting to talk, they once more find their old companionship, so that, when the saint again offers to give them sight, they refuse to accept his offer. Darkness with visions and hope is better than life with mental bitterness.

These two shorter plays led to one of the masterpieces of the twentieth-century theatre, *The Playboy of the Western World* (1907). Here we are in a small Irish village, to which comes a callow youth, Christy Mahon, who is reputed to have killed his father. He is treated as a hero, and Pegeen Flaherty casts off her loutish fiancé, Shawn, in favour of this grand picturesque figure. Suddenly, however, the father arrives, chastises his son soundly, and stalks out; in bitterness of heart, Pegeen rates poor Christy, and he, fired into an exhibition of courage, rushes out and murderously attacks the old man. The reality affects the villagers differently from the reported exploit. They seize and bind Mahon, intending to hand him over to justice, when in comes the old father again, takes his son's side, and releases him; eventually the pair march out together in fair good humour. Shawn now is confident that Pegeen will return to him, but her mind has been filled with a vision and she will have none of him; she has lost the only Playboy of the Western World.

Synge's cynical comedy, with its mixture of realism and fantasy, with its thoughts of death set alongside scenes of hilarious merriment, and the related plays of Lady Gregory—*Spreading the News* (1904), *Hyacinth Halvey* (1906), and *The Jackdaw* (1907) —may not have any very direct connexion with what was being produced on the English stage, but indirectly at least they aided in the later growth of comedy there. Despite the facts that they were dealing with an Irish peasantry far removed from the urban characters who, for the most part, were the choices of English dramatists, and that they exploited themes which these English dramatists could not touch, the spirit which informed them may readily be traced in many of the comedies produced for the London stage and for the stages of repertory theatres during the twenties and the thirties.

Among the playwrights who thus applied themselves to the writing of comedy Somerset Maugham first attracts attention. After, somewhat strangely, starting his dramatic career with a German play, *Schiffbrüchig*, in 1902, this author first gained public attention by a number of rather sentimentally conceived social plays. *The Tenth Man* (1910) deals with a financial giant who firmly believes that every man has his price; *Smith* (1909) contrasts upper middle-class 'society' and its manners with a healthy young Australian, Thomas Freeman—introducing a theme which, in slightly varied form, provides the core for *The Land of Promise* (1914). *Cæsar's Wife* (1919) is a drama of love and honour; love, murder, and retribution in the Malay Peninsula are full-bloodedly presented in *The Letter* (1927). All of these carry us far away from the comic, and for these Maugham will not be remembered.

As early as 1908, however, *Mrs Dot* had suggested other possibilities. Although farcically conceived, there is evident in it a conscious or unconscious following of Wilde's style. This was continued in *Penelope* (1909), with its charming picture in the 'manners' style of Professor Golightly, and with its frank air of intellectualism. Finally, in *The Circle* (1921) Maugham gave richer expression to this mood, with incisively drawn characters and dialogue delicately poised. Here he has clearly come within the environment of the Ethereges and the Congreves. The kinship between his comic approach and that of the late seventeenth century is even more clearly exemplified in *Our Betters* (U.S.A., 1917; London, 1923), which might almost have proceeded from Wycherley's pen. The wit may not be so sparkling, for the modern fashionables with whom Maugham deals are not so brilliant as the lords and ladies of Charles' Court, but the treatment of their intrigues, their jealousies, and their envies is of a kindred kind; the contrast between the social modes and the natural passions is fundamentally the same. Pearl is a true denizen of this world and Fenwick is just such a character as might have provided amusement for a Sedley or a Rochester:

> *Fenwick.* You've got a great heart, girlie. The world just thinks you're a smart, fashionable woman, clever, brilliant, beautiful, a leader of fashion, but I know different. I know you've got a heart of gold.
> *Pearl.* You're a romantic old thing, Arthur.
> *Fenwick.* My love for you is the most precious thing I have in the world. You're my guiding star, you're my ideal. You stand to me for all that's pure and noble and clean in womanhood. God

bless you, girlie. I don't know what I should do if you failed me.
I don't believe I could live if I ever found out that you weren't
what I think you.

Pearl [*with her tongue in her cheek*]. You shan't, if I can help it.

When Fenwick goes, the telephone rings; Pearl answers it:

You're speaking to Lady George Grayston. Tony! Of course I knew
your voice. Well, what is it? I'm not at all stern. I'm making my
voice as pleasant as I can. I'm sorry you find it disagreeable. [*She
gives a chuckle.*] No, I'm afraid I couldn't come to tea to-morrow.
I shall be engaged all the afternoon. What is the day after to-
morrow? [*Smiling.*] Well, I must ask Bessie. I don't know if she
is free. Of course I'm not coming alone. It would be most com-
promising. A nice-looking young man like you. What would
Minnie say? Oh, I know all about that. . . . I didn't promise anything. I merely said the future was everybody's property. A sleep-
less night. Fancy! Well, good-bye . . . Tony, do you know the most
enchanting word in the English language? Perhaps.

In the same style, although not so effectively, Maugham continued his comic studies in *The Constant Wife* (1927) and *The
Breadwinner* (1930), the latter concentrating upon the thoughtless and boring brilliance of the young. Judy's remark about love
affairs, that "since the War the amateurs have entirely driven
the professionals out of business," might be taken as Maugham's
last sardonic motto.

The conflict of young and old, the 'generations' theme, which
provided material for so many serious playwrights, has also given
much to the comic stage. Harold Chapin's *The New Morality*
(1920) is delightful Congreve where Maugham's plays are savage
Wycherley. The story of Betty Jones, who quarrels with every
one because of her appreciation of new standards, is excellently
and wittily told. The young generation found a fervent apologist
in Miles Malleson, whose *The Fanatics* (1927) made plea for
revised social concepts; it found its light-hearted exponent in
Noël Coward, with his wit, impertinence, and audacity. Starting,
like Maugham, with realistic dramas such as *The Vortex* and *The
Rat Trap* (both 1924), and occasionally turning later, as in *Caval-
cade* (1931), to serious themes, his true metier obviously lies in

the writing of easy, dallying, often inconsequential dialogue. *The Young Idea* (1921) well illustrates his earlier efforts in this sphere; *Private Lives* (1930) shows it fully fashioned; and *Blithe Spirit* (1941) exhibits it invested with an added delicacy.

Closely akin to Maugham, but lacking his incisive power, is Frederick Lonsdale. *Spring Cleaning* (1923), with its picture of a wife being misled by a wretched crew of bright young things and forcibly brought to reason by her determined husband, reminds us of the former's bitterly satiric style, and *The Last of Mrs Cheney* (1925) inevitably calls *The Circle* to mind. Other writers made their varied and often engaging contributions. St John Ervine, turning from serious drama, produced a charming and successful comedy of manners in *The First Mrs Fraser* (1929); Drinkwater gave us his delightfully topsy-turvy *Bird in Hand* (1927); and J. B. Fagan turned out some amusing costume and modern comedies, of which *And So to Bed* (1926) and *The Improper Duchess* (1931) deserve to be remembered. H. M. Harwood's comedies, from *Please Help Emily* (1916) to *The Man in Possession* (1930), and those of J. Hastings Turner, especially *The Lilies of the Field* (1923), with its portraits of the gay Catherine and Elizabeth, are light and crisp; Hubert Henry Davies, author of *Mrs Gorringe's Necklace* (1903), *Cousin Kate* (1903), and *The Mollusc* (1907), won success in the earlier years and Emlyn Williams' essay in romance and humour, *Spring 1600* (1945), attracted audiences four decades later.

Along with these should be noted the merry fantasies designed by Sir Alan Herbert—*La Vie Parisienne* (1929), *Tantivy Towers* (1931), and *Derby Day* (1932)—all indicating a desire to escape from formal realism and to indulge in wit and laughter. With them may be taken the extraordinarily diverse series of theatrical contributions which have come from that versatile actor, composer, playwright, and manager, Ivor Novello; with them, too, we may add to our general picture the pattern formed by revue from Albert de Courville's *Hello, Ragtime* (1912) onward. Nor should we forget the popularity of farce during this period— some of these farces, it is true, trite and planned in a painfully mechanical manner, but others exhibiting skill and fancy. The Aldwych Theatre presented a series of excellent entertainments in this kind; W. A. Darlington, in *Alf's Button* (1924), wrought an amusingly fantastic farce out of an Arabian Nights atmosphere, and later Terence Rattigan gave us his *French without Tears* (1936) and Gerald Savory his *George and Margaret* (1937).

Most of the dramatists from Shaw and Barrie onward who thus made contributions to the comic stage were the authors also of plays which either moved far from comedy or, more commonly, associated comic scenes with themes of serious import. Shaw wrote *St Joan*, Barrie *Mary Rose*, Milne *Success*, Synge *Deirdre of the Sorrows*; and, noting these works, we must bear in mind that the escape from the drab was being effected, during the first decades of the century, not only by the production of comedy and farce but also by the cultivation of themes, often fantastically conceived, which lay outside the range of the realistic social play and by the application of the dramatists to historical subject-matter.

Lennox Robinson's dramatic activities are in many respects typical. He is the author of several excellent comedies, in particular *The Whiteheaded Boy* (1916) and *The Far-off Hills* (1928), both charming and delightful. At the beginning of his career, however, he had devoted himself to the realistic social style, investing it with a characteristic cynical and ironic tone. *The Clancy Name* (1908) concerns itself with a stern old woman, filled with pride for the name she bears, and with her son, who, having killed a man, is prepared to give himself up to the police. She is in despair, for her family's reputation will be dragged into the mud; but suddenly, just as the lad is about to confess to the authorities, he rescues a child from a runaway horse and is himself killed. Thus he dies a hero, and the Clancy name is saved. In the same style Robinson wrote two other peasant dramas, *The Cross Roads* (1909) and *Harvest* (1910). A few years later, however, in *The Patriots* (1912) and *The Lost Leader* (1918) he discovered another, and a more fruitful, field for the exploitation of his talents. These two plays may be regarded as companion portraits of political leaders, and in both Robinson has, as it were, lifted the curtain into the past, even while keeping his action contemporary. In the former, the central figure is a James

Nugent, who, after having served a fifteen-year sentence in prison for his revolutionary activities, returns to his old haunts confident that he will be greeted as a hero; instead, he is met with chill indifference, and at the end, when he comes to address a rally, he finds that the hall is deserted except for its caretaker; every one else has gone off to the films. *The Lost Leader*, a more subtle study, deals with the legend that Charles Stewart Parnell was still living in 1918. In an old man resident in a remote village, this Parnell is supposed to have been found. Argument waxes fierce, some declaring their belief in him and others rejecting him as an impostor. At last, arrangements are made for a meeting at which the old man, Lucius Lenihan, will be confronted by some of Parnell's ancient associates. A political quarrel breaks out; there is a scuffle, and Lenihan himself is killed by a misdirected blow. Parnell's associates arrive, but they can say no more than that in the features of the dead man they can trace the lineaments of the political hero; beyond that, they can decide neither for nor against. We are close to the historical drama here, and it is not surprising that Robinson, in *The Dreamers* (1915), took a final step into the past.

Typical, too, in another way are two plays by an elder Irish writer, Edward Martyn. In 1899 appeared *The Heather Field*, a work cast in the prevailing realistic form. The plot tells of a certain Carden Tyrrell whose mind is dominated by a single vision —that of reclaiming the moorland round his farm. For years he wastes himself and his resources on an unending struggle, and in the end he seems to have won. At this moment he sinks down exhausted from the effort, the only thing keeping him alive being the thought that through his endeavours grass is now springing up on a tract which before had been desert; as he lies bedridden, his little son Kit comes gaily running in with a bunch of heather which he has gathered in this field, and, seeing it, Tyrrell's heart is broken, his mind cracks, and he dies a lunatic. The year following the production of this play, however, saw another of Martyn's works, *Maeve* (1900), and here we move into a different realm. The setting may be realistic and contemporary, but the real is now adorned with a mantle of the imagination. Maeve O'Heynes is a peasant girl, but to her is granted a vision of the fairy folk, of Queen Maeve who holds her court in a moorland haunt and who keeps in her hands all the secrets of loveliness. Maeve hears the call, and no human ties can be of avail to restrain her.

These plays remind us that, despite the strongly flowing current of the realistic, materialistic social drama, the early years of the nineteenth century produced a current hardly less powerful which ran counter to its direction, and that this current was directed not only by Irish playwrights. Lord Dunsany (E. J. M. D. Plunkett, Baron Dunsany) may be taken as one author who brings into association, as it were, the spirits of the Dublin and London stages. An Irishman, certainly, he may be, but there is to be found little in his work which can be traced back to the inspiration of the Abbey Theatre; his writings belong rather to the English than to the Irish stage, and in them he has been successful in conjuring up a strange imaginative world of his own, one in which the fantastic intrudes into the realm of the familiar. Thoroughly typical is his one-act, A Night at an Inn (1916), to which "The Toff," "Bill," Albert Thomas, and "Sniggers" have come after having stolen the jewel eye of an Eastern idol; they know that three Oriental priests are following them, and they believe that here they can dispose of their enemies. All goes according to plan, and the three priests are summarily disposed of. Down they sit to drink toasts to themselves, until "Sniggers" goes out to get some water and stumbles back in terror. As they try to get him to say what he has seen, the idol itself steps in, groping like a blind man, picks up the ruby, and moves off:

> The Toff. O, great heavens!
> Albert [in a childish, plaintive voice]. What is it, Toffy?
> Bill. Albert, it is that obscene idol [in a whisper] come from India.
> Albert. It is gone.
> Bill. It has taken its eye.
> Sniggers. We are saved.
> A Voice off [with outlandish accent]. Meestaire William Jones, Able Seaman.
>> [THE TOFF has never spoken, never moved. He only gazes stupidly in horror.

Bill. Albert, Albert, what is this?   [*He rises and walks out.*
One moan is heard. SNIGGERS *goes to the window. He falls
back sickly.*
Albert [*in a whisper*]. What has happened?
Sniggers. I have seen it. I have seen it. Oh, I have seen it!
                                                            [*He returns to the table.*
The Toff. [*laying his hand very gently on* SNIGGERS'S *arm,
speaking softly and winningly*]. What was it, Sniggers?
Sniggers. I have seen it.
Albert. What?
Sniggers. Oh!
Voice. Meestaire Albert Thomas, Able Seaman.
Albert. Must I go, Toffy? Toffy, must I go?
Sniggers [*clutching him*]. Don't move.
Albert [*going*]. Toffy, Toffy.
Voice. Meestaire Jacob Smith, Able Seaman.
Sniggers. I can't go, Toffy. I can't do it.   [*He goes.*
Voice. Meestaire Arnold Everett Scott-Fortescue, late Esquire,
Able Seaman.
The Toff. I did not foresee it.   [*Exit.*

We may, perhaps, smile at this and call it simply "theatrical,"
but the qualities here exhibited, no doubt rather crudely, are
those which inform the effectively simple *The Glittering Gate*
(1909), the ironically conceived *The Gods of the Mountain*
(1911), in which some beggars, after imposing on a superstitious
township, are turned into stone, and the fantastic *If* (1921). In
this last play, the theme is, as in Barrie's *Dear Brutus*, one of possibilities. "Let us," says Dunsany, "imagine a certain John Beal,
an ordinary, commonplace Londoner. Carry him back to any
point in his life. Suppose he did something ever so little differently from the way he did do it. What might not have happened
to him?" So we are taken back to an ordinary suburban railway-
station, and see John Beal catching the train which he once had
missed. Quite a small thing, apparently of no significance. For
Dunsany, however, character is not destiny; accidents shape our
lives. And so we see John Beal, from a chance meeting with a
stranger on that train which he had missed so long ago, led from
one thing to another until he finds himself a chieftain ruler in
the depths of Persia, wielding powers of life and death. He has

grown from a commonplace suburbanite into a being of romance.

This element of romance intrudes again and again, in widely differing forms, within the theatres' repertories during this period. Sometimes it includes the introduction of the supernatural, as in Benn W. Levy's *Mrs Moonlight* (1928), which is based on the idea that a certain woman has, by miraculous power, the ability to keep her looks and her figure eternally arrested at a particular age; more often it takes shape in a purely 'realistic' form with the introduction of adventure into the familiar daily routine, as in C. K. Munro's *At Mrs Beam's* (1921), H. V. Esmond's *Eliza Comes to Stay* (1912), and Arnold Bennett's *The Great Adventure* (1911). In Bennett's comedy the scenes are cast realistically, yet we know, and Bennett knew, that the events narrated could never have taken place. The entire plot, wherein a famous artist allows himself to be considered dead and watches his deceased valet buried, with full honours, under his name in Westminster Abbey, is delightfully impossible. In all sorts of ways this strain is exemplified. In some plays, such as Harold Chapin's *Augustus in Search of a Father* (1910), *The Marriage of Columbine* (1910), and *The Philosopher of Butterbiggins* (1915), it merely gives a slight colouring to the situations, which, as in the same writer's *The New Morality* (1920) and *Art and Opportunity* (1912) and *Elaine* (1912), show characters engaged in a voyage of discovery aimed at reaching inner truth. In some plays delicacy and quaintness is the goal, as in Louis Napoleon Parker's *Pomander Walk* (1910) and *The Minuet* (1922). In some we veer off to an imaginary realm, as in the charming *Prunella* (1904), written by Granville-Barker and Laurence Housman in collaboration; and in still others, such as Allan Monkhouse's one-act, *The Grand Cham's Diamond* (1918), romance is made to fly in like a bird. In this last little play, characteristic of numerous others, the setting is a dull lower-middle-class London suburb; through the window comes crashing in a great diamond thrown by a thief chased by the police. Mrs Perkins would fain keep it, not for its value, but because it is a symbol of something beyond her drab daily surroundings, but her daughter's fiancé, a detective, insists on taking it to the police-station. The bird has come flying, and has gone; quietly they all settle down again:

> *Miss Perkins.* I don't know what Albert'll think of you.
> *Mrs Perkins.* 'E's not going to marry me, thank 'eaven.
> *Mr Perkins.* D'y'want t'know what I think of yer?
> *Mrs Perkins.* Go on! Y've no 'magernation.
> *Miss Perkins.* I never thought to be ashamed of my own mother.
> *Mr Perkins.* Wantin' in the very el'ments of morality. I wonder 'ow Sossiety'd get on if they was all like you.
> *Mrs Perkins.* Polly, put up that blind. It's a bit chilly with them broken panes.
> *Miss Perkins.* Most unladylike as well.
>> [*They settle down into their chairs again.* MRS PERKINS *takes up her darning and* MR PERKINS *the paper. After putting up the blind* MISS PERKINS *returns to her puzzle.*
> *Mrs Perkins.* 'Ow much did y'say it was worth, Pa?
> *Mr Perkins* [*gruffly*]. Never mind.
> *Mrs Perkins.* Well, I 'ad my bit o' fun for onct.

In connexion with this trend, two related movements deserve attention. The first is the cultivation of what might be called the time-space theme, sometimes presented in a simple form, sometimes made more 'philosophical.' Reginald Berkeley's *The White Château* (1927) thus presents a time pattern with, as the central 'character,' not an individual but a building, and in a sense the author's object is to invest this object with an individuality of its own. Similar in style is H. F. Rubinstein's *The House* (1927). The connexion between such pieces and the aims of those dramas which we have just been considering receives emphasis when we look at another play of Berkeley's, *The World's End* (1925), which clearly puts him in the company of Barrie and Dunsany, and which, in fact, might almost be regarded as a variant of *Dear Brutus*, with the setting of a strange tavern, The World's End, and the intrusion of an Oriental magician who has the power of making wishes come true. In this play, each of the characters is granted his or her secret wish, and all remain dissatisfied. Out of this style of dramatic composition came numerous works in which the present merges into the past or assumes a dream-like atmosphere.

The dramatist who has achieved most in this sphere is John Boynton Priestley, and in his writings the 'philosophic' element is most definitely marked. Already in *Dangerous Corner* (1932) and *Laburnum Grove* (1933) he had given a suggestion of the topic which he was to make his own, and this topic was fully expressed in four plays written some five years later—*Time and the Conways*, *I Have Been Here Before*, *I'm a Stranger Here*, and *Music at Night*. In these, and in *They Came to a City* (1943), *Desert Highway* (1943), and *An Inspector Calls* (1945), he has sought to combine explorations both in the recesses of the human subconscious and in the concept of the 'time-continuum,' producing a series of dramas which establish him as one of the outstanding playwrights of his age.

The second feature of this general movement is that many of these playwrights have shown a tendency to find added scope for their efforts in periods other than the present. The historical drama during these years obviously made wide appeal; many of the most significant dramatic productions were those dealing with themes selected from ages that have passed by. That this exploitation of historical subject-matter is not merely the result of chance may easily be demonstrated: fundamentally it arose from the desire of numerous playwrights to escape from the trammels of the realistic stage. Clifford Bax puts this succinctly:

> The historical dramatist stands, in relation to the playwright of modern life, somewhat as a portrait-painter does in relation to a photograph. He gives—or tries to give—the essentials of human emotion and experience: not an exact rendering of somebody's actual speech but an impression of what that somebody is feeling.

In many ways, therefore, the cultivation of the historical themes may be looked upon as one other sign of dissatisfaction with the restrictions of the prose drama:

> The figures in a costume-play can be a little larger than life: that is to say that, without offending our sense of reality, they can express themselves a little more richly than figures which are

photographed, as exactly as possible, from the life which we see around us.

Already, in the very midst of the realistic movement during the first years of the century, experiments were being made in this form of play. Shaw deals with Cæsar and Napoleon and General Burgoyne; Lady Gregory develops her Irish folk-dramas; Lennox Robinson, in *The Dreamers*, turns from the contemporary political scene to that of the nineteenth century, L. N. Parker makes a study of *Disraeli* (1911). The full flourishing of the historical drama, however, did not come until the twenties and the thirties. In 1923 Shaw produced *St Joan*, Ervine wrote his costume play *The Lady of Belmont*, a sequel to *The Merchant of Venice*, in 1924, Clemence Dane essayed her *Will Shakespeare* in 1921, Rudolf Besier, after his earlier delicate studies of *Don* (1909) and *Lady Patricia* (1911), turned to win success with *The Barretts of Wimpole Street* in 1930, Reginald Berkeley gave us *The Lady with a Lamp* in 1929.

At the same time several individual playwrights applied themselves almost exclusively to this type of drama. One of these, John Drinkwater, had started his career with a number of varied experiments which indicated that he was groping towards a form in which best to express himself—*Rebellion* (1914), an allegorical work set in an imagined land, *The Storm* (1915), obviously inspired by *Riders to the Sea*, and $X = O$: *A Night of the Trojan War* (1917), an effective commentary upon war. In this last play two Grecian friends, Pronax and Salvius, and two Trojan friends, Ilus and Capys, are shown on the outskirts of their respective encampments. It is Pronax' duty to steal towards the Trojan walls in an effort to slay some one of its inhabitants; he sets off in the darkness, leaving Salvius reading a book. Similarly Ilus goes off in an attempt to assassinate a Greek, and he leaves Capys reciting some verses. Pronax comes upon Capys and kills him; Ilus slays Salvius as he is reading. Then we reach the ironic conclusion. Pronax returns, and in the gloom he does not realize that his friend is dead:

    Pronax. What, still awake, and reading? Those are rare songs,
To keep a soldier out of his bed at night.

Ugh—Salvius, sometimes it's horrible—
He had no time for a word—he walked those walls
Under the stars as a lover might walk a garden
Among the moonlit roses—this cleansing's good—
He was saying some verses, I think, till death broke in.
Cold water's good after this pitiful doing,
And freshens the mind for comfortable sleep.
Well, there, it's done, and sleep's a mighty curer
For all vexations.   [*The sentinel passes.*
                    It's time that torch was out.
I do not need it, and you should be abed . . .
Salvius . . .   [*He looks into the tent for the first time.*
                What, sleeping and still dressed?
That's careless, friend, and the torch alight still . . . Salvius . . .
Salvius, I say . . . gods! . . . what, friend . . . Salvius, Salvius . . .
Dead . . . it is done . . . it is done . . . there is judgment made . . .
Beauty is broken . . . and there on the Trojan wall
One too shall come . . . one too shall come . . .
                                        [*The sentinel passes.*

Then, in 1918, Drinkwater produced his *Abraham Lincoln*, and
at once his reputation, from having only a limited reach within
the repertory theatre field, soared; and he was induced, because
of its appeal, to write his *Mary Stuart* (1921), *Oliver Cromwell*
(1922), and *Robert E. Lee* (1923). In each of these a dominant
concept operates: they are all studies of men and women whose
natures rise above the commonplace. The first shows such a man
confronted by the problem of using force, which he abhors, to
achieve an idealistic end, and the same problem, with suitable
variations, controls the action of the plays on Cromwell and Lee;
in Mary Stuart, Drinkwater would have us see an exceptional
woman, one whose power of love is so great that it cannot be
confined to one object. Perhaps we may decide that these works
are not so profound as once they were deemed; but certainly they
were significant in giving dramatic expression to themes beyond
the range of the realistic plays of the time.

Somewhat later, Clifford Bax exhibits much the same kind of
development in his writing. His earlier pieces, from *Nocturne
in Palermo* (1924) to *Up-Stream* (1925), from *Midsummer Madness* (1924) to *Mr Pepys* (1926), were diverse in style, although

most of them revealed a predilection for the 'poetic' and fantastic. Then, between 1930 and 1931, he turned to offer the public a series of historical plays, *Socrates* (1929), *The Venetian*, *The Immortal Lady*, and *The Rose without a Thorn* (1931), the last of which won him a considerable amount of esteem. Although in some of his dramas he has tended to become too severely 'philosophical' and in others to lose grip with reality, his contributions merit a place alongside Drinkwater's.

A third playwright who had some influence at this time, both by reason of his own writings and through his practical stage activities, was Ashley Dukes, who won success with *The Man with a Load of Mischief* in 1924. The plot of this costume play is slight, but audiences delighted in the delicately turned prose of its dialogue. As the title of Dukes' later collection of dramas— *Five Plays of Other Times* (1931)—indicates, he was an author who consistently found his inspiration and means of expression in subject-matter taken from earlier periods. Success, too, attended the production of *Richard of Bordeaux* (1932) by Gordon Daviot (Elizabeth Mackintosh), which was followed by her other historical picture of *Queen of Scots* (1934).

Apart from these authors there were many others who similarly discovered fertile fields in historical themes. Shane Leslie takes the seventeen-nineties as the setting for his *Delightful, Diverting, and Devotional Play of Mrs Fitzherbert* (1928); in *Charles and Mary* (1930) Joan Temple deals with Lamb and his sister; the period of Henri IV is selected by Conal O'Riordan (Norreys Connell) in his cleverly handled *His Majesty's Pleasure* (1912; revised 1925); for the theme of *Krishna Kumari* (1924) Edward Thompson turns to India in 1806. English history for the most part interests Howard Peacey, in a series of plays neatly written and containing some effective scenes, although lacking in broader architectural strength. *Warren Hastings* (1928) has some dramatic force, but its orientation lacks precision; *The Fifth of November* (1924) suffers from its multiplicity of characters. Historical events have here not been moulded to theatrical requirements. Laurence Housman, with his skilful touch, his faintly cynical sentimentalism, and his subacid humour, after gaining considerable popularity among amateurs for his charming *Little Plays of St Francis* (1922) and his various short pieces based on the life of Queen Victoria, achieved wider commercial success with his *Victoria Regina* (1935), consisting of a set of one-act pieces bound together as a kind of chronological sequence. *Viceroy Sarah* (1934) and *The First Gentleman* (1945) by Norman Ginsbury belong to the same tradition.

The playwright who to a large extent sums up all these diverse activities is the Anglo-Scot James Bridie (O. H. Mavor). Starting his dramatic career under the influence of J. A. Ferguson, author of *Campbell of Kilmhor* (1915), and of John Brandane, author of *The Glen is Mine* (1923) and *The Lifting* (1925), it seemed at first as though Bridie were to restrict his sphere to that of the Scots dramatic movement fostered by the Scottish National Theatre Society and the Scottish Community Drama Association, but in the thirties he suddenly blossomed forth into a dramatist of wider appeal. Gifted with an individual sense of humour and a magnificent command of theatrical prose, he commanded attention because of his versatility, his appreciation of character values, and his fine dramatic sensitivity. Unfortunately, to these virtues he added a serious weakness: so active was his mind that constantly, as he was approaching the completion of a particular play, his imagination went leaping ahead to its successor—with the result that the vigour with which he had written his earlier acts was dissipated in his concluding scenes. Brilliant as his accomplishment was, he has thus left us no single drama which is thoroughly satisfying. The magnificent first act of *The Switchback* (1929) does not pass on its quality to the acts which succeed; the breadth of vision which has enabled him to present such a penetrating study of Edinburgh life in *The Anatomist* (1930), with its contrasting atmospheres of the sordid tavern, Dr Knox' consulting-room, and the prim, respectable parlours, does not carry through to the end.

The Anatomist is, of course, an historical play; and the trend of Bridie's genius is seen in his prevailing choice of subject-matter. *Tobias and the Angel* (1930) and *Susannah and the Elders* (1937) are inspired by Biblical material, the one 'historical' in treatment, the other carrying the ancient story into a Scots university setting. In *The King of Nowhere* (1938) we may be

materially in the contemporary world but it is a world transformed by fantasy; in *A Sleeping Clergyman* (1933) we may start
in the familiar surroundings of a present-day club, but soon we
are swept back into the past and forward into the future; in
Mr Bolfry (1943) we find ourselves in a Highland manse amid
characters belonging to the war years, but the chief person in the
action is the Devil himself, disguised as Mr Bolfry. Historical or
imaginative realms, the creations of fantasy, are those in which
Bridie most happily dwells.

Even if we put aside the later dramas written by Irish playwrights—for the setting up of the Eire state makes it improper
to consider these strictly as "British" drama—we can see that
this imaginative quality was amply reflected in many plays produced during these years in the London theatres. Paul Vincent
Carroll's Irish drama of *Shadow and Substance* (1934) may have a
precision and sensitivity difficult to find elsewhere; Sean O'Casey
may exhibit a fecundity of style which cannot be paralleled in the
writings of contemporary British playwrights; but plays such as
Sutton Vane's *Outward Bound* (1923), with its extraordinarily
skilful first-act surprise that the ocean liner is in fact the boat
of the dead, Laurence Housman's *Possession* (1921), a "peep-
show in Paradise," and, later, other imaginatively suggestive
works demonstrate that the same spiritual questing was potent
in the English playhouse.

4. THE POETIC PLAY

Obviously, many of the dramas surveyed in the previous section
were inspired by a spirit which might be called "poetic," and
some of their authors, such as Drinkwater and Bax, experimented in the penning of verse dialogue. These works, therefore,
serve as an introduction to the more determined efforts made
during the first half of the twentieth century to carry on the
tradition which, although often flagging, had remained an insis-
tent goal since the end of the sixteenth century.

When we turn to this sphere of dramatic activity, we are confronted by a definite paradox. On the one hand, it seemed as
though the theatre from 1900 to 1930 had rigorously set itself

against the poetic style, and yet, on the other hand, in the midst of all the trend towards realism there arose an almost underground attempt, more determined than we can find anywhere in the nineteenth century and certainly more deeply informed, to prepare the foundations for a new kind of verse drama. This paradox must be kept steadily in mind if we wish to assess correctly the spirit animating the playhouses of the period.

When the century opened in 1900 the star of Stephen Phillips glittered with momentary splendour, and there were many who believed that this writer was the herald of a vigorous, fresh development of poetic tragedy. *Herod* (1900) came first, to be succeeded two years later by the much-lauded *Paolo and Francesca* (written 1899, but not produced until 1902). Unfortunately, however, as these works were followed by *Ulysses* (1902), *The Sin of David* (1904), and *Nero* (1906), it had regretfully to be acknowledged that his work exhibited serious flaws which had passed unobserved in the first flush of enthusiasm. That Phillips was acquainted with the stage was certain, that his verse moved easily and melodiously could be admitted; but beyond that he had nothing. His characters were flat and artificially conceived, his situations often melodramatic. The result was that hardly any playwright has witnessed such a meteoric rise to fame, and such a rapid fall. From our point in time, we can more easily realize why this should have been so. The cardinal failing in his plays was that they were old. He looked backward, as the nineteenth-century poetic dramatists had done, and, like their works, his lacked true fire.

It might have been thought that Phillips' example might have warned others that any attempt to follow the same pattern was doomed to failure; but in fact the years between the production of *Paolo and Francesca* and that of Lawrence Durrell's *Sappho* (1960) are studded with plays, mostly now forgotten, which directly or indirectly attempted to follow the Elizabethan style. Rudolf Besier's *The Virgin Goddess* (1906) may be taken as one early specimen of the type, and J. E. Flecker's *Hassan* (1922) as another. The latter, with the aid of gorgeous scenery, of music and of ballet, was a success on the stage, but in reality it is only a patchwork of heterogenous elements without harmony and without form, hardly superior to a *Chu Chin Chow* or to Edward Knoblock's *Kismet* (1911).

Hassan and *Kismet* exploited Oriental subject-matter without introducing anything new; but another influence from the East did have the effect of starting something fresh. At the very beginning of the century a Japanese company brought a number of Nō plays to London; in 1913 a collection of translations of these plays was published; and the success of this volume led to the appearance of a second collection three years later. In these a new world was opened up before the poets. Hitherto the Elizabethan model alone had been available; now was discovered a strange and novel form of dramatic composition which provided a completely fresh orientation. Clearly, the technique of the Nō drama could not effectively be imitated directly, since it depended upon conventions which did not exist in England; but the general approach of these dramas certainly stimulated critical thought and led to experiments in styles different from those prevailing from *The Cenci* to *Paolo and Francesca*.

This influence of the Japanese drama may be traced in diverse authors of the time. It was not by chance that Masefield selected a Japanese theme for *The Faithful* (1915); although he does not, as some others do, introduce into his plays technical devices borrowed from the Nō, it seems clear that in *Philip the King* (1914), *Good Friday* (1917), *A King's Daughter* (1923), *The Trial of Jesus* (1926) and *Tristan and Isolt* (1927), he has, consciously and unconsciously, mingled the impress of the Japanese theatre with that of the classical. In the work of W. B. Yeats, on the other hand, this Japanese influence was freely acknowledged, and his plays provide an illuminating illustration of the way in which this influence produced a complete change in orientation. In his earlier writings Yeats had been dominated almost completely by the Elizabethan style, which he sought to mould into a new shape by his lyrical imagination. *The Countess Cathleen* (1892; acted 1899) is thus a kind of *tour de force*, based fundamentally on the outworn tradition which produced *Paolo and Francesca* but given life by Yeats' command of words. The plot bears us into a realm of fantasy, into a world racked by famine in which two Demon Merchants wander up and down buying

souls for bread. To thwart them, the Countess Cathleen, majestic
in her pity, offers to repurchase these souls at the terrible price
of her own. The Merchants willingly consent, but a divine pity
takes her into its folds, and she is granted a heavenly crown. This
story Yeats has invested with a rich lyrical utterance. Aleel, the
poet, shatters a looking-glass:

> I shatter you in fragments, for the face
> That brimmed you up with beauty is no more:
> And die, dull heart, for she whose mournful words
> Made you a living spirit has passed away
> And left you but a ball of passionate dust.
> And you, proud earth and plumy sea, fade out!
> For you may hear no more her faltering feet,
> But are left lonely amid the clamorous war
> Of angels upon devils.

And other characters who are not poets speak the same language:
Oona's words are cast in a similar mould:

> Tell them who walk upon the floor of peace
> That I would die and go to her I love;
> The years like great black oxen tread the world,
> And God the herdsman goads them on behind,
> And I am broken by their passing feet.

The Countess Cathleen is an impressive achievement for a young
poet, but basically it springs from the long, largely sterile romantic tradition. So, too, do the other early plays—The Land of
Heart's Desire (1894), wherein the matter-of-fact world represented in Bridget Bruin is contrasted with that of Mary, whose
mind is filled with "foolish dreams" of

> How a Princess Edane,
> A daughter of a King of Ireland, heard
> A voice singing on a May Eve like this,
> And followed half awake and half asleep,
> Until she came into the Land of Faery,
> Where nobody gets old and godly and grave,
> Where nobody gets old and crafty and wise,
> Where nobody gets old and bitter of tongue . . .

Cathleen Ni Houlihan (1902), in which a similar call comes to
Michael Gillane, The Shadowy Waters (1900; acted 1904), The

King's Threshold (1903), and *Deirdre* (1906). In all of these, despite their lyrical fervour, there is no inspiring force of a novel kind. Nor is there any greater inspiring force in Synge's *Deirdre of the Sorrows* (1910), even although in itself it is a work of power and vision.

When, however, we move forward a number of years to Yeats' *Four Plays for Dancers* (1916–17) and to some later works, we recognize that we are in contact with something new. This something new, in Yeats' writings and in the writings of others, requires to be very carefully considered. In its own time, undoubtedly, it had little to give to the public stage. Yeats himself has confessed that the playhouse began to be distasteful to him, that he shunned contact with its audiences, and that he came to dream of little plays, bound in conventional forms, which might be performed by a few players in a drawing-room before a score of privileged spectators. Our first thought, of course, is that in this dream there resides a definite anti-theatrical spirit, and unquestionably this first thought has right on its side. The drama can flourish only when the mind is set upon pit, box, and galleries—not a row of chairs arranged in somebody's drawing-room. Nevertheless, when we search deeper, we are forced to acknowledge that during this time when the poetic drama virtually disappeared from the playhouses, and when numerous critics declared that it had finally given up the ghost, a new foundation was being laid. Virtually for the first time, the poets started to inquire about things which in the nineteenth century had been taken on trust, and in particular two questions occupied their minds. In the past those who had applied themselves to the verse drama did so only because they were intent upon following in the footsteps of the Elizabethans: they did not stop to ask themselves what, in fact, were the virtues, if any, inherent in the casting of their plays in verse form. What we find in the early twentieth century is a determined effort to explore this problem: Lascelles Abercrombie's writings on the subject are merely among the first in a long series of essays from many pens designed to demonstrate the essential distinction between the poetic and the realistic prose theatre, to show the inevitable restrictions inherent in the latter and, above all, to stress the fact that the poetic drama, if it is to be effective, means much more than simply a play in which the dialogue assumes a verse form. Thus, we might say, the inner significance of this poetic drama was newly being examined, not merely its external form.

At the same time, it was recognized that the external form was a basic element, and, alongside the more general questions, there arose questioning concerning the relationship between verse measures and ordinary familiar spoken utterance. Hitherto, blank verse, because it had been used by Shakespeare, was tacitly accepted as the measure which had to be adopted by all poets anxious to apply themselves to the writing of plays. Now, in the new critical climate, those interested in the poetic drama came to realize that the Elizabethan blank verse had gained its power precisely because it was related to the ordinary speech of Shakespeare's age. They gradually were compelled to acknowledge that the Elizabethan prose utterance was far more richly patterned and less logically directed than the ordinary prose of later times and that, consequently, the Shakespearian blank verse might almost be regarded as a kind of heightened speech closely and intimately related to what he and his audiences heard in the world around them. With this discovery, they further were driven to admit that the imitation of Shakespearian, Marlovian, and Fletcherian cadences, such as had prevailed hitherto, was working against rather than for the revival of the poetic drama; these cadences, out of harmony with the speech forms of the modern age, instead of possessing a vital, impelling, creative force, were now dead things. They saw that Shakespeare's style possessed force and vigour because it was the organic outgrowth of a particular form of speech, and the strength resultant from that fact gave to his dialogue an energy which could make it appeal even in periods when familiar prose speech had materially altered; the modern poets, however, who sought to imitate him could gain no such power, and consequently their lines were bound to fall flat on the stage. Tacitly, therefore, those interested in a revival of the poetic drama confessed that the contemporary audiences who had come to feel a distrust of, and a distaste for, the 'poetic drama,' as that had manifested itself from Wordsworth to Swinburne, had full justification.

The important thing to observe is that the problem was thus being definitely posed and that the dilemma was being honestly faced. To escape from this dilemma two lines of development seemed to offer potential opportunities, and these may find illustration in the work of Lascelles Abercrombie and Gordon Bottomley.

The first of these lies in the conscious endeavour to adapt the earlier verse measures or to shape fresh measures in such a way as to make them vital for the theatre to-day. Abercrombie knew that, in the playhouse world of his time, when the 'poetic drama' was under a heavy cloud of disesteem, he himself had little hope of capturing the stage; but he was content to proceed with his task in the hope that, through his endeavours and the endeavours of others, a basis might be laid for something to come in the future. All his plays—from *Deborah* and *The Adder* in 1913, through *The End of the World* (1914), *The Staircase* (1920), *The Deserter* (1922), and *Phœnix* (1923), on to *The Sale of St Thomas* in 1931—are fundamentally concerned with this question of form. Unlike the nineteenth-century poets, he sought to escape from Shakespeare's impress; unlike Yeats, he tried to bring his verse into association with common reality. He aimed at achieving a new resonance, a welding of the familiar with the imaginative. In *Deborah*, for example, one character is speaking of the plague:

> But I within me
> Can see the thing, a ghost as grey as rain,
> Fleeces of shadowy air wrapping his shape,
> Tall as the winds, standing up over us,
> Smiling and idly bandying with his feet
> This way and that the writhing bodies like
> A man turns rats that have taken the bane he laid.

Quite clearly, a deliberate attempt is here being made, not to follow, but to escape from Shakespearian rhythms.

Perhaps because of this constant attention to the shape of the verse, Abercrombie's plays, as plays, have little theatrical value. In the treatment of his themes he tended towards the 'philosophic'; he was inclined to select subject-matter too far removed from the familiar—typical is the setting of *Phœnix*, placed in a distant Greece "in the times before the Trojan War"; only too often he allowed narrative to intrude unduly into his dramatic action, as, for instance, in *The Sale of St Thomas*. As a playwright, he is not of importance; as one who directed attention to the problems involved in the poetic drama and as an experimenter in new verse rhythms suitable for the stage he occupies a significant position.

This marks one way of approach; the other finds expression in the plays, especially the later plays, of Gordon Bottomley. Where Abercrombie aimed at a translation of ordinary speech into poetic terms, Bottomley decided to look for inspiration in other quarters. At the beginning, perhaps, no such object in his writing is immediately apparent. His early pieces, *The Crier by Night* (1902), *Midsummer Eve* (1905), *Laodice and Danaë* and *The Riding to Lithend* (1909), together with the two plays, *King Lear's Wife* (1915) and *Gruach* (1921; acted 1923), in which he has attempted to write introductions to *Lear* and *Macbeth*, exhibit little more than his own individual imaginative power, his grip of character values, and his manifest skill in creating scenes of suspense. The best of these are the two 'Shakespearian' plays. In *King Lear's Wife* an attempt is made to account for the situation presented to us at the start of *King Lear* itself: Lear is a rather wilful, amorous old man who has cast off his aged queen, Hygd, and taken the common, vulgar Gormflaith as his mistress. Goneril, virtuous and chill, seeks only vengeance; Cordelia's character is moulded by her mother's hatred and her father's excess of affection. In *Gruach*, the future Lady Macbeth is revealed as a girl reared in the chill rigours of a Scottish fortress who dreams of a golden world beyond its confines. She is about to be married to a man she despises, when a young soldier-courtier, Macbeth, arrives, and they go off together. The terrible figure of Lady Macbeth has thus been born in a girl full of life, ambitious, and striving for she knows not what.

In these plays Bottomley displayed a peculiar power of dealing with primitive nature. His early Britons and Scots are not just modern characters uttering their thoughts in verse; they are given an individuality of their own—a greater brutality, a sterner indomitability of purpose, and a greater simplicity. By exploring these qualities, Bottomley succeeded in doing what few authors of his time achieved, creating the atmosphere of another race and time. Yet in essence he was merely pursuing the old path: his plays were no more than variants of the style cultivated by so many in the previous century.

Then came a change. Partly through awakened interest in the Japanese Nō drama, he turned to write a series of choral plays with certain clearly defined objectives in view. After penning *Gruach*, he said, he "began to notice that the time is over for fitting a stylized speech [verse] to a naturalistic action that would fit a prose play equally well." In discovering this, he discovered another thing:

> that I love listening to poetry more than reading it. Then that the movement and colour of clothes and the incidence of light could, through my eyes, put my mind into a more efficient condition for listening to it.... As I see the theatre, every subject can be treated at two levels: (1) on the level of every day intercourse and colloquial speech, and (2) by making humanity vocal where it is unvocal, by making the stage a place where speech has become complete (regardless of external fact) and makes audible the grace of the soul, its grace of movement as well as of utterance.

The passionate search for theatrical poetic utterance, however, was accompanied by a further realization—that audiences willing to accept this utterance were few, and that the actors, trained in the naturalistic style, were incapable of giving full expression to the language he sought to give to his characters. As a result, he deliberately decided to turn to the amateurs, hoping among them to stimulate a spirit which might in time to come penetrate within the public playhouses:

> Insensibly I concentrated on something in which speech has as large a share as possible: then on narrative poetry, for which the Greeks found a valid place in drama: then on variety of verse-structure, which led me to see there is a place for lyric verse too.

"Look at any of the Greek masterpieces," he wrote,

> from the *Agamemnon* to the *Hippolytus* and you will see that all those men knew that a narrative element is a necessary factor in poetry's existing upon the stage. Our Jacobeans neglected or under-

valued it, with fatal results: but Shakespeare knew that it was better to tell of Ophelia drowning herself than to show her doing it. (The Japanese of his time, though, knew still more: they knew they could successfully show her in symbol drowning herself, when they could not realistically)... These considerations led me to attempt a new synthesis. It has two attractions for me: (a) it predicates an unrealistic treatment of the chosen theme—which seems to me reasonable, as verse is not a realistic form of speech and is not very comfortable in a realistic action—and, when realism is once abandoned, a delightful freedom in the choice of subject dawns for one: and (b) it frees performance from much of the modern theatre's expensive equipment.

Hence the creation of *Culbin Sands*, *Towie Castle*, and *Ardvorlich's Wife*. We are almost in the world of Yeats' *Four Plays for Dancers*, also inspired by admiration for the Japanese drama, but with one essential difference: Yeats' choice of a drawing-room and an audience consisting of a few selected friends was directed towards himself, an expression of his own fastidiousness, whereas Bottomley's turning to the amateurs was fed by the hope that thus he could build something of wider import.

Abercrombie, Bottomley, and others were, for the most part, working outside the walls of the theatres; but suddenly the effect of their labours came to view in the year 1935. The underground movement came to the surface. In the United States Archibald MacLeish produced his *Panic*, and Maxwell Anderson won high acclaim for his *Winterset*; during the same year T. S. Eliot aroused enthusiasm by his *Murder in the Cathedral*. Eliot's play formed an important milestone in the long slow journey towards the resuscitation of the poetic drama; here the poet who was regarded by many of the younger generation as their master turned to the stage and sought to apply his characteristic style to its purposes. The emotional power here exhibited gave assurance to those who had been pleading so long for the reintroduction of poetry to the theatre, and convinced those who had hitherto doubted the possibility of finding a dramatic speech based on the prevailing qualities to be found in modern verse. In this drama, Eliot had accepted the essential principle governing Bottomley's efforts, that the poetic drama should not

Design by Roger Furse for Shaw's "Cæsar and Cleopatra"

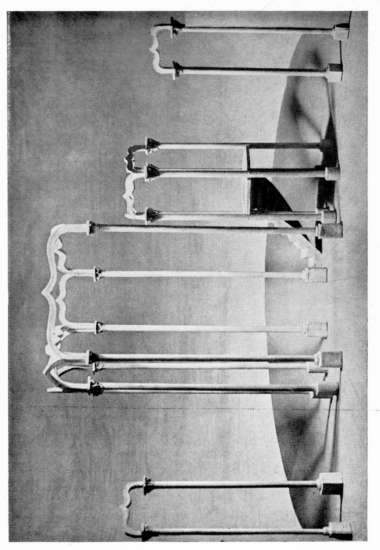

Design by Michael Warre for Shakespeare's "Richard II"

cringe and seek to crawl into the playhouses disguised as though it were prose, that it should boldly and vigorously employ all the devices proper to its form—emphatic melody, alliterative values, arresting imagery:

> I have smelt them, the death-bringers, senses are quickened
> By subtile forebodings; I have heard
> Fluting in the night-time, fluting and owls, have seen at noon
> Scaly wings slanting over, huge and ridiculous. I have tasted
> The savour of putrid flesh in the spoon. I have felt
> The heaving of earth at nightfall, restless, absurd. I have heard
> Laughter in the noises of beasts that make strange noises: jackal,
>   jackass, jackdaw; the scurrying noise of mouse and jerboa; the
>   laugh of the loon, the lunatic bird. I have seen
> Grey necks twisting, rat tails twining, in the thick light of
>   dawn.

The same year that witnessed the appearance of *Murder in the Cathedral* saw also the production of *The Dog Beneath the Skin*, by W. H. Auden and Christopher Isherwood, a play followed by *The Ascent of F6* in 1936 and by *On the Frontier* two years later. Of their value no one has doubts, yet the strange paradox is to be noted that the more these two authors have tried to incorporate the colloquial in their writing the farther they seem to remove themselves from the theatre. Numerous others applied their talents to a similar endeavour during the late thirties. Dorothy Sayers produced *The Zeal of Thy House* (1937) and *The Devil to Pay* (1939), in which Eliot's experiment in dealing with religious subject-matter was carried still further, while Stephen Spender presented *Trial of a Judge* (1938) on a political theme.

When war came in 1939 it certainly seemed that the revival of the poetic drama was becoming, if it had not actually become, a reality.

5. THE LATEST PHASE

A just assessment of the progress of the drama from the end of the war on to 1962 is rendered exceedingly difficult for many reasons, the most important of which is that in all periods contemporaries are but ill-equipped to measure and evaluate the worth of the writings produced during their own ages. In the general consideration of literature and art, perspective is needed before valid judgments can be reached, and, in particular, this gaining of perspective has special significance when dramatic works are being examined. No doubt the theatre rarely, if ever, offers us plays which, neglected in their own times, are seen later to have been masterpieces; within this realm authors such as William Blake are hardly ever to be found, and, with one or two very rare exceptions, all those dramas of the past in which we now recognize the presence of greatness were successful in appealing to their own generations. If, however, we are not confronted by this problem, its opposite counterpart remains constantly potent and perplexing: again and again in the theatre's history plays have attracted audiences and have received high critical praise which later audiences and critics have found undeserved. If we may judge from its extraordinarily numerous editions, Mucedorus, first printed in 1598, was one of the most esteemed dramas of Shakespeare's time, yet to-day we can look upon it only as a curiosity; The London Merchant excited eighteenth-century spectators, but, even when we make all allowances, it can scarcely be accorded any of the esteem with which once it was graced; we must ever keep before us as a warning the ecstatic cry of "Where's your Willie Shakespeare now?" which greeted the first Edinburgh performance of Douglas. These are not exceptional examples but they stand for hundreds of others; no one can read through critical essays of previous years without feelings of surprise and amusement at extravagant statements concerning what once were deemed to be works of genius.

Obviously, therefore, any effort to weigh and judge the merits of contemporary dramatic writings can at the best be no more than tentative. On the other hand, if perforce contemporaries cannot be granted the perspective view necessary for the reaching of valid conclusions, some measure of support and assistance may come if we seek, so far as is possible, to keep the past in mind while we are concerned with the present. This does not mean that we should ever be comparing new plays with old:

such procedure but seldom can yield useful judgments. What it does mean is that sometimes, perhaps indeed often, we are enabled to secure a kind of imaginative perspective if we endeavour to relate the conditions and general trends of the contemporary stage to conditions and general trends in certain selected earlier periods. The theatre may always be in movement and the playhouse of any one day may be markedly different from the playhouse of any yesterday; at the same time, if the playhouse is thus organic, it shares the qualities of other organisms, so that present conditions can often be explained and diagnosed by reference to what has now outwardly passed by and altered shape.

In seeking to look at the dramatic activities of the years 1945 to 1962, not as an entity in themselves but as part of the general historical development of the English theatre, two things seem to emerge. First, there is the fact that, despite the incidence of war, the dramatists in the years immediately following 1945 carried on, as it were, from where they left off. Maybe, however, that statement requires some modification, since the war years of 1939 to 1945 did not, in reality, create any essential chasm between post-war and pre-war. Although certainly the black-outs and the bombings interfered with the activities of the theatres, such performances as were given in these theatres did not differ markedly from the performances presented before 1939, and several dramatists continued to write plays which in style and content pursued paths which previously had been clearly signposted. *Blithe Spirit, Wind of Heaven, Mr Bolfry, They Came to a City* all belonged to this period. Thus, we might perhaps say that the war had no immediate and direct effect on the general playwriting trends which had been established during the thirties. Topical subject-matter, as in Ted Willis' *Buster* (1943), dealing with air raids, and Joan Temple's *No Room at the Inn* (1945), concerned with the problems of evacuation, certainly and understandably came into being, but only the subject-matter was different, not the style or the basic approach.

The second matter to be observed is that from the mid-fifties onward a new movement seized the theatre in its grip, and, when we examine this new movement carefully in relation to the twentieth-century playhouse as a whole, we suddenly realize that, in effect, it takes shape as a kind of condensed and accelerated repetition of the more long-drawn-out movement from 1900 to 1930. Clearly, this statement demands further elaboration and elucidation, but before devoting further attention to it we may first briefly consider the progress of the stage during the ten years from 1945 to 1955.

The thirties, as we have seen, were marked by three general styles of play—the relics of the old realistic social drama, now only rarely concerned with the problems which had captured the attention of the Galsworthys and the Ervines at the beginning of the century, and tending more and more to centre upon domestic issues; the various experiments in more imaginative styles, such as the series of dramas written by Priestley; and the sudden advent of a new poetic drama, signalized by the appearance of *Murder in the Cathedral*. It is precisely these three forms which characterize the drama for the decade 1945–55.

The ordinary realistic play, usually concentrating upon domestic issues, continued popular, even if it manifestly had lost its early vigour. Agatha Christie gave it a new twist in her numerous detective pieces, channelling into a fresh stream the combination of the 'ordinary' and the 'romantic' which had attracted the author of *The Grand Cham's Diamond* and other playwrights; numerous similar plays, such as Emlyn Williams' *Some one Waiting* (1953), kept the stage full of corpses, detectives, and suspense. Other authors carried on the style in divers ways, sometimes re-treating old themes, sometimes exploiting changed conditions. *Young Woodley* had been one of the first serious dramas about school-life, and the 'child' theme found various exponents: a schoolmaster who befriends a drifting boy forms the plot of Charlotte Hastings' *Uncertain Joy* (1955); a similar story is dealt with in R. C. Sherriff's *The Telescope* (1956); C. E. Webber, in *Be Good, Sweet Maid* (1957), turned to present a psychological study of a girl whose parents are separated; kindred dramatic essays were provided in Reginald Beckwith's *Child's Play* (1947), W. Chetham Strode's *The Guinea-pig* (1945), and, in variant patterns, in *Edward, My Son* (1947), by Robert Morley and Noel Langley, and Terence Rattigan's *The Winslow Boy* (1946) and *The Browning Version* (1948). This last-named author may be regarded as one of the chief and as one of the most skilled exponents of the realistic form, an author who at one and the same time exhibits both the virtues and the declining strength of the prose drama. His writings have vigour, certainly, yet, when they are looked at carefully, they are seen to have a mechanical rather than an organic being. *The Deep Blue Sea* (1952), for example, provides us with an interesting variant of the "triangle" theme, showing us Hester, wife of Sir William Collyer, living with a former R.A.F. man, Freddie Page; she is infatuated, yet she dimly realizes that he does not love her at her level, and her very understanding husband becomes at once her confidant and supporter. Like many earlier plays of the same sort, a careful consideration of the text appears to suggest that the piece, however theatrically effective, has been built upon an intellectual plan. Most of the modern triangle plays present similar features. This is true even of such works as Graham Greene's outwardly more ambitious *The Complaisant Lover* (1959) and Peter Shaffer's *Five Finger Exercise* (1958).

Numerous playwrights who had established their reputations continued along these lines, and others joined them in the penning of what, in effect, are modern drawing-room dramas, even if drawing-rooms have now ceased to have the significance which once they had. Clemence Dane provides a good acting part for an elderly actress in her *Eighty in the Shade* (1959), in which echoes of the past can be heard in the symphony wrought out of the 'grand old man' (in this instance a 'grand old woman'), the severe, self-tortured daughter who is her attendant, and the care-free vagabond. In all kinds of moods these plays were written, veering now to the documentary, now to the melodramatic. Van Druten trod one path in *I am a Camera* (1954), James Parrish another in *Message for Margaret* (1946), Mary Hayley Bell another in *Duet for Two Hands* (1945), Dorothy and Campbell Christie another in *Carrington, V.C.* (1953), Norman King another in *The Shadow of Doubt* (1955). Among these, the plays of Charles Morgan deserve some particular notice because of their attempt to infuse into the realistic form something of broader purpose. *The Flashing Stream* (1938), produced shortly before the outbreak of war, had tried to explore the complexities of man's intellectual and emotional life, showing passion entering into the world of strict science. Later, he came forward with a war play, *The River Line* (1952), concerned with the problem of loyalties, and two years later, in *The Burning Glass* (1954), he surveyed the impact of modern scientific inventions upon the soul of humanity. All are informed with a powerful command over words, but all fail as plays precisely because they give the impression of having been conceived according to ideas and not to imaginative perceptions.

Among these works, of course, there are numerous comedies, but on the whole the comic style yielded less than might have been expected. Far too many of such plays are of the school of Philip King and Falkland L. Cary's *Sailor Beware* (1955) or else succeed in reaching no farther than an engaging surface charm, as in the *Plaintiff in a Pretty Hat* (1956) of Hugh and Margaret Williams. One writer, however, managed to evolve something new out of the comic form. In 1942 Peter Ustinov had first attracted public attention with his sensitively written study of Russian exiles, *House of Regrets*, and during the war he had added to that reputation with his 'generations' play, *The Banbury Nose* (1944). Then, some seven years later, came *The Love of Four Colonels* (1951), a lively political allegory which, unlike most theatrical allegories, permits its laughter to play on all alike. Its fantastic story of the English, Russian, French, and American officers each anxious to take over as his headquarters a castle in which a Sleeping Beauty lies in state is treated with a peculiar mingling of wit and humour. The American faith in psycho-analysis, the Frenchman's confidence in his knowledge of women, the Russian's assurance in the use of force, and the Englishman's prime interest in dogs are gaily put before us. This highly individual kind of comedy finds further exemplification in another fantastic piece, *Romanoff and Juliet* (1956), this time set on the frontier between East and West, once more drawing thoughtful laughter out of the fairy-tale-like contrast between two worlds divided by their ridiculous curtain. Some other writers have, in their own ways, followed this style, but, in spite of the merits of a few among their plays, without seriously challenging Ustinov. Benn W. Levy's mythological fantasy, *The Rape of the Belt* (1957), illustrates the political present with the imaginary past and, structurally, sweeps us back, with its framework provided by Zeus and Hera, to the four-centuries-old *Rare Triumphs of Love and Fortune*. The imaginary past, too, offers William Golding material for his similarly inspired *The Brass Butterfly* (1958).

In spite of the preponderating number of realistic plays contributed to the stage during these ten years, and in spite of the many comedies both thoughtlessly frothy and pregnantly thoughtful, that which gives particular character to the period is the continuance and growth of the poetic drama. The war had barely ended when, in August 1945, Martin Browne opened the Mercury Theatre as a "poets' playhouse," and although the Mercury is a tiny place, and although the 'Poet's Playhouse' had not long endurance, its establishment may be regarded as symbolic. In 1945 and 1946 it caused poetic dramas to come forward in number —Peter Yates' *The Assassin*, a psychological study in the insanity of the man who murdered Lincoln, Norman Nicholson's *The Old Man of the Mountain*, a modern treatment of a Biblical story, Ronald Duncan's *This Way to the Tomb*, on the story of St Anthony, and Anne Ridler's *The Shadow Factory*, also religious in theme. Meanwhile T. S. Eliot remained actively engaged within this sphere. Already, in 1939, he had followed *Murder in the Cathedral* with *The Family Reunion*, in which the Orestes tale was put into contemporary terms. Not only the movement from the past to the present, however, distinguishes his first dramatic work from his second; in *Family Reunion* quite obviously he was intent upon toning down the 'poetic' element, and this intent he has later carried to a further stage both in critical statement and in creative practice. *The Cocktail Party* (1949), *The Confidential Clerk* (1953) and *The Elder Statesman* (1958) confessedly aim at evolving a verse style so close to familiar conversation as to seem at times indistinguishable from it. In Eliot's mature judgment, the fortunes of the poetic drama will best be served by shaping the dialogue in such a way that audiences are not made conscious of the fact that they are listening to verse at all.

Sharply opposed to this approach is the poet who soared into prominence immediately after the end of the hostilities, Christopher Fry. Just before the war's declaration, Fry had produced a short religious play in verse, *The Boy with a Cart*, but this did not attract any immediate general attention. The year after the war ended, however, came *A Phœnix Too Frequent*, and this drew at least informed opinion to recognize the brilliance of his individual style. Then, with *The Lady's not for Burning* (1948) and *Venus Observed* (1950), together with *Ring Round the Moon* (1950), based on a play by Anouilh, he suddenly won wide popularity. Since then he has written the interestingly experimental *A Sleep of Prisoners* (1951), *The Dark is Light Enough* (1954), and *Curtmantle* (1961), besides adapting a work of Giraudoux' as *Tiger at the Gates* (1955). Fry's distinction is that he makes his dramas float on a constantly moving foam of words, and the appeal his works made to audiences in the early fifties most certainly was due to the fact that ears long wearied by the metallic and reiterative prose utterance of the current realistic plays of the time were suddenly made aware of a new music. There are some critics now who say that in his writings the words are sometimes superfluous in their excess, as though the poet had become lost in his own melodies, and had almost forgotten the stage and its action; yet in more ways than one this excess formed a rich and indeed necessary contribution to the theatre. Through it, audiences were once more taught that the poetic in drama need not mean the dull, that dullness resided rather in the relics of realism around them. Moreover, as Fry has advanced in his dramatic career he has tended to make his words firmer, more intimately related to current speech patterns, while still leaving himself the opportunity of moving from this to richer forms. The dialogue of *Curtmantle* well illustrates this:

> *Marshal.*   And how
> Does the aggrieved heart of the Archbishop take it?
> *Henry.* Look, Marshal: I am making enough concessions.
> And here we stand in Normandy, ready to float him
> Again towards England. And God knows I have shown him
> Plenty of reverence—Louis could hardly do better—
> Holding his stirrup for him while he dismounts,
> Acknowledging that the less should serve the greater.

I only ask him to treat me with tolerable respect
In front of these men who are watching us from their places.
                                        [MEN *are standing behind. Enter* BECKET.
Let us show each other all the good we can
And forget our quarrel.
    Becket.   I am very willing.
    Henry. The days behind us are thoroughly rebuked.
If we ever remember them
It will be with such fierce pain, the days ahead
Will double their virtue to overcome it.
There have been many kings of England before me,
Some greater, some less than I am. And many good
And holy Archbishops. Behave to me as the most
Holy of your predecessors behaved
To the least of mine, I'll be satisfied.
    Becket. I am touched by this. Yet we mustn't forget
That if our predecessors had settled everything well
We should never have had to undergo
These fearful years, of such harm to us both.
    Henry. Maybe so. Also remembering
That Providence is a great maker of journeys,
And whoever refuses to go forward is dropped by the road.
    Becket. At least I take hopefully to the sea with you;
And surely England will take us up
Like a palm-branch in its hand, to see us riding
Together again on the road to London.

Thus we reach the close of the first decade following the end
of the war, when the second dramatic movement begins to take
shape. In this second movement, the progress of the poetic drama
has been summarily halted. A few stray experiments in the
writing of verse plays have been made sporadically, but virtually,
in so far as this type of theatre is concerned, we are back where
we started. That does not mean, however, that the poetic drama
has been finally slain, as some enthusiasts fondly believe: rather,
if a comparison between the present and the past has any
validity, we might almost be prepared to hazard the suggestion
that the time is now almost ripe for a further manifestation of
its efforts.

The special character of the years 1955–61 has been provided
by the sudden upsurge of a new realism, distinct from the old yet

strangely reminiscent of the realistic endeavours at the beginning of the century. Just as *John Ferguson, Chains, Rutherford and Son*, and all the various essays in the depiction of lower-middle-class life aroused excitement betwen 1900 and 1915, so a similar excitement has been evoked in at least certain quarters by the "kitchen-sink" school of recent years. And the parallel goes beyond just a general outline: numbers of the new dramatists are demonstrating in their plays that consciously or unconsciously, in revolting against both the poetic play and the 'drawing-room' drama, they are exploiting themes, situations, and characters which already had been freely put upon the stage in the earlier years; the impact made by the Manchester Repertory during the first two decades of the century is mirrored in the impact made by the Royal Court Theatre and, to a certain extent, by the Stratford Theatre Royal; angry young men and women were sponsored both by the one and the other. As we read some of the early 'advance-guard' notices of the social-realistic plays being produced during the century's earlier years we feel we might almost be reading kindred reviews of plays produced to-day; the statement made by P. D. Campbell in an article printed by *The Stage* in 1929:

> The success that has fallen to the lot of *Journey's End* registers the first definite and important step in the development of the propagandistic drama—

reminds us irresistibly of a statement printed in *The Twentieth Century* in 1961:

> The first night of John Osborne's *Look Back in Anger* at the Royal Court on May 8, 1956, was a turning-point in the history of the modern British theatre.

Look Back in Anger startled the public in 1956 by its retreatment of the old theme concerning the well-brought-up girl who marries a man out of her social milieu; here was a fresh orientation and a vehicle in which the author's vituperative abilities were offered full scope. *Look Back in Anger* was followed by the would-be symbolic *The Entertainer* (1957), which makes use of the music-hall tradition, associated with the presentation of realistically drawn scenes; by *Epitaph for George Dillon* (1958;

written in collaboration with Anthony Creighton), a rather old-fashioned work based on a theme freely exploited by Edwardian dramatists but coloured richly by Osborne's clamorous upbraidings:

> Have you looked at them? Have you listened to them? They don't merely act and talk like caricatures, they *are* caricatures! That's what's so terrifying. Put any one of them on a stage, and no one would take them seriously for one minute! They think in clichés, they talk in them, they even feel in them—and, brother, that's an achievement! Their existence is one great cliché that they carry about with them like a snail in his little house—and they live in it and die in it!

The lines, plentifully bespattered with exclamation marks, pour forth in an unending stream. And the stream becomes a flood in the unsuccessful *World of Paul Slickey* (1959), wherein the author's attack upon the audience misfired.

These plays of Osborne's set the pace. They made their impact in the theatre by their abusive wrath and self-centredness as well as by their shock tactics. Both qualities are reproduced in Arnold Wesker's somewhat adolescent *The Kitchen* (1959) and in his later ambitiously titled "Wesker Trilogy," consisting of *Chicken Soup with Barley, Roots,* and *I'm Talking about Jerusalem* (1960). Other playwrights followed suit. Keith Waterhouse and Willis Hall produced *Billy Liar* (1960), an inconclusive documentary; John Mortimer infused a dash of irony into *Lunch Hour* and *Collect Your Hand Baggage* (1960); Doris Lessing experimented in *Each His Own Wilderness* (1958), a rather confused play of ideas with the usual angry overtones; a new *Journey's End* was provided by Willis Hall in *The Long and the Short and the Tall* (1958); the documentary style enriched by Irish eloquence was cultivated by Brendan Behan in *The Quare Fellow* (1956); a prison 'comedy-drama'; another attempt at the documentary enlivened by colourful language appeared in John Arden's *Live like Pigs* (1958), varied structurally in *Sergeant Musgrave's Dance* (1959); Shelagh Delaney attracted attention for her *A Taste of Honey* (1959) and *The Lion in Love* (1960); Alun Owen took a kindred way in *Progress to the Park* (1960); Stephen Lewis aimed at the ultra-naturalistic in *Sparrers Can't Sing* (1960).

These, and many other similar plays, were eagerly praised by a number of the critics, being hailed, as we have seen, much as the realistic plays of the early nineteen-hundreds had been hailed. It was almost as though there had been no Gorki to write a *Lower Depths* in 1902. Certainly the outspokenness of the modern authors brought upon the stage episodes and references such as could never have been heard in the past, but fundamentally the shock-tactics were not different in kind. When *The Long and the Short and the Tall* appeared there were numerous derogatory allusions made to the "sentimentalism" of *Journey's End*; but undoubtedly this modern play bears the same relationship to the audiences of the sixties as Sherriff's drama bore to audiences of the twenties. Roger Gellert can now present his *Quaint Honour* (1958) in which homosexuality in a school is sympathetically treated; the 'shock' on spectators of to-day is almost identically similar with the 'shock' which for a time caused *Young Woodley* to be banned by the censor in 1928.

While all these playwrights sought in their own ways to cultivate the realistic drama, interpreting 'realism' mainly by reference to the class of characters introduced and by the nature of the social message incorporated in the action and in the lines, and while some critics at least, lauding this movement as though there had been no realistic movements in previous years, called for further developments of the "journalistic theatre," the interesting thing is that in many ways the playwrights showed that they themselves soon came to see that realism was not sufficient. Already in 1959 there were signs within the group which had been sponsored by the Royal Court Theatre that fresh attention was being paid to the possibilities of the historical theme; and in 1961 this Theatre's director drew attention to "a movement away from modern-dress naturalism." Thus, in a sense, the pattern of the years 1900 to 1935 was being repeated. Historical plays, of course, were at this time sporadically being written by playwrights who did not belong to the advance guard—plays such as Julian Green's *South* (1955), concerned with the American Civil War, Sherriff's thoughtful *The Long Sunset* (1955), dealing with the end of the Roman occupation of Britain, and plays with subject-matter closer in time, like Rattigan's *Ross*

(1960). These, however, may be looked upon as works belonging to the older tradition. What is interesting is the fact that Osborne turns to write a *Luther* (1961), applying his vituperative style to a character from the past, that John Whiting pens *The Devils* (1961), that Robert Bolt reverts to Sir Thomas More for the central character of *A Man for All Seasons* (1960), and that various members of the younger playwrights group have expressed their intention of similarly exploring diverse episodes and persons of the past.

Even more significant are the efforts of those who have turned from the straight realistic to more imaginative methods of play construction. Bernard Kops thus deliberately goes for inspiration to Jewish folk-drama in *The Hamlet of Stepney Green* (1958) and *The Dream of Peter Mann* (1960), the first a somewhat crude but yet impressive "sad comedy with some songs" dealing mainly with the ineffective would-be crooner David Levy and the strangely evocative figure of his father, who appears both as dying man and as ghost; and the other moving, somewhat less impressively, in a similar world between the material-real and the imaginative. The 'grand-old-man' theme, which had been frequently exploited in the past, notably in *The Truth about Blayds*, is taken up again by several writers and given symbolic touches. Angus Wilson in *The Mulberry Bush* (1956) chooses as his central character the retiring president of a university college and uses his drama to reflect the downfall of the liberal tradition. An aged scientist occupies the stage in Doris Lessing's *The Truth about Billy Newton* (1960), and in this the symbolical elements become more pronounced. John Whiting, after giving us his delightfully fantastic *A Penny for a Song* (1951), produces his peculiar *Saint's Day* (1951), with its octogenarian poet, Paul Southman, waiting to go to his celebration dinner amid an atmosphere heavily burdened by even greater symbolic connotations.

Whiting himself has said that he regards the story of *Saint's Day* as "simple" and that its "so-called symbolism"

> is no more than the use of people, places, things, even ideas and quotations from literature, which have a personal significance.

And this statement may serve as a cue for the consideration of a further and still more significant development in the non-realistic theatre in our times. There can be no doubt that one of the most striking recent movements has been towards what is now being labelled as "the theatre of the absurd." N. F. Simpson writes his nonsense play, A Resounding Tinkle (1957)—with an almost 'sophomoric' cleverness reflected in the character-names of Mustard Short, Denzil Pepper, Miss Salt and Miss Vinegar—and follows this with the more mature cleverness of One Way Pendulum (1959), which might be regarded as a fantastic re-treatment of the excellent American comedy-farce, You Can't Take It with You. In spite of their shortcomings, however, these plays demonstrate their inherent quality when they are compared with some other similar pieces, such as Nigel Dennis' absurdity-satire, Cards of Identity (1956) and The Making of Moo (1957). The style itself, of course, belongs to the same environment which produced the much-discussed and somewhat repetitively boring Waiting for Godot by Samuel Beckett, as well as Harold Pinter's The Dumb Waiter (1960), The Birthday Party (1958), The Room (1960), and the much more vital The Caretaker (1960).

Two aspects of these plays immediately demand attention—aspects which are, paradoxically, antagonistic to each other. First, it seems clear that some of the authors are devoting themselves to this form of drama for much the same reasons as induced their predecessors in the thirties to explore the possibilities of the poetic drama. Kops' attempt to mould a new structure out of the musical folk-play is one example of this, and another appears in Arden's note to Live Like Pigs, in which he categorically asserts that in writing it he "was more concerned with the 'poetic' than the 'journalistic' structure of the play." Because of this trend, associated with the latest gradual re-approach to historical subject-matter, we may well wonder whether the next step may not be in the direction of a fresh assault on the penning of verse dialogue.

On the other hand, the second aspect of these plays runs wholly counter to this tendency. In Doris Lessing's The Truth about Billy Newton, the key figure is a youth who is almost completely inarticulate and who moons about the stage playing tunes on his flute. It has been said, rightly, that in Harold Pinter's plays we have "the lowest common denominator of human speech." In numerous works by the younger writers we recognize that an attempt is being made to deny the very validity of language, not only in the theatre but in life as well. Hitherto we have assumed that man separates himself from the animal world in general by the fact that, through his command of ordinary logical speech for the communication of fact and intellectual concept, and through his command of emotionally evocative 'magical' speech, he has the power of conveying to others of his race both ideas and passions. Now, however, stress is being laid on precisely the opposite—it is averred that no individual man has the opportunity, through words, of entering into communion with any other person. The title of Doris Lessing's *Each His Own Wilderness* thus might be taken as characteristic of much more than its own stage action. The development of this new concept has two results. The first is suggested in the comment by Whiting, already quoted, concerning his *Saint's Day;* many of the "people, places, things" in it, he says, "have a personal significance." The attitude inspiring this statement underlies Pinter's declaration that he does not "write with any audience in mind" and it is reflected in Osborne's plea that playwrights should have "complete artistic freedom" so that they "don't have to please audiences or please critics or please anybody" but themselves. All of this, however, bears destructively down on the very essence of drama. The lyric poet, may, if he wishes, move in a dream world of his own imagining; his images may be 'private' as well as 'public'; but the drama is something which by its basic nature must be designed to appeal to an audience, and those authors who apply themselves to the stage must accept the fact that 'public' utterance alone can serve its purpose.

Serious as are the implications here, the implications of the second result are considerably greater and more dangerous. The claim that by the means of words man cannot communicate with man means that several playwrights and critics are tending in various ways to deny the very foundation of drama. In 1958 Ann Jellicoe produced *The Sport of My Mad Mother* and in 1961 carried its style a step farther in *The Knack*. In both of these the lines given to the actors are almost completely meaningless, and, defending her method, the authoress has explained that she is striving to communicate "with the audience through their senses," divesting words of all their values save their sounds. Other authors, anxious to reveal loneliness, nothingness, meaninglessness, have selected inconsequential conversations in their dialogue—believing that "in a world that has become absurd it is enough to transcribe reality with meticulous care to create the impression of extravagant irrationality." They have forgotten that transcription is not sufficient, that the drama demands interpretation; many centuries ago *King Lear* concentrated on the lonely, the irrational, the absurd, but through the use of words it made its vision meaningful. Obviously, however, if words are regarded as fundamentally useless, the logical procedure is to do without them altogether, and such procedure is being adopted by still others. It is almost as though we have here another instance of the connexion between our own period and that period when the silent film seemed to some enthusiasts the supreme art form. Wesker thus tells us that in *Chips with Everything* he is "working very much towards a reduction, not only of scenery, but of dialogue as well"; he proudly states that "there is a whole scene in this play in which absolutely nothing is said." A critic, Martin Esslin, who has devoted a detailed study to the "theatre of the absurd," speaks of "a return to the really basic elements of drama, the suspense created by the elementary ingredients of pure, pre-literary theatre"; for him, as for others, the word 'poetic' undergoes a strange metamorphosis, so that this "pre-literary theatre" is equated with a "more original approach to a poetic theatre"—"the type of play in which the language is deliberately flat and unpoetic and the poetic element is made to reside in the power of the action itself as a poetic image." Robert W. Corrigan, another student of this "theatre of the absurd," declares, in fact, "that the dramatic idea of *Waiting for Godot* is that the drama is no longer possible." Evidently some at least of the modern playwrights are doing their very best to put themselves out of business.

Odd things, of course, have happened in the long history of

the drama, and have been forgotten. In considering these latest ventures, the essential thing is that we should consider them, not in isolation, but in connexion with what has gone before, and also in association with the principles operating within the stage as a whole. Most certainly we may agree that the theatre embraces much more than the drama; most certainly skilled performers may create powerful impressions, both pathetic and comic, by the exercise of wordless mime; yet we cannot, because of this, deny that in the performance of drama the theatre has reached its highest power, and we assuredly should not confuse the issue by applying such terms as 'poetic' to spheres with which these terms have nothing to do. Moreover, we must seek to be logical: if a dramatist finds that he has not the ability to express his concepts in words, then the only thing for him to do is to step back and give his place to the actors.

Above all, we should concentrate upon the relationship between these present developments and kindred movements in the past. During earlier years excited groups of intellectuals have acclaimed all sorts of -isms—expressionism, futurism, and what not—which, after their brief moments of esteem, have passed away. At the moment, hardly anyone can speak of master playwrights other than Brecht and Ionesco, but continually the drama has been engaged in discovering new authors who have seemed for the moment to offer the final answer and who have soon been dismissed. And the peculiar thing is that very frequently the apparently novel, when examined and reflected upon, has disclosed a definite basis in the past. Thus, for example, to-day's cult which seeks to deny the potentiality of speech to provide a medium of communication between man and man was being vociferously and raucously voiced years ago by the devotees of Dadaism, while the use of words for their sound values alone was being exploited by the Surrealists at least thirty years ago. If we think that the angry young men of the moment are unique, born of a period in civilization the like of which has not been witnessed before, we need only cast our minds back to the years immediately after 1600 and look at the early seventeenth-century young men who rebelled against the previous current of the stage; they, too, found their spiritual home in the 'private'

theatres of the time, many of them displayed an anxiety to cultivate 'private' themes, most of them eagerly grasped whatever
opportunities there might be for the exercise of vituperative
rhetoric, and a few of them, at least, embraced stylistic 'obscurity' as an ideal. In noting these parallels, however, the
parallel which becomes most significant for a broader picture of
the present-day stage is that between the dramatic excitements
of 1956–61 and the dramatic excitements of 1900–30. The
repetition of the earlier pattern by the later is that which gives
to much of the 'advanced' drama, from the appearance of Look
Back in Anger onward, its slightly old-fashioned air.

In saying this, of course, we must freely recognize that the
new drama takes its shape because of the many and serious
concerns and worries and fears which now are bearing down
upon us. Play-titles such as Farewell, Yesterday and Goodbye,
World tell their own story. Without doubt, a menace hangs over
our planet, and it is quite possible that humanity will have to say
good-bye to the world, or that the world will say good-bye to
humanity. Nevertheless, we should perhaps remember that ever
since the time of Noah men have periodically faced this threat.
The present fears and imaginings are hardly different in kind
from those which confronted civilization in the fifth century, or
which, some centuries later, swept in with the Black Death, or
which, later still, inspired Dekker's terrible description of London's charnel-house streets during the plague. The lone and level
sands stretch far away, covering many majestic monuments of
the past. So far as the theatre is concerned, if our civilization does
perish, the drama will have to endure long dark ages before it is
again called into being: but if our civilization endures, it is
almost certain that much of what is now arousing ardent enthusiasm will change shape just as the objects of previous
enthusiasms have been absorbed within the stage's inherent
traditionalism.

In the meantime, we must recognize that the 'advanced'
drama of the past few years has accomplished much. Many of the
plays written under its influence will assuredly seem in the
future sentimental in concept and execution, but at least some
will be remembered. The only real danger rests in the possible

alienation of the public. Even now, the managers of theatres intent on cultivating the 'advanced' styles are confessing sadly that these styles are not attracting to the auditoria the large numbers of young people to whom specifically they address their appeal; and, despite the crowds which, at least in London, have been going to see these works, partly out of curiosity, it seems clear that dramas of this kind are not likely to increase the playgoing public or even to hold existing playgoers within the theatre's orbit. For what some of these dramas have achieved we may welcome the new movement; but, in doing so, we must preserve our sense of balance, recognizing that the same sort of thing has manifested itself before, that what at the moment gives the impression of novelty is not so new after all, that basically the playhouse must depend upon the audience, and that at least some of the objectives sponsored by this new movement are not only oriented away from the audience but are basically antitheatrical and anti-dramatic.

Critical and Historical Studies

I. PLAY-LISTS AND GENERAL REFERENCE WORKS

COMPLETE, or almost complete, lists of English plays are provided in Sir E. K. Chambers' *The Mediaeval Stage* (2 vols., 1903) and *The Elizabethan Stage* (4 vols., 1923), G. E. Bentley's *The Jacobean and Caroline Stage* (5 vols., 1941–56), and the present writer's *History of English Drama, 1600–1900* (6 vols., 1952–59). For the period up to 1700, A. Harbage's *Annals of English Drama* (1940) is a useful handbook, and up to 1660 Sir Walter Greg's massive *Bibliography of English Printed Drama to the Restoration* (1939–59) is an invaluable detailed study. *The Oxford Companion to the Theatre* (ed. Phyllis Hartnoll, 1951) contains numerous short entries on theatres, dramatists, and actors; more detailed material is included in the Italian *Enciclopedia dello spettacolo* (1954–, to be completed in 10 vols.). B. Ifor Evans has a *Short History of the English Drama* (1948), and W. Bridges-Adams a fuller survey, *The Irresistible Theatre* (1957, in progress).

II. THE MIDDLE AGES AND EARLY TUDOR PERIOD

Sir E. K. Chambers' two volumes remain a standard authority, although they are now supplemented by Karl Young's *The Drama of the Medieval Church* (2 vols., 1933), Hardin Craig's *English Religious Drama of the Middle Ages* (1955), and by numerous specialized studies. All the extant English manuscript plays have been edited, and several anthologies print specimen pieces (J. M. Manly, 1900–1903; A. W. Pollard, 1923; J. Q.

Adams, 1924). For the staging, R. Southern's *The Medieval Theatre in the Round* (1957), G. R. Kernodle's *From Art to Theatre* (1944), and Glynne Wickham's *Early English Stages* (1959–62) present much detailed information. Folk drama is dealt with by Sir E. K. Chambers in *The English Folk Play* (1933), and by R. J. E. Tiddy in *The Mummers' Play* (1923).

The Tudor moralities and interludes, after long neglect, are beginning to attract more attention. Most of the plays are included in the invaluable "Malone Society" series and J. S. Farmer's "Tudor Facsimile Texts." Important critical contributions are A. P. Rossiter's *English Drama from Early Times to the Elizabethans* (1950), T. W. Craik's *The Tudor Interlude* (1958), Bernard Spivak's *Shakespeare and the Allegory of Evil* (1958), and D. M. Bevington's *From Mankind to Marlowe* (1962). In *The Huntington Library Quarterly*, xxii, 1958, F. H. Mares has a significant essay on the pervasive character of the Vice.

III. THE ELIZABETHAN, JACOBEAN, AND CAROLINE PERIOD

The prime authorities are Sir E. K. Chambers and G. E. Bentley. The Elizabethan stage has been much discussed, and certain of its features are still matter for controversy. Among early studies may be mentioned W. J. Lawrence's *The Elizabethan Playhouse* (2 vols., 1912–13), and *The Physical Conditions of the English Public Playhouse* (1927), A. Thorndike's *Shakespeare's Theater* (1916), J. Q. Adams' *Shakesperean Playhouses* (1917), A. Thaler's *Shakspere to Sheridan* (1922); and, among later investigations, J. C. Adams' *The Globe Playhouse* (1943), C. W. Hodges' *The Globe Restored* (1953), and Leslie Hotson's *Shakespeare's Wooden O* (1959). Related subjects are dealt with in A. Harbage's *Shakespeare's Audience* (1941) and *Shakespeare and the Rival Traditions* (1952), B. L. Joseph's *Elizabethan Acting* (1951), and Muriel C. Bradbrook's *Elizabethan Stage Conditions* (1932). The staging of the Court masques is discussed in P. Reyher's *Les Masques anglais* (1909), the present writer's *Stuart Masques and the Renaissance Stage* (1937), Lily B. Campbell's *Scenes and Machines in the Renais-*

sance (1923), and Enid Welsford's *The Court Masque* (1928); many of Inigo Jones' original designs are reproduced in *Designs for Masques and Plays at Court* (1924), a catalogue prepared by P. Simpson and E. F. Bell. Sir Walter Greg, in *Dramatic Documents from the Elizabethan Playhouses* (2 vols., 1931) gives the texts of, and analyses, the surviving prompt-books and associated material.

Most of the plays are now available in well-edited form, some printed separately, and others in collections; general studies abound; many volumes treat of the work of individual dramatists, and others examine particular dramatic forms. F. E. Schelling's *Elizabethan Drama* (1908) and F. S. Boas' *Shakespeare and His Predecessors* (1896) still have value, but these early studies have largely been superseded by such later works as H. W. Wells' *Elizabethan and Jacobean Playwrights* (1939), Una Ellis-Fermor's *The Jacobean Drama* (1936), and A. Harbage's *The Cavalier Drama* (1936). F. S. Boas has a handy *Introduction to Stuart Drama* (1946). Elizabethan tragedy has been much discussed in general, and special aspects—for example, Willard Farnham's *The Medieval Heritage of Elizabethan Tragedy* (1956), W. Clemen's *English Tragedy before Shakespeare* (1961), Muriel C. Bradbrook's *Themes and Conventions of Elizabethan Tragedy* (1935), F. L. Lucas' *Seneca and Elizabethan Tragedy* (1922), F. Bowers' *Elizabethan Revenge Tragedy* (1940), and H. H. Adams' *English Domestic or Homiletic Tragedy* (1943). L. B. Campbell covers wide ground in *Shakespeare's "Histories"* (1947), and I. Ribner has a comprehensive survey of *The English History Play* (1957). Comedy is dealt with in Muriel C. Bradbrook's *The Growth and Structure of Elizabethan Comedy* (1955). Tragicomedy is examined by F. H. Ristine (1910), E. M. Waith (1952), and M. T. Herrick (1955), pastoral drama by Sir Walter Greg (1906) and the 'jig' by C. R. Baskerville (1929). The principles underlying the dramatic practice of the period are explored by Madeleine Doran in *Endeavors of Art* (1954) and by Mary C. Hyde in *Playwriting for Elizabethans, 1600–1605* (1945). The social background of the early seventeenth-century stage is discussed by L. C. Knights in *Drama and Society in the Age of Jonson* (1937).

The vast library of critical works on Shakespeare cannot be dealt with here, even selectively, but some attention may be drawn to the considerable number of recent studies relating to the writings of his predecessors, fellows, and successors. Marlowe's achievement, both in general and in particular, has found many interpreters (notably Una Ellis-Fermor, 1927; F. S. Boas, 1929 and 1940; Tucker Brooke, 1930; M. K. Mincoff, 1937; J. Bakeless, 1942; R. W. Battenhouse, 1941; P. H. Kocher, 1946; and F. P. Wilson, 1952). Among contemporaries, Jonson's reputation rivalled that of Shakespeare, and his writings, too, have been closely studied; apart from the invaluable critical material in the great edition of his works edited by P. Simpson and C. H. Herford, mention may be made of the analysis of his methods by H. W. Baum (1947), A. Sackton (1948), and J. J. Enck (1957). Other playwrights have had their lives and careers closely examined: Marston (G. Pellegrini, 1952; A. J. Axelrad, 1955), Dekker (M. T. Jones-Davies, 2 vols, 1958), Heywood (F. S. Boas, 1950; A. M. Clark, 1931; M. Grivelet, 1957), Middleton (S. Schoenbaum, 1955; R. H. Barker, 1958), Chapman (P. V. Kreider, 1935; J. W. Wieler, 1949; J. Jacquot, 1951; E. Rees, 1954), Beaumont (C. Gayley, 1914), Fletcher (C. Leech, 1962), "Beaumont and Fletcher" (E. H. C. Oliphant, 1927; D. McKeithan, 1938; W. W. Appleton, 1956), Massinger (A. H. Cruikshank, 1920; M. Chelli, 1923; T. A. Dunn, 1957), and Ford (J. Sarjeaunt, 1935; S. B. Ewing, 1940; G. F. Sensabaugh, 1944; R. Davril, 1954; H. Oliver, 1955; C. Leech, 1957). In mentioning these, it should also be noted that a great deal of penetrating analysis of the Elizabethan stage has appeared in article form.

IV. THE RESTORATION PERIOD

Leslie Hotson's *The Commonwealth and Restoration Stage* (1928) presents valuable material on the fate of the theatre during the time (1642–60) when the drama was officially banned. A general survey appears in the first volume of the present writer's *History*, and M. Summers covers the period in *The Restoration Theatre* (1934) and *The Playhouse of Pepys* (1935). G. C. D. Odell in

Shakespeare from Betterton to Irving (2 vols., 1920) and A. Thaler in *Shakspere to Sheridan* (1922) deal with the staging of plays and theatrical conditions; Eleanore Boswell meticulously analyses *The Restoration Court Stage* (1932). Bonamy Dobrée has a critical study of *Restoration Tragedy* (1929). Naturally, the comedies of the time have received most attention: special note may be made of Bonamy Dobrée's *Restoration Comedy* (1924), Ten Eyck Perry's *The Comic Spirit in Restoration Drama* (1925), Kathleen M. Lynch's *The Social Mode of Restoration Comedy* (1926), L. I. Bredvold's *The Intellectual Milieu of John Dryden* (1934), J. H. Smith's *The Gay Couple in Restoration Comedy* (1948), D. Underwood's *Etherege and the Seventeenth Century Comedy of Manners* (1957), and N. N. Holland's *The First Modern Comedies* (1959). The chief dramatists have all had their works recently edited in collected editions, and special studies have been devoted to several: D'Avenant (A. Harbage, 1935; A. H. Nethercot, 1938), Thomas Killigrew (A. Harbage, 1930), Congreve (D. C. Taylor, 1931; J. C. Hodges, 1944), Wycherley (C. Perromat, 1922; W. Connely, 1930), Farquhar (W. Connely, 1949), Shadwell (A. S. Borgman, 1928), Southerne (J. W. Dodds, 1933), Otway and Lee (R. G. Ham, 1931).

V. THE EIGHTEENTH CENTURY

For many years John Genest's ten-volume *Some Account of the English Stage* (1832) has been the standard season-by-season record of performances, but this is now being supplanted by the majestic *London Stage, 1660–1800* (1960, in progress), and it is supplemented by D. MacMillan's *Drury Lane Calendar, 1747–1776* (1936) and C. Beecher Hogan's *Shakespeare in the Theatre* (2 vols., 1952–57). D. MacMillan also has a valuable *Catalogue of the Larpent Plays* (1939). On the theatre, R. Southern's *The Georgian Playhouse* (1948) and *Changeable Scenery* (1952) should be consulted, together with D. F. Smith's *Plays about the Theatre in England* (1936) and *Critics in the Audience* (1953). Colley Cibber's *Apology* (1740; ed. R. W. Lowe, 1889) is a revealing record of stage affairs, and much other similar material may be found in the lives and autobiographies of later actors. Sybil

Rosenfeld's *Strolling Players and Drama in the Provinces* (1939) and *The Theatre of the London Fairs* (1960) offer a great deal of information concerning performances outside of the major London playhouses.

A general survey of the drama appears in the second and third volumes of the present writer's *History*. F. W. Bateson deals with *English Comic Drama, 1700–1750* (1929). Several individual playwrights have been specially studied, notably Sheridan (W. S. Sichel, 1909; W. A. Darlington, 1933; L. Gibbs, 1947), Garrick (T. Davies, 1780; P. Fitzgerald, 1899; Elizabeth Stein, 1938), Fielding (W. L. Cross, 1910), Steele (G. Aitken, 1889; L. Loftis, 1952), Home (A. E. Gipson, 1917), Colman the Elder (E. R. Page, 1935), and Colman the Younger (J. F. Bagster-Collins, 1946). The origins and development of the sentimental drama are traced in Sister Rose Anthony's *The Jeremy Collier Stage Controversy* (1937), J. W. Krutch's *Comedy and Conscience after the Restoration* (1924), and in several wider surveys by E. Bernbaum (1915), F. O. Nolte (1935), and A. Sherbo (1957). Ballad opera is examined by E. M. Gagey (1937) and by W. E. Schultz (1923), and farce by L. Hughes (1956).

VI. THE NINETEENTH CENTURY

The fourth and fifth volumes of the present writer's *History* attempt to give a general conspectus of the drama during this period. E. Reynolds discusses the early Victorian drama (1936), and C. Rowell deals with the later parts of the reign (1956). A lively picture is presented in C. Rice's *London Theatre in the Eighteen-Thirties* (ed. A. C. Sprague and B. Shuttleworth, 1950). There are many informative lives of players such as Mrs Siddons (J. Boaden, 1827; T. Campbell, 1834), Edmund Kean (H. N. Hillebrand, 1933), J. P. Kemble (H. Baker, 1942), Macready (W. Archer, 1890; *Reminiscences*, ed. Sir Frederick Pollock, 1875), Phelps (J. Coleman, 1886; W. M. Phelps and J. Forbes-Robertson, 1886), Charles Kean (J. W. Cole, 1859), Irving (A. Brereton, 1905), and Ellen Terry (Gordon Craig, 1931; C. St John, 1907). Playwrights' autobiographies, too, such as those of Planché (1872) and Fitzball (1859), are of prime importance. E. B. Watson deals with theatrical conditions in *Sheridan to Robertson* (1926). The popular stage is discussed by F. J. H. Darton in *Vincent Crummles* (1926), by M. W. Disher in *Blood and Thunder* (1949), and by A. E. Wilson in *East End Entertainment* (1954). W. Archer's *English Dramatists of Today* (1882) has particular significance as a contemporary assessment of the 'new' playwrights; Robertson's writings are examined by T. E. Pemberton (1893), Jones' by R. A. Cordell (1932), and Pinero's by Hamilton Fyfe (1930), and much has been written on the subject of the "Savoy Operas." The influence of William Poel on the stage generally is outlined by R. Speaight (1954).

VII. THE TWENTIETH CENTURY

The drama since 1900 has attracted a good deal of discussion, and only a few of the numerous studies can be mentioned here. E. Reynolds has a short comprehensive *Modern English Drama* (1951). Among earlier works, J. T. Grein's *The New World of the Theatre* (1924), A. E. Morgan's *Tendencies of Modern English Drama* (1924), Ashley Dukes' *Modern Dramatists* (1912) and *The Youngest Drama* (1923), and F. Vernon's, *The Twentieth-century Theatre* (1924) are all worthy of note, but these are only a few out of many. The pervasive influence of Gordon Craig is outlined by Enid Rose (1931). *The Irish Dramatic Movement* (1939) is surveyed by Una Ellis-Fermor. The work of Shaw and Barrie has, of course, been much discussed; Granville-Barker's methods and ideals are closely examined by Marjory M. Morgan in *A Drama of Political Man* (1961), and a study of this author's theatrical career has been written by C. B. Purdom (1955); Priscilla Thouless (1934) and R. Peacock (1946) deal with modern poetic drama. R. Findlater's *The Unholy Trade* (1952) is a vigorous indictment of modern theatrical conditions. The many volumes of collected reviews prepared by dramatic critics are of special importance in any endeavour to relate contemporary opinions to later judgments.

The achievements of the past few years have been examined for the most part chiefly in periodical articles (particular attention may be drawn to the special 'Theatre' issue of *Twentieth*

Century, February 1961). Three broader studies are of considerable service: R. W. Williams' *Drama from Ibsen to Eliot* (1952), F. Lumley's *Trends in 20th Century Drama* (1960), and L. Kitchin's *Mid-century Drama* (1960).

[Among numerous studies, both general and specialized, which have been published during the past three or four years, the following may be particularly noted:

I. *General Reference Works*

John Russell Taylor has prepared a useful *Penguin Dictionary of the Theatre* (1966). A. Harbage's *Annals of English Drama* should now be used in the new edition (1964), considerably revised by S. Schoenbaum. The catalogue of the 'Larpent' plays executed by D. Macmillan (1939) is supplemented by the British Museum's *Plays Submitted to the Lord Chamberlain, 1824–1851* (1964).

II. *The Middle Ages and Early Tudor Period*

M. D. Anderson introduces much fresh material in her *Drama and Imagery in English Medieval Churches* (1963). Anne Righter's *Shakespeare and the Idea of the Play* (1962) is an important study of the relationship between playwrights and spectators from medieval times to the latter years of the sixteenth century.

III. *The Elizabethan, Jacobean, and Caroline Period*

Those who are interested in the question of collaborative authorship during this period should note Cyrus Hoy's significant series of articles published in *Studies in Bibliography* between 1956 and 1961, as well as S. Schoenbaum's historical survey of *Internal Evidence and Elizabethan Dramatic Authorship* (1966).

V. *The Eighteenth Century*

Kalman A. Burnim presents a wide conspectus of theatrical method during the latter part of this period in his *David Garrick, Director* (1961).

VI. *The Twentieth Century*

On the latest styles of drama three studies are of special value—John Russell Taylor's *Anger and After* (1962), Martin Esslin's *The Theatre of the Absurd* (1961), and Bamber Gascoigne's *Twentieth-century Drama* (1962).]

Index